THE DEVELOPMENT OF
A RUSSIAN LEGAL
CONSCIOUSNESS

THE DEVELOPMENT OF
A RUSSIAN LEGAL
CONSCIOUSNESS

Richard S. Wortman

THE UNIVERSITY OF CHICAGO PRESS
Chicago & London

RICHARD S. WORTMAN is associate professor of
history at the University of Chicago. He is
the author of *The Crisis of Russian Populism.*

THE UNIVERSITY OF CHICAGO PRESS, CHICAGO 60637
THE UNIVERSITY OF CHICAGO PRESS, LTD., LONDON

Library of Congress Cataloging in Publication Data

Wortman, Richard.
  The development of a Russian legal consciousness.

  Bibliography: p.
  Includes index.
  1. Courts — Russia — History. 2. Lawyers — Russia.
3. Justice, Administration of — Russia — History.
I. Title.
Law   347'.47   76-600
ISBN 0-226-90776-7

To Marlene,

Жить с толь милою женою
Раи во всякои стороне;
Там веселия сердечны,
Сладки, нежны чувствы там;
Там блаженствы бесконечны,
Лишь приличные богам.

Г. Р. Державин Препятствие
к свиданию с супругои

Indeed, it is especially military power that makes the man in Russia; all other types of energy depend on manners and institutions, which Russia, in its present state, has not yet developed at all.

Madame de Stael

From the work close at hand, we moved to the distant: we analyzed all the branches of activity—one promised to elevate the military name of his ancestors through science; another to bring all the knowledge of Europe to our industrial world; another to sacrifice his life in the tsar's service, either on the field of battle or in painful civil labors. We trusted ourselves and the others, for our thoughts were pure and our hearts knew no calculations.

Prince Vladimir Odoevskii,
New Years' Day

CONTENTS

ABBREVIATIONS

*GBL	*Gosudarstvennaia biblioteka imeni Lenina (otdel rukopisei)* (Lenin State Library — Manuscript Division)
*GPB	*Gosudarstvennaia publichnaia biblioteka imeni Saltykova-Shchedrina (otdel rukopisei)* (Saltykov-Shchedrin State Library — Manuscript Division)
*IM	*Gosudarstvennyi istoricheskii muzei* (State Historical Museum)
*LOA	*Leningradskii oblastnoi arkhiv* (Leningrad Regional Archive)
*Materialy . . .	*Materialy po preobrazovaniiu sudebnoi chasti* (Materials on the reform of the judicial branch)
*PD	*Pushkinskii dom* (Pushkin House)
PSZ (IP)	*Polnoe sobranie zakonov rossiiskoi imperii s 1649, Izdanie pervoe: 1649–1825* (Complete Collection of Laws of the Russian Empire, First Part: 1649–1825)
PSZ (IV)	*Polnoe sobranie zakonov rossiiskoi imperii s 1649, Izdanie vtoroe: 1825–81* (Complete Collection of Laws of the Russian Empire, Second Part: 1825–81)
SZ	*Svod zakonov rossiiskoi Imperii* (Digest of Laws of the Russian Empire)
*TsGADA	*Tsentral'nyi gosudarstvennyi arkhiv drevnikh aktov* (Central State Archive of Ancient Documents)
*TsGAOR	*Tsentral'nyi gosudarstvennyi arkhiv oktiabr'skoi revoliutsii* (Central State Archive of the October Revolution)
*TsGIA	*Tsentral'nyi gosudarstvennyi istoricheskii arkhiv* (Central State Historical Archive)

*Broken down into coded sections in the first part of the bibliography, "Archival and Other Unpublished Sources" (p. 323).

ACKNOWLEDGMENTS

I would like to thank all those who made this work possible and helped me to deal with its imperfections. The Inter-University Committee on Travel Grants and the International Research and Exchange Board enabled me to have two extensive stays in the Soviet Union. The University of Chicago, through its Social Science Research Committee, College Research Committee, and Slavic Committee, provided generous support for my various research needs. I want to thank the archivists of the various repositories where I worked for their patience and assistance, especially the staff of the State Historical Archive in Leningrad who located and made available to me the numerous tomes of service lists and materials on the judicial reform.

I owe a great debt to the many Soviet scholars who shared their vast knowledge and understanding of Russian history and sources with me. P. A. Zaionchkovskii has been a kind and learned advisor of my research on this subject since its beginning in 1966. His assistance in directing me to little known archival and published sources was crucial in opening new avenues of interest. I. I. Dmitriev helped me with valuable advice on historical materials and varied approaches to them. V. G. Chernukha and V. R. Leikina-Svirskaia also were generous with their bibliographical knowledge and suggestions on my research.

I want to thank the many scholars who have read all or part of the manuscript at various stages of preparation: Leopold Haimson, Richard Hellie, Arcadius Kahan, Emile Karafiol, Herbert Klein, Walter Pintner, Marc Raeff, S. Frederick Starr, and Marlene Stein Wortman. I am deeply grateful for the time and energy they spent and for the candid and searching criticisms that spurred me in the revisions of this work.

GENERAL INTRODUCTION

THE HISTORY OF RUSSIAN LEGAL INSTITUTIONS AND THE RUSSIAN LEGAL profession has in large part been the history of the Judicial Reform of 1864. The reform created a modern court system in the midst of tsarist despotism, introducing independent public courts, an oral adversary procedure, and the jury system. It made possible a defense of the accused, establishing limits to the tyranny of the police. It brought into being a trained legal profession that could make the new system work. The Judicial Reform appears as a brilliant flash of light, illuminating the gloomy background of tsarist institutions, and completely adventitious to their prior development.

Historians have sought the causes for so sudden a break with the past exclusively in the circumstances of the emancipation era. Liberal scholars, who contributed most of the literature on the reform, understood it as a result of the new spirit that led the government to take heed of public opinion, and the needs of society after the Crimean War.[1] Soviet works have followed a similar interpretation, but with emphasis on the effects of the revolutionary movement.[2] Even prerevolutionary official historians, who highlighted the autocracy's previous commitment to reform, could explain the shift in attitudes toward the judiciary only by reference to the emancipation.[3] The copious literature on the reform has been summarized in Kaiser's comprehensive study.[4]

Nearly all works on the reform assign the emancipation of the serfs central importance in determining its fundamental nature. According to this explanation, the emancipation, ending the landlords' judicial authority over the peasants, created conditions necessitating an independent judiciary.[5] While it is undoubtedly true that the emancipation compelled some kind of court reform, nothing in it dictated the character of the new judicial system. Kaiser points out that the old courts served the needs raised by the emancipation between 1861 and 1866 adequately, and refutes the other reasons given for connecting the judicial reform directly to the emancipation.[6]

So obvious has it been to historians that emancipation should lead to an independent judiciary that they have given little attention to one of the most important facts in the evolution of the reform: that the reformers *thought* the emancipation necessitated a system of independent courts governed by modern, liberal principles of court procedure. Sharing the thought processes of the reformers, historians of reform could only depict their heroes as sincere, learned, self-sacrificing men, struggling for the right.[7] They described the reformers with the kind of romantic adulation that reduces motivation to a quest for good or evil. As a result, they left unanswered the crucial question of who these men were who drafted so successful a reform and how and why they were present in the tsarist administration in the 1860s.

The present work is an attempt to throw light on that question. It shifts the focus from the structural and procedural reforms of the courts to the problem of personnel and professionalization. It stresses that a crucial change making the Judicial Reform possible was the appearance in the tsarist administration of men capable of drafting and implementing such a reform—a group of legal experts who strove to assume the attributes of a profession. As a result, the reform appears here not as the beginning, but as the culmination of processes of change taking place within the officialdom.

The formation of a group of legal experts within the tsarist administration represented a major break with the institutional traditions of the Russian state. European judicial systems, whatever their failings, enjoyed a certain reverence that had accrued over the centuries to courts and the law in the West. The tsarist state, ever insistent on the supremacy of the executive power, had held the judicial function in disdain, and this disdain was shared by the officialdom and the nobility. A low opinion of the judiciary well suited officials reluctant to have their actions limited by law, and a nobility accustomed to seeing authority wielded by august figures, impersonations of might, whom they as estate owners could emulate. In the era of reforms, it was common to speak of the peasants' lack of respect for law. But a lack of respect for formal legal remedies also pervaded the attitudes expressed in government and society before the emancipation. The veneration accorded to judicial authority in the West, and even in many primitive societies, was not a feature of prereform Russia.

The beliefs in the supremacy of the executive and the subservience of the judiciary are elements in the "traditional pattern of institutional behavior" that has persisted in Russia through the course of modernization.[8] This pattern has survived judicial reform, industrialization, and revolution. The Judicial Statues of 1864 sowed conflict between executive and judicial authorities, as the autocrat became increasingly distrustful of the independent judiciary. Lenin, himself a lawyer by education, regarded bourgeois law as an instrument of the old state order, and after 1917, the new Soviet power reduced the judiciary to its own compliant instrument.

The work of dispensing justice carried a low status in Russia. The tsarist state did not need the corporations of jurists that western monarchs utilized to consolidate their authority at the expense of local, feudal privilege. Military concerns remained uppermost, and the Russian nobility shared their monarch's military disposition. As a result, long traditions of legal apprenticeship and training, and corporations of privileged, and often powerful, judges did not exist in Russia. The contrast with the Prussian model, whose military and absolutist features Russian monarchs tried to adopt, is most striking. Jurists were the first academically trained officials to serve in the new Prussian administrative state in the eighteenth century. The Hohenzollern kings worked to institute high standards for the legal profession as early as the late seventeenth century. By 1775, every candidate for judicial position had to pass examinations given by the university and the State Examination Board. Russia would not even begin to approach such rigorous standards until the end of the nineteenth century.[9]

As a result, legal professionalization marked a more radical innovation in Russia than it did in Europe. Legal professionalization brought throughout the West a new emphasis on formal university education, and greater state involvement in enforcing legal standards during the nineteenth century. But in Russia, such formal legal education would represent the *first* systematic preparation of judicial officials. Before the reign of Nicholas I, training in the law meant learning to copy and fulfill chancellery formalities. It was a menial task, low in status, and unlikely to confer distinction. The establishment of a strong judiciary required a completely new image of the judge and a new esteem for legal expertise.

Treatments of the Judicial Reform, emphasizing the importance of external factors—disgruntled public opinion, the emancipation of the serfs, the aftermath of the Crimean War—have all but ignored changes within the tsarist administration. The assumption has been that the oppressive administration of Nicholas I was stagnant, and that change could be provoked only by outside forces that would compel the officialdom to work for new goals. This liberal view has received its most effective statement in the works of Marc Raeff and Hans-Joachim Torke. Torke's monograph on the Russian officialdom during the reign of Nicholas I shows a great expansion in the size of the imperial administration, but little change in the character of the officials, and stresses the absence of a legal ethos among them.[10] Like Raeff, Torke sees change coming only with the reforms, when new liberal views began to affect the administration as well. But Torke, like others who have advanced this interpretation, has had to rely for sources on accounts written by contemporaries who were openly hostile to the system and who used all their literary abilities to indict it. There is no doubt that the judiciary was corrupt and inefficient, and that personnel left much to be desired at the close of Nicholas's reign. But this does not mean that officials in the 1840s and 1850s remained identical to those of the beginning of the century in all other respects as well.

A more recent approach examines the administration as a social grouping rather than as a disembodied organization. The Soviet historians S. M. Troitskii and P. A. Zaionchkovskii, and the American historian Walter Pintner have utilized service lists to give profiles of the social characteristics and backgrounds of officials.[11] The work of these scholars has made it possible for the first time to deal with the administration as a historical agent itself, participating in the acts of reform, rather than as a machine responding automatically to social and economic pressures from without. Their research has also made it possible to understand the characters and attitudes of officials themselves, whether they were conservative or reformist in orientation.

Recent work on the officialdom has described changes in its composition and attitudes that helped prepare the way for reforms. Walter Pintner has shown the rise of young bureaucrats with higher education to high positions in the government in the last decades before the reform. Emphasizing the changing nature of the officialdom, he suggests that the new officials, who had been exposed to intellectual influences in the university, began to regard state interest as paramount.[12] Bruce Lincoln has examined the intellectual interests and aspirations to reform of the rising generation of bureaucrats in the last decades of Nicholas's reign.[13] Daniel Field and S. Frederick Starr have analyzed the roles of particular groups of officials in the evolution of the emancipation and the *zemstvo* reforms.[14]

This book is an inquiry into the changes in composition and attitudes that took place in the Russian judicial administration in the decades leading up to the Reform of 1864. I have endeavored to determine how personnel changes affected the composition of different levels of the judicial system, and for this reason have analyzed the data from different periods separately according to office. The material suggests that a new type of official was beginning to appear at all levels of the system before the reform. Chapter 3 describes changes in officials' social backgrounds, educational preparation, and career patterns.

But such changes in composition would have had little significance if they were not accompanied by changes in attitudes. The personal materials left by legal officials — state papers, memoirs, letters, literary and philosophical works — attest to changes in their goals, values, and approaches to their service obligations. Part 2 deals with the views and experiences of officials of different generations. It examines the personal factors that made possible the adoption of new approaches to law and service, and the cultural influences that would shape a new ethos.

The era of reforms brought reassessments of autocratic policy, and allowed the new judicial cadres to devise a reform based on their own principles. The Judicial Reform of 1864 introduced a court system patterned on recent European models. But the Russian autocrat, though made aware of the importance of judicial expertise, never fully accepted the enhanced role of the judiciary within the autocratic system, or the new type of official who would staff it. He and his advisors continued to see the independent judiciary as a usurpation of autocratic prerogatives, threatening to the very basis of the tsar's power. Unlike the monarchies of central Europe, the Russian tsar never came to terms with his judiciary.

This study attempts to examine how the processes of legal modernization fit into the traditional patterns of Russian statecraft. The dynamic element was the autocracy's effort to strengthen and rationalize its apparatus as it strove to approximate western models of the absolute state. This tendency is what George Yaney has described under the general rubric of the "systematization" of Russian government.[15] The barrier to change resided in the danger that such a tendency might entail to the power of the monarchy and the nobility. Part 1 describes the evolution of the policy of absolutist autocracy which led the monarch to use law as a means to extend the authority of the state. During this phase, the effective working of the state and the precise implementation of the laws became a way for the autocrat to extend his own power and to enhance his image and legitimacy. Specialization and legal expertise began to assume importance and to affect the personnel of legal institutions. Part 2 considers the subjective side of this process, the changing mentality, feelings, and aspirations of the generations of officials who had to deal with the problem of acting in behalf of the law in the Russian administration. Part 3 is a discussion of the reform era. It analyzes the politics of reform that permitted the officials in the legal administration to achieve their goals, and the difficulties that awaited an independent judiciary within the framework of Russian autocracy.

I
AUTOCRACY AND THE LAW

1
ABSOLUTISM
AND JUSTICE
IN EIGHTEENTH-CENTURY
RUSSIA

With what sorrow, we, with our love for our subjects, must see that many laws, enacted for the happiness and well-being of the state are not implemented due to the widespread internal enemies, who prefer their own illegal profit to their oath, duty and honor. What sorrow we must feel that such deeply rooted evil is not extirpated. The Senate, as our first governmental office, according to its obligations and vested powers, should long ago have eliminated the many disorders that are multiplying unhindered in subordinate offices to the great harm of the state.

The insatiable greed for profit has grown to such an extent, that some offices, established for legal justice, have turned into market places for bribery. Partiality has become the guide of judges and connivance and dereliction encouragements to outlaws. Many cases and people oppressed by injustice are in a truly pitiful condition; we sincerely lament this and also that our gentleness and moderation in the punishment of criminals has brought so ungrateful a requital.

Imperial Decree of Her Majesty
Elizabeth Petrovna to the Governing
Senate, 16 August 1760

IN THE EIGHTEENTH CENTURY, RUSSIAN AUTOCRACY TOOK ON A NEW GUISE. IT began to appear as a dynamic, secular force in the life of the country. The Russian tsar and emperor went beyond the roles bestowed upon him by tradition. He undertook vast new responsibilities in the developing of the economy, the strengthening of institutions, and the supervision of the moral life of the population. The Russian rulers of the eighteenth century emulated the examples of western monarchies. They embarked on what might be called the "absolutist" phase of Russian autocracy. The model for Russian government became the absolute "police" state of the West, whether exemplified in Sweden, Prussia, or Napoleonic France. Like the monarchs of the evolving European police states, the Russian tsar sought to extend his own authority to regulate state and society. He attempted to take over the direction of the moral life of the nation, to realize the "dream of a city where moral obligation was joined to civil law within authoritarian forms of constraint."[1]

The new image of authority was a new source of legitimization for the monarch's power. Not only the annointed of God, he would be the guardian of his nation's well-being. Peter the Great's assertion that he had "to labor for the general welfare and profit" was typical of the eighteenth-century justification of legislation. The monarch was directing the state to work for the general welfare (*obshchaia pol'za*), ensuring the economic well-being, security, and happiness of the citizenry.[2] The ruler's power was justified by the concern for the welfare of the citizenry. The state could secure the general welfare by making government operate according to law. Laws would govern the work of the institutions of state and direct the efforts of officials toward the goals set by the ruler. Peter the Great began the long effort to establish legality (*zakonnost'*) as the basis of the operations of the state.

In the attainment of the general welfare, the securing of legal justice (*pravosudie*) was a principal, if not the principal, component. Peter's General Regulation, the statute defining the work and procedures of the colleges, cited the protection of justice first in its listing of the goals of his new institutions. Feofan Prokopovich's *Law of the Monarch's Will* (*Pravda voli monarshei*), the chief ideological manifesto of Petrine absolutism, stressed that the first of the monarch's obligations in seeking the national welfare (*vsenarodnaia pol'za*) was to care for legal justice — to safeguard the wronged from those who were wronging them.[3] After Peter, the protection of justice would remain a prominent feature of the absolute monarch's image of protector of the nation's welfare. Elizabeth, Catherine the Great, Alexander I, Nicholas I, all would voice urgent concern for the condition of justice and the insufficiencies of Russian courts.

The absolute monarch's heightened sense of responsibility for justice made him only more suspicious of judges, whose knowledge, impartiality, and honesty had always been open to question. Here, as in all areas of state life, the ruler aimed to control the acts of officials who were implementing his policies. Judges were intermediaries who applied the monarch's law, at best imperfectly, and whose discretion should be limited as much as possible. To western rulers and thinkers, the legal profession had come to represent a residue of traditional habits and attachments acting to thwart the will of the rational legislator. An antilegalist spirit animated Frederick the Great to try to abolish lawyers in Prussia, and Jeremy Bentham to find a rational legislation that would eliminate the need for lawyers' obfuscation. Leibnitz had set forth the rationalist ideal when he had written to Leopold I of Austria describing "a summary of Roman law," the size of a large Dutch map, "which contains all the main rules in such a way that from their combination all forthcoming cases should be decided. . . ."[4]

Eighteenth-century antilegalist attitudes reinforced and dignified the Russian autocrat's traditional disdain for the judicial function. Judges provoked the monarch's exasperation, and on occasion rage, as evinced in Empress Elizabeth's decree of 16 August 1760. In 1697, Peter the Great expressed what was to become the Russian tsar's fundamental notion of the perils of litigation. The courts were a breeding ground for chicanery and every kind of fraud.

> From the plaintiffs and defendants there is much injustice and conniving. Many have started suits to no purpose. Defendants have answered with untruths. . . . Other plaintiffs and defendants involved in the same perfidy hire for the confrontation [*poval'nyi obysk*] their brothers and boyar children, those chicaners and contrivers, those thieves and despoilers of souls, who force the weak to go through red tape, bribes, losses and ruin.[5]

The greater the monarch's desire to bring the benefits of law to Russia, the greater his determination to narrow the role of the judge. Catherine the Great, who early in her reign presented herself as the champion of a new expanded role of law and legal equality, was most suspicious of the nefarious ways of judges. Like the philosophes, she regarded the legal profession as just another private interest, inventing mysteries and complexities to obscure the rational pronouncements of the legislator. One of her favorite texts, Beccaria's *Crimes and Punishments,* provided many articles for her famous *nakaz,* the Instruction to the Legislative Commission of 1767. Beccaria's contribution is best known as the source of her pleas for an end to torture and corporal punishment. But in addition to humanitarian considerations, Catherine found in Beccaria strong statements of the need to control the judges, and these found their way into the *nakaz.* "No inconvenience that may arise from a strict observance of the letter of penal laws is to be compared with inconveniences of subjecting them to interpretation," Beccaria wrote. The judge was to make a syllogism: the first proposition being the law, the second whether the law applied to the facts, and the last the all but automatic verdict. Article 98 of the *nakaz* declared, in words borrowed directly from Beccaria, "The Power of a Judge consists only in the due execution of the laws to the end that no doubt may arise with respect to the Liberty and Security of the Citizens." Article 153: "Nothing is so dangerous as this general Axiom: The Spirit of the Law ought to be considered and not the Letter." Article 178: "Where the laws are precise and clear, the office of a judge consists only in ascertaining the Fact."[6] The Provincial Reform of 1775, with its dispersion of judicial authority, would bring additional assertions of the limits of judicial discretion. Article 184 of the reform declared that "the decision of a case is reached not otherwise but on the strength of laws and according to the words of the law."[7]

The Russian tsar did not face the deeply rooted private law traditions of the West and did not have to rely upon corps of jurists to buttress his own claims to authority. His strictures were not attacks on entrenched and conservative corporations, but threats issued at the actions of subservient, if wayward officials. His legislation aimed at limiting the role of their fallible judgment in applying the law. In principle, it banished legal interpretation from the judicial system. The judge was to adhere to the statutes and, when in doubt, turn to higher state organs for elucidation. Russian procedural law until 1864 would exclude judicial interpretation or reference to precedent as grounds for judicial decisions.

Lawyers, as private individuals who could manipulate the law, appeared even more dubious in official eyes. Legislation discouraged the use of representatives in the courts. Those who took on the task of representing litigants in the courts were usually marginal individuals in the judicial system, retired clerks practiced in the formalities of paper work and the ways of bribery, or serfs of wealthy noblemen trained to watch out for their masters' interests. The retired clerks often collaborated with their former colleagues in the chancelleries to the disadvantage of their clients, or worked for both parties in civil suits. They existed at the edge of the system, the barely tolerated Frol Skobeevs of the Russian autocracy.[8]

In the West, William Bouwsma has shown, lawyers served as protectors of order and property, mediators between stability and change, and most important, agents of secularization, who could deal with the imperfections of the real world within a rational intellectual framework.[9] In Russia this concession to the secular world was not easily received. The autocrat, whatever his personal weaknesses, remained the moral guardian of the nation, and lawyers as instruments of moral compromise always remained suspect. Peter the Great's Military Statute of 1716 tried to ban advocates from criminal trials: "By their worthless, prolonged arguments, they are a burden to the judge, and extend cases to enormous length, rather than bring them to swift conclusions."[10] "Lawyers," Catherine the Great wrote, "depending on when they are paid and who pays them now defend what is true, now what is false; now what is just, now what is unjust." The role of lawyers in the French Revolution only confirmed earlier fears. "Lawyers and procurators do not legislate here and never will legislate while I am alive. After me, my principles will be followed." Catherine's successors were no more sympathetic to lawyers. Nicholas I was terrified of them and would not hear of their introduction to Russia. During his reign, the word *lawyer* (*advokat*) was banned from the press.[11]

The autocrat's concern for justice and distrust for judges led to the creation of institutions to watch over the dispensation of justice. One of the principal functions of the institutions of the Petrine state was to oversee the work of judicial offices. Peter's highest governmental organ, the Senate, received its first assignment to act as an appeal organ, which was "to judge without deceit and to punish unrighteous judges by stripping them of their honor and all their possessions."[12] In the decree establishing the colleges, Peter declared his intention "to bring civil government into the same good order as the military," and thus prevent the abuses of the judges in the old *prikazy* who had amassed so much power that they "did whatever they wanted."[13] The colleges, established under the Senate, partly at Leibnitz's prompting, were supposed to control the actions of officials. The eight to ten members of each college would watch over each other's conduct and direct the work of subordinate institutions. The Justice College and the Land College (*Votchina Kollegiia*) would supervise the handling of legal cases and act as appeal instances.

The Senate and colleges, however, proved poor watchdogs over justice. Peter found frequent and flagrant examples of disregard of his laws. Irritated, he declared, in a decree that would be quoted throughout the eighteenth and nineteenth centuries, that "it is pointless to write laws when they are not safeguarded or are played with like cards so that those of the same suit are placed together...." He commanded that the General Regulation of the colleges be glued on boards with pedestals and kept on the desks in all the judicial offices of the empire, "like a mirror before the eyes of the judge." Finally, he commanded in 1724 that those responsible for injustice in the courts would be punished by death, "natural or political," and the deprivation of all estates.[14]

Peter's vexation resulted in the creation of a new official, the procurator-general, whose duty became the overseeing of the Senate and the entire civil administration. The procurator-general was to sit in the Senate and "to watch closely so that the Senate preserves its office, and dispatches all cases that are subject to its review or decision truthfully, zealously, decorously, promptly, and according to the regulations and decrees." He was to ensure that "cases are not completed only at the desk, but are executed in real action."[15] He was assisted by a corps of procurators who reported to him on failures to observe the law. The procurator-general was virtually a military officer placed in command of the Senate, which was instructed to obey him in all matters. The procurator-generals themselves were ex-military men. Lieutenant-General Pavel Ivanovich Iaguzhinskii, the first to hold the office, was a former guard's officer. All his successors as procurator-general in the eighteenth century would be products of military training and service, most of them attaining high rank before they shifted to civil duties.[16]

The problem of controlling justice in provincial institutions was especially difficult. When Peter came to the throne, justice was among the responsibilities of the officials in charge of all local administration—the provincial chiefs—*voevedy*. In short, legal remedies were sought from administrative authorities. Peter tried to create separate judicial offices in the provinces that would be directly responsible to the Justice College. He instituted a system of separate royal courts (*nadvornye sudy*)—usually translated as Aulic Courts—that were under the authority of the Justice College and presumably outside the purview of the administration. But this attempt to create a discrete judicial sphere in the Russian state was premature. The provincial administrative heads, civil governors or *voevody*, quickly used their preeminent power in the area to direct and dominate the operations of the courts. On occasion, governors even had themselves appointed chairmen of these courts. Once the Justice College itself was invaded by a corps of dragoons sent from the Petersburg Provincial Chancellery to remove a petitioner protesting a ruling of the governor.[17] After Peter's death, the hierarchy of Aulic Courts was eliminated, and full authority over justice in the provinces restored to the *voevody* and governors. Until Catherine's reform of provincial government in 1775, justice in the provinces remained a function of administrative offices. On the lowest level, the *provintsiia*, the *voevoda*, and particularly his chancellery decided legal cases. Above him the governor, *gubernator*, in the *guberniia* received appeals. The highest instances remained the Justice College and the Senate.

Catherine the Great, in her endeavor to free local authorities from the excess of tasks burdening them and to ensure "the unobstructed course of justice," introduced the first exclusively judicial institutions to the provinces. The Reform of 1775 created local courts in the new districts, *uezdy*. There were separate courts for each class and the judges were elective. Above the district there were appeals courts, the highest of which, the Civil and Criminal Chambers, received appeals from all districts and heard certain cases, such as official crimes, as first instances. The Provincial

Chambers assumed the functions of the Justice College, which Catherine dismantled. Members of the chambers were appointed by the Senate, which continued to serve as the highest instance in the system.[18]

The new provincial institutions were subjected to elaborate devices of control. The reform introduced a procurator in each province, who was responsible to the procurator-general and the local Provincial Bureau (*gubernskoe pravlenie*). He was to be aided by two assistants, called *striapchiia,* for criminal and treasury cases. District *striapchie* were to supervise the legality of operations of district courts and institutions. At the same time, Catherine affirmed the governor's obligation to oversee justice. The new eminence she established in the provinces — the commander-in-chief, governor-general, or *namestnik* — also had extensive responsibilities for watching over the dispensation of justice. As the personal plenipotentiary of the empress, he was to punish irregularities in the courts, protest unjust decisions to the Senate or the empress, and confirm sentences involving deprivation of life and honor.[19]

Three separate offices were thus supposed to ensure that officials enforced the law in the province. In fact, the procurators usually reached a modus vivendi with the governors, who were concerned primarily with avoiding disruption and allowing ordinary corruption to continue in judicial offices. Procurators were of lower rank than governors and found it easier to join than to fight them. Campaigns to root out dishonesty and illegality, like that undertaken in the first decades of Catherine's reign, consequently had little effect, and most of the supervision became limited to the fulfillment of formalities. "The circle of serving people in each governmental office, in the bureaucracy, in the provinces, in the districts, represented a more or less solid union, with mutual protection and services."[20]

To keep the judges from straying from the law, the eighteenth-century monarch introduced a written, inquisitorial procedure, which presumably permitted easy verification by higher organs. Peter I issued the legislation that would define the procedures governing Russian courts down to the Judicial Reform of 1864. Peter adopted the inquisitorial procedures in use at the end of the seventeenth century, systematized them, and used them to curb the discretion of the judge. The rules governing the operation of courts were set forth in the Military Process section of the Military Statute of 1716. The statute, borrowed from Swedish, Danish, and German military codes, sought to incorporate the most recent principles of closed canonical procedure and proofs into a generally tightened system of military organization and discipline. Though it stipulated that its rules would apply only to military personnel, a decree ordering its dissemination, issued eleven days later, extended their effect to civil courts as well.[21] The Military Process made no distinction between civil and criminal cases;

it ordered trials to be closed and secret: all present "must keep what happened in court secret and tell no one, whoever he may be, anything about it."[22] The suit could be initiated either by a plaintiff or a judge. Defendants were to respond orally to the charges; written statements were optional.

The Process required that the judge comply with formal proofs established by the law. The best proof was voluntary confession, then followed witnesses' testimony, written statements, and the purifying oath. The Process enumerated at great length the types of witnesses to be excluded. The social standing of the witnesses would determine the weight to be given to their testimony and the outcome of the case.[23] Peter followed both European models and previous Russian practice in allowing torture to be used to induce confession, and in surrounding this permission with numerous limitations to prevent its abuse. He specified that the judge was to apply torture only in cases where he felt "complete suspicion" — where there was strong evidence from two eyewitnesses. In civil cases, the judge was to order torture only when evidence of a criminal act came to light: "if, in great and important civil cases a witness becomes difficult, or confused, or changes the expression on his face."[24] More specific definition of inquisitorial process awaited a new codification. Materials prepared for a code in the 1720s included rules for evidence, punishments, and use of torture.[25]

The Military Process was only the first of many statutes and decrees aiming to regiment judicial officials and force them to apply the law. A plethora of rules came to define every stage of the trial. The system of correspondence between courts, the keeping of protocols, were defined down to the most petty detail. The courts had to confirm their observance of these rules in writing; "every step of the court had to leave a trace on paper."[26] How to keep the written formalities of the court was described in the decree, On the Form of the Court.

On the Form of the Court provided rules to guide the court secretary in following the proper forms, and assigned to him the responsibility for observing correct written procedure. The decree established strict formal requirements for official proceedings. Testimony was to be written down in "points." Secretaries must prepare two notebooks, one for the testimony of the plaintiff, the other of the defendant, and sign and impress their seal on each page. Litigants were to present their testimony orally, but only so the secretary could record it according to the rules established in the decree.[27]

The procedure governing cases, both civil and criminal in eighteenth- and nineteenth-century courts, consequently, was closed and inquisitorial. Litigants saw the secretary and the chancellery staff, but usually not the judge, and decisions were reached behind closed doors. The judge became dependent on the chancellery workers, who reviewed the facts of the case as transmitted by the police, and knew the laws and rules necessary to express the case in the proper form.

The ideal the absolutist state aspired to in the eighteenth century was a judiciary faithful to statute law, whose actions were monitored by supervisory institutions intent on protecting that law. Needless to say, the reality fell far short of the ideal, as the accounts of prereform courts make clear. This was partly due to the usual divergence of life from the system prescribed for it by reforming rulers. But it was also the result of an ambivalence in the ruler's own attitudes toward legality in Russian institutions. The Russian tsar never completely adopted the values of the European absolute monarch. He borrowed western forms but disregarded them when he saw fit.

Seeking to institutionalize authority, the autocrat never abandoned his reliance upon personal authority. On the one hand there was a movement toward order in the state; on the other, there was resistance to order when it would constrain the exercise of the tsar's personal whim or will. This fundamental ambivalence would limit the effect of the effort to transform the Russian state, to establish the rule of law in place of the rule of men.

The ruler's personal power could at any time overrule and cancel the action of law or procedures. What is perhaps more important, the desire of the ruler when expressed by his subordinates could have the same effect. Down to the end of the empire it remained impossible to distinguish a law (*zakon*) from an administrative ruling (*razporiazhenie*), which had the force and often the scope of law. The tsar could make the recommendation of a subordinate law by issuing an imperial command (*vysochaishchee povelenie*). Repeated efforts to distinguish between laws and administrative rulings failed, as the monarch's decree (*ukaz*) could give any ruling he chose legislative force, whether or not it had gone through prescribed channels or conflicted with earlier laws.[28]

The tsar's attachment to his personal power made him chary of all legal definition of authority. As a result, while law was supposed to be the basis for the new state, the attempts to order, compile, and disseminate the law were performed perfunctorily at best. Codification was a cause that every Russian monarch subscribed to, but which most pursued less than enthusiastically. Peter the Great began work on a new codification. It was initiated a total of nine times in the eighteenth century, but without result. The repeated failures were in part due to an eighteenth-century approach to codification, which sought to combine moral principles derived from natural law with existing laws of each country.[29] This presented enormous difficulties in practice, as suggested by Peter's attempt to use Swedish legislation as a model and Catherine's to follow the teachings of the philosophes. But another, and perhaps more important stumbling block was the ruler's reluctance to delegate power over codification to officials and institutions that might seek to usurp legislative authority.

The Empress Elizabeth had provided an example of the dangers of allowing an institution to undertake its own review of the law. She had ordered the Senate to examine all laws promulgated since the death of Peter the Great in order to determine which were "not in keeping with the condition of the time" and which were "in conflict with the well-being of the state." Deviations from Peter's legislation were to be eliminated. The senators used this assignment to interpret and alter many laws without Elizabeth's knowledge and consent, and her successors found her leniency deplorable.[30] Peter III decreed on 1 June 1762, "We, by the Grace of God ... most highly command that from now on the Senate issue to the public no decree with the force of law, or [which] even serves to interpret previous laws without submitting it to Us and obtaining Our approval for it." In 1764, Catherine also complained that the Senate had exceeded its authority and issued laws.[31]

The codifying commissions of the eighteenth and early nineteenth centuries were under similar pressures. They had both to reform and preserve without giving the appearance of arrogating judgment to themselves as to what constituted the golden mean. The autocrat in turn avoided entrusting this work to a stable group of officials whose exclusive task was codification. Those officials assigned usually held other responsibilities as well and could not give it undivided attention. They were replaced before they had ample time to familiarize themselves with their duties, and on occasion the entire staff of the agency assigned to codification was changed without apparent reason.[32]

The same distrust extended to works describing or explaining the Russian law. No such work was published until the reign of Catherine the Great. This was due in part to the lack of publications on secular subjects in general by the state. But published collections of decrees also were rare, covering only the years 1714 to 1725, and 1717 to 1728. Even guides to legal forms and contract were lacking; the first, a guide to writing letters, appeared in 1789.[33]

Thus a judicial system based exclusively on statute law had to operate without available ways to determine what statute law was. The court system functioned in the chancelleries, where clerks kept notebooks of decrees, which they exchanged among themselves and sold for high prices.[34] Derzhavin, when serving as governor of Saratov in 1785, could not find a single book of laws in the entire province. At his request, his friends searched Moscow but could find only copies of military regulations to send him.[35]

The autocrat's distrust for the judiciary thus arose from two contrary premises. First, that the judges would not adhere to the institutions and rules set up to implement his authority; second, that the judges might use institutions and rules to curtail his personal power. The informal, patriarchal image of the tsar, however it might fade in the eighteenth

17

century, still retained a great appeal. This appeal was particularly potent for members of the nobility, many of whom prided themselves on a special relationship with the crown, which conferred grace and favor that placed them above the law. Thus, the tsar appeared in two guises — as the absolute monarch directing institutions and insisting on compliance with the law, and as the patriarch-autocrat whose supreme power enabled him to bestow favors on those close to him. As patriarch-autocrat, he could subvert his own absolutist princples, while the emphatic solemnity with which he pronounced those principles lent a peculiar pathos to his acts of personal grace.

The Russian nobility shared the ruler's disdain for the judiciary and the judicial function. They had attained their position not on the basis of traditional privileges but by service to the autocratic sovereign, and they sought their interests through the exercise of his untrammeled executive power. A strong judiciary could only subject their own position to the standards of an external law, and threaten whatever benefits had accrued to them through personal connections and their own ruthlessness or enterprise.

But the attitudes of the Russian nobility represented a serious obstacle to the goals of absolutist justice. The absolute states of central Europe had consolidated their authority over justice by asserting their power over noble corporations and other groups that had traditionally carried on legal functions. The estates came under increasing royal control, allowing the central power to direct and yet make use of the legal authority and experience of local corporations. The Russian nobility, lacking such traditions, could not serve as an intermediary assisting the extension of royal justice. It was a warrior class which Peter the Great created out of the diverse groups that had provided service to the Muscovite state. Arms were the nobleman's metier and pride. Thus, Prince Shcherbatov extolled the nobility's contributions to Russia's greatness: "Who after all was it who lent you a helping hand at the time of your greatest calamity? Those, your faithful sons, the ancient Russian noblemen! They, defending everything and sacrificing their lives, they, freed you from the alien yoke and regained your old liberty." Law was a grasping for profit, *nazhivochnoe delo,* scarcely appropriate to a nobility that had won the tsar's gratitude by sacrifice on the battlefield.[36]

Peter the Great urged the nobility into judicial positions, and noblemen would in fact rule over judicial offices during the eighteenth century. But they took on judicial office only after initial training and service in the military, and it became customary for retiring officers to apply directly to the Senate for judicial positions. Peter drew the initial membership of his new civil service from the officer corps that had achieved success in the Northern War. Similar practices continued after his death. In 1738, less than one-quarter of the 211 members of the colleges had not served in the military. In 1755 only about 22 percent of the highest officials of the government had begun their career in the civil service or had studied in non-military educational institutions; 61.5 percent began in the military or military schools; 16.5 percent in some office connected with the tsar's court (*dvor*). The great majority of these high officials were hereditary noblemen.[37]

Much the same pattern prevailed in local institutions. Peter's Aulic Courts were staffed predominantly by officers; the Nizhnii Novgorod Aulic Court, for example, consisted of one colonel, one major, three captains, and one *tsaredvorets* (designating a member of the Moscow serving class of the previous century). Most of the *voevody,* who were in charge of local justice in the time between Peter's death and the reform of 1775, were military men. The second provincial instance, headed by governors and vice-governors, appears to have had much the same composition. Of sixteen heads of provincial administration whose lists were examined by Troitskii, thirteen had previously served as soldiers in the army or sailors in the fleet. Though the Provincial Reform created a distinct hierarchy of courts, the military remained the initial career for most judges. Of sixty-seven chairmen of provincial judicial chambers in 1788 discussed by Givens, fifty-seven or 85 percent had begun their service in the military; forty chairmen had spent over fifteen years in military service. About the same proportions prevailed at the beginning of the nineteenth century. Of thirty lists for chairmen, twenty-five or 83 percent indicate initial military service, and fourteen, military service of more than fifteen years.[38]

The highest judicial offices, the Senate and the Justice College, were dominated by wealthy and powerful noblemen who had reached their positions through connections they enjoyed in Petersburg. Seven of the eleven senators in 1754 belonged to the titled aristocracy. Titled noblemen also served as heads of the colleges and as ambassadors and governors. These leading families belonged to the richest 3 percent of the nobility and were related to each other through an intricate system of family ties. Some of the great families boasted old lineages, others had recently come to favor and received extensive estates, but all owed their continued wealth and political standing to the throne.[39]

As serf owners, the nobility, from the smallest landlords to the greatest magnates, shared the ruler's executive predispositions and were inclined to be suspicious of a strong judicial authority. Noble landlords held judicial as well as administrative authority over their serfs, and as masters preferred their power over their peasants to be undefined. The unconditional nature of their serfs' obedience gave them the exaltation of participating in power and allowed them to identify with their sovereign's aversion to institutional limits. The intrusion of justice, applied by impartial judges, could only impeach their claims to power and importance. The administrative hierarchy protected and bolstered their authority; it provided swift and ruthless repression when the serfs became unruly and threatened to break into uncontrolled rebellion.

The monarch's position was too vulnerable to allow him to be severe with influential noblemen. The elimination of the succession law by Peter the Great created an insecurity in the monarch's own position, making him dependent on cliques in the court and the guard to maintain power. He rewarded his favorites with large grants of land and high positions in government, and was not wont to allow them to be judged by the institutions of the state. The Empress Elizabeth was thus not exaggerating her leniency in her decree of 1760, and her resolve to combat dishonesty and introduce strict punishment proved largely limited to words. Her procurator-general, Iakov Shakhovskoi, sought futilely to stop the illegal machinations of Peter Shuvalov, a favorite and president of the War College.[40] Catherine the Great's unsuccessful attempt to punish Governor Arshenevskii, and Alexander I's to prosecute Governor Lopukhin (see chapter 4) were examples of how helpless the autocrat was in coping with flagrant and unquestionable transgressions by the powerful.[41]

Provincial noblemen would protect their interests by appealing to eminent and powerful members of their class, and perhaps to the tsar himself. This sense of personal dependence and relationships in turn made them even more wary of formal institutionalized legality.[42] Behind the facade of the autocratic state, there existed an intricate system of protection and influence dominated by the wealthiest and most influential members of the nobility, reaching to the throne itself. David Ransel's analysis of an eighteenth-century letter-book has provided evidence of the importance of patronage hierarchies in protecting the individual nobleman against the arbitrariness of the system. A lesser nobleman could defend himself against criminal charges or safeguard his interests in a civil suit by securing the protection of an important figure in the hierarchy of patronage. In Petersburg, the influence of these hierarchies was so strong that the Senate was reluctant to convict members of the nobility of crimes. Early in her reign, Catherine had to appear personally at Senate sessions to convince the senators to enforce her decisions in legal cases.[43]

The provincial nobility in the eighteenth century seemed to prefer informal settling of disputes where this was possible. Unfortunately, this practice has left few traces in the sources. Personal mediation was one means of settling disputes, though it is difficult to tell how frequently it was used. Gogol's judge, Demian Demianovich, who advised the two Ivans to settle their differences amicably at a drinking party to which he would be invited, was a caricature of what must have been a familiar type. When mediation failed, there could be resort to armed confrontation; force was a common arbiter of disputes in the eighteenth century. In the 1750s, private wars took place between armies as large as six hundred men organized into regular military formations and observing military ceremonies.[44] Defendants would use armed men to intimidate government officials seeking to enforce court decisions. The descriptions of force as an element dominating the countryside in Aksakov's *Family Chronicle* and Pushkin's *Dubrovskii* were not mere literary inventions.[45]

The provincial nobility complained bitterly about the conditions of local judicial institutions in their *cahiers,* their *nakazy* to the Legislative Commission of 1767. Of 134 *nakazy* examined by Jones, 80 expressed grievances about the condition of justice.[46] The nobility of Riazhsk district pointed out that the local court — the chancellery of the *voevoda* — had not settled a single suit in fifteen years. The strong people in the countryside were impudently seizing the lands and serfs of their neighbors, knowing full well that the courts would not protect the victims.[47] The Epifanov nobility voiced similar complaints, claiming that lesser landlords could receive redress of their grievances at best after waits of ten to twenty years. "Receiving no satisfaction," the *nakaz* declared, "the poor and helpless endure want and deprivation, because of these deficiencies and the numerous appeals that seldom if ever are decided."[48]

Yet, however great their distress at the dispensation of justice, it is clear that they did not see the solution in a strong judiciary. Their proposals called for judges from the local nobility who would be sympathetic to their needs and apart from the formal administrative system. These judges would decide disputes not according to law, written or customary, but by the exercise of their personal judgment. The nobility wanted "a wise father, a protector, a guardian, and not at all a bureaucrat." The *nakaz* of Serpukhov-Obolensk-Tarusa declared, "The *zemskii* judge must be like a guardian to the district and defend its inhabitants." The provincial nobility wanted disputes to be settled in a family manner. The Iaroslav *nakaz* asked for a noble commissar "who will try to reconcile [opponents] by calling them unto him . . . explaining to both of them which cause is in the right and leading the stubborn party to a reasonable admission. . . ." The Rostov and Tula nobility wanted meetings of neighboring landlords to settle disputes.[49]

The Russian nobility, with its aversion to legal procedures and legal institutions, had to preside over courts that demanded an expertise — a mastery of forms and procedures, and an ability to find laws and connect them with the facts of the case. Such paper work was not to the taste of the noblemen, many of whom, in any case, were illiterate. They left it in the hands of the clerks and the office staff — the chancellery. Eighteenth- and early nineteenth-century courts were consequently comprised of two almost separate worlds. The judges, predominantly of military background, who preferred informal methods, knew little about the law, and had little experience in the courts, held the power of decision. The chancellery, the repository of knowledge of the law and bureaucratic routine, would prepare the case and often the decision that the judge would sign.

The functional division between judge and chancellery marked a social division as well. Peter tried to train young noblemen to serve as secretaries in the colleges and the Senate, but the repeated complaints of the Senate in the first half of the century indicate their reluctance to do so.[50] After the nobility's emancipation from service in 1762, the government seems to have relinquished this effort. In the provinces, the chancelleries of judicial offices were non-noble throughout the century. The chancellery staff of the *voevody* was comprised of sons of chancellery workers—the *prikaznye liudi*—who had served as clerks for generations. Their numbers were augmented by sons of clergy, who had left the church and obtained the right to work in the civil administration.[51]

In the course of the eighteenth century, judicial expertise came to be associated with the low social status of those who performed clerical work. The class of clerks dominated the chancelleries and set the tone for recruits from the clergy, who came to resemble them. Clerical workers entered service young, between the ages of nine and twelve, as copiers and learned the arts of handwriting, filling out forms, and finding laws. They pursued the same task through their lives, learning to avoid the appearance of thought or interpretation. Their argument was limited to "so speak the laws," and they disposed of a cover of legal citations that permitted them to turn a case in any way they deemed desirable. Interpretation of the law thus proceeded, but under cover, precluding the references to prior practice that would permit the evolution of a cumulative legal experience.

The chancellery workers of the eighteenth century were even more confined than their Muscovite forebears. The new notion of nobility set them apart from the dominant class of the Russian state. In the seventeenth century, they owned small plots of land and even serfs, but in the course of the eighteenth century, land and serf holding became a noble privilege, though a few were able to evade restrictions. During the eighteenth century, it also became increasingly difficult for them to rise to positions above the chancellery, which were occupied by nobles.[52]

The clerks formed an isolated caste without a sense of its own importance or dignity. Their freedom from the soul tax set them apart from the lower classes, whom they despised. They envied the members of the hereditary nobility whose privileges and wealth tantalized them with possible, if highly unlikely rewards for service. They wanted above all to regain the right to own serfs, to spare their wives the humiliating trials of public manual labor, such as leading their cows to the town watering hole each morning. Those who rose to the fourteenth rank became personal nobles. They then enjoyed the right to sue for insult. But they still faced the scorn of hereditary noblemen, who called them "pettifoggers" (*krapivnye semena*). They still had to scrape before them in their own homes when the quartering obligation forced them to house officers assigned to their town.[53]

The members of the chancellery class lived by values of a status most of them could not hope to attain. Their worship of hierarchy, their grasping dishonesty — often resulting from a condition of dire poverty — provoked the sneers of noblemen and provided the material for the literary stereotype of the almost inhuman office worker in nineteenth-century Russian literature. For the members of the chancellery class, the only escape from this situation was to be ennobled, and the only way to be ennobled was, in some manner, to excel in subservience and gain the protection of an influential nobleman. "The power and authority of the magnates [*vel'mozhi*] can bring the greatest of advantages to the subordinate able to endure, to suffer, to obey, to execute," wrote Gavriil Dobrynin, the son of a poor priest who followed this precept to rise out of the chancellery to become counselor and procurator in provincial courts.[54]

During the eighteenth and early nineteenth centuries there were several conspicuous examples of non-nobles who reached prominent positions in the state: Dmitrii Volkov, the state-secretary of Peter III; Count Alexander Bezborodko, the secretary to Catherine II; Dmitrii Troshchinskii, chairman of the Permanent Council and minister of justice; and Michael Speranskii. It is indicative that none of these figures rose through the chancelleries of state institutions. Each achieved recognition by his faithful and able service to a great nobleman, who, when he came to favor, brought his protégé to the attention of the ruler. Those who succeeded in this manner received hereditary nobility and, during the eighteenth century, estates with serfs. With the exception of Speranskii, they tried to resemble the great noblemen whom they served. The few non-nobles at the summit of the government could not constitute a discrete bureaucratic nobility with their own pretensions and esprit de corps. Nor like the noblesse de la robe did they bring outside commercial interests or education to the legal system, as in the lower levels of the French parlements.[55] The Russian bureaucratic nobility could have no leavening effect; they were merely a dutiful class of servants who helped their noble protectors operate the Russian administration.

The low social status of the chancellery prevented the clerks from developing their own sense of self-respect as defenders of the law. When they were appointed to judicial positions, they had to make clear that their allegiance was to the hierarchy of power and not to the law. The first president of the Justice College, A. A. Matveev, was one of the men of humble background whom Peter the Great had raised. A member of the chancellery class, Matveev immediately felt the difficulties of imposing formal justice. He wrote to Peter,

> The college, despatching everything correctly, according to its oath and obligation before Your Highness, and not catering to the wishes of any others, has gained many foes who are always seeking to do harm, both secretly and openly.

One aristocrat was all but waging war on him:

> And there are other aristocratic figures who have cases brought against them by the fiscal officers, or against their relatives and friends. Seeing that I, without deceit and self-interest, refuse to cater to them in their cases, they, with their friends and relatives, plot against me and threaten to do me irreparable harm both before Your Highness and in the Senate. As a result, I, a mere orphan, am always in peril from them. For Hercules himself could hardly withstand two.[56]

But the loyal servant could expect little support from his sovereign, himself the most prominent member of the elite. The ruler was forgiving of the misdeeds of the magnates and cooperative in assisting them to wield influence. Matveev was the last of his kind to be president of the Justice College. All eight of his successors were noblemen, several from such illustrious families as the Golitsyns, Shcherbatovs, and Trubetskois.[57]

The nobility, however great their reluctance to prepare for a civil career, jealously guarded high offices against the rise of able members of the chancellery. Attempts to open high offices on a regular basis to chancellery workers evoked strenuous protest from noble circles. With the nobility's emancipation from service, Volkov, Peter III's secretary, tried to introduce a "professionalization" of the upper ranks of the bureaucracy by filling them with experienced officials who had risen through the administration. Volkov's policy was one of the factors leading to his and his sovereign's swift downfall.[58] Speranskii would experience similar problems in his effort to raise the quality of officials in the early nineteenth century.

Improvement of judicial officials thus depended on a change in the attitudes of the nobility toward judicial office. The Russian ruler tried in various ways to create the kind of concern for justice in the Russian nobility that was evident in their European counterparts. Throughout the century, official statements importuned the nobility to begin work in the chancellery, and asserted the dignity of chancellery work, despite all indications to the contrary. Intellectuals and jurists, spokesmen of westernization, extolled the calling of the law. These views, at odds with the dispositions and tastes of the ruler and the nobility, introduced conflicting elements into the mentality of those noblemen who took them seriously.

Peter had hoped that noblemen would in fact take on secretarial positions and learn to work in the chancellery. The General Regulation established junker schools under each of the colleges for members of the nobility, *shliakhetsvo,* who would, "by the assiduous copying of cases, learn writing and arithmetic." They would study under the direction of the secretary, like clerks, and would rise by degrees to higher ranks, "so that aristocratic and noble families will not suffer reproach." Peter hoped to make the position of secretary a noble one. In 1724, he issued a decree restricting the secretary's position, which carried the tenth rank in his new Table, to members of the hereditary nobility, unless no qualified nobleman was available. If a non-nobleman had to be appointed secretary, he would be awarded hereditary nobility.[59]

The Empress Elizabeth made the first effort to attract the nobility to systematic study of the law. She brought to Russia the jurists Fredrich Strube de Piermont and Phillippe Henrich Dilthei. Strube de Piermont, a Belgian, taught at the Academy of Sciences. Dilthei, an Austrian, became the first professor of law at Moscow University when it was founded in 1755. Both taught Roman and natural law, though in 1770 Dilthei began to teach Russian law as well, on the basis of the Naval and Military statutes.[60] To attract students to his classes and private pupils, Strube composed a brief program showing "the Equal Benefit of Military and Legal Sciences." Strube repeated an argument first stated by Peter—that the judiciary was as essential to the power of the state as the military. But he went further, insisting that the law was a pursuit superior to the bearing of arms. He argued that those countries which valued legal talent above military were to be considered even more advanced than those where only military skills were esteemed. The glory and benefit of military exploits were so evident that the military disposition was most characteristic of a people "that reasons by external feelings." On the other hand, "that perspicacity which is exercised in the establishment of useful laws and order and brings benefit from them is not so visible, but is attained only by the mind."[61]

Efforts to encourage active noble involvement with law gained momentum in Catherine's reign. Catherine, whose own title to rule was more than dubious, used the image of wise legislator bringing law to the empire as a basis of her appeal. The improvement of laws and the protection of rights were means for her to establish a firmer relationship between herself and her subjects. Count Nikita Ivanovich Panin, one of her supporters in the overthrow of Peter III, submitted a project for the reform of governmental institutions that tried to ensure that the state would operate on the basis of fixed and regular laws. Catherine, while not adopting the project, seemed to approve of its goals and sought even more than her predecessors to use the image of defender of the law to enhance her position as monarch.

Catherine endeavored to spread legality by gaining the active support of the nobility in the defense of their own interests.[62] Her reforms introduced noble legal institutions and tried to inculcate the European example of local nobilities concerned for the defense of their own rights. The Provincial Reform established district courts, which were run by a judge and two assessors elected by the district nobility. By bringing the first distinctly judicial institutions to the provinces, the reform made it possible for the nobleman to defend his life and estate without appealing to administrative authority. The Charter of the Nobility of 1785 vested the nobility with rights to protect in the courts, and most important, gave them a complete right of property for the first time.[63] It created noble corporations in the districts and thus instituted the kind of social organization that characterized western nobilities.

Such reforms, however, could not effect a sudden change in noble sentiments. The noble deputies to the Legislative Commission seemed more interested in bolstering and protecting their own privileges than improving laws. The new district courts were in a regular judicial hierarchy, and to many noblemen seemed extensions of the administrative system rather than congenial gatherings to settle disputes. As a result, elective service appeared as compulsory service in disguise. Catherine dealt with the resistance to law as she did with all kinds of ignorance. She emphasized enlightenment and tried to instruct the nobility in the importance of the science of the law. With Catherine, a familiarity with the law began to be presented as part of the cultural equipment the nobleman was supposed to have, a necessary skill to dispatch his obligations to the state.

To attract the nobility to the university, Catherine, at the urging of the rector, the poet Kheraskov, had special noble classes taught at Moscow University in 1779. In 1783 these classes were moved out to a separate building, marking the establishment of the Noble Pension under Moscow University. The pension was a secondary school, devoted mainly to the teaching of language and literature. But it also provided the opportunity to hear law professors from Moscow University, some of whom presented their courses at the pension as well.[64]

Catherine's most active spokesman for legal enlightenment was S. E. Desnitskii, the first Russian professor of law. Desnitskii, the son of a petty burgher, was a student of Dilthei. He completed his studies at Edinburgh and on returning to Russia, received a teaching position at Moscow University. A disciple and translator of Blackstone, he championed the cause of university education in the law in Russia. But there were few noblemen enrolled at Moscow University in the eighteenth century and few of them wanted to devote themselves to the law.[65] Desnitskii's public speeches exhorted the nobility to change their attitude to the law. His address to the ceremonial assembly of Moscow University in 1770 developed a theme set forth in Catherine's *nakaz;* it praised the achievements of Russian arms, but insisted that the arts of peace were as worthy as those of war:

> To capture and subdue many peoples and spread one's power is only to prove military art and its excelling force; but to maintain limitless conquests in singleminded obedience and universal satisfaction is the type of work that proves human wisdom and the happy gift of the governing to achieve great deeds.

Previous generations had distinguished themselves on the field of battle; it would be the task of contemporaries to provide effective civil institutions. The true unity of the empire depended on "proper legal statutes," and Desnitskii went on to enumerate reasons for studying "legal art" (*zakonoiskusstvo*).[66]

In an address of 1778, Desnitskii tried to dispel the moral stigma attached to the study of the law. "We should not disparage and call chicanery a science which defends the sacredness of the property, the possessions and the life of those living under the nation's laws." He assured Russians eager to study the law that no one at the university was so corrupt as to teach under this science "the chicaner's eloquence."[67] Noblemen, as property owners, needed to study the law "for the defense of one's life and estate, for the compliance of one's acts with the general rules prescribed by the regime, and for the knowledge of the mutual obligations of society, without whose execution society cannot defend the tranquil life of its members." The law would show the nobleman how to effect sales and mortgages of his estates, how to fulfill his role as judge over his peasants, and how to conduct suits against his neighbors.[68]

But Desnitskii hoped that the knowledge of the law would do more than help the noblemen on their estates and enable them to serve as district judges. It would also permit them to serve in administrative and, particularly, chancellery positions. Peter, he recalled, had reserved secretarial posts for members of the nobility and Catherine had urged chancellery positions in the new provincial governments upon them. Desnitskii, himself from the estate of petty burghers, tried to convince noblemen of the honor of serving in clerical posts, and the benefit of such work for civil government.

> This office in Russia, and especially under the Justice College is, without doubt, of great importance and may justly be honored for the refinement of theoretical reason in practical legal process and the most reliable preparation of noblemen as skillful judges. By despatching this office, he [the nobleman]

can learn not only how to know the law well, but how to apply it in actual legal process.[69]

Desnitskii well understood that his high words on the office of clerk were in conflict with the nobility's own attitudes. "The inattentiveness of many to both their own and the general welfare has left this essentially noble position, that has been so exalted by monarchs, to chancellery people."[70]

Vasilii Novikov, a nineteen-year-old Kaluga nobleman, expressed similar ideas in a speech he prepared for the Kaluga nobility in 1786. Like Desnitskii, Novikov responded to Catherine's reform by urging the nobility to participate in the new institutions and assume a civil role. Their forefathers had undertaken the defense of the fatherland and the extension of its borders. Now, with the borders of the empire ensured, they should turn their attention to internal well-being. They should combat ignorance and strive to improve the lot of their peasants. He called upon them to elect the best and most experienced to serve as judges.[71]

To assist the nobility, Novikov compiled the first Russian guide to being a judge: *Theater of Court Conduct or Reading for Judges and All Lovers [Amateurs] of Jurisprudence, Containing Remarkable and Interesting Court Cases, the Judicial Investigations of Famous Practioners of the Law and other Events of This Type Able to Enlighten, to Touch, to Move to Virtue, and to Furnish a Useful and Pleasant Pastime.* The *Theater* was a collection of cases, most of them from a recent French compendium. It instructed future judges how to determine the truth in court cases, advising "caution in conclusions, perspicacity in the investigations of crimes, and respect for humanity."[72]

Law for Novikov played much the same instrumental and didactic role as did literature in the eighteenth century. Culture and study had the goal of teaching and spreading virtue. Novikov considered it would be a great triumph of his labors "if this book took the place of card playing and other empty wastes of time so unbecoming to the judicial calling." His good judge would be able to correct human vices so that in the future courts would be less necessary. The judge's obligation was "the establishment of good conduct, which will prevent crimes and disputes and reduce the demand for legal justice."[73] Novikov too regarded justice as the dirty work of administration, as an unfortunate necessity to cope with the residual of human ignorance and vice.

Similar didactic motifs ran through the literature of eighteenth-century Russia. Theater and verse strove to correct and cultivate — to uplift the Russian nobleman to the levels of European culture. The writers of the eighteenth century showed that the nobleman could be useful to the country only if educated. True nobility depended upon knowledge. Alexander Sumarokov, the court playwright of Elizabeth and Catherine, declared that learning, or science—*nauka*—was the only grounds of nobility. *Nauka* enabled the nobleman to promote the good of his country and attain a genuine rather than a specious glory. Knowledge was most necessary for the nobleman who would serve as a judge.

> *All wisdom has a distant goal,*
> *Though we strive eternally towards it,*
> *We will find treasures along the way*
> *Pericles and Alcibiades were not ashamed*
> * of their science,*
> *The chiefs of their armies were adorned by*
> * science,*
> *Alexander was great also from it,*
> *The bold crowned Frederick reveres it,*
> *Peter sweetened the Petropolis by it,*
> *Catherine cultivates science anew.*
> *One can never scorn science:*
> *And it is hard to find truth without it.*
> *Such a judge is like a blind man,*
> *Who signed the case decided by the clerk*
> * [pod"iachii]*
> *Like a baby, who can be led anywhere,*
> *Yet one to whom fate gave high rank.*
> *Nobility was not a matter of blood.*
> *If I am suited to no office,*
> ***Then, though born a nobleman** [dvorianin],*
> *I am not noble [blagoroden].*[74]

In his "satire," *On Bad Judges* (*O khudykh sudiakh*), Sumarokov wrote with contempt of judges who slept through the hearing of cases, weary from the previous night of card playing. They unthinkingly signed decisions prepared for them by clerks. "An illiterate judge," he wrote, "should not be in charge of a court."[75]

The ignorant and irresponsible judge appears frequently in the satirical literature of the eighteenth and early nineteenth centuries. *Chicanery* of Kapnist, the works of Gogol and Suhkhovo-Kobylin, all followed a tradition of describing the hypocrisy of legal justice that had originated with Aristophanes' *The Asses*. It was the conviction of eighteenth-century writers that such satire could lead to moral improvement and impel the Russian nobleman to educate himself to assume his new civil role. Perhaps the most striking example of the bad judge is the character of the counselor in Denis Fonvizin's *Brigadier*. The counselor declares,

> In my day, every person with a just or unjust case went to the department and could, once he got friendly with a judge,

receive a favorable resolution. In my day you didn't poke your
nose any further. We used to have a saying: To God it is high,
to the tsar far.[76]

His notion of justice was simple. When asked why an innocent person
should be declared guilty, he replies,

> Because all people are sinners. I myself was a judge. It used to
> to be that the guilty paid for his guilt and the innocent for
> his innocence. In my time everyone was satisfied that way: the
> judge, the plaintiff and the defendant.[77]

Fonvizin, who in his youth had been close to Nikita Panin's circle, gave
his answer to the problem in the letters from his character, Starodum
(old thought)—the fount of traditional wisdom. In Starodum's letters,
Mr. Zdravomysl' (Mr. Common Sense) says that sometimes judges could
not understand cases because they lacked practice and the ability to
understand. The ability could only be acquired by reading and study.

> I do not ask for learned judges, but I think a judge should
> definitely be enlightened and able to read and write, that is
> he should at least know spelling, which I notice few here do.[78]

An appeal directed more sharply at the provincial nobleman was a
satirical dialogue written by Mikhail Khrapovitskii, "A Conversation of
District Noblemen about Elections to the Courts." In the conversation,
Mr. Zdravomyslov (Mr. Common Sense) is appalled to hear the description of local elections given by Mr. Prostiakov (Mr. Simpleton). Mr.
Prostiakov tells how all the candidates for positions were chosen at a special
meeting of important noblemen at the house of a powerful landlord of the
district. Mr. Nevezhin (Mr. Ignorant) had been selected district judge,
because, Prostiakov argues, he is too poor and stupid to engage in
chicanery. Mr. Nevezhin has read nothing but the Bible. Zdravomyslov
replies that the secretary will lead Nevezhin by the nose, take bribes, and
very quickly relieve him of his entire salary. He proposes Mr. Den'gov (Mr.
Money). Prostiakov objects that a rich man would not take such a post.
"And is it lowly to serve as a judge?" asks Zdravomyslov. "What a strange
notion! The judge is appointed to be the preserver of sacred justice, the
basis of all prosperity. He is entrusted with the security of our property and
therefore his very position becomes important and respected." Prostiakov
pleads that not he, but Mr. Naglov (Mr. Impudent) had proposed
Nevezhin to be judge and he was helpless to object. Other local positions
were also filled with incompetents and drunkards, for, Prostiakov explains,
landowners at the meeting would not put up with brainy people
(umnitsy).[79]

The Cadet Corps was where a nobleman was most likely to learn about the law in eighteenth-century Russia. Catherine, disbanding the Junker Schools, tried to encourage study of civil subjects in the Corps.[80] The courses taught were in natural law and sought to convey to the noblemen the importance of the law and a general understanding of its basic principles. The cadets used the textbooks of Strube de Piermont and Vladimir Zolotnitskii. Based on the theories of Pufendorf, Wolff, and Gundling, these were moral primers concerned above all with defining the nature of obligations, both public and personal, for the nobleman. Zolotnitskii explicitly stated the close connection between morality and law typical of eighteenth-century thought. "[Natural law] consists in the knowledge of good and bad acts, in the logic of their internal state. Consequently, it provides law that compels us to fulfill the former and avoid the latter."[81] He went on to show natural law as a striving for the good. Strube described love as the primary motivation of mankind. Pleasure was obtained by submission to the laws of nature contained in the passion of love, and these laws dictated the fulfillment of obligations. Man's obligations were to his spouse and friends, as well as to society.[82] Each book had briefer sections on rights, particularly on the acquisition and defense of property. Zolotnitskii also provided a defense of monarchical government. Such natural law theory dominated university teaching as well in the last decades of the eighteenth century.

But if the nobility was to heed the sovereign's call and develop a practical knowledge of the law, there would have to be books of laws for them to consult, and such books were not available. Without books, one could learn about the law only in the chancellery. Desnitskii himself admitted that clerical work was poor preparation for legal officials. He pointed out that clerks never progressed beyond the mechanical tasks of assembling and transferring legal citations. "No one, not only of wealthy background, but even a student, would wish to subject himself to the yoke of work and the endless copying of mountains of papers." As a result, the law had turned from "a lord's" into "a slave's science."[83]

Catherine's own commitment to the spread of legal enlightenment helped to moderate misgivings about publications on the law, and law books began to appear in her reign. The first description of Russian laws for practical use was Professor Dilthei's *Juridical Exploration of the Rightful Place of the Court, on Judicial Authority, on the Judicial Office, on the Judicial Petition and Proof* . . . , published at the press of Moscow University in 1779.[84] The book's preface gave eloquent testimony as to why such a study was so long in coming. The learned Austrian felt he was writing in a hostile atmosphere and tried to defend his effort. "This book has experienced the cruelest enemy, who has charged the author with the greatest guilt—that he has dared to write laws." He argued that he wrote not laws, which only the sovereign could issue, but commentaries on them for the benefit of students. Other enemies charged that his book might take the place of the laws in the courts. He rejected this contention by declaring most emphatically his intention to remain within the bounds of his discipline. "What teachers of the law assert about the reason and interpretation of the laws and their application to cases represents only an opinion and it is forbidden to transfer it from school to court. For one is School Jurisprudence, and the other Court." Another objection denied the need for instruction in the laws. This criticism, which he received more tolerantly than the others, held that a good mind and a good heart were sufficient to perform the obligations of the judge. He replied that they were not, "for cases should be decided according to laws and not one's own reason." The final objection, that the book contained nothing that was not already known, was more to the point, for Dilthei, careful not to press his claims to interpretation too far, kept his exploration as vague and abstract as possible. His description of types of courts and their obligations, types of suits, and proofs was based on Roman law with an occasional reference to Russian legislation, mostly to decrees of Peter and Catherine the Great.[85]

Dilthei began offering the first courses in Russian law in the 1770s. But these were limited to an examination of the Military and Naval statutes. Practical training in the law would have to be conducted by a clerk, who would know the laws through experience and be able to teach legal procedures. In 1786, Denis Fonvizin, then rector of Moscow University, enlisted Z. A. Goriushkin to give a course in "the practical art of the law" (*prakticheskoe zakonoiskusstvo*). Self-taught, Goriushkin had learned about the law in the chancelleries of the Moscow *voevoda* and the Justice College. His classes consisted of readings from the laws and then attempts to apply them to actual cases. The students composed legal papers, which he corrected. Then trials were presented in dramatic form. From Goriushkin's own description of these trials, it is clear that he attempted to make them as faithful as possible to current practices. The judge, in his account, is a retired military officer. The secretary provides him with all the advice he needs, much of it drawn verbatim from the laws. The judge sees himself as a docile servant of the law; the judicial power, he declares, consists only in "the execution of the laws, for in this way the innocent are saved from the hands of the unjust." He strives to apply the laws "without the change of a letter." The secretary confirms these remarks by reading article 152 of Catherine's *nakaz,* which asserts that the judge's obligation is to follow a syllogism comprised of the law, the fact, and the logical conclusion.[86]

The first guide to Russian laws, Chulkov's *Juridical Dictionary,* came out in 1788, and was followed by several others in the 1790s.[87] The best known of these was Fedor Pravikov's *Memorial from the Laws (Pamiatnik iz zakonov)*, which began to appear in 1798, and received several editions and numerous supplements. Pravikov set forth laws issued since the Code of 1649 by category, then beginning with 1798, presented them year by year. The *Memorial* was a published version of a clerk's notebook. Himself a clerk, and the son of a rural priest, Pravikov had attended Moscow University, and entered the Senate as a copyist in 1766 at the age of fifteen. He had learned about the laws in the Senate chancellery, where he served all his life, reaching the position of secretary in 1797.[88]

Pravikov's compilation was followed by others, such as Maksimovich's widely used *Guide to the Laws* (*Ukazatel' Zakonov*). The numerous works of this kind, published at the beginning of the nineteenth century and often in several editions, attest to the quickening demand for legal guides. But though answering a need, these were individual efforts and could not in themselves make order out of the chaos of Russian legislation.[89]

At the end of the reign of Alexander I, it was still difficult to locate particular laws. This was the experience of Przheslavskii, who spent long hours in Petersburg chancelleries trying to protect a relative's estate from confiscation. He searched through all the compilations and made inquiries among friends but could find no law concerning the confiscation of estates. Then he learned from an old man who worked as a representative in the courts that it could be found in the statute of the Treasury College, an institution which had been finally abolished by Alexander in 1802. But no one in Petersburg seemed to be able to locate a copy of the statute. Przheslavskii tried the Senate bookstore, but he was assured that no such law existed. Requests elsewhere were equally fruitless. Finally, an appeal to the management of the Senate bookstore brought a search of the premises, which revealed the statute in a dusty corner of the shop, at the bottom of a large heap of rubbish.[90]

2
BUREAUCRATIZATION, SPECIALIZATION, AND EDUCATION

Count Peter Vasil'ievich!
Knowing that the type of legal process existing till now, instead
of safeguarding legal justice with its procedures and making it
more effective, has been an obstacle to the successful course of
justice; that the majority of complaints have been about the
slowness of decisions; that the rules of procedure, being
scattered through so many laws are unknown in all their detail
even to the best legal experts; finally that the most varied cases
are subject to one and the same form, which is unsuitable to
their substance, numbers, the times, and the present level of
legal enlightenment, and drag on necessarily for years so that
the simplest open and shut cases turn into onerous and ruinous
suits, I have found it necessary to bring this to the attention of
the Governing Senate.

Imperial Decree of His Majesty
Alexander Pavlovich to Count
Zavadovskii, "On the Composition
of a Project for a Law on the Form
of the Court," 25 August 1801

THE REIGN OF ALEXANDER I BEGAN WITH A BOUT OF REFORM ACTIVITY. Educated in the ideals of the enlightenment, the young tsar made a fresh attempt to show the autocracy as the legitimate guardian of the nation's well-being and happiness. He borrowed his methods from the repertoire of absolute monarchy. He tried to deal with the disorder and inequity characteristic of Russian institutions by rationalizing organization and centralizing power. He tried to provide officials capable of making the new apparatus work by improving and expanding the Russian educational system.

Alexander was also disturbed by the condition of justice and the lack of adequate laws. The decree of 25 August 1801, establishing the tenth commission to codify the laws, placed priority on the reform of legal procedure. He ordered the head of the commission, Count Zavadovskii, to give it preference before all other matters, "as the most necessary and so essential in purpose."[1] But like his predecessors, Alexander saw the solution to governmental problems in an enhancement of executive power, and the reform of legal procedure was quickly subordinated to the general administrative reform and then forgotten. Speranskii justified the postponement of attempts to improve the courts in a memorandum of 1803. He set forth a cameralist argument, contending that reform of the courts and the law should await reform of "police" and "economy." The courts worked poorly because the judges and the police officers were untrained and ignorant. It was no use striving to improve the laws if the administration and the courts were staffed by individuals incapable of applying them. Courts could operate properly only after government had been transformed and the citizenry uplifted.[2]

Both the revision of legal procedure and codification gradually lost their urgency. The Codification Commission received broad assignments and made changes in legal procedure part of the collation and review of all legislation. It then proved impossible to agree on the first principles underlying the general review, and the discussions reached an impasse. Codification proceeded only when Speranskii took over direction of the work. But his hastily prepared project, heavily borrowed from the French *Code Civil,* evoked general condemnation when submitted in 1812 and had to be withdrawn. The commission continued in existence and carried out technical tasks of gathering the laws under the direction of Baron Rosenkampf, but it no longer enjoyed the monarch's active support or interest.[3]

The tsar and his young friends on the Unofficial Committee sought the happiness of the citizenry in a restructured state apparatus working on clear and rational principles. "The means for insuring the enjoyment of what constitutes happiness are contained in the administrative regulations." The reformers sought to determine these regulations according to a conception of the entire system, rather than piecemeal.[4]

The model for Alexander's reform became the neat and symmetrical division of functions in the ministerial system of Napoleonic France. The monarch now saw his interest in strengthening the authority of heads of institutions. The eighteenth-century collegial institutions had sought to limit their chiefs' power, which might rival the monarch's; the nineteenth-century ministerial institutions would seek to enhance their authority as means to make central power more effective. Establishing ministries, the tsar aimed "to divide state matters into various parts, corresponding to the natural bond between them, and for their most successful operation to assign them to the authority of Ministers chosed by Us." The reform allotted the administrative authority previously held by the procurator-general and the Senate to ministries. It tried to create separate administrative hierarchies for care of finances, internal well-being, and justice. The minister of interior, who directed the "police" authority, was responsible for ensuring the happiness of the population, and was the most powerful of the ministers. The minister of justice supervised the operation of all the legal offices in the empire. He inherited the title of procurator-general and his role as presiding officer of the Senate.[5]

The reform thus created a branch of the central administrative apparatus devoted to the dispensation of justice. The Senate, shorn of its most important administrative powers, remained the supreme judicial instance in the hierarchy, but it came increasingly under the power of the minister of justice. The minister presided over the Senate and enjoyed the right of direct access to the tsar, the chief sign of supreme authority in the Russian state; the members of the Senate lost this right in practice, if not by law. His subordinates, the chief-procurators (*ober-prokurory*), could object to the decisions of the Senate's departments, and refer them to one of the General Sessions of the Senate. If the General Session also ruled in a way unacceptable to the minister, the case could be referred to the Committee of Ministers, which was not bound by legislative enactment as was the Senate, or to the State Council, or finally to the tsar.[6]

But the preeminence of the minister of justice did not extend to the provinces. There his authority competed with the governors', who were responsible to the minister of interior. The attempts of Derzhavin, the first minister of justice, to defend an official in a provincial court against removal by the governor failed, when the minister of interior, Victor Kochubei, took the governor's side.[7] As a result, the governor enjoyed a de facto power over appointments to provincial court positions. He was also responsible for appointments to the chancelleries of district and provincial courts, where most legal work went on. He held direct authority over the local police, who carried on investigations for the courts and executed their sentences. Finally, his unlimited personal power in the province made it possible for him to intervene freely in the courts, to influence or reverse their decisions in those cases where he did not have such power by law.

The great importance of one of the tsar's friends, Victor Kochubei, as minister of interior, is indicative of the persistence of the personal element in the new ministerial system. Symmetry and regular administrative procedures appeared the best means to create a well-functioning state, but Alexander preferred to deal with individuals he trusted, even if it violated procedure. Thus, he established the Committee of Ministers as a supreme state institution, and at the beginning attended its meetings, which he called frequently. But he soon reverted to dealing with ministers individually and informally, a practice that would continue throughout the century. After 1810, the meetings of the committee were less frequent. In the last years of Alexander's reign, the power of his personal secretary, Alexei Arakacheiev, overshadowed the ministers', as the favorite ruled over the administration with a power that was unconstrained and undifferentiated.[8]

The same fate befell Alexander's effort to establish separate supreme judicial and legislative organs in the central government. The State Council was established in 1810, the only part of Speranskii's scheme for governmental reorganization to be instituted. The council was to examine and consider legislation initiated by the tsar or the ministers. Alexander attended the State Council in 1810 and 1811, then he lost interest, whereupon its significance declined.[9] The tsar continued to issue decrees on the recommendation of individual ministers without submission to the council, thus perpetuating the sway of the executive and the personal in the administration. But while the council's legislative influence diminished, it took on considerable judicial functions. The minister of justice would refer cases to it, sometimes through the Committee of Ministers, for legislative pronouncements. But, more important, the tsar could be prevailed upon to move cases from the Senate to the council when important dignitaries so wished. Count Gur'ev complained in 1826 that the State Council, the Senate, and the Committee of Ministers were all handling the same kinds of cases depending upon the immediate circumstances.[10] Thought and behavior remained apart in Alexander's statecraft. The image of efficient, ordered government gripped his imagination, but impulse, sentiment, and fears determined his actual conduct of affairs.

If administrative reform was to provide the organization for better government, a new enlarged educational system then would provide the men to work in it. Europe offered the example of administrations that required university degrees or examinations for civil office, and European administrative models prompted attempts to emulate European official-doms. Alexander began his reign with the establishment of three institutions of higher learning — Kharkov and Kazan universities and the St. Petersburg Pedagogical Institute (named a university in 1819). The preliminary rules for the new educational system announced the first goal of higher education to be "the preparation of youth for the state service."[11]

Initially, Alexander tried to attract the nobility into the new institutions. The decree of 24 January 1803 stipulated that no one in any province, five years after it had become a part of an educational district, could be appointed to civil posts "requiring juridical and other knowledge," without completing public or private school (*uchilishche*).[12] But the majority of the nobility continued to regard university education as unbecoming. Speranskii reported to Alexander that the nobility were responding to the appeal less than other classes. They were avoiding thorough study because they were concerned only with achieving high ranks. In France, England, Austria, and elsewhere, he pointed out, "no one can be a judge, lawyer or procurator without a certificate and test administered by specific offices."[13]

At Speranskii's instance, Alexander decreed the controversial Examination Law of 1809. "To our enormous sorrow," the tsar stated in the preamble, "we see from the reports of the Ministry of Education that the nobility, accustomed to lead other estates by its example, will take part in these useful institutions less than others." Henceforth, the law declared, ascent of the Table of Ranks was to depend not on seniority or birth, but on "merits and exceptional knowledge." The law made a university degree or the passing of an examination administered at a university requisite to attainment of the eighth civil rank, and therefore to the attainment of hereditary nobility and the higher ranks necessary for important governmental positions. The examinations covered a broad range of subjects — verbal sciences (Russian grammar and composition and one foreign language), jurisprudence, history, mathematics, and physics. The section on jurisprudence was to test knowledge of natural law, Roman law, private law, state economy, and criminal law.[14]

The education that Alexander tried to introduce was general and philosophical. This approach brought a great expansion of the educational establishment, but it also led to the submergence of the law in broader, more speculative subjects. Alexander's ambitious goals created difficulties. The University Statute of 1804 assigned the teaching of law to the faculty of moral and political sciences. These were to convey the universal truths of political life that would breed an enlightened citizenry and officialdom. Natural law doctrines, based on such universalistic principles, continued to dominate the university curriculum. At Moscow University, Lev Tsvetaev gave traditional Roman and natural law courses. To teach law at the new universities, the government recruited professors in Germany. But the number of faculty proved insufficient, and professors of law had to spend much of their time teaching subjects such as political philosophy and political economy. At Kazan and Kharkov, the German professors quickly quarreled with the authorities and departed, leaving teaching responsibilities to young careerists who taught everything. The few conscientious professors remaining were ferreted out by Magnitskii and Runich during the reactionary purges of the second half of Alexander's reign.[15]

The achievements at the St. Petersburg Pedagogical Institute were more impressive. The Hungarian scholar, M. A. Balugianskii, became professor of political science and then first rector of St. Petersburg University. Balugianskii succeeded in assembling an excellent faculty to teach political economy, philosophy, and law. But here too law was slighted. The talented Alexander Kunitsyn, who had studied natural law theory and law at Göttingen and under Balugianskii, was burdened by extensive teaching responsibilities that left him almost no time to teach law courses. The purge of St. Petersburg University by the mystic minister of education, Prince Alexander Golitsyn, led to Balugianskii's resignation and the undoing of his work. In 1825 only eighteen students were studying law at Petersburg University, and the curriculum included no course in Russian law.[16]

Practical training in the law was offered only at Moscow University. There N. N. Sandunov continued Goriushkin's tradition of staging mock court trials. Sandunov was interested only in procedure; "Practice is the only science" was his motto. He began his class with readings from Pravikov's *Pamiatnik,* then explained the meaning of the laws according to his own system. An actual Senate case was then read and processed through several instances, the students playing the roles of the various officials from the copier to the chairman. Sandunov emphasized clear speech, handwriting, and style above all. He taught the students how to fill out the necessary forms and acquainted them with the prescribed order of the court. The young noblemen at the university and Noble Pension, bored by Tsvetaev's abstruse lectures, became completely absorbed in their roles in what one of them called "this type of useful comedy." Indeed, these cases, like well-rehearsed plays, were performed at the annual assemblies of the university and pension. Sandunov himself had an active interest in the stage and wrote translated plays. His brother was a famous actor.[17]

Alexander also made an attempt to introduce a systematic legal education. In November 1801, Procurator-General Bekleshov drew up plans for an institute which would train students principally in "jurisprudence" (*pravovedenie*) and a pure writing style "appropriate for legal cases." Up to thirty students were to be chosen from poor noblemen, up to fifteen from the chancellery class. The former would become secretarial assistants upon graduation, the latter chancellerists (*kantseliaristy*). The institute was attached to the Codification Commission and opened in 1806. But it received only perfunctory support from the government, and students rarely attended classes. Its operations were suspended in 1809 and in 1816 it was officially closed.[18]

Despite the examination laws, Alexander's efforts to attract noblemen into the universities met with little success. Noble parents complained that universities did not teach military science or confer military rank. They would have preferred the opening of new Cadet Corps.[19] At the beginning of the century, of about 100 students registered at Moscow University, approximately half were nobles. By 1825, enrollment had risen to 714 students, 219 of them noblemen. In the political sciences faculty, where law was taught, 101 of 267 students were noble. Most of the noble students were from the service nobility. Members of the landed nobility rarely matriculated in these years, though some would audit lectures to prepare for the service examination or simply out of interest.[20] The new universities, first filled by seminarians, appear to have been even less popular among the nobility than Moscow University.[21]

Alexander won little noble sympathy for his pursuit of educational standards in the bureaucracy. Education threatened the nobility's patriarchal image of the tsar, the personal and family connections that guaranteed them access to desirable positions.[22] Reluctant to train for the service themselves, they nonetheless opposed surrendering high positions to non-nobles. The threat to their position in Alexander's reign came in the person of Michael Speranskii. Speranskii approximated the European type of state-secretary of humble origin who had gained authority as the monarch's talented and knowledgeable aide. Just as the Ministerial Reform represented the autocracy's effort to emulate the developments of absolutist state organization, Speranskii represented the western type official that members of the nobility feared would rise in the new state. Speranskii gave these fears substance by placing his protégés in important positions, particularly in the Ministry of Interior, where a special bureau was established to check on the recruitment of educated personnel.[23] This was one of the aspects of Speranskii's activity that brought his downfall and exile in 1811. Nicholas Karamzin expressed a widely felt sense of misgiving:

> Where work had been carried out by eminent officials such as
> a president and several assessors, men with long training and a
> strong sense of responsibility for their whole office, we came
> to see insignificant officials, such as directors, filing clerks,
> desk chiefs, who, shielded by the Minister, operated with
> utter impunity.[24]

Karamzin argued that the choice of officials from the nobility, and especially the well-to-do nobility, was advantageous for the state. "Noble status should not depend upon rank but rank upon noble status; that is the attainment of certain ranks should be made unconditionally dependent on the condition of being a gentleman." Only noblemen, he insisted, had the wealth necessary for high position and the desire for distinction that would impel them to serve well.[25] Nonetheless, he agreed that the only way to improve the administration was by selection of men according to merit. The civil service thus could be improved only by improving the quality of noble officials. Yet Karamzin shared the distaste for the universities, redolent of German professors and uncouth seminarians.

It was such sentiments that Victor Kochubei carried to the ear of the tsar. There would be no one to study in the universities, Kochubei claimed, especially since they had been founded on German models. "A system of lycées is the best system Russia could adopt."[26] In 1809, the lycée at the summer palace at Tsarskoe Selo opened with the goal of training a select group of noblemen for the civil and military service. Graduates received the ninth rank (while graduates of the university received only the fourteenth) and were especially favored once they entered the service.

As at the universities, law in the lycée was taught as a "moral science."[27] Teachers were borrowed from the faculties of St. Petersburg University, and in the first decade of its existence, the lycée had the services of Kunitsyn as an instructor of law. Kunitsyn taught natural law with an emphasis on the liberty and equality of mankind, and his courses, critical of both despotism and serfdom, were popular among the students. The liberal views he set forth in his writings on natural law made him repugnant to the authorities and he was removed in 1821. But Kunitsyn conveyed more than seditious ideas in his courses. The notebooks of Dmitrii Zamiatnin contain detailed summaries of Russian civil law and procedure and the history of Russian criminal law, with citations of legislation since the law code of 1649.[28] Kunitsyn inspired many of his students with a genuine devotion to the law, and several entered judicial posts directly upon completing the lycée. The first three classes graduated forty-six of seventy-eight pupils into the civil service. Eleven entered the Ministry of Foreign Affairs and ten, judicial institutions—the Ministry of Justice, the Codification Commission, or the Senate.[29] That group included Dmitrii Zamiatnin, Baron Modest Korf, and Ivan Kapger, all of whom would play an active role in the administration and reform of justice during the subsequent reigns.

Aside from the lycée, Alexander's effort to create a corps of educated noble bureaucrats brought little change in the traditional noble career patterns. Despite the examination law, St. Petersburg's official society continued to be sharply divided. At the top, the *znat'*, or notables, monopolized access to the high positions of government. Such individuals regarded paper work as onerous and demeaning, and they never served in the chancelleries. They sought power through the imperial court. Even after Speranskii's law required imperial court officials to hold civil or military positions, they were able to find sinecures that would ease their ascent through the Table of Ranks. Beneath were the poor noblemen or chancellery workers' sons working in governmental offices, living spare and difficult lives, hoping for the connections that would lift them into the elite.[30]

The progress of bureaucratization hinged on the attitudes of the nobility. The immediate effect of the new structure on provincial offices seems to have been a sharp rise in the number of non-noble judges, as we shall see in the next chapter. If the nobility did not heed the monarch's call, there were only two possible outcomes: a non-noble state apparatus potentially hostile to the tsar's social values; or a relinquishment of the absolutist views the autocracy used to justify its authority. It was this dilemma, among many others, that confronted Tsar Nicholas Pavlovich when he ascended to the throne in 1825.

Nicholas I's accession to power was greeted by the Decembrist Revolt, an armed uprising led by noble guards' offices. The dread of revolution continued to haunt Nicholas throughout his reign, giving his rule its characteristic oppressive tone, its antagonism to anything liberal, free, or expansive. The Third Section of his personal chancellery, his political police, came to symbolize the general atmosphere of distrust and the fear of new ideas that Nicholas represented. But Nicholas's obsessive preoccupation with revolutionaries and his stern martial style should not conceal the other fundamental problems that his statecraft endeavored to solve.

The Decembrist Revolt not only threatened the tsarist state, it also made the dilemma of absolutist monarchy in Russia more acute. The state as the guardian of the interests of its citizens now had to face the demands of the politically aware members of the population who could point out how it had not kept its promises. The ideals of Catherine had been answered by Radishchev's depiction of injustice and inhumanity. Alexander's visions had ended in the guard's officers' assertion that autocracy was incompatible with the general welfare. Nicholas I's reign was a last effort to make good on the absolutist promise. He was determined to make the state work by strengthening authority, supervision, and respect for law.

For Nicholas, law was an extension of the autocrat's personal will. Shortly before his accession, he told Balugianskii, "I want to place all the force and strictness of the laws at the base of the system of state and government." He set a bust of Peter the Great on his desk and declared, "This is the model I intend to follow throughout my reign."[31] Nicholas regarded the law as a sacred expression of his own authority, and its enforcement as a moral as well as a civil obligation. The Decembrists' allegations about the condition of Russian courts struck him as true. As a youth he had heard of the inadequacies of legal justice, of bribery and chicanery in the courts, of the absence of laws, and the contradictory nature of those that were available. He considered legal justice the fundamental necessity of every state and was determined to do something about it.[32]

Nicholas's answer to the problems of government was to watch as closely as possible over his officials. After his accession, he took codification under his "direct authority," and established a new branch of his own chancellery, the Second Section, to carry on the work of codification. He assigned Speranskii and Balugianskii to take charge of the Second Section, but he also remained actively concerned himself. He helped set the basic principles, and reviewed the results at every stage.[33] Thus he dealt with the problem of delegating authority over codification by trying to delegate very little authority and to direct the operation himself.

The Decembrist Revolt showed Nicholas the danger of the abstract universal concepts of justice that had influenced previous attempts at codification. Instead, he adopted historistic and national views that simplified the task of codification and did not threaten the monarch's monopoly of authority. This approach, argued in Russia by Karamzin, and formulated by Savigny and the German historical school of jurisprudence, presented the laws of each nation as expressions of that nation's particular characteristics and needs. It banished the notion that law had to conform to universal natural norms, and consecrating the statutes issued by the autocrat, exempted them from outside judgment. Codification then became the ordering and compilation of the ruler's legislative acts, the precondition to the precise implementation of his will.

Under Nicholas's close supervision, the Second Section utilized the materials of previous codification commissions and worked quickly to meet his demands. In 1830, it published an ostensibly complete collection of Russian laws, set forth chronologically. Two years later, it completed and released the *Digest of Laws,* which systematically presented those laws still in effect. In 1845, under the direction of Count Bludov, it published a penal code, which removed some of the anomalies and brutality of the previous system of punishments. The old procedural laws, including On the Form of the Court, provided the basis for the closed inquisitorial process prescribed in the *Digest.* In the early 1840s, Bludov began his work on new laws of court procedure.[34]

Nicholas showed the same personal involvement and desire for total control in his approach to the operations of the administration. He tried to make the structure left by Alexander work according to rule. He insisted that "all matters come to the throne according to the order established by law."[35] Here too his method was to try to keep a close watch on the operations himself, though in the administration this would raise many more complexities than it did in the work of codification. He strengthened the authority of the minister as the agent of his supervisory power, and developed mechanisms to check on the operations of each ministry. Thus the minister of justice became responsible for overseeing the proper dispatch of cases in all the judicial offices of the empire. The device that Nicholas used to tighten supervision was "accountability" (*otchetnost'*). Accountability meant rigorous surveillance of governmental offices on the basis of statistical reports. It was introduced both in the police agencies under the Ministry of Interior, and in the courts under the Ministry of Justice in the early 1840s. The records of the number of criminal cases at each instance were forwarded through the Senate and the minister of justice and received in the First Section of the tsar's chancellery. Each month the Senate would submit thick registers, every page of which had to be signed by the minister himself. In addition, the minister initiated numerous investigations to check on the speed, efficiency, and honesty of the courts. These supplemented the special senatorial investigations, which inspected all aspects of the administration in those provinces where trouble had been revealed.[36]

Nicholas also strengthened the authority of the ministries over provincial government. The Instruction to Civil Governors of 1837, formulated by Count Bludov, abolished the governor-generals and concentrated greater power in the ministries. A law of 1845 made the governor responsible for seeing that ministerial decisions were executed, as well as supervising the general course of local government. Both of these laws had the effect of increasing the governor's responsibility at the expense of the provincial bureau's (*gubernskoe pravlenie*). But the governor's power was now limited to surveillance (*nadzor*) rather than administration (*upravlenie*). Like decision-making power, responsibility for appointments devolved increasingly upon the ministries. As we shall see in the next chapter, the authority of the minister of justice and his influence began to be felt in an increasing number of provincial appointments. The result of the tendency toward centralization was a steady increase in the size of the administration and a burgeoning of paper work, beyond the capacities of any organ to understand or even to examine.[37] Nonetheless, corruption and influence continued to play a considerable though perhaps diminished role. These were the limits and shortcomings that were becoming evident in the absolutist style of governing.

Specialization of administrative offices required increased specialization of personnel. The Decembrist Revolt helped Nicholas to overcome the autocrat's traditional distrust of specialized legal expertise. He thought the general education of the previous decades had planted revolutionary intentions in the minds of the youth; it had familiarized them with the liberal universalistic notions of the enlightenment and prevented them from learning the specific skills necessary to make the administration work. He regarded specialized education as an instrument to inculcate habits of obedience and the ability to understand and apply statute law. As a result, he tried to introduce a legal training that would teach the youth the laws of the nation rather than general concepts of law subversive to authority. Starting out from the assumption that education could create a subservient and responsive officialdom, Nicholas took the first steps toward building a strong judiciary in Russia.

At the beginning of Nicholas's reign, Speranskii had reported that the two prerequisites "for the establishment of legal justice on solid grounds" in Russia were firm and clear laws, and knowledgeable judges and jurists.[38] Both of these became the task of the Second Section. Speranskii claimed that it was necessary to assign at least one professor of Russian law to each university for the training of future officials. But in 1828 no university course in Russian law was being offered in the empire. The first generation of Russian law professors, therefore, had to be trained by those working on the compilation of laws. In 1828, Nicholas ordered that six outstanding students, chosen from the Moscow and St. Petersburg religious academies, be sent to the Second Section for training in the law. Another six were assigned in 1829. In the Second Section, they studied Roman law, Russian public law, and political economy. Their teachers were Balugianskii and his associates from Petersburg University—Kunitsyn, Plisov, and Klokov. They also were acquainted with the laws being compiled by the Second Section and assisted in the preparation of indexes. Under the guidance of Modest Korf, they learned to compose memoranda on the basis of old Senate cases. After completing their studies in Petersburg, they were sent—their numbers augmented by Redkin and Kalmykov from the Professors' Institute at Dorpat—to Berlin for general training in the law under the personal supervision of Savigny. When they returned they were examined, granted doctorates, and assigned chairs in the universities—the first contingent of professors of Russian law. While no member of the group became a great jurist, nearly all were conscientious and knowledgeable, and several, like Peter Redkin, Constantine Nevolin, and Nikita Krylov succeeded in inspiring genuine interest in the study of the law in their students.[39]

The University Statute of 1835 made the teaching of the law a major function of the universities. It created separate law faculties, which were supposed to consist of seven chairs. In accordance with Nicholas's views, courses in natural law were banished from the law curriculum and the students were to occupy themselves instead with the mastery of the details of Russian legislation.[40] The political aims of this approach were manifest and have been pointed out in the liberal historical literature. The students were to study "laws" (zakony) rather than the general subject of "law" (*pravo*), a policy which was reflected in the names of the chairs in the statute. The mastery of specific laws was supposed to turn the students into obedient technicians, and many professors insisted on rote memorization and recitation of the *Digest of Laws*.[41] But the limitations of the new curriculum were often more formal than real. Courses in encyclopedia of law in fact transmitted the principles of natural law, and Roman law remained in the curriculum. Many of the new chairs would remain vacant, leaving whole areas of the law untaught, but legal education was more comprehensive than ever before. As we shall see in chapter 8, those professors who wished were able to use their courses to convey theoretical and philosophical approaches that often had a greater impact on the students than the study of laws.

Like his predecessors, Nicholas sought the new officials in the nobility. But Nicholas addressed the nobility without the old supplicant, pleading tone. Faced with a defective judicial system that was discrediting the autocracy and with the possibility of a non-noble judiciary, Nicholas returned to Peter's manner of command. His Manifesto of 13 July 1826, deploring the methods employed by the revolutionaries, urged the nobility to devote themselves to improvement by participating in the work of the state. He promised that all paths to "honor" and "merit" would be open to them. "Just courts, military forces, the various parts of the internal administration — all of these demand, all depend upon earnest and knowledgeable executors."[42]

His appeal was directed at the lower and middle nobility, and represented an attempt to break free from the alliance with the noble elite. The lessons he was trying to convey were set forth bluntly in highly popular novels of Faddei Bulgarin, the regime's chief literary propagandist. The villains of Bulgarin's works were the rich members of the elite and the powerful landlords, who saw all improvements in institutions and law as against their interest. Prince Kurdakov, in *Petr Ivanovich Vyzhigin*, secures the intervention of the powerful Count Khokhlenkov to have charges against a wealthy contractor dismissed. When a young official objects that this is arrant injustice, Kurdakov condemns such talk as the spread of freethinking. "Count Khokhlenkov *has taken an interest* in the contract and so it is not for you to speak here of injustice! I cannot understand what ideas have been spread among young people! They want to judge about everything, themselves decide about everything, talk about law and legality." He tells the young man that he should do as he is told and not think. "What kind of worker are you that you can't find the laws that I need?" But these younger lesser noblemen are standing in the wings, reluctant to select laws to suit their masters, awaiting the moment when they can prove themselves the true descendants of Peter the Great — men who see Russia's greatness not in luxury and excess but in their devotion to the good of the fatherland.[43]

Powerful noblemen dominate the corrupt courts that appear throughout Bulgarin's writings. The story "The Elected Judge" satirizes a court much in the manner of the eighteenth century. The judge has taken his position without knowledge or understanding of the laws, and has to turn to the secretary for help. He has been forced to serve as judge by a powerful nobleman who plunders and intimidates his neighbors. Unlike Khrapovitskii's Nevezhin, however, Bulgarin's judge is an intelligent and understanding man—a victim of circumstance. He listens sympathetically to the narrator's reproving comments, then asks how he and other noblemen can be expected to understand the law when private pensions and other institutions do not teach Russian legislation. The narrator answers that noblemen should "train [*vospityvat'*] their children in the universities where general and private Russian legislation is taught, without which it is as impossible to be a nobleman as to be an officer without a sword." The judge replies,

> Well, brother, have there been universities in Russia for a long time? And would our young man, our little gentleman, whom no one is going to compel, sit on a student's bench when his comrades are prancing about in sewn uniforms? In Russia, boys who have hardly mastered penmanship are already counting the minutes lost in attaining rank and try to make time to catch up to their comrades. Is there time to think of laws?[44]

The narrator's relative, futilely trying to conduct his own case, is shocked at what he has seen. He vows that his children shall learn the law.

> Now my first duty is to teach my children Russian legislation and to instill in them the rule that courage and strength are as necessary to a civil servant as to a soldier. My sons, when they go out into the world, must vow that they will stand as firmly for justice in the court as for their banner on the battlefield.[45]

Nicholas, however, did not stop at attempts at persuasion. His goal, as expressed by Minister of Education Uvarov, was to remove noble youth from the influence of foreign tutors, and "the close circle of domestic prejudices," and bring them into schools where their moral upbringing could be supervised by the state.[46] In his eyes, the private tutors and pensions, which taught the well-to-do nobility, were responsible for the contagion of European ideas in Russia. He also wanted to discourage the early entry into the service, which as Bulgarin's judge pointed out, left the young nobleman ignorant and untrained. Pushkin confirmed these views in a special memorandum he wrote for the tsar.

> All youth should be drawn into public institutions, subject to the supervision of the government; they should be kept there (for a considerable number of years) to give them time to be

fully baked, to be enriched with knowledge, to mature in the quiet of the schools rather than the noisy idleness of the barracks.... There is no reason to hesitate; private instruction must be crushed at all costs.[47]

The government launched an attack on all noble education that was outside state control. In 1833, Uvarov forbade the founding of private boarding schools, except in the case of extreme necessity, and allowed foreigners to maintain them only if they became Russian subjects. He brought existing boarding schools under the supervision of the ministry, which insisted that instruction be carried on in Russian and include classes in Russian history. The pensions at Moscow and Petersburg universities (the latter was established in 1819) were made gymnasiums. In 1853 noblemen accounted for 80 percent of the pupils in Petersburg gymnasiums.[48]

To discourage early entry into the service, the government introduced new incentives to study at the universities. A law of 1822 raised the ranks to be awarded to university graduates. Attendance at a university conferred the fourteenth rank; completion of the course of studies (*deistvitel'nyi student*), the twelfth; graduation with special distinction, the candidate degree (*kandidat*), the tenth; master's received the ninth rank; doctor's the eighth. Nicholas supplemented these rules with measures that reduced the years to be spent achieving the lowest, the fourteenth rank, on the basis of birth and pre-university education, thus making swift ascent to the Table of Ranks possible for noblemen who had finished primary or secondary school.[49] He also continued the policy, begun by Alexander, of introducing quotas on lower-class students.

The government introduced educational standards even for the lowliest clerical positions. A law of 1827 required all new recruits to clerical positions who had not completed a primary education to pass an examination testing their reading, writing, grammar, and arithmetic. The comprehensive act of 1828 ordered that office heads give graduates from state schools and those with secondary education preference over those with primary schooling. In addition, new schools were established for sons of indigent chancellery clerks, preparing them in clerical skills and office procedure.[50]

In the decades after the Decembrist Revolt, noblemen and even members of the elite began to appear at the universities, especially Petersburg and Moscow, in increasing numbers. In the 1830s, young aristocrats, brought in carriages and often accompanied by servants, began to sit in lecture halls alongside lesser nobles and commoners. Noblemen were most numerous in the juridical faculties, which, it was thought, provided suitable training for the future official. The Russian nobility was beginning to view the law as a gentlemanly science.[51]

But though a university education became respectable for the nobility in these years, their numbers increased only as the university enrollment itself rose. The available figures give no indication of an increase in the proportion of hereditary noblemen to total enrollment at the university, or even in the juridical faculty.[52] For the legal profession to become fully noble, a stronger stimulus was necessary; an elite school of the law had to create a model of the noble legal official. This was the purpose of the School of Jurisprudence (*Uchilishche pravovedeniia*), which opened its doors in 1835 in response to proposals advanced by the tsar's nephew, Prince Peter Oldenburg of Denmark, and Michael Speranskii.

During his service in Petersburg, Oldenburg had observed "the lack of educated and informed officials in the chancelleries of judicial offices." Young noblemen aimed "for ministerial departments, where the kinds of glory and the size of the pay flatter their hopes." Some would then take high judicial posts; thus they would "bypass chancellery positions without receiving necessary information about the system of clerical procedure [*deloproizvodstvo*]." Oldenburg's solution to the problem was to establish an elite secondary school devoted to the law. The school would train young noblemen for the key chancellery positions in the judicial administration and thus remove the stigma from clerical work. Oldenburg offered to contribute the funds for the school's building.[53]

Speranskii seconded Oldenburg's suggestions. Now reconciled to noble domination of the government, he argued, in 1832, that only a corps of educated noblemen, trained to work in the chancellery could make the Russian judiciary work.

> Able and well-bred clerical workers [*deloproizvoditeli*] are needed everywhere to help judges; they are needed in Russia more than anywhere else, for we have no educated judges or learned lawyers nor will we have them for a long time.

Educated clerks would help maintain the system of elective judges and noble control of the courts.

> With a good clerical worker, a judge—chosen by the trust of an estate—who has common sense and a clean conscience, though he may lack technical knowledge, generally can be more useful than one who is simply educated. But the same judge, chosen by the trust of his estate, with a bad clerical worker will merely conceal the latter's partiality or ignorance.[54]

Oldenburg proposed that the school train noble youths for six years in both "practical legal administration" and "auxiliary sciences." He hoped it would provide them "actual experience of the chancellery system and the forms of clerical work," and teach "the correct and precise presentation of cases and how to decide them in accordance with the laws." He recommended that upon graduation they serve six years in the judicial administration, beginning in "low chancellery offices."[55] Nicholas approved Oldenburg's project and appointed him preceptor — a position he held until his death in 1881.

The school, according to Oldenburg, worked toward "the ennoblement of service in judicial offices." Admissions' requirements were based on the principles of birth and service. The permanent statute of 1838 required that candidates for admission be from families registered in the sixth section of the genealogy books — those listed among the serving classes before Peter the Great — or be sons of officials of the fifth rank or officers of the sixth rank and above.[56] The school gave what was in most respects a secondary education. Pupils entered at ages ranging from twelve to fifteen and remained for six (later extended to seven) years. The first three years they took language, history, mathematics, and other general elementary subjects. The second half of their curriculum was devoted to the study of the law, based on a curriculum similar to, but on a lower level than, the university's (see chapter 8).[57]

Self-supporting pupils, upon completion, were obliged to spend four years in the Ministry of Justice, and state-supported pupils six years. Their final examination was heard by the minister of justice and other high functionaries. They received the ninth, tenth, or twelfth rank according to their grade record. During the school's first forty years, 44 percent of the graduates received the ninth rank — that awarded to university masters — and 35 percent the tenth, awarded to university candidates.[58] After entering the service, graduates enjoyed the special protection of both Oldenburg and the minister of justice, which brought them preferences in promotions and bonuses. Needy graduates received financial assistance.[59]

The universities and the School of Jurisprudence provided a route for lesser noblemen through the legal administration to high governmental positions. The institutional and educational reforms of the first half of the nineteenth century prepared the way for a fundamental change in the character and attitudes of legal personnel. In 1801, Procurator-General Bekleshov had pointed out "the extreme lack of sufficiently educated people" in judicial offices. By the end of Nicholas's reign, an anonymous critic of the legal administration remarked, "There is hardly any branch of government that can boast so splendid a staff as the Ministry of Justice. Many educated people hold positions in the center and in the provinces."[60] The Russian judiciary at the dawn of the reform era looked quite different than it had at the beginning of the century. We shall now turn to an assessment of these changes.

3
THE COMPOSITION
OF THE RUSSIAN
LEGAL ADMINISTRATION
IN THE FIRST HALF
OF THE
NINETEENTH CENTURY

Why, fate, do you hold me on a chain like a mad dog? Why do you tempt me with sweets and delicacies and then torment me with hunger and cold? Why do you drag money in other men's pockets, wealth, plenty, past my nose? Fate, may you be damned for your works! There is no justice on earth, there is no compassion; the strong oppresses the weak, the stuffed devours the hungry, the rich scalp the poor! I would like to take you, hateful world, and set you on fire, from one end to the other. I would like to don my uniform, and march over your ashes; that's what you'll get, you son of a devil!

Final soliloquy of Kandid
Kastorovich Tarelkin,
A. V. Sukhovo-Kobylin,
The Case (*Delo*)

THE RUSSIAN JUDICIARY AT THE BEGINNING OF THE NINETEENTH CENTURY WAS geared to serve the interests of the social and political elite. Judgeships were rewards, primarily for military service, and went usually to noblemen who represented the hierarchy of privilege in the legal system. Men with little experience or interest in administering justice left the actual processing of cases to an army of clerks, proficient at accommodating the law to the dictates of those who wielded wealth or influence.[1] "For us the judiciary is service, for [the secretaries] it is a profession," M. A. Dmitriev, himself a judge, wrote. "For them it is a matter of life."[2] The legal administration was split between judges, who held power and responsibility, and clerks, equipped with knowledge and experience but only rarely promoted to the bench. Social barriers within the system thus precluded an officialdom united by a common commitment to justice.

It will be the thesis of this chapter that the specialization of functions and centralization of authority introduced by the Ministerial Reform began to eliminate the rift within the judicial system. The creation of a separate Ministry of Justice worked toward the isolation of a discrete judicial sphere staffed by educated officials. The concentration of authority in the central offices of the ministries during Nicholas's reign enabled the minister of justice to extend his influence over provincial institutions and encourage the growth of a corps of officials with loyalties to the ministry rather than to local executive authorities. By the middle of the century, a group of legal officials had appeared who possessed a common experience in legal institutions and similar social and educational backgrounds.

The data presented in this chapter suggest a growing reliance on professional considerations and a declining importance of status in determining appointments to positions in the legal administration. This trend is prominent in the material on three variables—landed wealth, career patterns, and formal education. The evidence is more conclusive for some offices than for others, but the trend is in the same direction for all appointive offices of the Ministry of Justice. The trend corresponds to changes in the civil service in general at this time. Whether this resulted in tendencies to specialization in other branches as well will have to be answered by future research.

The legal administration during the first half of the nineteenth century retains the homogeneous character of the administration of the eighteenth century, drawing principally on noblemen, sons of chancellery workers, and clergy.[3] This was partly the result of the legal prohibitions of most members of other classes entering civil service. The privileges granted to university graduates created exemptions from these prohibitions, but the number of merchants' and peasants' sons remained negligible.

Important changes in the social characteristics of legal personnel take place at the highest level of the judicial system. In the Senate, a diminishing role is played by the members of the noble elite — officials owning five hundred souls or more, whose wealth and standing opened the way to high positions.[4] By the middle of the century, lesser noblemen are rising to positions of chief-procurator of the Senate and even senator. It is clear that this change reflects a shift in priorities within the state and not economic trends among the nobility. The number of landholders in the empire owning over one hundred souls and over five hundred souls probably did not decline from the late eighteenth century; both categories actually grew in number from 1834 to 1858.[5]

The most significant changes appear in the career patterns of these officials, occuring at nearly every level of the legal administration in the first half of the century. The usual noble career of the late eighteenth century began with early registration in the military, often at infancy. The nobleman would then shift to the civil service after having risen to a rank that would guarantee him a suitable office. His initial career experiences and training were thus in the military, even if he resigned relatively early. Military service enabled noblemen of all economic layers to avoid the lower levels of the civil service where technical ability and practice in applying the law might be acquired. In the last years of the eighteenth century and the first decades of the nineteenth, the Archive of the College or Ministry of Foreign Affairs and the Kremlin Expedition served similar purposes for members of the elite. While not instilling a barrack mentality, these offices permitted noblemen to gain rank easily and to assume judicial positions without judicial knowledge or experience.

Such practices gave way to civil service career patterns. An increasing number of officials in judicial offices began their careers in civil offices and an increasing number specialized in judicial service. A greater number of central officials received appointments to provincial positions. In this way, the minister extended his authority over provincial offices at the expense of the governors'.

Finally, the data point to a rising educational level for almost all appointive offices under the ministry. Before 1849, service lists did not require information on education, and it is therefore difficult to make direct comparisons between the later and earlier periods. But age of entry into service gives a useful index of the level of formal educational preparation. The practice of entering service early, deplored by Pushkin, Bulgarin, and Nicholas himself, became less frequent as education began to confer greater advantages. My research supports Uvarov's boast that in 1843 one could see noble youths studying in educational institutions at an age when their fathers had been in service.[6]

The purpose of this chapter is to examine when and how these tendencies contributed to the advance of legal specialization in the ministry. I have found it useful to analyze the composition of the ministry by office rather than rank, which often subsumed diverse offices under the same or approximate *chiny*. This approach permits us to locate the positions where changes took place and to determine the approximate time they occurred. It allows us to connect these changes with the particular responsibilities of the offices affected by them, and in turn, shows us the type of service experience the new officials underwent.

THE SENATE

With the establishment of the ministries, the Governing Senate lost most of its administrative authority and became a primarily judicial institution. Its prestige also declined, to match the low valuation of the judicial function in the autocratic system. But, specialized in function, the Senate, like most Russian institutions at the beginning of the century, was not specialized in the personnel assigned to it. The position of senator was used to pension eminent bureaucrats and officers. Its membership at all times would include a complement of generals; in 1853, they would comprise over 30 percent of the total number of members. Knowledge and expertise resided in the senate chancellery, but even there assignments, early in the century, often merely bestowed rank and salary upon those providing services to the elite, such as the famous Moscow tailor Zimulin, and an English tutor, neither of whom ever appeared in the Senate.[7]

The senators' lack of experience and zeal in their work gave cause for the minister to try to influence and even determine their decisions. Derzhavin initiated the practice of having procurators read long reports on cases to brief the senators thoroughly on the details. His successors favored shorter reports that would give the senators less food for thought and indicate which way they were supposed to vote. By the middle of the century, the minister of justice, Count Panin, would withhold reports until the last moment so that the senators would find it simplest to approve the ministry's opinion. Panin even intimidated them directly.[8] But despite these efforts, the senators continued to insist on their own opinions and disgruntle the minister. The frequent disagreements in the departments of the Senate and the minister's frequent challenges of their rulings indicate that senators still played an important role in the judicial process, however ill-informed and time-consuming their participation might be.

After its reorganization at the beginning of the century, the Senate consisted of ten departments. The first dealt with administrative justice and other administrative matters that remained within the Senate's discretion. Departments 2, 3, 4, 7, and 8 exercised jurisdiction over civil cases; departments 5 and 6, criminal. There were also heraldry and cadastral departments and regular general meetings of all. The first five departments, as well as the heraldry and cadastral departments, met in

Table 3.1. Social Origins of Officials in Legal Departments, 1826–56[a]

Origin	Senators		Chief-Procurators			Chief-Secretaries			Secretaries	
	1826	1846	1826	1845	1856	1826	1846	1856	1826	1846
Noble	34[e](94)	43[f](96)	11(100)	5(72)	8(80)	11(50)	8(44)	13(86)	7(33)	14(38)
Officers[b]	2(6)	1(2)	...	1(14)	1(10)	5(23)	6(33)	1(7)	7(33)	4(11)
Chancellery	...	...	...	...	...	2(9)	...	...	1(5)	2(5)
Clergy	...	...	...	...	...	3(14)	...	...	2(10)	3(8)
Merchant	...	...	...	1(14)	1(10)	...	...	...	2(10)	2(5)
Burgher[c]	...	...	...	...	...	...	...	1(7)	...	4(11)
Other taxed classes[d]	...	...	...	...	...	1(4)	4(23)	...	2(10)	7(19)
Foreigner	...	1(2)	...	...	...	...	...	...	...	1(3)
Totals	36(100)	45(100)	11(100)	7(100)	10(100)	22(100)	18(100)	15(100)	21(100)[g]	37(100)

[a] Service lists for Senate officials in the legal departments in 1826 are scattered through the individual alphabetical listings in *opis'* 3 of *fond* 1349. Service lists for the 1840s are assembled by department in *opis'* 5 of *fond* 1349. My sample of senators is thirty-six of seventy-two deliberating members in 1826, forty-five of fifty-five in 1846. There were twelve chief-procurators for the departments under consideration. There were a total of thirty-six chief-secretaries in 1826, thirty-three in 1846, twenty-seven in 1856 in these departments; the number of secretaries is difficult to determine for 1826 since the *adres-kalendar'* did not give a complete listing of this office. In the 1840s there were fifty to sixty secretaries in the legal departments.

[b] Refers to *ober-ofitserskie deti. Ober-ofitsery* held ranks from the fourteenth to the ninth in the civil or military service. In the military service the fourteenth rank conferred hereditary nobility, but nobility could only be passed on to children born after that rank was attained;

the others would be designated officers' sons. In the civil service those ranks, up to 1845, conferred personal but not hereditary nobility and children of officials in those ranks would be designated officers' sons.

[c] *Meshchanin.*

[d] Includes freed peasants, soldiers' sons, court servants.

[e] Eleven are titled.

[f] Seven are titled.

[g] Since percentages have been rounded to the nearest whole number, totals are sometimes slightly above or below 100.

Petersburg; departments 6 through 8 met in Moscow. A chief-procurator (*ober-prokuror*) represented the ministry in each department, and took charge of the department's chancellery, which was headed by a chief-secretary (*ober-sekretar'*). I examined service lists from the Senate's legal departments (2 through 8) from 1826 and 1846, and will discuss each office separately, in descending order. In this way I will attempt to give a profile of the changes taking place at each level of the Senate hierarchy.

Senators were the highest judges in the Russian legal system. Appointed by the tsar himself, they had attained the top ranks of the Russian administration (privy counselor, *tainyi sovetnik,* the third rank or actual privy counselor, *deistvitel'nyi tainyi sovetnik,* the second; the first rank was given rarely and was a special honor). Each senator participated in a department, a seven-member body which deliberated collegially. There were also nondeliberating members, whom I have not included in my calculations.

The membership of the Senate in 1826 was comprised preponderantly of hereditary noblemen, many of them from the wealthiest layers of their class (tables 3.1 and 3.2). In subsequent decades, the social composition of the Senate remained much the same, with some decline taking place in the number of large landowners (owning over five hundred souls) and some rise in the number of small (eleven to one hundred souls) and middle landowners (table 3.2).[9]

Table 3.2. Serfholding of Senators in Legal Departments

No. of Souls	1826	1845	1846	1855
0	10(29)	11(23)	15(33)	12(32)
1-10	...	3(6)	...	1(3)
11-100	2(6)	3(6)	2(5)	5(14)
101-500	9(27)	10(21)	14(31)	11(30)
501-1,000	4(12)	13(27)	8(18)	4(11)
1,001-10,000	8(23)	7(15)	5(11)	4(11)
10,000-	1(3)	1(2)	1(2)	...
Totals	34(100)	48(100)	45(100)	37(100)

NOTE: Figures for 1826 and 1846 come from service lists. Figures for 1845 and 1855 come from the listings in the *Spiski grazhdanskim chinam pervykh chetyrekh klassov* and include all senators holding civil ranks. Those senators who retained military ranks after appointment to the Senate are not included. Since the military spirit of Nicholas's reign often made it advantageous to retain military rank, there is a decline in the number of senators with civil ranks. Serfholding includes all souls mentioned as the official's own. I have combined hereditary (*rodovye*) and honorably acquired (*blagopriobretennye*) because of the few cases in which the latter appeared, and because some officials appeared to ignore the difference between the two in their listing. Also, it was a frequent practice to turn hereditary into acquired estates by fictional sales and other legal devices in order to gain greater freedom of disposal. See Aleksandr Liubavskii, *Iuridiches-kiia monografii i issledovaniia* (St. Petersburg, 1875), pp. 12, 31.

Table 3.3. Initial Service of Senate Officials, 1826-56

Initial Service	Senators			Chief-Procurators			Chief-Secretaries		
	1826	1846	1856	1826	1846	1856	1826	1846	1856
Military	30(83)	30(67)		4(36)	2(29)	1(10)	4(17)	...(...)	...(...)
Civil	6(17)	15(33)		7(64)	5(71)	9(90)	18(78)	17(94)	15(100)
Teaching	...	...		...	...	...	1 (5)	1 (6)	...
Totals	36(100)	45(100)		11(100)	7(100)	10(100)	23(100)	18(100)	15(100)

NOTE: For source of data, see table 3.1, note a.

Table 3.4. Service Experience of Senate Officials, 1826–56

Mean	Senators		Chief-Procurators		
	1826	1846	1826	1846	1856
Age	61.2(31)[a]	60.3(43)	39.3(9)	48.4(7)	43.6(10)
Years military service for ex-officers	20.5(29)	16.8(31)	11.0(4)	10.5(2)	8.0(1)
Age of retirement from military of ex-officers	27.4(29)	28.8(32)	23.3(3)	27.5(2)	24.0(1)
Years of civil service	23.1(35)	27.3(45)	22.9(11)	29.4(7)	22.5(8)
Years in provincial offices	3.3(35)	7.0(44)	2.4(11)	3.9(7)	.3(8)
Years in central offices	19.7(35)	20.2(44)	20.5(11)	25.6(7)	22.2(9)
Years of previous civil service[b]	14.7(35)	19.0(45)	17.2(11)	23.7(7)	19.0(8)
Age entry to civil service (all)	33.3(29)	31.1(43)	16.7(9)	17.6(7)	20.0(8)
Age entry to civil service (lifetime civil servants)	14.6(5)	12.8(14)	13.0(6)	13.6(5)	19.4(7)
Years in office	8.2(33)	8.4(45)	6.3(11)	5.7(7)	4.0(10)

Mean	Chief-Secretaries			Secretaries	
	1826	1846	1856	1826	1846
Age	51.1(22)	46.4(18)	37.3(13)	38.5(21)	36.9(37)
Years civil service	33.4(23)	29.4(18)	16.5(15)	23.6(21)	18.7(37)
Years in provincial offices	4.3(23)	9.0(18)	1.7(15)	5.5(21)	5.0(37)
Years in central offices	29.1(23)	20.4(18)	15.5(15)	18.1(21)	13.7(37)
Years previous civil service	24.0(22)	22.7(18)	10.3(12)	17.2(21)	13.9(37)
Age entry to civil service (all)	16.3(22)	15.9(18)	18.6(13)	15.3(21)	18.1(37)
Age entry to civil service (lifetime civil servants)	13.8(18)	15.9(18)	18.6(13)	15.3(21)	18.1(37)
Years in office	9.5(22)	7.0(18)	6.4(12)	6.6(21)	5.2(37)

[a] Parentheses indicate number.

[b] Years before appointment to present office.

Notable changes occur in the senators' career patterns. The percent of senators who had begun their service in the administration rises from 17 in 1826 to 33 in 1846, and the number of years spent in the civil service before appointment as senator also increases (tables 3.3 and 3.4). But the most striking change would be the appearance in the middle of the century of senators who had risen through the judiciary. Earlier, such a pattern appears to have been rare. In 1826, military service provided the route for poor and lesser noblemen into the Senate. Of ten senators without land, in 1826, eight were noblemen who had begun their service in the military, where they had remained for an average of 22 years. All but one of the eight assumed their first civil position at the fifth rank (*statskii sovetnik*) or above, which placed them high enough to avoid chancellery positions. The two senators with the smallest holdings, 75 and 91 souls, had served 47 and 34 years in the military, respectively. Two landless noblemen had begun in the civil service. One had worked in a court for five years, then spent 35 years in the military before returning to the civil service. Thus only one senator in my sample for 1826 owed his position exclusively to his service in the civil administration.

The judicial administration was not a path to membership in the 1826 Senate. Of the five senators who had not served in the military, none had risen through the judicial administration. Of all the senators, only six had served in a judicial office previous to their appointment. They had been chief-procurators of the Senate — the only judicial position that could lead to designation as senator. But it is clear that these senators owed their appointments to their social standing and not to their prior legal service. Five of the six came from elite families; three of them held hereditary estates of over 1,000 souls, two between 500 and 1,000. All five had begun service in the military, then shifted to such high civil service positions as vice-governor, membership in the Foreign Affairs College, or assistant to the chief-procurator. One of the six, an officer's son, Zakhar Nikolaevich Posnikov, held no land and rose through the customs administration. But his wife, the daughter of a General Arkhipov, owned estates populated with 2,608 souls.[10] The Committee of 6 December had found that the Senate was "frequently filled with people without skill in civil cases, those who never had been prepared for the calling of judge, and who had spent their whole life in another field."[11] The service lists for 1826 indicate that this description was probably true for nearly all senators. The highest judicial positions in the land appear to have been virtually barred to judicial officials.

In 1846, the general pattern is the same. Again senators with no serfs represent a group of successful noble officers. Thirteen of the fifteen without serfs began in the military and they averaged over twenty-seven years of military service. Of the fifteen senators who had not served in the military, only one had reached his position after extensive service in the judicial administration. But there are indications that new types of officials are receiving appointments as senators. Eleven of the 1846 senators had served as chief-procurators, and three of them had served previously in another judicial position. By 1846, service in the judicial administration was no longer incompatible with appointment to the highest judicial instance.

The data for 1855 show that the effects of Nicholas's policy were reaching to the Senate. While it is true that the educational level of senators remained low, in the 1850s, as Zaionchkovskii shows—with three-quarters of the members without higher education or any training in the law—senators now appear who have spent their careers as legal officials. For the first time landless noblemen who owe their positions to legal service have been appointed senators. Five senators with no serfs in 1855 have served only in civil institutions, and, more important, three of them have risen through the judicial administration. Two of the three smallest landlords, owning 25 and 45 souls, are also products of the legal administration. Typical of the new officials are two former heads of the Department of the Ministry of Justice, Boris Karlovich Danzas and Matvei Karniolin-Pinskii. Danzas was a graduate of Tsarskoe Selo, Karniolin-Pinskii of the St. Petersburg Pedagogical Institute, and both had assisted the Second Section in its review of criminal legislation. Danzas had served sixteen years in the Ministry of Justice before his appointment in 1851; Karniolin-Pinskii, twenty-three years before his appointment in 1850. Neither held land.[12]

The rise of a new, noble, civil servant is more apparent in the office of chief-procurator. The chief-procurators acted as the minister's agents in the Senate; they supervised the flow of cases through the departments and the departments' chancelleries, and were responsible for the selection and promotion of chancellery personnel. They read reports on cases to the members of the departments, usually presenting materials in a manner conducive to the minister's opinion. If a chief-procurator objected to the department's ruling, he would move the case to one of the "general meetings," and submit a "conciliatory proposal" for consideration. If he disapproved of the general meeting's decision, he could have the minister refer the case to the State Council.[13] The chief-procurator could wield considerable influence over the Senate. The features of the officials in this position at a given time give a clue to the minister's determination and ability to use this influence.

The chief-procurator's office carried high rank—the fourth or fifth—and considerable prestige. At the beginning of the nineteenth century, the office was held by young members of the elite, and scattered references to the late eighteenth century indicate that it was an elite office then, too. It was regarded as a route to swift advancement. Chief-procurators were expected to avoid conflict with senators and court their favor. The poet I. I. Dmitriev, a chief-procurator during the reign of Paul, entered into almost weekly quarrels with the senators and watched with dismay as he was passed over while his more docile colleagues received decorations and bonuses. Before long he submitted his resignation. When he became minister of justice in 1811, Dmitriev found that his chief-procurators were mostly young people from the court or military service. They were "well-bred but inexperienced and strove to excel mostly in securing advantageous connections."[14] The chief-procurator's influence on the fate of a case could be great, but as one petitioner, O. A. Przheslavskii, remarked, "Since most of the chief-procurators were from the notables [znat'] and had little experience in making sense of cases cleverly composed to obtain a particular intention, they submitted to the influence of the clerical workers." A procurator would influence the decision only if he was appealed to in his capacity as a member of the patronage hierarchy. Przheslavskii received the good will of a chief-procurator by surrendering his seat to him at a crowded concert.[15] Alexander I tried to change this pattern. In an instruction to one of his chief-procurators, he complained that many young noblemen held that position without actually serving. He ordered that such individuals be advised, in accordance with the will of the tsar, that "it was more suitable to their class and dignity to enter the military."[16]

Service lists for the period 1826 to 1856 show a new type of chief-procurator appearing during the reign of Nicholas I. The position was dominated by noblemen both at the beginning and the end of the period, but the chief-procurators of 1856 came from a different stratum than those

Table 3.5. Serfholding of Chief-Procurators in Legal Departments of the Senate, 1826-56

No. of Souls	1826	1846	1856
0	1(9)	3(43)	7(70)
1-10	...	...	...
11-100	...	1(14)	2(20)
101-500	5(46)	1(14)	1(10)
501-1,000	2(18)	1(14)	...
1,001-10,000	3(27)	1(14)	...
Totals	11(100)	7(100)	10(100)

NOTE: Serf-listing after 1849 was supposed to include the parents' serfs when the parents were living, though it is not certain that all officials observed this requirement. If they failed to, it would mean an artificially low estimate of serfholding for younger officials. But in the many cases where lists have been available for an official both early and late in his career, I have found no examples of such omissions.

of 1826. The large landlords of the elite and middle landlords disappeared from the office, replaced by landless and small noblemen (see tables 3.1 and 3.5). The number beginning service in the military also declined.

Striking changes took place in the pattern of previous civil service. The most frequent beginning for the careers of the 1826 chief-procurators was in the College of Foreign Affairs (five of the eleven), and it was through the easy and elegant service under the college that they gained the high rank that enabled them to become procurators. Those who began in the civil service entered young, none after the age of sixteen (see table 3.4). Only three provide educational data, listing the Page Corps, a private pension, and the pension at Moscow University. Their service career was long, averaging about twenty-three years. It was concentrated in central institutions; only one had begun service in provincial institutions and only three had served at all in provincial institutions. But it is notable that only about one-third of their civil service previous to their appointments was in the legal administration. Most of their legal service, moreover, was spent in the office of the chief-procurator (za ober-prokurorskim stolom), an assignment with light and undefined responsibilities which members of the elite assumed while they awaited promotions in rank.[17] None had served in the Senate chancellery.

Twenty years later the service lists show a different profile (see tables 3.4 and 3.5). The office is no longer a berth for rich aristocrats; landholding has dropped. The chief-procurators are older and have served longer terms in the civil service, again almost exclusively in central institutions. The number of years in judicial offices has increased to about two-thirds of their total civil service. Two of the seven have served in the Second Section, three in the Ministry of Justice. Two are graduates of Tsarskoe Selo, two of Moscow University, both of them candidates; one was a graduate of the Pedagogical Institute.

By 1856 the shift to a civil service pattern has become still clearer (see table 3.4). The chief-procurators fit the category of the new career bureaucrats with higher education, who, as Pintner has shown, began to fill high administrative positions in Nicholas's reign. They have entered the civil service much later and have had longer formal education than their predecessors. Four are graduates of Moscow University (three of them candidates), two of the School of Jurisprudence, one of the Engineering Cadet Corps; only one mentions no formal education.[18] More of the chief-procurators are products of the legal administration; five have spent the principal part of their careers in the Ministry of Justice or the Senate. All of their service is in central institutions, with the exception of a three-year term one spent in the provinces. The number of years in the chief-procurator position continues to drop as a result of Panin's practice of frequent reassignments.

The chief-procurator of 1826 was a wealthy or middle landowner, a member of the *jeunesse dorée,* favored with a high position en route to even more distinguished and prominent offices of state. The chief-procurator of 1856 was a lesser or middle nobleman who had risen through the Ministry of Justice or other organs of internal administration. Prince Pavel Pavlovich Gagarin and Alexander Vasil'evich Kochubei are examples of the first type. Gagarin was a member of the ancient Gagarin family; Kochubei, a cousin of the minister of interior, Victor Kochubei, and a member of the family whose wealth and standing derived from their relationship with Catherine's favorite, Count Bezborodko. Gagarin owned two thousand souls, Kochubei, seven hundred. Both were educated at home. Gagarin studied as well at the Jesuit school of the abbot Nicholas. Both began their careers in the College of Foreign Affairs, and then served in brief assignments in various branches. They were appointed chief-procurators in 1818, Gagarin at the age of twenty-nine, Kochubei, thirty-one. Both became known as enlightened individuals with a respect for human rights. Gagarin distinguished himself as an able and energetic official. At the close of the 1820s, he ruled over the Moscow legal institutions, it was said, like a minister. His ability to conduct criminal hearings and investigations of institutions impressed both Michael Dmitriev and Ivan Aksakov.[19] But he remained at all times aloof, an outsider, destined for higher positions, checking up on the operations of governmental offices. In 1831 he was appointed a senator, and in 1844 a member of the State Council. He served on numerous committees for Nicholas and on the commission investigating the case of the Petrashevtsy. His success removed him further from the details of legal administration. Chief-Procurator Lebedev wrote in 1850 that Gagarin had "little experience in the processing of cases, and this concerns both chancellery matters and matters of state importance."[20] Kochubei too rose to the Senate and the State Council. In the late 1850s, the two old officials would participate in the deliberations of the State Council about the judicial reform, and, baffled by the complexity of the subject, would have to accept the leadership of the younger generation.

Andrei Efimovich Matiunin's life was one example of a new career pattern. Though a nobleman with 378 souls, he was educated at the university and rose through the civil administration. Matiunin completed Kazan University with a degree of candidate in 1832 and entered the Department of State Economy and Public Buildings of the Ministry of Interior in the same year. In 1839, he became a secretary in the Department of the Ministry of Justice, and in 1840 began serving on the Ministry's Consultation. In 1846, assigned to the chief-procurator's desk of the First Department, he carried out an investigation, *reviziia,* of the offices of the ministry. In 1848, he was appointed to be chief-procurator of the First Section of the Third Department.[21]

Baron Nikolai Egorovich Tornau was typical of the three Lutherans from the Baltic provinces serving as chief-procurator in 1856. Tornau held neither land nor serfs. He finished the lycée at Tsarskoe Selo in 1829, and entered the College of Foreign Affairs. In 1830 he was assigned to the Second Section. In 1833, he shifted to the Asiatic Department, and in 1840 was appointed assistant chief of the Caspian region. At this time he was participating in the compilation of a digest of Moslem laws. In 1847 and 1848 he served in the Ministry of Justice and then transferred to become director of the chancellery of the governor-general of Lifland, Estland, and Kurland. He was appointed to serve as chief-procurator in 1851. During these years, Tornau devoted himself to the compilation and translation of Moslem laws, for which he received the Demidov prize of the Academy of Sciences.[22]

Among the chief-procurators in 1856 was a protégé of Count Panin, Kastor Nikiforovich Lebedev. Lebedev's father was a teacher in the Penza *gimnasium;* his mother was the daughter of a bankrupt landlord. As a student in the philological faculty of Moscow University, Lebedev became known as a habitué of literary circles and a talented satirist.[23] He entered service in the War Ministry in 1835, but his interest was soon attracted to comparative jurisprudence and criminal legislation, and in 1841 he transferred to the Ministry of Justice. In 1842 he became a division chief and in 1848 he was appointed to the position of chief-procurator of the First Section of the Sixth Department.[24]

Lebedev was uncomfortably dependent upon his position for income and unhappy with his demeaning assignments. His yearning for security, his lack of the aristocrat's calm finesse made him repugnant to the members of the elite who had dealings with him. Lebedev was immortalized as Tarelkin in Sukhovo-Kobylin's comedies *The Case* and *Tarelkin's Death.* Sukhovo-Kobylin described the chief-procurator as a grasping, craven bribe-taker, motivated solely by the impulse to climb out of his humiliating condition of need, dehumanized by the hell of the tsarist bureaucracy. But Sukhovo-Kobylin, the wealthy aristocrat, the lion of the Moscow salons, was inspired by more than satirical malice. Accused of the murder of his French mistress, Sukhovo-Kobylin tried the traditional aristocratic devices to free himself of guilt. He bribed the secretary in the Moscow Aulic Court and succeeded in having testimony suppressed, altered, or coerced so the charge could be pinned on one of his household serfs. But the Senate was no longer as amenable to aristocratic persuasion as it had once been, and Lebedev, a chief-procurator in the Sixth Department, was one of those who would not accept the concoction of evidence Sukhovo-Kobylin had purchased.

Lebedev, however distasteful his appearance and mannerisms, believed that landlords could be brutal and should be punished for their misdeeds. Later he wrote a report about the difficulty of convicting landlords who had murdered their peasants. In Sukhovo-Kobylin's case, he understood who was the guilty party.[25] "There is no doubt that the murder was completed with calculation, with intent, and in cold blood," he wrote, pointing to Sukhovo-Kobylin's guilt.[26] Sukhovo-Kobylin finally had to invoke the influence of contacts close to the empress to have the charges quashed, but his rage against the functionary who did not yield to his bribes and pressure knew no bounds. Tarelkin expressed his vengeance against Lebedev. The playwright turned the chief-procurator into a groveling clerk who did not even get to enjoy the fruits of his evil, "a special kind of viper that inhabits the Petersburg swamp." "The movement of his jaws gives cause to think that some of his teeth, and perhaps all, are acquired and not inherited. He speaks like Demosthenes when the latter stuffed his mouth with stones."[27] Art elevated his rage into an indictment of the tsarist bureaucrat that would delight future readers and audiences. But Tarelkin was in fact his retaliation — the revenge of an aristocrat who found that he too might be brought within the sphere of formal justice and was to be subjected to the indignity of judgment by the likes of Kastor Nikiforovich Lebedev.

When we turn our attention from the chief-procurator to the chief-secretary of the early nineteenth century, we cross a vast social gulf. We move from the world of the court and the mansions of the elite to the cold apartments of *chinovniki,* dreaming, as Vigel' described them, of the promotions and medals that might reward their long service. It was the gulf between the world of power and the world of work. The chief-secretaries had attained the sixth or seventh ranks after a life of service in the chancellery. Further advancement was barred, since chief-procurators were not appointed from the chancellery staff. On the other hand, the chief-secretary had at his disposal the law and procedure that the nobleman disdained. He headed the clerical workers who had the actual responsibility for preparation of cases. He directed the formulation of the memorandum, the *zapiska,* which detailed the circumstances and the pertinent legislation for cases, and as a result he could and did influence their outcome.[28] When senators or chief-procurators could not be enlisted in support of a suit, it was necessary to purchase or win the sympathy of the chief-secretary. Przheslavskii described him as "the mainspring of the Senate's operating mechanism."[29]

The changes in the social composition and career paths of the chief-secretaries' offices during the subsequent thirty years proceed in a direction opposite to those taking place among the chief-procurators'. The social profiles of the two offices converge, so that by 1856 we witness the formation of a relatively homogeneous cadre of personnel staffing legal institutions. While the social characteristics of the chief-procurators change between 1826 and 1846, the chief-secretaries' remain much the same. Then a shift takes place, reflecting the assignment of students from the School of Jurisprudence. Both class composition and serfholding by 1856 are similar to the chief-procurators'.

Table 3.6. Serfholding of Chief-Secretaries in Legal Departments of the Senate, 1826-56

No. of Souls	1826	1846	1856
0	12(55)	10(56)	10(84)
1-10	6(27)	3(17)	1(8)
11-100	3(14)	2(11)	...
101-500	1(4)	2(11)	1(8)
501-1,000	...	...	...
1,001-10,000	...	1(5)	...
Totals	22(100)	18(100)	12(100)

In this period, the chief-secretary's position becomes a noble office. Chief-secretaries of 1826 come from the lesser nobility and chancellery workers, the groups that had traditionally staffed the lower and middle echelons of the Russian bureaucracy (see table 3.1). The proportion of noblemen declines slightly from 1826 to 1846, then rises sharply. By 1856, the representatives of other classes have almost disappeared and the chief-secretaries, like the chief-procurators, tend to be almost exclusively from the lesser nobility (see table 3.6). During this period, the average age falls (see table 3.4). In 1826, the chief-secretaries have a significantly higher average age and number of years of civil service than do the chief-procurators, their superiors in rank and office. By 1856, they are somewhat younger and have spent fewer years in the civil service.

The decline in age reflects a significant change in career pattern. In 1826, most chief-secretaries had reached the culmination of a long career in chancellery service under the Ministry of Justice. Eighteen of twenty-two had begun their careers in offices under the ministry; twelve of the twenty-two had been recruited from provincial offices. The materials for 1836 and 1846 show an increased reliance on chancellery workers from other branches; only eleven of twenty-one in 1836 and eleven of eighteen in 1846 began under the ministry, about two-thirds of them coming from provincial chancelleries. After 1846, chief-secretarial appointments are made from among the recent graduates of the universities and the School of Jurisprudence, recruited to work in central institutions: twelve of the fifteen 1856 chief-secretaries have come out of the central institutions of the Ministry of Justice.

Educational qualifications appear to rise during the period; however, data on the early period are fragmentary. In 1826, only ten provide information on education: four had completed the university; one the pension at Moscow University; one the Cadet Corps; two the seminary;

one a religious academy. From the early age of entry (see table 3.4), it appears that few had received higher education. Only two had entered the civil service after the age of sixteen. Data are similar for 1836 and 1846, but the age of entry rises to 18.6 years, suggesting increased educational attainments. When Stoianovskii entered service in 1841, he claimed there were only six individuals with higher education in the chancelleries of the St. Petersburg departments of the Senate.[30] In the next decade, however, there is a decisive rise in the educational level of the chief-secretaries. The age of entry increases sharply. Of twenty-seven chief-secretaries in 1856, twenty-one were graduates of the School of Jurisprudence, four of the university. Two mention no formal education.[31]

Similar trends are evident among the Senate secretaries, who held the office immediately beneath the chief-secretaries. Serfholding corresponds closely to the chief-secretaries' in 1826 and 1846 (see table 3.7). We observe a decline in age and total length of service, and a rise in the age of entry into civil service (see table 3.4). An increasing proportion have received their initial experience in the Senate chancellery, or the central offices of the Ministry of Justice, rising from 6 of 21 in 1826, to 20 of 45 in 1836, to 22 of 37 in 1846, to 34 of 52 in 1856, or about two-thirds.

Table 3.7. Serfholding of Secretaries in Legal Departments of the Senate, 1826-46

No. of Souls	1826	1846
0	13(62)	32(89)
1-10	5(24)	1(3)
11-100	3(14)	2(5)
101-500	...	1(3)
Totals	21(100)	36(100)

The rise of the age of entry to the civil service — from 15.3 to 18.1 years — suggests increasing educational attainments of Senate secretaries. In 1846, ten are university graduates (two candidates), seven from the School of Jurisprudence. From the complete information available for 1856 (see table 3.8), it becomes clear that the Senate chancellery had changed considerably since Stoianovskii had begun his service there in 1841. Over three-quarters of the secretaries had attended the university or the School of Jurisprudence.

The changes in the character of the heads of the Senate chancellery become clearer when we examine examples of officials who held the chief-secretary's office. Nobleman Aleksei Fillipovich Fial'kovskii was born in 1778 and, at the age of fourteen, entered the chancellery of the Chernigov Lower Tribunal *Nizhnaia Rasprava* (a district court for state peasants, *odnodvorty* and *raznochintsy,* which was abolished by Paul).

After four years he was raised to the fourteenth rank, *gubernskii regis-trator,* and moved to the Chernigov district court. In 1799 he was appointed to the Senate. By 1808 he had risen to the position of secretary and had achieved the eighth rank, collegiate assessor, which exempted him

Table 3.8. Education of Senate Secretaries in 1856

University	25(44)
School of Jurisprudence	22(39)
Richelieu Lycée	1(2)
Lycée--Prince Bezborodko	1(2)
Provincial gymnasium	2(4)
None indicated	6(11)
Total	57(100)

SOURCE: *Spisok chinam pravitel'stvuiushchego Senata za 1856 g.*

from Speranskii's examination law, issued the following year. As secretary he worked with Senators Karneev and Sivers on a Senate investigation. Participation in Senate investigations was well rewarded, and in 1819 at the age of forty-one, after twenty-seven years of service, Fial'kovskii received promotion to chief-secretary and the rank of *kollezhskii sovetnik,* the sixth. His service list of 1822 ascribes to him three souls and two wooden houses, one of which he acquired himself. His service list of 1831 mentions thirteen souls.[32]

Fial'kovskii enjoyed the favor of his superior, Chief-Procurator Prince A. A. Lobanov-Rostovskii. In a report of 1822, Lobanov-Rostovskii praised him for his "honest and noble character" and his firm knowledge of the practice of the law (*zakonovedenie*). "He observes the strict order, precision and activeness in the processing of cases, and prepares them with praiseworthy care, zeal and skill." Fial'kovskii had processed 109 investigations and 1,196 cases in the preceding year. Lobanov-Rostovskii recommended him for the order of Anna, second class.[33]

Officer's son Alexander Petrovich Reisler entered the Senate as copier in 1805, at the age of thirteen. By 1813 he had reached the twelfth rank of *guberskii sekretar'.* In 1815, he assisted in the investigation of Voronezh and Penza provinces and was raised to the ninth rank, *tituliarnyi sovetnik.* In 1817, he was appointed secretary, and in 1819 served also as treasurer of his department.[34] Reisler was a victim of the examination law. Lobanov-Rostovskii wrote of Reisler, and another officer's son in the same situation, that both, "by their diligence, by their art in preparing and processing cases, their thorough knowledge of the practice of the law, their noble and honorable conduct could be worthy chief-secretaries," but by giving so much of themselves to service they had no time to prepare for the examination.[35] Nonetheless, in 1825, an exception was made and Reisler was appointed chief-secretary at the age of thirty-two, though he had attained only the ninth rank. The next year Nicholas issued a decree allowing exemptions from the examination requirement for those with long service at the ninth rank.[36]

The chancellery later in the century presents a quite different pattern. Alexander Nikolaevich Shakhov was from an old but impoverished gentry family, and had, according to his service list, one wooden house, acquired by himself. Among the first graduating class of the School of Jurisprudence, he entered the ministry in 1841 at the position of junior assistant to the secretary of the Second Department. In 1844, he was raised to senior assistant, and a year later became acting secretary of the Fourth Department. Two years later, at the age of twenty-six, he was appointed chief-secretary. By 1856, Shakhov had already attained the fifth rank.[37] Shakhov's brother, Ippolit, was graduated from St. Petersburg University in 1843, and rose to chief-secretary of the Fifth Department after only ten years of service.[38]

Karl Karlovich Peters, a landless Baltic nobleman, was graduated from the School of Jurisprudence in 1845 at the age of nineteen and became a junior assistant to the secretary. In 1846, he shifted to the ministry's department. He was appointed assistant chairman of the Orel Criminal Chamber in 1848. In 1850 he was reassigned to Petersburg as secretary of the first division of the Senate's Fifth Department. In the same year, at the age of twenty-four, he was promoted to chief-secretary. Graduates of the School of Jurisprudence, Shakhov and Peters were assured of swift success in the service. They also received a bonus of 240 silver rubles a year, which Nicholas had ruled in 1842 should be granted to graduates of the School of Jurisprudence once they were confirmed in the office of chief-secretary.[39]

The reign of Nicholas I saw the disappearance of the gulf between chancellery and superior office in the Senate. Nicholas's determination to improve the dispensation of justice led him to eliminate the stronghold of landed wealth at the top of the Senate hierarchy and to encourage the advancement of men of education and experience from the nobility. Members of the lesser nobility began to choose the civil rather than the military service as a route to distinction.

THE MINISTRY OF JUSTICE

Representatives of the new legal cadres began to staff the offices of the Ministry of Justice as well. The ministry's highest office, the Consultation, was a collegial body established to provide the minister with expert opinion for his recommendations on cases before the Senate. The Consultation was comprised of members, who included the chief-procurators of the Senate, and consultants. Members deliberated and determined the recommendation to the minister; consultants composed the reports and advised the members. In 1849 most of the members of the Consultation represented the elite. The composition of its membership resembled the Senate's.[40] Ten members were noblemen, one was from the clergy, one the son of a court baker. Most of the members held land, and several, like Count Lev Viktorovich Kochubei, Count Ivan Avgustovich Ilinskii, and Count Lev Grigorevich Saltykov, were great landlords who had risen in the guards and Ministry of Foreign Affairs (see table 3.9). Several lesser noblemen who had served in the ministry, such as Tseimern and Illichevskii, were also members.

Table 3.9. Serfholding and Education of Officials of the Ministry of Justice in 1849[a]

Office	0	1-10	11-100	101-500	501-1,000	1,001	Totals
Members of Consultation							
Higher education[b]	1	0	1	2	0	0	4
No higher education	2	0	1	2	0	3	8
Totals	3	0	2	4	0	3	12
Stolonachal'niki							
Higher education[b]	11	0	0	1	1	1	14
No higher education	2	0	0	1	0	0	3
Totals	13	0	0	2	1	1	17

[a]The listing is complete for 1849, in 1349-5-4501.

[b]Higher education included the universities, the School of Jurisprudence, the lycée at Tsarskoe Selo. Three of the members of the Consultation completed the university (two of them had candidates' degrees). One attended Tsarskoe Selo. Of the *stolonachal'niki*, thirteen completed the university (five of them had candidates' degrees); four were graduates of the School of Jurisprudence; one of Tsarskoe Selo.

The new types were most evident in the ministry's department, the central office of the ministry's administrative machine (see table 3.9). The heads of the various sections of the department were desk chiefs (*stolonachal'niki*), who also on occasion drafted the reports that influenced and often determined the Consultation's rulings. Of seventeen *stolonachal'niki* in 1849, fifteen were noblemen, and most of them were landless. Their average age was twenty-seven and all but a few had served exclusively in the ministry. Their educational level is striking.

The most notable of the desk chiefs was Sergei Ivanovich Zarudnyi, later to become the leader of the effort of judicial reform. Zarudnyi was in many ways typical of the new group. From an old Ukrainian noble family, he had been left without means of support besides his service. His grandfather had owned a large part of Kharkov province, but by the 1840s most of the family's holdings had been fragmented and sold off. Zarudnyi's service list of 1847 indicates that his father held one hundred souls. But his later service lists show that he received none of these in inheritance and remained without land or serfs. Zarudnyi received a candidate's degree in mathematics from Kharkov University, then came to Petersburg hoping to find a position at the Pulkovo observatory. His hopes were frustrated, however, and he had to take a position in the Ministry of Justice instead, which he secured with the help of the chief of the department, B. K. Danzas, his relative. Once in the ministry, Zarudnyi became passionately interested in the law. His abilities at logical exposition, together with the protection of Danzas, brought him to the attention of Panin, who relied increasingly upon him to write his reports. At the end of the forties, Zarudnyi was already dominating the deliberations of the Consultation. In late 1849, he was promoted from *stolonachal'nik* to chief judicial consultant. He initiated a weekly "school" for the young jurists in the ministry, where he explained and analyzed the various cases to be discussed in the Consultation.[41]

THE SECOND SECTION

The changes in composition of the codification section of the tsar's chancellery took a different direction. Speranskii had been placed in charge of the initial work of codification when the Second Section was established in 1826, though he never received an official position on the staff. He and its official chief, Alexander Balugianskii, formerly the rector of the Petersburg Pedagogical Institute, chose the officials and

Table 3.10. Serfholding and Education of Officials of the Second Section in 1835 and 1847[a]

Education	0	1-10	11-100	101-500	501-1,000	1,001-	Totals
1835 officials							
Higher education	6	0	1	1	0	0	8
No higher education	4	0	0	0	0	0	4
Totals	10	0	1	1	0	0	12
1847 officials							
Higher education	8	0	2	2	1	4	17
No higher education	3	0	0	1	0	2	6
Totals	11	0	2	3	1	6	23

[a]Materials were available for twelve of fifteen of the 1835 officials scattered through *fond* 1349 and in the *Russkii Biograficheskii Slovar'*. Materials are complete for 1847 officials in 1349-5-7753.

[b]The 1835 officials include six with university educations--three of them doctors, and two from the lycée. The 1847 officials include sixteen from the universities, five of them with candidates' degrees, one a master's. One official had completed the lycée.

set the tone of the Second Section in its first years when it accomplished the work on the complete collection of laws and the *Digest of Laws.* Its membership then was comprised predominantly of academic jurists and officials who had advanced in the service due to education or merit during the periods of Speranskii's preeminence. Its composition in 1835 showed Speranskii's continued influence. Only four noblemen, two held land — Zamiatnin 150 souls and Tseimern, 75. Four of the eleven non-nobles, Balugianskii, Kunitsyn, Plisov, and Klokov, had taught at a university or the Pedagogical Institute.[42]

After Speranskii's death in 1839, the character of both the Second Section's work and its personnel changed radically (see table 3.10). The major effort at codification had been completed. There remained the tasks of preparing new editions of the *Digest,* periodical supplements, and the penal code of 1845, which Bludov called "a modified digest." The Second Section was also responsible for the reform of court procedure, which never assumed the same significance in Nicholas's eyes as codification. Dmitrii Nikolaevich Bludov was appointed head of the Second Section in 1840, and proceeded to replace the experts who had worked on codification with his own appointees.

The service lists of the Second Section in 1847 indicate that Bludov's preferences were quite different from Speranskii's. Fifteen of the twenty-three members were noblemen, five of them titled. Eleven noblemen had completed the university, and eight owned land, several of them extensive estates. Bludov turned the Second Section into a haven for educated and cultivated members of the elite. Assigned to the favored work of codification and preparation of reform projects, they avoided contact with the daily work of administration and the ordeal of serving under Victor Panin. Among them were Prince Vladimir Odoevskii, the novelist-philosopher, and the poet, Count Alexei Konstantinovich Tolstoi, who together with his cousins, the two Zhemchuzhnikov brothers, composed Koz'ma Prutkov's parodies of the thoughts and expressions of more serious-minded officials.[43]

PROVINCIAL OFFICES

Provincial judicial offices also felt the impact of the government's new administrative policies. Administrative centralization brought increasing specialization of judicial personnel. Governors and provincial bureaus paid little attention to the place or nature of earlier administrative work in making assignments. But as the minister of justice asserted his authority over judicial positions, he wielded a growing influence over assignments and succeeded in filling provincial judicial offices with individuals affiliated with the ministry and with himself. With the weakening of governors' power over appointments, we discern the outlines of a distinct judicial administration in the provinces, staffed by officials who are taking on the features of a legal cadre.

The Criminal and Civil Chambers were the highest judicial instances in each province.[44] Early nineteenth-century Judicial Chambers consisted of two judges appointed by the Senate — a chairman and counselor (*sovetnik*) or assistant chairman. Two assessors elected from the gentry and two from the merchantry were supposed to assist in the decision of cases pertaining to members of their own class, though in fact their role was never more than negligible. The law of 6 December 1831, increased the property requirements for voting in gentry assemblies. As a concession to the nobility, it made the chairman's office elective in most provinces. Minister of Justice Count Panin, however, opposed election of judges and succeeded in gaining the right to appoint the chairman when the candidates did not meet the ministry's ethical standards.[45]

I will discuss the aggregate data from the offices of chairman, assistant chairman, and procurator for three points in time, presenting the peculiarities of the individual offices where relevant. Data from the beginning of the century suggest the composition of the provincial courts during the late eighteenth century. Results were not affected by the flow of noblemen from the military during the period of Paul's terror, since only 4 of 78 officials had entered the civil service after his accession. The data

Table 3.11. Social Origins of Provincial Judicial Officials in the First Half of the Nineteenth Century

Origin	Beginning	Quarter	Middle
Noble	63(81)	38(67)	45(75)
Officers	8(10)	7(12)	4(6)
Chancellery	1(1)	5(9)	2(4)
Clergy	2(3)	6(10)	4(6)
Merchant	1(1)	...	1(2)
Taxed classes	1(1)	1(1)	4(6)
Foreigner	2(3)	...	...
Totals	78(100)	57(100)	60(100)

SOURCE: Provincial and district lists are from *opis'* 4 and 5 of *fond* 1349.

NOTE: The total number of such officials in each period is 210 to 230. The breakdown of my sample is as follows: beginning--30 chairmen, 38 assistant chairmen, 11 procurators; quarter--23 chairmen, 23 assistant chairmen, 11 procurators; middle--26 chairmen, 27 assistant chairmen, 12 procurators. I have mentioned the divergences of individual offices from the aggregate data in the text. Lists were not available for each province in each period. Since these positions were centrally appointed, however, I believe that regional differences, except for Siberia, should not be significant. My lists are from the following provinces, beginning (B), quarter (Q), and middle (M): Tver (BQM), Kostroma (BM), Novgorod (BM), Moscow (BQM), Vladimir (BQM), Smolensk (BQ), Kursk (BM), Orel (BQM), Tambov (BQM), Riazan (BQ), Saratov (B), Kazan (B), Orenburg (B), Vologda (BQM), Arkhangelsk (BM), Chernigov (BM), Kiev (BQ), Pskov (QM); Nizhnii-Novgorod (Q), Voronezh (QM), Poltava (M), Simbirsk (M).

from the end of the first quarter and the middle of the century show the impact of the personnel policies of Alexander I and Nicholas I.

The materials on Provincial Chambers suggest that the government succeeded in limiting the social changes accompanying the process of specialization of legal officials. The proportion of hereditary noblemen declines during the first quarter of the century, perhaps as the result of Speranskii's influence and the examination law (see table 3.11). Such a decline affects all three positions. Nicholas's personnel policies appear to have arrested this tendency. The proportion of hereditary noblemen rises slightly during the second quarter of the century. This increase, moreover, occurs in the appointive assistant chairman and procurator positions. Despite the law of 6 December 1831, the proportion of noble chairmen in my sample decreases.[46]

Table 3.12. Serfholding of Provincial Judicial Officials in the First Half of the Nineteenth Century

No. of Souls	Beginning	Quarter	Middle
0	20(25)	23(42)	27(45)
1-10	14(18)	8(14)	...
11-100	25(32)	17(31)	12(20)
101-500	17(22)	6(11)	19(32)
501-1,000	2(2)	...	2(3)
1,001-10,000	1(1)	1(2)	...
Totals	79(100)	55(100)	60(100)

NOTE: For source of data, see table 3.11 note.

Data on serfholding indicate that the government succeeded in keeping landed noblemen in provincial judicial offices (see table 3.12). There is a sharp decline in landholding, paralleling the social shift that takes place during the first quarter. Then it rises again to somewhat above its initial level. At the beginning of the century, 43 percent have fewer than ten souls; at the middle, 45 percent (when the category of one to ten souls virtually disappears due to the prohibition of holding serfs without land). The increase in the number of middle landlords (one hundred to five hundred souls) takes place in the chairman's position. Middle landlords rise from 17 percent at the end of the first quarter to 50 percent of chairmen at mid-century, as a result of the election law of 6 December 1831. The landholding of assistant chairmen and procurators remains constant during the second quarter.[47]

Changes in career pattern, however, appear to progress without interruption. At the beginning of the century the court personnel have the military background typical of eighteenth-century judicial officials. After the examination law the proportion of military men declines in all provincial judicial offices (see table 3.13). The average number of years they have spent in the military decreases by half (see table 3.14). The practice of assigning officers directly to one of these positions—as was the case with nine of the officials at the beginning of the century—disappears by mid-century. The growing role of the ministry tells with an increase in the proportion both of officials who had begun their careers in central institutions and of those who had served in central institutions.[48] Only one official at the beginning of the century had served in the Senate chancellery, at the end of the first quarter 10 of 57 had (17.5 percent), at mid-century 24 of 65 (36.9 percent).

Table 3.13. Initial Service of Provincial Judicial Officials in the First Half of the Nineteenth Century

Initial Service	Beginning	Quarter	Middle
Military	52(67)	17(30)	11(18)
Civil	24(31)	35(61)	44(73)
Church administration	1(1)	1(2)	1(2)
Teaching	...	4(7)	4(7)
Imperial court	1(1)	...	...
Total	78(100)	57(100)	60(100)

NOTE: For source of data, see table 3.11 note.

The change in career pattern is accompanied by a rising educational level. The age of initial entry to the civil service increases from 16.0 to 18.0 years at mid-century, suggesting longer educational preparation. Again there is only limited information on education before mid-century. At the beginning of the century, of fourteen giving information on education, two had attended the university, ten the Cadet Corps. At the end of the first quarter, six indicate they had attended the university, only two the Cadet Corps, and three, religious academies. Of the forty-four lists available for mid-century, eleven were from graduates of the School of Jurisprudence, thirteen of the university. The proportions correspond to those for all chairman's, assistant chairman's, and procurator's offices in the empire in 1850, when 18.6 percent had attended the university and 19.5 percent the School of Jurisprudence.[49]

By all accounts, the assistant chairmen played the most important role in the operation of the courts in the middle of the century. Most chairmen played no part in the proceedings and some, like Sumarokov's judge, slept through them.[50] Stoianovskii wrote of the courts of the 1840s, "Cases usually were decided without a report, by the assistant chairman alone, the single member appointed by the government and in the last years before the reform the only jurist. All the other members, with the occasional

Table 3.14. Service Experience of Provincial Judicial Officials in the First Half of the Nineteenth Century

	Beginning	Quarter	Middle
Age	49.0(76)	49.1(57)	42.2(60)
Years military (ex-officers)	19.6(57)	11.9(18)	9.5(11)
Age leaving military (ex-officers)	31.5(57)	25.4(18)	25.6(11)
Years civil service	20.4(78)	27.8(57)	22.0(60)
Years in this province	11.8(76)	14.8(57)	7.7(60)
Years in other provinces	6.0(76)	8.6(57)	10.2(60)
Years in central offices	2.5(76)	4.6(57)	3.8(60)
Years prior civil service	15.7(78)	23.7(57)	18.8(60)
Age of entry into civil service (all)	28.8(75)	20.9(57)	20.5(60)
Age of entry into civil service (lifetime civil servants)	16.3(21)	16.0(35)	18.0(44)
Years in office	4.6(78)	4.4(57)	3.3(60)

NOTE: For source of data, see table 3.11 note.

exception of the chairman, only signed the prepared decision about the defendant, whom not one of them had seen."[51] The new type of educated noble legal official was most prevalent among the assistant chairmen. According to the complete listings of 1850, their educational level was the highest of the three provincial judicial offices: 18 of 74 (24.3 percent) had attended the university, 22 of 74 (29.7 percent) the School of Jurisprudence.

During the first half of the nineteenth century, the noble provincial judge who had vaulted to his position by his military service began to give way first to an official, often non-noble, with long administrative experience, and then to a nobleman who owed his position to education and civil service. By the end of the 1850s, a group of officials sharing a common educational experience with officials in central judicial institutions was beginning to emerge in provincial courts. The change is well illustrated by the differing characteristics of officials who held the assistant chairman position. Peter Ivanovich Pritupov illustrates the type who began his career in the military service, and received his initial training and education as an officer. A nobleman owning four souls, Pritupov entered the military service in 1772 at the age of seventeen. He served eleven years, then in 1783 joined the staff of the Novgorod Police Administration. In 1789 he was appointed a police captain; in 1790 he became *striapchii*, or assistant procurator, in the Novgorod magistrate's office, where he remained until 1803 when he was appointed to the position of counselor in the Novgorod Civil Chamber. In 1805, he held the seventh rank—*nadvornyi sovetnik*.[52] The counselor of the Riazan Criminal Chamber, Ivan Federov Ponoplin, held 102 souls. He began his career in 1764 as a soldier and remained in the military until 1785. In 1786 he was elected district police chief (*zemskii ispravnik*) and a year later sheriff (*gorodichii*). He was appointed to his position as a counselor in 1801.[53]

A second type is a product of the civil service. He is distinguished primarily by long experience in the routine of chancellery work and represents the penetration of responsible legal positions by chancellery personnel. Alexander Nikolaevich Ivanov, the counselor of the Nizhnii-Novgorod Criminal Chamber in 1825, was a landless nobleman who had risen through the chancellery. Ivanov entered service in 1803 as a copier in the Saratov Provincial Bureau and Criminal Chamber. In 1805, he was assigned to the Military College in Petersburg, and in the same year took a position in the chancellery of the Senate's Fourth Department. He served there until 1814, when he was elected district police-chief in Saratov province. He then worked in the Department of State Lands, and in the Treasury Chamber of the Caucasus. There he received the special exemption from the examination law given to those who served in the Caucasus, and attained the eighth rank without a university education or examination. In 1822, at the age of thirty-three and after nineteen years of service, Ivanov was appointed counselor and raised to the seventh rank (*nadvornyi sovetnik*).[54]

The third type is an official, usually from the lesser nobility, who rises swiftly due to educational and social advantages accorded to him in the general effort to upgrade the staff of the judiciary. Mikhail Dmitrievich Iazykov, acting assistant chairman of the Vladimir Criminal Chamber in 1851, was only twenty-one years of age and had reached only the tenth rank (*kollezhskii sekretar'*). A nobleman, owning one hundred souls in Nizhnii-Novgorod province, he had graduated from the School of Jurisprudence in 1847 and had begun work in the chancellery of the First Department of the Ministry of Justice, and in 1850 was assigned to serve as counselor in the Vladimir Criminal Chamber.[55]

Grigorii Ivanovich Grebenshchikov listed his origin as from the taxed estates. A graduate of Kazan University, he became a teacher of law and legal process in a provincial gymnasium in 1837, and shortly thereafter in a Penza Noble Institute. He was appointed to the chancellery of the second division of the Fifth Department of the Senate in 1845, and in 1849, at the age of thirty-one, to his position as assistant chairman in the Kursk Criminal Chamber. He had attained the eighth rank, entitling him to hereditary nobility.[56]

The office of secretary of the Provincial Chambers shows a similar trend to greater control by the ministry over appointments. Until the 1840s, provincial bureaus, under the governors' direction, had responsibility for appointments to the Chambers' chancelleries. The governor and his staff would recruit clerical workers, often outside the province. As minister, Panin decried the low quality of the personnel of the Chambers' chancelleries and succeeded in extending ministerial authority over provincial chancellery appointments. A decree of 1846 gave him the power to appoint the secretary of the Chambers from three candidates proposed by the provincial bureaus.[57] In 1852, an opinion of the State Council, issued as law, assigned the Chambers the authority to appoint, relieve, and replace members of their clerical staff with the confirmation of the minister of justice. A committee under the chairmanship of Prince Gagarin had recommended that the Chambers be given the right to appoint chancellery workers in the district courts as well. But Panin objected, claiming that such a rule would conflict with the provincial bureaus' right to remove chancellery personnel in district institutions.[58]

Service lists of secretaries show an increasing proportion of officers' sons, probably a result of the greater number of chancellery officials who had attained officer rank in the expanding administration of the early nineteenth century (see table 3.15). The secretaries are increasingly products of the legal administration, the number who had spent all their careers in

Table 3.15. Social Origins of Secretaries in the First Half of the Nineteenth Century

Origin	Provincial Courts			District Courts		
	Beginning	Quarter	Middle	Beginning	Quarter	Middle
Noble	6(22)	5(19)	9(27)	15(16)	10(12)	25(22)
Officers	...	5(19)	14(41)	6(6)	22(27)	40(34)
Chancellery	8(30)	9(33)	1(3)	26(27)	30(36)	13(11)
Clergy	9(33)	5(19)	8(23)	37(39)	20(24)	39(33)
Merchant	1(4)	...	...	2(2)	...	...
Taxed classes	2(7)	2(7)	2(6)	8(8)	1(1)	...
Foreigner	1(4)	1(4)	...	2(2)	...	...
Total	27(100)	27(100)	34(100)	96(100)	83(100)	117(100)

NOTE: There was a total of about one hundred secretaries of
provincial chambers and about five hundred secretaries
of district courts in the empire.

For source of data, see table 3.11 note.

Table 3.16. Service Experience of Secretaries in the First Half of the Nineteenth Century

Mean	Provincial Courts			District Courts		
	Beginning	Quarter	Middle	Beginning	Quarter	Middle
Age	38.4(27)	38.9(26)	37.7(34)	35.8(96)	36.8(82)	35.3(117)
Years civil service	22.8(28)	23.3(27)	18.3(34)	20.1(97)	22.2(82)	18.3(117)
Years prior civil service	17.4(28)	17.3(27)	14.3(34)	15.3(87)	14.3(78)	13.4(117)
Age of entry into civil service	15.1(27)	14.7(26)	19.0(34)	15.7(96)	14.6(81)	17.3(117)
Years in office	5.9(28)	5.6(27)	4.8(34)	4.7(88)	7.1(78)	5.2(117)

NOTE: For source of data, see table 3.11 note.

courts rising from 15 of 28 (53.6 percent) at the beginning and 15 of 27 (55.5 percent) at the quarter, to 24 of 34 (70.6 percent) at mid-century. The number of secretaries spending all their service in their current place of work triples, increasing from five to seven to fifteen. There is also a sharp drop in the number of those serving outside the province, falling from eight at the beginning of the century and nine at the quarter to two at mid-century. By the middle of the century, there are thus strong indications that the Chambers were taking over control of appointments to their own chancelleries. The rising age of entry (see table 3.16) suggests an increase in their years of education as well. Of the twenty-one secretaries who give information on education at mid-century, six list primary education; five, secondary; eight, the university (two of them candidates); two, seminaries. Secretaries of the Chambers, too, are beginning to resemble other judicial personnel in the education they receive and in the nature of their previous service.

District Courts

The authority of central institutions to bring about change was less effective at the lowest judicial instance—for the nobility, the elective district (*uezd*) court.[59] District judges were elected for terms of three years before 1831 and six years after by the members of the district nobility qualified to sit in the district assembly. They were assisted by two deputies (*zasedateli*) whose participation in trials was nominal or nonexistent. The Charter of the Nobility specified that only those who had attained the first officer's rank (the fourteenth or lowest on the Table) were eligible for election, thus excluding noblemen who had not served. Since the great mass of provincial gentry received their ranks in the military, retired officers provided the majority of recruits for the office. Though district judges were supposed to hold the eighth rank, the service lists show them at every rank from the sixth down. The judge in Bulgarin's story exclaims, "a corporal [twelfth rank] can be a Marshall of the Nobility, while a Police Chief may be a colonel [sixth rank]."[60] Many retained military rank, and after 1831, retention of military rank became mandatory until an elective judge had served long enough to warrant promotion.

Immediately after the provincial reform, the nobility recognized elective service as a new onerous and demeaning obligation. Publicists like Shcherbatov were quick to interpret election as a way to reimpose obligatory service on the nobility. The poorer or more hapless noblemen of a district were those who could be induced to take this office, and even they were resourceful at finding reasons to decline or to resign. So many noblemen withdrew because of poor health in the first years of the new elective institutions that the Senate issued a decree requiring medical certification for resignation. Others arranged for themselves to be prosecuted for some fictitious offense, which exempted them from the obligation. "Better to be on trial, only to be free from elective service," was a common saying. The governor of Smolensk Province complained in 1817, "Many noblemen, pleading poor health or other pretenses, find means to avoid service without even taking their position, or after filling it for only a short time. This is met with so often that for many positions there are not even candidates."[61] In some districts all the landholders were wealthy and no one would serve. Frequently, fewer than a quorum of twelve could be asembled and a judge had to be elected by the noblemen of a neighboring district.[62] After resignations, or when no noblemen were available to serve, the governor would appoint an interim replacement, whom the gentry would later elect to the position. These frequently were non-nobles serving in the provincial administration. The Charter of the Nobility and later legislation, though specific about suffrage requirements, demanded only the attainment of the fourteenth rank with an unblemished service record to hold elective office.[63]

The district judge remained a creature of the powerful figures in his province, the pawn of the governor or the powerful landowners in his area. Koshelev and Koliupanov described district marshals of the gentry who reduced their neighbors to a kind of vassalage and ruled over local institutions as late as the 1850s.[64] Nicholas and his advisors thought that this situation could be remedied by reducing the weight of poor nobles in the assembly. Wealthier electors, they reasoned, would be independent enough to choose honest judges. Senator Durasov, after investigating Kostroma province in the mid 1820s, reported that the poor nobility

> encounter many reasons and cases compelling them to be obligated to rich landlords. The latter, making use of their influence upon them, organize them into parties, and in this way they are able in elections to posts, upon which the fate of many people depend, to multiply the number of election balls at their disposal. And those who do not want to take such reprehensible steps, must, for all their merits, surrender the advantage.

As a result, officials were elected who were not always worthy of their position, and many showed this in their later conduct on the bench. Durasov recommended raising the requirement for voting in district assemblies from an income of one hundred to one thousand rubles a year.[65]

Such considerations prompted the Election Law of 1831, which sought to ensure that electors would have sufficient property to ensure their "striving for the general good." The law raised the suffrage requirements for nobles from one hundred rubles a year income to ownership of one hundred souls and three thousand *desiatiny* of land. Those with smaller holdings would vote indirectly, through a deputy, one for each group of one hundred souls and three thousand *desiatiny*. Personal nobles could be elected, but only if they were of "honorable and irreproachable conduct," and not under suspicion of wrongdoing. Those on trial could be elected when the offense was no more than "minor oversights" in service. All those who received more positive than negative votes became candidates for the district judgeships, and the governor selected one of two senior candidates.[66]

But in spite of these measures, the district court remained a dismal prospect for most noblemen. It had the combined disadvantages of low prestige, remoteness from centers of power and culture, and meager pay. The district judge was at best regarded as a well-meaning fool, like Gogol's Demian Demianovich, who signed secretaries' reports without listening. The lifting of suffrage requirements seems to have had little effect on the prestige of district courts despite the Election Law of 1831 (see tables 3.17–3.20).[67] The average number of years as judge rises, but remains below the length of a single term in office. Noble judges continue to preside over most courts, but there is a clear increase of non-noble judges. As a result, while more district judges hold medium-sized estates, there are also more without land.

Service patterns remain close to those for the beginning of the century. There is a moderate decline of those beginning in the military, but this is a result of the greater number of non-nobles. Among the nobles, the tendencies that appear in the data are opposite to those characterizing provincial and central institutions. There is a slight fall in the proportion of noblemen beginning in the civil service from 8 of 50 (16 percent) to 6 of 41 (14.6 percent). The years spent in the military remain constant and the age for leaving military service rises. The proportion of judges with no civil service experience previous to their appointment rises sharply from 10 of 52 (19.2 percent) to 19 of 56 (33.9 percent). The age of entry for civil servants falls, reflecting the increase in non-nobles who began their careers as copiers.

The data suggest that district judges in noble provinces were not conforming to the new patterns of service observable in appointive posts. Rather, district judges more and more tend to fall into two categories: the retired officer with no or little civil service experience, and the non-noble appointee of the local administration, with no or little contact with the local nobility. The prevalence of both types bespeaks the increasing reluctance of the local nobility to serve in the district courts. The shortage of candidates was such that a decree of 1841 permitted reserve officers to hold elective office, a measure that may have led to the increase in number of those without previous civil service experience.[68] Both types suggest that the local judge, even more than before, was becoming a puppet of the local

Table 3.17. Social Origins of District Judges in the First Half of the Nineteenth Century[a]

Origin	Five Landlord Provinces[b]		Vologda Province[c]			Arkhangelsk Province[c]	
	Beginning	Middle	1800	1824	1848	1799	1849
Noble	50(96)	41(73)	7(70)	5(50)	3(38)	3(38)	1(11)
Officers	...	6(11)	1(10)	1(10)	1(12)	1(12)	1(11)
Chancellery	...	1(2)	...	1(10)	2(25)	1(12)	1(11)
Clergy	1(2)	5(9)	...	2(20)	2(25)	...	3(33)
Taxed classes	1(2)	3(5)	1(10)	1(10)	...	3(38)	2(23)
Foreigner	...	...	1(10)	...	...	...	...
Merchant	...	...	...	...	...	...	1(11)
Totals	52(100)	56(100)	1C(100)	10(100)	8(100)	8(100)	9(100)

[a]For source of data, see table 3.11 note.

[b]This is a small sample of about 15 percent of district judges in landlord provinces, and can only give a rough approximation of the changes in the district courts in this period. It is made up of the following provinces, which contained a total of sixty-two districts: Kostroma, 1800 (67 percent of the population landlords' serfs) and 1847 (61 percent); Novgorod, 1805 (51 percent) and 1849 (45 percent); Kursk, 1802 (46 percent) and 1850 (42 percent); Orel, 1800 (63 percent) and 1842 (52 percent); Tambov, 1799 (49 percent) and 1848 (44 percent). Figures are from the fifth *revizia*, of 1795, and the ninth, of 1850, as cited in V. M. Kabuzan, *Izmeneniia v razmeshchenii naseleniia Rossii v XVIII -- pervoi polovine XIX v* (Moscow, 1971).

[c]Vologda and Arkhangelsk provinces contained ten *uezdy* each.

Table 3.18. Initial Service of District Judges in the First Half of the Nineteenth Century

Initial Service	Five Landlord Provinces		Vologda Province			Arkhangelsk Province	
	Beginning	Middle	1800	1824	1848	1799	1849
Military	43(83}	38(69}	10(100)	4(40}	1(13}	6(75}	...(..}
Civil	9(17}	13(24}	...	6(60}	7(87}	2(25}	7(78}
Teaching	...	4(7}	...	...	...	...	1(11}
Church administration	...	...	...	...	...	...	1(11)
Totals	52(100)	55(100)	10(100)	10(100)	8(100)	8(100)	9(100)

NOTE: For source of data, see table 3.11 note.

84

Table 3.19. Serfholding of District Judges in Five Landlord Provinces

No. of Souls	Beginning	Middle
0	3(6)	12(21)
1-10	8(15)	9(16)
11-100	34(66)	24(43)
101-500	7(13)	11(20)
Totals	52(100)	56(100)

NOTE: For source of data, see table 3.11 note.

administration. The officer without civil service experience did not meddle in the operations of the court. Non-noble judges, many of whom served in the district courts of the provincial capitals, were usually creatures of the governor. Appointed to finish an incomplete term, they were frequently re-elected by the district nobility who were unwilling or unable to reject their governor's choice.

Table 3.20. Service Experience of District Judges of Five Landlord Provinces in the First Half of the Nineteenth Century[a]

Mean	Beginning	Middle
Age	41.1(51)	45.9(56)
Years military service--ex-officers	12.8(45)	12.7(41)
Ex-officers age of leaving military	27.2(42)	29.9(41)
Years of civil service	12.4(51)	14.3(56)
Years of service this district	5.9(51)	11.0(56)
Years of service outside district	6.5(51)	3.2(56)
Years prior civil service	10.2(50)	9.8(56)
Age of entry into civil service (all)	28.1(49)	29.4(56)
Age entry to civil service (lifetime civil servants)	16.1(8)	14.8(12)
Years in office	2.0(47)	4.4(56)[b]

[a]For source of data, see table 3.11 note.

[b]Increase is due to increase in term from three to six years, due to the election law of 1831.

The two types emerge clearly in the service lists for Tver and Tambov province at mid-century.[69] The lists for Tver (not among the provinces in the sample), from 1827 and 1851, show little change in social composition — ten of twelve are noblemen in 1827, and eleven of twelve in 1851 — and in landholding. But there is an increase of former officers serving as judges from nine of twelve in 1827 to twelve of twelve in 1851. There is also a decline in the number with previous civil service experience, from nine in 1827 to five in 1851.

In Tambov province, the change proceeds in the direction of class diversification. In 1799, all nine of the judges for whom lists were available were noble officers, with small landholdings. In 1825, nine of ten are nobles and former officers; landholding remains about the same. By 1851, noblemen fill only five of the twelve positions, three — all of them former teachers — were from the clergy, two were officers' sons, and one each from among the chancellery workers and free estate.

The large number of non-noble district judges does not signal the emergence in these courts of a group of judges who had been apprenticed in court chancelleries; the gap between judges and chancelleries was maintained despite the absence of noble judges. The judges in these courts were selected not from court personnel, but from officials working in important administrative positions in the provinces — six of the seven non-noble Tambov judges had been serving in the provincial bureaus or the local offices of the Ministry of State Lands. Only one had risen through the court chancelleries to become a judge. The local functionaries' disdain for legal expertise and experience thus persisted in the district courts, the interests of the local administration prevailing where the nobility withdrew from active participation.

The shift away from noble judges was more pronounced in provinces with few or no noblemen. There, too, the non-noble judge was usually an administrator with no or little court experience. The composition of courts in Vologda (25 to 29 percent serf population) and Arkhangelsk (no landlords' serfs) provinces changes from the beginning to the middle of the century (see tables 3.17 and 3.21).[70] In Vologda at the beginning of the century, judges are predominantly small noble landholders who had been through the military service. In Arkhangelsk there are only three noble judges, but the initial service for six of the eight judges is military. In the middle of the century there are fewer noblemen in both provinces' courts. The principal initial service is civil, and they have served considerably longer in the administration (see table 3.21). This is also the pattern at mid-century for other non-noble provinces farther from the center, such as Perm and Tobolsk.[71]

The civil service background of these judges, however, does not point to increased involvement with the judicial system, or a pattern of apprenticeship in the courts. These judges, too, had risen through the administration. Few had begun their service in court chancelleries and those who had, had spent long terms in other, nonjudicial provincial institutions. In Arkhangelsk, only four judges, and in Vologda three judges, had risen through the courts; in the Siberian courts where there were no noble judges, there was an even greater reliance on administrative personnel: five of the eleven Perm judges and six of the nine Tobolsk judges had never served in judicial offices before. They had served predominantly in the fiscal administration and the provincial bureaus.

Most judges in non-noble districts were provincial officials who had proved themselves loyal and obedient administrators. They had risen out

Table 3.21. Service Experience of District Judges in Vologda and Arkhangelsk Provinces in the First Half of the Nineteenth Century[a]

	Vologda Province			Arkhangelsk Province	
	1800	1824	1848	1799	1849
Age	48.3(10)	50.4(10)	50.9(8)	56.1(8)	46.8(9)
Years military service--ex-officers	15.5(10)	7.8(4)	11.0(1)	20.0(6)	...(9)
Years civil service	19.5(10)	31.2(10)	30.9(8)	22.8(8)	28.4(9)
Years prior civil service	11.7(10)	27.5(10)	23.5(8)	12.6(8)	21.5(8)
Age of entry into civil service (all)	28.8(10)	17.9(10)	17.0(8)	32.0(8)	17.5(9)
Age of entry into civil service (lifetime civil servants)	...	13.2(6)	15.1(8)	14.0(2)	16.4(7)
Years in office	5.2(10)	2.2(10)	7.4(8)[b]	1.8(8)	4.6(9)[b]

[a]For source of data, see table 3.11 note.

[b]Increase is due to increase in term from three to six years, due to the election law of 1831.

of the chancellery but retained the chancellery worker's adherence to routine and the wishes of his superiors. Here the system of patronage, contacts, and friendships that could protect the nobleman from bureaucratic arbitrariness in European Russia did not operate. The judge had the litigants at his mercy. The result was a corruption and incompetence unheard of even in the district courts of European Russia—the embodiment of the nobleman's nightmare of the untrammeled sway of the clerk.[72]

The pattern for the secretaries of district courts is closer to that for other appointive officials. Like the provincial secretaries (see tables 3.15 and 3.16), there is an increase in officers' sons—chancellery workers who had been promoted during the previous decades—serving as secretaries of district courts. The age of secretaries' initial service rises sharply from the end of the quarter to the middle of the century, suggesting that the measures discussed by McFarlin had succeeded in prolonging the education of chancellery personnel. More secretaries came out of the court system. Like the provincial secretaries, a greater number were serving in those courts where they had begun their service (12 percent at the beginning of the century, 22 percent at mid-century). Fewer had served in the provincial bureaus (39 percent at the beginning of the century, 27 percent at mid-century). These tendencies were incipient, but they suggest that even in the lowly chancelleries of the district courts officials were appearing, who in their educational attainments and service patterns resembled personnel at other levels of the judicial administration.

By the end of Nicholas's reign, an administrative-legal elite had emerged whose members' status depended upon their position in the administration, rather than their position upon their status. They were mostly noblemen with little or no land, or sons of officer workers, and depended upon their administrative work for their livelihood. They owed their position to their education and service in the legal administration and other civil offices. These officials brought new preconceptions and attitudes to their assignments. The change in the personal, subjective world of the officialdom will be the theme of part 2.

II
THE MEN

INTRODUCTION:
THE NOBLE LEGAL OFFICIAL

But this manner of offering gratitude to the ALLCHERISHING
MOTHER OF THE FATHERLAND *and* SOVEREIGN, *who is so great a*
BENEFACTRESS *to all her subjects, is insufficient for the heart
of one who breathes with zeal to prove by the shedding of his
blood that he feels the very deepest devotion.*

Dedication of Vasilii Novikov's
Teatr sudovedeniia to Catherine II

THE NEW SERVICE PATTERNS IN THE RUSSIAN LEGAL ADMINISTRATION reflected a change of attitudes among the Russian nobility. During the first half of the nineteenth century, members of the nobility began to relinquish purely military conceptions of their role and to regard careers in the civil service and in the legal administration as suited to their noble dignity. Part 2 will be devoted to the changing ethos of noble officials. It will describe how they came to adopt different ways of understanding the world, and how these affected their attitudes toward service and the law.

The young nobleman formed his ethos as he passed from childhood into maturity and assumed the obligations that would comprise his life service. Due to the importance of service, state institutions played a considerable part in shaping this ethos. Service in the guard, preparation in the Cadet Corps or the university, taught the obligations to state and society. The family, on the other hand, seemed to be a negligible influence on social attitudes. In many cases the father was away in service, or had children late in life and died before they grew up.[1] Whether such a pattern typified the nobility as a whole is a question that lies beyond the bounds of this study. But the absent father, whether deceased or away in service, is a recurrent theme in the life histories of the legal officials examined here.

These officials seem to have felt little or no identification with their fathers. In several cases, the mother exerted a strong moral influence. But young noblemen had to find the values and personal models that they would use to define themselves as men in the world they encountered after they left home. This pattern could lead to a blind acceptance of the official outlook as it was transmitted in state institutions. But it could also open the youth to new views and attitudes when these became available in noble society.

Consequently, cultural and intellectual influences played an extraordinary role in shaping the mature identities of young noble officials cut off from family traditions and preconceptions. They would receive their initiation into the adult world from their reading, education, association with peers, and first experiences in service. From the literary and philosophical currents of the time, they fashioned an ethos that explained and justified the world to them and gave them values to live by. Their ethos made sense both of the private world of emotions and the world of service, and connected the two in a meaningful way. It enabled them to understand their feelings of love, friendship, and social obligation and to cope with the great problems of life, death, and immortality.

It will be a theme of this section that the weakness of generational solidarity among the officials from the lesser and middle layers of the Russian nobility allowed them to adopt the new notions of social roles that would appear in the intellectual world and educational institutions. The agents of legal modernization in Russia thus would come from a social grouping not customarily oriented toward the civil service and from families who did not succeed in transmitting traditional values. The novelty of their institutional role, and the lack of parental guidance would impel them to seek new definitions of their goals and values. Over the first half of the nineteenth century, there would take place a change in the personal character of the Russian legal official—the evolution of a new sense of self and of a dynamic spirit necessary to reform and create institutions.

We will see this evolution reflected in two signal changes in the attitudes of officials. First, a shift would occur from an ethos that emphasized reverence for authority and glorified subservience and resignation to one that emphasized fidelity to truth and ideals and glorified self-assertion. Second, an attitude that regarded the law as a secondary or auxiliary concern would give way to one that stressed the sufficiency and dignity of service in the legal administration. The evolution took place slowly, and, as in all such changes, clear lines of demarcation are difficult to find. But for the purpose of elucidating the mentalities described in the subsequent chapters, I will distinguish three dominant types of officials. These types would make their appearance consecutively, though the earlier types would never disappear completely from the scene.

The official who served at the end of the eighteenth century still approached his work in the judicial administration with the mentality and responses he had acquired in his military training. This official of the military-absolutist type had not received legal training, and regarded the law as little different from other commands, requiring no special respect or skill at understanding. Thus Gavriil Derzhavin, the first minister of justice, would come to his administrative assignments with the temperament and expectations of the military officer. Just as Peter the Great had likened the fight against injustice in the courts to a battle against internal enemies, Derzhavin looked upon his service as a struggle against the forces of wrong. Derzhavin saw his civic duty as a matter of faithful enforcement, but this attitude would make him incapable of comprehending or coming to terms with the illegality and evasion of law that he found everywhere around him in the administration. His experience highlights the difficulties that officials committed to the ideals of Petrine absolutism encountered in the Russian administration.

A noble civil-service identity first began to emerge in the opening decades of the nineteenth century. It appeared first among the officials of the College of Foreign Affairs, who cultivated sentimentalist tastes and mannerisms, what may be called the "diplomat-sentimentalist" type. Young noblemen began to enlist as junkers in the Moscow Archive of the College of Foreign Affairs when Tsar Paul terrorized the guards' regiments and most important, forbade the registration of children as guardsmen.

The Moscow Archive was not affected by the frightening events in the capital and made light demands on the junkers. They had to appear at most once a week, and their assignments were simple translations.[2] The archive provided a comfortable place for them to collect the years of seniority necessary for high rank and position. Michael Dmitriev, himself a junker, thus justified service in the archive: "The government demands service from all noblemen without exception. Where was one to find so many positions? What kind of tasks would be suited for young people with breeding, fit only for high society? And without service they would receive no rank and without rank they would enjoy no significance in society."[3]

Young noblemen now began to enter service in the College of Foreign Affairs rather than the military, as we have seen in the careers of Pavel Gagarin and Alexander Kochubei. Deprived of the military personae, they reached out for a new definition of nobility that was not connected with the bearing of arms. They found this definition in sentimentalism, which dominated Moscow literary life at the turn of the century.[4] Both at the Noble Pension and at the archive, noble youths were open to sentimentalist influences and read sentimentalist literature. They learned to look upon nobility as a refinement of feelings—sensibility—which was shown in an exquisite sense of literary expression—taste. Though the nobleman had to serve, nobility was the result not of his service, but of his inner qualities. Sentimentalism made a personal ideal of the poet elevated in feeling and literary gifts.

The service life of the diplomat-sentimentalist type existed outside the charmed circle of personal feelings. His fastidiousness did not touch his official obligations. Sentimentalism gave rise to a moral dualism, which as formulated by Nicholas Karamzin, permitted the official to serve in the judicial system and civil adminstration without involving himself in its repugnant complexities. It enabled him to accept the law as an expression of authority belonging to the public sphere that was beyond his capacity to influence or even to judge.

The most prominent representatives of the new noble civil servants were the young officials who led the literary society Arzamas. Arzamas has been known primarily for its literary contribution, as the champion of the linguistic ideas of Karamzin. But the Karamzinians also represented a whole new official mentality. The core of its membership was a group of rising young bureaucrats serving under Capo d'Istria, the minister of foreign affairs. From Arzamas came some of the leading figures in the administration of Nicholas I: Dashkov served as minister of justice; Bludov as minister of interior and chief of the Second Section; Uvarov as minister of education; Zhukovskii as court poet.

Arzamas emphasized the personal role of literature, and its meetings were diversions, emphasizing conviviality, wit, and elegant expression. The members opposed the followers of Admiral Shishkov in the Symposium of the Lovers of the Russian Word, who saw literature as an official and ceremonial matter. They composed and recited parodies of the Shishkovites' grandiloquent perorations.

The diplomat-sentimentalist type was part of a culture of literary expression, and simple and elegant writing was his speciality. His skills accorded with the tsar's desire to improve the style of state papers. Alexander needed officials who could write clearly and convey the facts of cases and the details of commands. He was meticulous about writing himself, and would demand several drafts of decrees from his state secretaries, choose one whose style and clarity pleased him, then edit it to his taste before signing it. The Senate's involved and obscure memoranda irritated him. The minister of justice, I. I. Dmitriev, who was a friend of Karamzin, informed one of his chief-procurators that

> His imperial Highness, finding that the reports brought for Imperial review often contain details that comprise nothing essential and that the sense is obscured with superfluous repetitions and clumsy style, has deigned to command that some lessons be given to the chancellery in the composition of such reports.[5]

Dmitriev assigned the task of improving the style in the Ministry of Justice to Dashkov. In 1820, Bludov and Dashkov undertook the translation of Russian diplomatic documents for the years 1814 to 1822 from the French with the goal of creating a Russian diplomatic language. Assisted by the Karamzinians, Alexander succeeded in introducing a new "ministerial" writing style that presented state matters clearly and directly. The laws and official documents of the first half of the nineteenth century carried an elegant polish that would disappear later in the century.[6]

Where Alexander valued form, his brother Nicholas valued content. Nicholas emphasized the sanctity of the law and the obligation to enforce it faithfully. The legal-ethical type appeared in response to this emphasis of official policy. During Nicholas's reign, noble officials began to look upon work in the legal administration as a sufficient fulfillment of their noble obligations. They came to appreciate the need for legal expertise, and many were trained in the law. Their dedication to their work arose out of a new sense that it possessed a personal meaning for them and they began to regard it as a life commitment. In this way, they brought to an end the dualism of the sentimentalist mentality, and found in their civil service an expression of their individual worth.

The new sense of obligation to the law manifested itself in two ways. For some, especially those officials educated before Nicholas's reform of legal training and the university curriculum, it meant a renunciation of individuality and an unquestioning acceptance of the legal authority of the state. Such officials saw their obligation as the faithful and resolute enforcement of all statutes and rules; civil service became for them a regimen imposed by duty. Thus Count Panin accommodated himself to the legal administration by subjecting his personal impulses to a literal adherence to rule. Kastor Lebedev adopted a similar attitude but with greater doubts and personal conflict.

The recruits from the institutions of higher learning took a different view of their personal obligations to the law. They retained the sentimentalist's sense of the importance of personal feeling, but, in a new romantic world view, saw personal feelings being fulfilled only in union with a greater force of history—the evolution of universal justice. Law came to represent for them not the prescriptions of the *Digest* but the realization of justice in institutions and the goal of their personal strivings. The administration of the law became a way to unite the individual with the ideal.

The graduates of the School of Jurisprudence felt it their mission to advance justice within the ministry and looked upon old procedures and understanding with contempt. The universities, despite the restrictions Nicholas imposed, spread the teaching that justice resulted from the unfolding of the ideal on earth. Students learned to see the study of the law as demanding the knowledge of universal norms and the mastery of science and philosophy. Their model became the teacher, the bearer of knowledge, rather than the poet. Thus Constantine Nevolin, one of the staid and conservative graduates of the Second Section Institute, made the students of the 1840s aware of the philosophical and historical processes that shaped legal institutions.

> All positive legislations, as expressions of one general idea,
> are in essence, identical. All of them develop in one and the
> same order, rising from limited to more general principles.
> They all present a striking similarity to each other at similar
> stages of development.[7]

The cultivated noble official of the beginning of the century was sentimentalist in his tastes, little concerned with philosophy, and most likely to enter the Ministry of Foreign Affairs. The young noble official of Nicholas's reign was idealist in his philosophy, romantic in his literary tastes, and regarded the law in exalted terms, hardly compatible with the existing legal system. He began to ponder ways to change the system, so that legal expertise could assume its proper prestige and authority. Thus, by bringing the principle of legal specialization to Russia, Nicholas helped to spread the notion of the high calling of the legal official. In this way, he inadvertently sowed the seeds of a new judicial system.

4
RUSSIA'S FIRST
MINISTER OF JUSTICE

An official dies but his decorations remain on the face of the earth.

Koz'ma Prutkov

IN THE LATE EIGHTEENTH CENTURY, MANY RUSSIAN NOBLEMEN SOUGHT A model of noble manhood in the works of classical philosophy. Marcus Aurelius was especially popular; his *Meditations* came out in five editions between 1740 and 1798. Selections from other classical philosophers appeared frequently in the journals.[1] Classical philosophers provided descriptions of civic virtue befitting a martial temperament. They wrote of courage and strength, and emphasized the imperative of acting in accordance with duty and reason for the public good. The attributes of virtue—courage, valor, manliness—would retain their validity in the civil service. It became possible to carry the mentality of the warrior into the administration—to make the administration the field of a struggle in behalf of the law. For noblemen devoted to the law, this struggle became a matter of personal ethics, decisive for their own self-respect.

Alexander Radishchev, Russia's first radical philosopher, and Gavriil Derzhavin, Russia's greatest court poet and first minister of justice, were heirs to this military mentality. Sons of officers, they served, though in different connections, under the military. Derzhavin spent fifteen years as a soldier and officer; Radishchev, who was chosen to study abroad, served a brief period in the military administration. But both entered the civil service with the predispositions of their noble forebears. Cherishing the qualities of courage and valor, they felt impelled to fight heroic struggles in defense of their principles in the inhospitable circumstances of the Russian civil service.

Radishchev and Derzhavin learned from classical philosophy that true courage could be attained only by an understanding and coming to terms with death. To face life as men, they, like warriors, had to be able to confront death, the chief deterrent to manly daring. Each tried to conquer his fear of death in a way that expressed his commitments in life. From differing conceptions of death and immortality, they drew the strength and inspiration to attack the ugly realities of Russian institutional life and to accept mockery, condemnation, and disgrace.

Radishchev coped with death by envisioning it as a welcome outcome to life, a guarantee of the beautiful, harmonious, and just. His was a Stoic-Christian notion of death that gave him the strength to condemn Russian institutions. Whatever the result of his challenge, the ability to part with life voluntarily—the heroic act of Cato—gave him the assurance to proclaim himself a man.

> If outrageous fortune hurl upon you all its slings and arrows,
> if there is no refuge left on earth for your virtue, if, driven to
> extremes, you find no sanctuary from oppression, then re-
> member that you are a man, call to mind your greatness and
> seize the crown of bliss which they are trying to take from you.
> Die.[2]

In death Radishchev found his ultimate utopia, the alternative to the here and now. His faith in a good society, based on man's natural instincts, was sustained by a belief in a beautiful afterlife. Death was liberation from misery and wrong. Like Goethe and Herder, he saw death as welcome rather than horrific, as an opportunity to unite with the peace and beauty of the universe.

> Life extinguished is not annihilation. Death is destruction, transformation, rebirth. Rejoice, dear friends. The disease has disappeared, the agony has passed; there is no more room for misfortune and persecution, burdensome old age has faded, the bodily form is dissolved but renewed.[3]

Death assumed a different aspect in the poetry of Gavriil Derzhavin. It appeared with a terrifying visage, as a thief whose "fateful claws" would seize man from his temporal glory (*On the Death of Prince Meshcherskii*); as an ominous outsider peering through the fence at the gaiety and good spirit of the feast (*Invitation to Dinner*). If Radishchev's notions of death were stoic, Derzhavin's were epicurean, reflecting the Horatian currents of the eighteenth century, the influence of English death poetry and the verse of Frederick the Great. Derzhavin coped with the menace of death, as was typical in the enlightenment, by reasserting the value of life. Death enhanced the appreciation of life and the desire to live. At the feast, death's presence was a reminder to enjoy the moderate, possible pleasures of life — good company, golden sturgeon, *borshch, kaimak,* wine, and punch. The awareness of death awakened a love for the present and made man sensitive to the immediate.

> *While the roses perfume the garden,*
> *We will hurry to enjoy their scent,*
> *So we will delight in life,*
> *And take comfort from what we can,*
> *Cut the clothing to the cloth.*

Derzhavin showed little concern for the hereafter. His was the temporal notion of immortality characteristic of the enlightenment: Man lived on through the good he did on earth, which would earn the gratitude of posterity. His ode, *The Waterfall,* written on the death of Prince Potemkin, used the waterfall as a symbol of the vanity of the spectacular glories won by military triumph. Its mighty torrents, ruining the shoreline and leaving nothing after them, were shamed by the tiny rivulets "nourishing fields of golden grain." Potemkin's grandeur, though momentarily impressive, proved spurious for it brought only bloodshed and wreckage. Death was the awful force that moved man to do what moderate good he could while he lived.

> *"To merits Truth alone gives out,*
> *Laurels that never wither."*[4]

Radishchev's views of justice grew out of his stoic notion that this life and world were mere expressions of a greater order of the universe. He was the heir to the natural law content of Catherine's thought. During his study in Germany, he became converted to the more radical natural law theories of the enlightenment, and he embraced and elaborated them with little regard for his own personal interest or well-being. His *Journey from St. Petersburg to Moscow* applied the standards of justice and equality to Russian conditions and his condemnation of serfdom and autocracy enraged Catherine, bringing him the loss of his position in the St. Petersburg customs' bureau and exile to Siberia. Law and institutions, he thought, had to be measured against natural law, and, if necessary, changed. Statute law had strayed from its original principles and often was in open conflict with justice and the needs of society. In 1801, when he was allowed to return to Petersburg and appointed to the codification commission, he pursued the same views. He wrote in one memorandum for reform,

> In time cerebration and chicanery obscure the laws' true meaning; impudence and contrivance thwart their action, lending them false interpretations and making mockeries of their vain threats. As laws grow decrepit, their effect dies, and rights and obligations become insecure.[5]

The moment was opportune for introducing new laws, for "the reason of wisdom guided by the lamps of science has spread its beneficent influence through the society of nations and even to the government of nations."[6] He asked for true equality before the law, open justice, juries, and an end to corporal punishment. The codification commission, however, was engaged not in changing, but in assembling the laws, and Radishchev's proposals were received coolly. He heard stern warnings to abandon his efforts or be returned to Siberia. In September 1802, he kept his resolve and took refuge in death.

Derzhavin's attitude toward life enabled him to prosper in the very system that Radishchev forswore. Ambitious, appreciative of the good things in life, he used his verse to gain entrée to high circles and led a successful, if stormy, bureaucratic career. He introduced new personal elements into the ceremonial ode, and thus was able to make his verse a subtle instrument of both praise and criticism. He would sing the glory of the powerful, but often in ambiguous bantering tones.[7] His ode, *To Felitsiia*, written in 1782, captivated the empress and won him imperial favor by flattering her self-image as an enlightened monarch. He showed her as a benefactress, bestowing freedom and wise laws on her subjects and encouraging learning and the arts. "Felitsiia's glory is the glory of a God," he wrote. *To Felitsiia* also contained allusions to the wealth and personal excesses of such magnates as Potemkin and Aleksei Orlov, which so amused Catherine that she had copies sent to them with the relevant passages marked in pencil.[8] After *To Felitsiia,* Derzhavin's rise was swift. He served as governor, state-secretary, and senator. He encountered many setbacks, and on several occasions fell from favor, but he was always able to recoup his losses with a skillful piece of flattering verse. On 8 September 1802, ten days after Radishchev's suicide, Alexander I appointed Derzhavin Russia's first minister of justice.

Derzhavin's service to the autocracy had enabled him to rise out of the lesser rural nobility. His father, an army officer, died in 1754, less than a year after retirement from service, and before he had managed to register the eleven-year-old Gavriil in the Cadet Corps. Derzhavin first attended the Kazan gymnasium, then, at the age of nineteen, entered service as an ordinary soldier. He rose to officer rank, distinguishing himself during the campaigns against Pugachev. But his violent temper antagonized his superiors and deprived him of the rewards he thought he deserved. Nonetheless, his service gained him the necessary connections to secure his material position. By petitioning the empress directly, he received a grant of estates with three hundred souls. He purchased more land and serfs at estates undergoing sale for foreclosure. Derzhavin's parents had owned a total of sixty souls; by the early 1780s, or before, he had achieved reknown as a poet, he owned about one thousand souls, and was a member of the wealthiest one percent of the nobility.[9]

Derzhavin was convinced that the system that had made possible his success was sound. It was the individuals who ran it who willfully obstructed its goals. Derzhavin had early encountered such individuals. He was eleven when his father died, and he saw the neighboring landlords take the opportunity to seize parts of the family's property and flood others in order to build a mill. He remembered trudging from office to office with his mother, waiting for hours in antechambers, trying futilely to secure justice. "Such suffering of his mother from injustice remained imprinted on his heart," Derzhavin wrote of himself. He felt helpless rage against the petty officials who ignored his mother's pleas. "They all cruelly passed by her, and she had to return home in tears with nothing, in extreme grief and sadness...."[10]

Derzhavin brought a spirit of vengeance to his lifelong struggle against those he saw as doers of wrong. He bore a personal responsibility for showing them their error and ensuring their punishment. His role would be that of heroic defender of justice against those officials who were indifferent or antagonistic to the law. When he entered the civil service in 1778, at the age of thirty-five, he continued to view himself as a soldier pursuing his combat for a just cause in the administration. He later wrote his own epitaph.

> *Here lies Derzhavin,*
> *Who upheld legal justice* [pravosudie],

> *But crushed by wrong* [nepravda],
> *Fell in defence of the laws.*[11]

The ethos of eighteenth-century absolutism gave Derzhavin a way to put his righteous anger at wrongdoing in the service of a cause. He adopted the goal of "precise enforcement," propounded by Russian monarchs, and was a convinced adherent of the principle affirmed in Catherine's *nakaz* that the judge's duty was to do no more than to apply the law issued by the legislator.[12] By ensuring enforcement of the laws, Derzhavin was able to identify his own sense of indignation with the autocracy's goal of legality. The monarch's laws became his instruments to combat wrongdoing.

Derzhavin waged his struggle against the individuals who were not faithful to the system. His pursuit of legality, like his notions of immortality, had limited goals. His secular immortality would be achieved by inducing officials to obey the laws (*zakony*). Law in its general sense, *pravo, droit,* remained a notion foreign to him. It was the duty of the ruler, he wrote in *To the Rulers and Judges,* to keep the laws (*sokhraniat' zakony*). Justice depended on the correct application of the laws—legal justice (*pravosudie*). And legal justice could be attained only by appointing virtuous judges.

It was moral quality that distinguished the good judge in Derzhavin's eyes. The ideal judge had to be honest and true to the law. He was impartial and incorruptible. In his *Righteous Judge* (*Pravednyi sud'ia*), adapted from Psalm 100, he described the qualities of the good judge, which he was striving to attain. He promised to avoid thoughts of criminal entanglements and contact with the evil, the debauched, and flatterers. He would associate with the "just, honorable, and well-behaved," while "liars, bribe-takers and the proud" would be banished to the ends of the empire or sent to the grave. The good judge ("Pokhvala za pravosudie") is swayed neither by the entreaties of friends nor the promises of medals, luxuries, and, "unsparing of his health, sits nights over piles of books." The law is clear; the judge must learn it and strive to overcome the pressures against applying it equitably. He must achieve a godlike objectivity.[13]

However Derzhavin relied on flattery and intrigue to advance himself in the service, he remained true to his faith in the laws. Contemporaries respected him for his honesty and impartiality, and frequently chose him to serve as the conscience judge to mediate their disputes. Suvorov referred to him as Aristides. The cause of law, Khodasevich observed, became almost a religion for him. Like Peter the Great, he liked to see the laws respected and surrounded with visible, sacerdotal signs of their importance, as arks.[14]

But Derzhavin's faith that statutes could be enforced precisely, or even respected, proved as illusory as Radishchev's that the system could be transformed. Though he may have had the lofty moral qualities of his ideal judge, Derzhavin had never studied the law and had only a vague understanding of the problems of legal interpretation. His views raised particular problems in the Russian system, where, due to the confusion in the laws, there was often no statute, or only several contradictory statutes to govern a given situation. As a result, Derzhavin's understanding of the law was often no more than subjective whim.[15] Nonetheless, with his wonderful naïve sense that his personal progress and success were identical to the cause of justice and national well-being, he would entertain no doubts about his own judgments.

Derzhavin's confident self-righteousness unleashed storms of opposition, resentment, and intrigue wherever he was assigned in the administration. He encountered Russian officials' distaste for all legal limits to their power, their tendency to regard questions of legality as challenges to authority. So when he left his muse to serve in the administration, it is hardly surprising that his zeal was not well received by his superiors and subordinates. He disrupted the working relationships that had little to do with formal law, and began a process of mutual recrimination and vilification that could end only in power struggles to the finish. His experience in government is a vivid example of the difficulties of imposing the Petrine system upon the tangle of power relationships and corruption that governed the dispensation of justice in late eighteenth- and early nineteenth-century Russia.

Derzhavin's memoir of his service career is a tale of thwarted righteousness, as full of outrage as is Radishchev's *Journey*. But whereas the *Journey* took the form of the eighteenth-century sentimental novel, Derzhavin's account was written in the manner of an official report. Entitled *Memoirs from Occurrences Known to All about the Authentic Cases Comprising the Life of Gavriil Romanovich Derzhavin,* it is, in effect, a series of government briefs that vindicate Derzhavin's position and condemn his opponents' on all matters.[16] There is in it none of Radishchev's powerful sense of sympathy for the victims of pervasive justice. The dominant feeling is rage against the violators of the law, as Derzhavin understood it—a paranoid self-righteousness that fixed all evil upon the faithless human beings who served, rather than on the system itself.

Derzhavin lacked Radishchev's philosophical education and appreciation of general concepts. His poetry, Eikhenbaum observed, excelled in depicting specific material visions—the crimson skies of combat, the shimmering of water, dazzling sunlight, the aromas of food—but was unsuccessful in describing the abstract. Likewise, his memoir focuses on specific wrongdoings without touching on causes or general implications. To emphasize the enormity of abuses and the distance between his righteousness and the turpitude of others, Derzhavin invoked his characteristic literary device—the hyperbole; in defense of the law, Khodasevich remarked, Derzhavin's poetic hyperbole became political.[17] The hyperbole helped Derzhavin turn a specific infraction, devoid of general meaning, into a spectacular wrongdoing, a personal altercation into a conflict over the law.

No one, including the ruler, was exempt from his angry criticism. He compared rulers to gods, but the flattery was in the simile, and the monarch was praiseworthy only to the extent that he or she approached the image of a god. The monarch was mortal too, and his failings appeared on a grander scale, particularly in the sphere of justice. In his famous paraphrase of Psalm 82 (Psalm 81 in the orthodox Bible), *To the Rulers and Judges,* he wrote,

> *Tsars! I imagined you mighty Gods,*
> *That no one sat in judgment of you,*
> *But you are ruled by passions too,*
> *And are just as mortal as am I.*

The earth shakes; the heavens reel with wickedness. The monarchs blinded by bribery, ignore ubiquitous wrongdoing. Justice will reign when God himself descends, and, as "tsar of the earth," sits in judgment.[18]

The gap between godlike ideal and man's mortal imperfection is the tragic theme of much of Derzhavin's verse. In *On the Death of Prince Meshcherskii,* he wrote, "We are pride and indigence together, / Today a god, Tomorrow, dust."[19]

He regarded rulers as fallen gods, and tended to address them as such. Toward lesser mortals, he showed even less tolerance of error or short-comings. One after another, his superiors in the administration failed to measure up to his high standards of compliance with the law.

His first disillusionment was with his patron, the procurator-general, Alexander Viazemskii. Viazemskii had secured for Derzhavin a post in the Senate chancellery, where Radishchev, too, had gotten his first glimpses of state service. Derzhavin soon became aware of what Viazemskii was up to. The procurator-general was the head of the apparatus of legal control: He was supposed to ensure that the operations of the entire state administration corresponded to law. But as presiding officer of the Senate, he also was the highest official in the executive hierarchy, and when administrative necessity required, he usually found it expedient to overlook the law. Derzhavin first found that his immediate superior, under instructions from above, had ceased drawing up the monthly reports on local Fiscal Chambers that were required by law. He heard rumors about misappropriation of the Chambers' funds. He indignantly protested and threatened to resign. Feelings ran high, but in the end, the matter was smoothed over, Derzhavin apologized and all was forgiven.[20]

The second more serious episode occurred at a moment when Derzhavin was emboldened by the success of *To Felitsiia.* His immediate superior had become Serge Viazemskii, related (by marriage) to the procurator-general. Serge Viazemskii announced — clearly at the procurator-general's bidding — that it would be too difficult to compile new budgets for all the provinces for 1783, and therefore the budgets for the previous year would continue in effect. Serge Viazemskii claimed that the financial reports from the provinces were lacking, making the calculation of income and expenditures impossible. Derzhavin knew that such figures were available, and furthermore, that they should, as a result of the recent census, involve a considerable increase in the tax collections. Additional sums should have been forthcoming from new taxes levied since the previous budget. Derzhavin reported that he was sick, took some of the necessary materials home, and drew up a project showing that such budgets could be easily compiled. The presentation of his report caused an uproar in the Senate. The state treasurer suggested that it was not clear that the additional sums could be located. But Derzhavin knew that they had the funds and were holding them in reserve against a shortage, when they would surprise the empress and earn her gratitude. The procurator-general also hoped to blame the governor-generals he chose for not submitting the required reports. In any case, Derzhavin sensed that he "should not try to get along in a place where justice is not loved," and resigned his position.[21]

In return for his services in the Senate, Catherine appointed him governor of the newly formed Olonets province. Upon hearing of this assignment, Viazemskii is said to have remarked, "Worms will crawl out my nose, if Derzhavin lasts long," and, indeed, Derzhavin lasted less than a year. As governor, Derzhavin was subordinated to the *namestnik,* or governor-general. The governor-general was not only superior to the governor in the administrative hierarchy, but enjoyed special status as the empress's personal envoy in the provinces. He had direct access to her and, while he was in Petersburg, had the right to attend the Senate. While he was in the province, his presence was surrounded with unusual pomp and social activity. Governor-generals usually were charged with two provinces. They ruled like potentates and troubled little with legally established procedures.[22]

Like Derzhavin, the governor-general of Olonets and Arkhangelsk provinces, Timofei Tutolmin, had risen through the army, then had transferred to civil service. He had gained the reputation of a liberal, enlightened official, and he hoped to introduce new procedures in the provinces. Difficulties arose almost immediately between him and Derzhavin. Tutolmin sent a new chancellery procedure to the Olonets provincial bureau (*gubernskoe pravlenie*), over which Derzhavin presided. Derzhavin described this as "whole books of laws, which [Tutolmin] had written and which had not been confirmed by Imperial authority." Derzhavin "doubted about implementing these laws and, visiting [Tutolmin] in his home, took him the printed decree of 1780 which forbade the governor-general from adding any of his own laws but ordered him to execute only those promulgated by imperial authority."[23] Derzhavin protested to Viazemskii and to the empress, pointing out the discrepancies between Tutolmin's and the officially established procedure. Tutolmin's instructions for registering laws, he claimed, conflicted with accepted form and represented an arrogation of authority by local officials. He particularly objected to the registration of the governor-general's orders in the same journal with imperial decrees. Only imperial decrees, he believed, had the status of laws and were entitled to the respect owed to legislation. He urged that in the future, when the governor-general's bureau (*namestnicheskoe pravlenie*) received a decree signed by the sovereign, a copy should be made, while the original, "out of especially reverential respect for the legislative power, should be preserved in an ark on a table of the office."[24]

Tutolmin had viewed his orders not as laws (*zakony*) as Derzhavin had contended, but as administrative regulations (*rasporiazheniia*). The distinction between the two was rarely made in administrative practice. Local authorities had always issued such orders and rarely would an inferior official dare to consider them less than authoritative. Indeed, the governor of Arkhangelsk province seems to have raised no questions. Tutolmin argued that when he had assumed power, he had been commanded to issue instructions on "the system of maintenance and office procedure for cases."[25] And his orders concerning taxes had followed the listing of Catherine's *nakaz* of 1764.

Viazemskii replied evasively to Derzhavin that "what is not in the law cannot be." There followed a desperate power struggle, with Derzhavin trying valiantly to defend his authority as governor. But here, too, the statutes offered no clear guideline, and it was difficult to disentangle the responsibilities of the governor from those of the governor-general. The governor-general's role was described as one of supervision (*nadzor*) of inferior instances, while the governor's, according to the decree of 1764, was both supervisory and administrative. In practice, it proved impossible to distinguish the two, and the governor-general, possessing the authority to watch over the governor's acts and to remove lesser officials in the province, wielded supreme administrative power as well.[26] Derzhavin angrily accused Tutolmin of exceeding his authority. His statement is a good description of the devolution of authority everywhere in Russia after the reform of 1775.

> Tutolmin tried to draw all the powers of the governor-general's bureau to his own person. He forbade acting without his permission not only when his claim justified respect, but even

> when moving chancellery workers from one position to another. He never sought the bureau's approval on requests to the Senate for awarding ranks.... He wanted the bureau to consider his proposals decrees, for he demanded accounts of them like those for Senate decrees. Likewise he removed the real powers belonging to other chambers, and became at once a clerical chief [*deloproizvoditel'*], judge, director [*pravitel'*], and, I even dare say legislator.[27]

Finally, Derzhavin entered into a lengthy imbroglio with Tutolmin over the question of the equalization of the landholdings of state peasants in the province. Tutolmin initiated this conflict in response to a Senate decree of 1785, commanding such equalization. But the decree was ambiguous, and once redistribution began, Derzhavin made every effort to obstruct it, accusing Tutolmin of exceeding his authority. He also charged the director of economy, Ushakov, with issuing orders beyond his competence, and in one village ordered that redistribution be halted forthwith. But Derzhavin was no more punctilious in observing the limits of his own authority. When the redistribution nearly provoked a disturbance among the angry peasantry, Derzhavin rushed to the scene and ordered that several peasants be punished "bodily." The Senate, at Tutolmin's prompting, inquired why such punishment was inflicted without court verdict. Though this was the common practice of governors, Derzhavin was, in fact, without legal grounds. In his defense, he could only cite several articles of the Provincial Reform, irrelevant to the case. He concluded with the assertion that "a court is nothing but the act of the criminal compared with the laws and the decision or sentence resulting from a responsible office [*prisutstvennoe mesto*] by written order, as to what is to be done with the criminal," an argument vaguely derived from Article 152 of Catherine's *nakaz*.[28]

Derzhavin issued orders to his subordinates to ignore Tutolmin's instructions, but they, knowing their own best interest, ignored them. One by one his supporters deserted them. He began to investigate the operation of agencies under Tutolmin's authority, but then Tutolmin countered with an investigation of his subordinates. He sought the intervention of Prince Bezborodko, but to no avail. In the autumn of 1785, he took a leave of absence to the capital, and never returned.[29]

The following year, Derzhavin received his second position, as governor of Tambov province. There he found Governor-General Gudovich more to his liking. Gudovich, a former general, was mild-mannered, unobtrusive, and attentive to the laws. Derzhavin wrote to a friend, "Although I have not gotten to know Ivan Vasilievich Gudovich well, having seen him only briefly in Petersburg, I like his papers because there are references to the laws everywhere. The laws are used as the only grounds for decision — and this is close to my heart."[30]

Given the chance, Derzhavin proved an energetic administrator, determined to bring culture and good administration to Tambov. He introduced schools for noble children and began a theater in his home, where "noble youths and girls presented various moralistic dramas." He brought a dancing master from St. Petersburg, and took it upon himself to school the young provincial noblemen in European style sociability (*liudkost'*) and deportment. He succeeded with great effort in establishing a people's school in Tambov, and five others elsewhere in the province. He had the ovens in the court, hospital, and other public buildings repaired, so that people could sit indoors during the winter without wearing heavy fur coats. He improved the prison and had numerous stone buildings constructed in the town, including a public theater.[31]

Local society welcomed Derzhavin's efforts at bringing culture to Tambov. But his reforming activity in the government won him few friends. From the beginning, he was dissatisfied with the provincial administration: tax arrears were too high; the officials were ignorant and corrupt. Most disturbing, he could find no collection of laws in any provincial office. He wrote to a friend in Moscow, "In Tambov province there is a great lack of laws. What is unknown is whether they have ever been in use here." He asked his friends in the capitals to send him law books. But he received only two volumes, *The Admiralty Regulation* and the *Battalion Instruction*.[32]

Derzhavin became especially troubled about the disorganization of the account books. He found that sums received were usually not entered. He reorganized the keeping of accounts and introduced monthly audits. Such fastidiousness about accounts disturbed the relaxed dishonesty of Tambov administrative procedures. It was common and not reprehensible practice in Tambov, as in other provincial towns, for officials to make use of state funds for their own investments. His subordinates soon became disgruntled about his "desire and passion to tie down his fellow serving people and cause them unpleasantness," and began to cause trouble for him.[33]

Difficulties began when Derzhavin discovered that Matvei Borodin, a Tambov merchant, had received a government contract, signed by the vice-governor, which allowed him to cheat the treasury of thirty thousand rubles. Borodin had been exceedingly generous and bighearted to all the Tambov functionaries. He had made special efforts to win Derzhavin's favor, treating the entire Tambov population to a lavish feast and celebration on the day of the opening of the people's school. But neither this, nor the knowledge that the contract had been made with Gudovich's connivance, could dissuade Derzhavin from pursuing the matter. He tried to have Borodin prosecuted, but the vice-governor and Gudovich's secretary acted to protect him. Then he placed an arrest on Borodin's property, whereupon Gudovich protested to the Senate. Prompted by the urgings of Viazemskii, the Senate fined Derzhavin heavily. Another period of harassment began, and again he found his subordinates disregarding his commands. In an effort to cultivate support in the capital, he assisted one of Potemkin's aides to secure provisions for Potemkin's army. But then Gudovich accused him of exceeding his authority and misappropriating funds, accusations that were technically correct, though such irregularities would ordinarily have gone unnoticed.

The Senate reprimanded Derzhavin, in the meantime dropping the case against Borodin. But this was only the beginning. Once Derzhavin had challenged him, Gudovich was ready for war to the finish. He bombarded the Senate with accusations against Derzhavin, most of them false, but all useful to Borodin's allies in discrediting Derzhavin's position. He was accused of exceeding his authority, disobeying a superior's orders, accumulating tax arrears, and embezzlement. All of Tambov's society turned against him. Tensions rose. At a social gathering, Derzhavin's wife, angered at the innuendos, struck the wife of the chairman of the Civil Chamber, who then addressed a complaint to the empress. Finally, Gudovich snubbed Derzhavin by not inviting him to the opening of the noble assembly in Tambov. In response, Derzhavin wrote an indignant note asserting that he would no longer be responsible for what might happen. This was a bad mistake, for it allowed Gudovich to declare Derzhavin a menace to the social tranquillity of the province. Such words were all that was needed to throw terror into the officials of the central government. Derzhavin was removed from his post and brought to trial in the Senate for misappropriation of funds.[34]

He was acquitted, probably due to Potemkin's influence. But the struggle cost him dearly. He had to bribe a clerk two thousand rubles. Gudovich also brought a number of lesser suits against him; all of them were defeated but at high cost. By this time, it is true, Derzhavin was a wealthy nobleman. But like other members of the elite, he regarded his serfs and land less as a source of income than as a surety to contract extensive debts. And once he had lost favor, the opportunities for enrichment disappeared, as he came to be regarded as a poor risk.[35] His debts to a private moneylender were recalled. For three years, he could secure no position in the service. He felt himself close to ruin.[36]

Nor did his courage win the admiration of the empress. In both Olonets and Tambov, he had disrupted the normal harmony of mutual interests and protection in the province. He had questioned his superiors on the grounds of a fealty to the law, but this did not interest Catherine. At his audience, she was irked at his self-righteousness and impatient with his excuses. "Isn't there something obstinate in your ways that you don't seem to get along with anybody?" she asked. She remarked that he had quarreled successively with Viazemskii, Tutolmin, and Gudovich, and she remained unimpressed with the facts of the episodes. She remarked later, "I said to him that rank respects rank [*chin chin uvazhaet*]. In his third position he still couldn't get along with anyone; he should seek the reason in himself. He lost his temper even in my presence. Let him write verse. *Il ne doit pas être trop content de mon conversation.* Let him write verse."[37]

But Catherine could not always appear so casual about the laws, and the time came when Derzhavin's cantankerousness would prove useful. On occasion, the autocrat's leniency toward errant functionaries would be tested, and it would become necessary to reassert the punitive power of the sovereign. If Derzhavin fit poorly into the executive hierarchy, he was ideally suited to fulfill the function of control, to be a watchdog defending the law. In 1791, Catherine discovered that the Second Department of the Senate was allowing the transfer of cases from one province to another. She had prohibited this practice in the Reform of 1775, for it had permitted the wealthy and influential to shift cases to the most advantageous venue. She was distraught to find her own reform disregarded, and called upon Derzhavin to investigate and eliminate these abuses. She appointed him her secretary (*stats-sekretar'*), and, briefly, he was one of the most powerful figures in the government. For a few months, he passed on the legality of all Senate recommendations. Each Saturday he would lecture the assembled chief-procurators on the correctness of their resolutions. When these meetings were discontinued, he required the members of the Senate chancellery to submit reports on their work (*spravki*), an irritating formality that had usually been ignored.[38]

Derzhavin reported regularly to Catherine about important cases. At first she received him often, but soon her distress about Senate procedures and other irregularities passed, and the complexities of legal cases wearied her, especially when they touched the interests of her favorites. She said to Alexander Khrapovitskii that "Derzhavin comes crawling to me with every kind of rubbish." The cases, Derzhavin wrote, "were of an unpleasant type, that is petitions about miscarriages of justice, rewards for meritorious service, or alms for poverty." The empress was interested in questions of foreign policy, war, and the building of cities, and found the administration of justice dull. She claimed that he was bothering her with matters too trivial for her attention, and met with him infrequently.[39] He found it increasingly difficult to summon the old image of godlike ruler and to compose odes in the manner of *To Felitsiia.* "For from afar those objects that seemed divine and fired his soul appeared to him, once in direct contact with the court, really human and unworthy of the great Catherine...." Intrigue and the influence of the favorites seemed to determine her position on cases. Her concern for the law seemed as insincere as her servitors'. "She ruled the state and the administration of law more according to politics and her ambition than sacred justice." The phrase on her lips was always "live and let live." She seemed indifferent toward her favorites' defaulting on loans, both from the state and private sources. Often she would assign him to investigate abuses she knew existed, then after he had assembled the necessary evidence, she became nonchalant and secretly protected the culprit from prosecution. He was assigned to the commission established to investigate the theft of funds from the Loan Bank. The chairman of the commission was Count Zavadovskii, the head of the Loan Bank. After his appointment, Derzhavin claims he was informed by Catherine, through an intermediary, that Zavadovskii had been seen one night taking two trunks home from the bank, one full of silver, the other of gold. He succeeded in collecting enough evidence to incriminate Zavadovskii, but the empress ignored his report. It remained in her private office at her death, and neither Paul I nor Alexander I saw fit to pursue the matter. Under Alexander, Zavadovskii became the head of the Commission for Codifying the Laws and Russia's first minister of education.[40]

Derzhavin lost no opportunity to impress Catherine with the importance of the law. But Catherine wanted the laws kept in their place, and to be reminded of them only when it suited her needs. When the Senate, after the Peace of Jassy in 1792, discussed how to thank the empress for her care of the welfare of her empire, some senators suggested that she again be offered the title of "Great and All-Wise Mother of the Fatherland," which she had declined in 1767; others thought that a statue should be erected in her honor. Derzhavin proposed that a digest of all the laws and reforms promulgated since she had come to the throne be compiled, "adding to it continuously all her heroic achievements and keeping it in a specially constructed ark so that in time this may serve as a true basis of history, drawn from the cases themselves, rather than from popular traditions and often falsely disseminated and absurd tales." The senators approved the idea but the thought did not flatter the empress. When he told her of it, she merely smiled and changed the subject.[41]

In his audiences with Catherine, he earnestly tried to explain where her duty lay. He would lecture her about remaining true to her stated trust in law. When she remained unmoved by his arguments, he often would break into loud scolding, and she, too, would lose her temper, screaming back at him and sending him from the room. On one occasion, it was said, he seized her by the collar and began shaking her angrily. She had to ring for help, and afterward, in Derzhavin's presence, always kept someone else in the room. The day after this episode, however, she was contrite.

> "You are so hot-headed. You are always arguing with me," she said.
> "Why should I argue, Sovereign? I am only reading what is in the case, and it is not my fault that I have to report to you such unpleasant cases."

"Well, enough. Do not get angry, forgive me. Read what you have brought."[42]

In 1793, Catherine removed him from the post of secretary and appointed him senator. Derzhavin only vaguely understood how the empress was using him. He explained her behavior by the influence of favorites or the frivolousness of her character. But Catherine merely was performing the two complementary roles of the autocrat, now the righteous severe absolutist, now the merciful, forgiving mother. Mercy cannot be shown without the threat of conviction, and Derzhavin, with his fundamentalist fervor, helped to keep this threat credible. Formal justice enhanced the appeal of the monarch's forgiving grace, but only if it was not sufficiently effective or institutionalized to demand respect itself.

In the first years of Alexander I's reign, Derzhavin played much the same role, and met with much the same frustrations. The young tsar was eager to enforce the laws and to curb abuses in his administration. But he had no desire to allow Derzhavin to rob him of his own legal discretion or to throw the administration into disarray. Derzhavin again faced the quandary of what to do about an administration that refused to enforce its own laws, but was beyond questioning or criticism. Again he responded in the only way he knew, and directed his anger and bile at those individuals who did not act according to his preconceived patterns.

Tsar Alexander called upon Derzhavin early in his reign to direct one of the first of his senatorial investigations, of Kaluga province, where, it was said, the governor, D. A. Lopukhin, led nightly drunken expeditions against the population and had perpetrated other serious abuses. But Lopukhin had strong allies in the capital—his relative Peter Lopukhin, the chairman of the Permanent Council (*nepremennyi sovet*); Bekleshev, the procurator-general; and Troshchinskii, the head of the chancellery of the Permanent Council. D. A. Lopukhin's wife was from the powerful Sheremet'ev family. Derzhavin demurred,

> "What?", answered Alexander, "You do not wish to obey me?"
> "No, your majesty. I am ready to execute your will, even at the cost of my life and the truth will be placed on this desk before you. But be so good to enable me to defend justice. For all cases are done through the boyars. Catherine and your father were repeatedly deceived by them so that in regard to my many assignments ... though I did all that honor and loyalty demanded, justice was always eclipsed and I was disdained."[43]

Derzhavin reluctantly accepted the assignment. He discovered that Lopukhin had borrowed thirty thousand rubles from a Kaluga merchant, Goncharov, then, threatening the merchant with exile to Siberia, demanded the return of the IOU. Derzhavin assembled the evidence to bring thirty-four separate charges against Lopukhin, among them bribetaking, illegal confiscation of property, and murder. But when he returned, he found that the tsar had turned against him. Lopukhin's allies charged that he had exacted confessions by torture, which Alexander had recently prohibited. Derzhavin succeeded in proving the falsity of the reports, and a commission convened at his request validated all thirty-four charges for prosecution. But the Senate had difficulty reaching a decision. Its deliberations continued for five years. In 1806, when the minister of justice was Peter Lopukhin, the charges were dismissed.[44]

In the Senate, Derzhavin continued his recriminations against what he saw as illegal acts. When Procurator-General Bekleshev asked the Senate to rescind a salt contract that was disadvantageous to the state, but legally concluded under Paul, Derzhavin declared,

> In observance of the sacredness of the laws, it was extremely dangerous for the new reigning monarch's first step to violate the public trust. But since the procurator-general was, on the one hand a despot and an impudent and insolent loudmouth, and on the other, a base fondler of political aims, with which he meant to besmirch the previous administration, he announced that his proposal, which had been prepared for the Senate, was already approved by the tsar; then the whole assembly agreed with him and the contract was annulled.[45]

He admonished Alexander to keep the promise made in his manifesto on his accession to the throne, to rule "according to the laws and the heart" of his grandmother. Alexander, at the moment, was receiving the projects for reform of the Senate, which he had invited at the opening of his reign. Most of them provided the Senate with legislative powers, which was not at all Alexander's intention.[46] Derzhavin's method of personal address appealed to him much more, and he invited him to submit a project.

Derzhavin's project, as many commentators have remarked, was distinguished neither by consistency nor originality. Rather it betrayed his rather rudimentary sense of political theory. Like most of the projects submitted, his was devoted to establishing a proper "division of powers" in government. But since he wished to see all "power" remain in the hands of the autocrat, he really outlined a plan to divide only functions. It was, Korkunov noted, merely an application of the principles of Catherine's local reform to central institutions. The procurator-general, Derzhavin claimed, had assumed all the powers of government during the course of the eighteenth century, and this precluded the effective dispatch of any of them. He had taken over executive, legislative, judicial, and "preservative" (*oberegatel'naia vlast'*) authorities — the last referring to the responsibility to protect the law, the control function. It was clearly the procurator-general's failure to exert effective supervision that disturbed him the most, and his project was merely a proposal to free and enhance the procurator-general's control authority, but couched in the fashionable political jargon of the day. Derzhavin proposed that the four powers be assigned to four ministers, who would preside over the corresponding departments of the Senate, and would have the right of direct access to the tsar. But he concluded that "all of these powers from the ministries flow to their one center, to the tsar, through the intermediary of the procurator-general," and thus returned to the procurator-general all of the powers he had taken away.[47]

Derzhavin's plan, nonetheless, pleased the tsar. Alexander and his young friends were drafting the Ministerial Reform, which also aimed to divide responsibilities without touching the ruler's monopoly of power.[48] Derzhavin became, for the moment, most valuable to the emperor — a prominent senator, devoted to upholding the law, but opposed to extending the Senate's prerogatives. Like Alexander's friends, he saw the problem of government as ensuring the effective enforcement of the monarch's will. This made him ideally suited to fill the post of minister of justice (though he claims Alexander had originally intended him to be minister of finances), who according to the reform, would serve ex officio as procurator-general, and inherit his functions.

As minister, Derzhavin stood by Alexander in his single confrontation with the Senate. This well-known clash occurred over the Senate's right to object to imperial decrees. According to the Senate Regulation of September 1802, such objections were allowed against general state decrees when they presented difficulties of execution, and against decrees about individual judicial cases when they conflicted with existing legislation.[49] Some Senators interpreted this provision as similar to the parlements' right of remonstration. The opportunity to exercise the right arose with a decree, approved by the tsar, that would have required noble non-commissioned officers to serve in the ranks for twelve years. The Senate at first gave little attention to the decree and approved it. Then a group led by Count Severin Potocki, objected, on grounds primarily of law — that it clashed with the Charter of the Nobility. Derzhavin was enraged. He saw Potocki and his followers as a group of ambitious aristocrats seeking only to usurp power. His was the traditional view of the lesser nobility — that the autocrat was the only force in Russia that could rise above self-interest. He considered the right of protest in the new rules to mean an orderly process of approaching the emperor through the procurator — a right to present an opinion. Again, he sought concrete symbols of the law. He took the relics of Peter the Great from the chest on the procurator-general's desk: the hourglass and the gavel that Peter and later his procurator-general, Iaguzhinskii, had used to maintain order in the Senate. He pounded with the gavel to "lend greater importance to a matter in which, so to speak, monarchical government was at war with aristocratic." The gavel did bring order to an unruly Senate meeting, but the senators, nevertheless, voted to protest. Derzhavin wanted to prevent them from presenting their opinion to Alexander, but Alexander yielded and received a deputation. He listened in silence, then let the matter rest, and later, in March 1803, prohibited all such protests.[50]

As minister of justice, Derzhavin seemed to have attained a position that would enable him to enforce his notion of the law throughout the administration: The Ministerial Reform assigned the minister of justice the formidable powers the procurator-general held by previous legislation. He was presiding officer of the Senate, and the Senate, according to the Ministerial Reform, could receive reports from the ministers, request additional information from them, and pass on evidence of their malfeasance to the tsar. The procurator-general could easily sway the Senate's decision, and thus could challenge the acts of other ministers. The minister of justice also had the limitless competence, assigned him by Peter the Great, to be "the sovereign's eye," with authority over "all civil and state cases," and with power to supervise the entire administration.[51]

But the power of supervision, if wielded seriously, would supervene the executive power, creating a new, alternative source of authority in the government, which the monarch could only regard with misgiving. Alexander, happy to have Derzhavin as an ally in preserving his legislative monopoly, was not eager to create in him a policeman of the highest echelons of his government. Since he was still determined to introduce major changes in government, Alexander was more than wary of formal legal controls that would allow the Senate to obstruct the work of his new executive hierarchy. The Senate's right to watch over the ministers became law only after he had voiced strong objections in the meetings of his Secret Committee, and he never allowed this power to be exercised effectively. Still less did he wish to see the procurator-general meddling in the affairs of the other ministries and interfering with his own direct personal relationship with his ministers. When Derzhavin began to assert his supervisory authority, he alienated the sovereign's favor, and embroiled himself in protracted, acrimonious conflicts with the other ministers.

He undertook this obligation with his customary indelicacy and indiscretion. He discovered that contracts concluded by the Naval and Finance ministries exceeded the amount permitted without Senate approval, yet had received imperial confirmation. "The Ministers took it upon themselves to loot the treasury, each according to his own desires," he complained.[52] The minister of finances did not submit his annual report to the Senate, concealing, Derzhavin believed, significant abuses, especially among the liquor concessionaires. In the Committee of Ministers, Derzhavin attacked proposals of Minister of Interior Kochubei to allow Jesuit missionary activity among the Moslem and other nonorthodox nationalities. He ridiculed the foreign minister's proposal to declare war against Sweden because the color the Swedes painted a border bridge was not permitted by

Russian legislation concerning the decoration of public structures. Derzhavin's challenges and criticisms were uttered at men who regarded their own spheres as personal trusts bestowed by the ruler, not as open to the criticism of others. They took his intrusions as effrontery, and the tsar shared their views.[53]

Most annoyed was Kochubei, who was one of Alexander's intimates and responsible as minister of interior for bringing effective administration to provincial government. Kochubei resented what he considered petty, legalistic harassment. He did not mind, he claimed disingenuously, calling ministers to responsibility before the Senate, but it was Derzhavin and his procurators who were making judgments and not the Senate. "No Minister has been brought to court, but many have been subjected to chicanery by the procurators for forms, statements, etc." He scorned Derzhavin's "petty clerks' tricks [tours de podiachii], that comprise the basis of all governmental matters here." Like Alexander and the other friends on the Unofficial Committee, Kochubei was striving not for adherence to formal legality but for a new system and order in government, and he called Derzhavin "the personal embodiment of the opposition to all system and method."[54]

Control in the Russian administration was likely to consist of little more than petty formalities, and in this sense, Kochubei's objections were probably justified. But at the same time, Kochubei took a dim view of all legal restraint, whether petty or significant. Law as an abstraction had great meaning for him: he saw it as a means to ensure that lesser officials complied with the wishes of those in authority. But he showed little readiness to be burdened by it himself, and ran his office like other figures of great power and wealth in the government. The relations between the ministries of Interior and Justice were particularly strained, since the ministerial reform had left their jurisdictions only vaguely defined. The two ministries were supposed to divide the functions of the old procurator-general. The Ministry of Interior was to inherit his executive power, the Ministry of Justice his control responsibilities. But nowhere was this distinction spelled out. The powers of the minister of interior seemed almost limitless. "The office of Minister of Interior obliges him to care for the general well-being, tranquillity, quiet and order of the empire." All parts of the provincial administration, including the governor, were to address themselves to him, which in effect made them his subordinates. But the provincial bureau (gubernskoe pravlenie), which consisted of all the leading officials of the province, continued to bear broad formal responsibilities and remained directly responsible to the Senate.[55]

The Ministry of Interior was in charge of local administration; the Ministry of Justice of ensuring the legality of central and local administration. But justice and administration were indistinguishably fused in Russia. The parameters of authority, left undefined in the legislation, were set through conflict between the two new institutions. Derzhavin wrote about himself,

> The Ministers, especially Count Kochubei, slandered him, because the office of Interior Minister clashed with the obligations of the Procurator-General in the courts and especially in the Provincial Bureaus. They walked together as if entangled, knocking each other from the path, fighting to get ahead of each other through shoving and trickery.[56]

Derzhavin had to contend not only with Kochubei, Alexander's friend and confidant, but with Michael Speranskii, who already enjoyed considerable prestige in the administration for his knowledge and administrative talent. Speranskii headed the Second Department of the Ministry of Interior, which held a broad competence over police affairs and "the welfare of the realm."[57] Derzhavin became convinced that Speranskii's spies had infiltrated his ministry in order to sabotage its operations and report to Kochubei and Alexander. In any event, the struggle between the ministries was unequal and the outcome swift.

The most significant clash occurred over the question of the governor's authority over the provincial courts. The governor could review criminal cases, and held certain supervisory powers, but had no statutory authority over provincial judicial officials themselves, who were elected by the provincial gentry or appointed by the minister of justice and responsible to the Senate. Nonetheless, Derzhavin found that Kochubei, at the governor's urging, had persuaded the tsar to decree the removal of the chairman of the Nizhnii-Novgorod Criminal Chamber. One of the members of the court, an assessor, had been arrested for brawling in the streets of Nizhnii-Novgorod, and the governor had ordered that he be beaten with a stick. The chairman of the court had challenged the governor's order, on the grounds that the assessor could be punished only by court verdict. The governor had complained to the minister of interior, accusing the chairman of disobedience, though the courts were not legally subject to his authority. The chairman turned to the minister of justice for defense. Derzhavin went to the tsar and pointed to the lack of legal grounds for the removal. The tsar appeared to be convinced, but took no step to reverse his decision. Derzhavin again came before him and succeeded in securing from him a signed decree upholding his position. But Kochubei then pronounced an oral decree of the tsar, reaffirming the removal before the Senate. Though a written superseded an oral decree, Derzhavin, understanding that Kochubei could have spoken only with the tsar's consent, conceded.[58] Judges in the provinces remained under the sway of the governors, as they had been previously. The primacy of the executive in the Russian administration was reasserted, and the judicial system was reduced once more to a compliant part of the administrative apparatus. Derzhavin, for all his irascibility and narrowness of outlook, had sought to endow law with an integrity within the administration. The futility and triviality of his efforts, the hostility of the tsar and other high officials gives a picture of the ambiguous and inferior role assigned to legality at the beginning of the nineteenth century. Limited to the defense of formal rules, law was disdained for a carping formalism, which the powerful, wealthy, and the enlightened could proceed to ignore.

Derzhavin also tried to tighten his own control over the observation of the law within his ministry and the Senate, and his efforts met a similar fate. He introduced the "Legal Consultation," consisting of the chief-procurators and legal consultants, to advise him on cases requiring his opinion, that is, where there was a disagreement within the Senate or between the chief-procurators and the Senate. This innovation, which was supposed to present him with knowledgeable judgments, soon followed the pattern of all such institutions in the autocracy, and became merely another instance, extending the already labyrinthine course of adjudication without adding new elements of expertise. Derzhavin blamed his successors, and particularly Dmitriev, for its failure, but it was clear from the outset that it could do little to eliminate shortcomings that were rooted in the system. The aristocrats who staffed the consultation were dependent on the chancellery for their understanding of the case, and could have only a limited influence over the decision of the minister. Their presence merely demoted the Senate another rung in the judicial hierarchy.[59]

By the autumn of 1802, Derzhavin's relations with the tsar had become strained. Alexander took every opportunity to object to Derzhavin's chancellery procedure. Derzhavin defended his procedures and continued to lecture Alexander about remaining true to Catherine's principles. "You always wish to instruct me," Alexander shouted at him angrily. "I am the autocratic sovereign and I so wish."[60] But it was probably Derzhavin's effort to oppose the law on free agriculturists that finally tested the tsar's patience. The law, providing conditions for voluntary emancipation of serfs, aroused Derzhavin's strong sense of social conservatism and moved him to oppose the legislator's will openly. It was passed by the Permanent Council, then, with imperial approval, sent to the Senate for promulgation. But Derzhavin demurred and tried every stratagem to block it. First he used persuasion. He told Alexander that "it was dangerous to rule about freedom before our uneducated rabble," and repeated the traditional conservative argument that emancipation would hurt the interests of the state and of the peasants themselves. Alexander agreed to refer the measure back to the council, but when Derzhavin returned home, he found Novosil'tsev awaiting him with an oral decree from the tsar ordering implementation. He then tried to induce the Senate to object on the grounds of the very right of protest whose exercise he had previously condemned. But the senator he asked to initiate the protest took fright and failed to appear. Then he ordered the measure from the First Department to the general assembly for further discussion. Finally, Alexander reprimanded him and commanded him to have the law promulgated forthwith.[61]

On 8 October 1803, thirteen months after his appointment, Derzhavin was relieved of his post as minister. His successors would be docile figures. Prince Peter Lopukhin, who succeeded him as minister, came from the very circles he had tried to oppose. Lopukhin, too, had begun his career in the military, but he had none of Derzhavin's respect for law, and merely complied with the wishes of the powerful figures in government. During his seven years as minister, he made no effort to interfere in areas outside his own competence.

Alexander begged Derzhavin to remain in service as a senator and member of the Permanent Council. Derzhavin replied that he would not be heard in the Senate or seen in the Council. In such a capacity, "it could have been necessary to sacrifice justice [*spravedlivost'*] in order to cater to someone's caprice ... it is good to serve when storms cannot trouble smooth waters, i.e., when partiality cannot violate the laws." In his poem, "Freedom," the metaphor for his official obligations was a hill, which while dreaming, he felt resting on his shoulder.

> *The sacred authorities,*
> *Ordered that I bear this yoke,*
> *Promising all earthly laurels,*
> *Titles, gold and honor,*
> *No! Arising from slumber,*
> *I said I won't.*[62]

Derzhavin preferred to withdraw from state life. After 1803, he spent little time in Petersburg, choosing to live in Moscow or on his Novgorod estate. He had a lingering feeling of the defeat of his efforts in behalf of the laws. He apostrophized the goddess Justice in 1808 ("K pravde"),

> *For sixty years I, your consort,*
> *Have beaten my head against the wall for you,*
> *To pass for your faithful servant;*
> *But I see, splendid daughter of heaven,*
> *That my faithfulness is in vain:*
> *With you I am only a simple fool.*[63]

In his last years in government, the tone of his verse changed. Close contact with the figures he had to extol made it difficult to infuse his public poetry with personal meaning. As Jane Harris has shown, the personal and public became increasingly separate in his work. On the one hand, he wrote formal odes, on the other, he turned to more intimate forms, the elegy, and other meditative lyrics.[64] This reflected a general change in his attitude toward service—the view he and Radishchev had held—that personal virtue should be realized in courageous service of government and society. When Radishchev despaired, he took his life. Derzhavin, though regretfully, withdrew from the government and sought fulfillment in poetic expression, rather than in his dedication to service. He came to see his poetry as his contribution to mankind, as the guarantee of his immortality. The friendly lyric muses had inspired him to sing hymns for posterity. A few months before his death, in 1816, his apostrophe was to a congenial, affectionate muse, Polyhymnia,

> *An enchanting dream,*
> *Fills all my soul,*
> *With your singing in my songs,*
> *I will be, I will be immortal.*[65]

5
THE QUIET
SHELTER

My friends! Walk with decisive steps along the path leading to the temple of harmony, and overcome the impediments met on the way with the courageous tenderness of the lion.

Koz'ma Prutkov

THE FIRST YEARS OF THE NINETEENTH CENTURY WERE AN ERA OF EMOTIONAL awakening in Russia. It was, as George Florovskii has aptly remarked, "an epoch of signs and visions, of premonitions and apparitions." It was a time of the discovery of the heart, when the mind was neglected, and feeling was often used to dispense with principle — a time of the "irresponsibility of the heart."[1]

The new awareness gave rise to an official culture that would replace the neoclassical culture of the previous century. The new culture responded to the needs arising in the administrative elite. It gave a world view to those who no longer looked upon military service as their destiny. The talents that the nobleman could put at the disposal of the state would be the products of his superior sensitivity and taste. His mastery of style would permit communication within the bureaucracy and help the monarch to understand the operation of his administration. The education and elegance of the new bureaucrats would lend distinction to the new, reformed, civil administration.

The "irresponsibility of the heart" encouraged a new attitude toward the law and its administration. The simple stubborn literalism of Derzhavin gave way to a new nonchalance, a sophisticated and detached acceptance of the frailties of the system. This nonchalance is evident in the careers of Dashkov, Bludov, and others of the diplomat-sentimentalist type, like M. I. Dmitriev and P. P. Gagarin, who went on to work in the legal administration. These officials viewed law as one part of their general, gentlemanly education. They regarded their role as to act in a manner suitable to the sensitive, enlightened official. But they did not view the elimination of injustice as their personal responsibility, and they remained aloof from its demeaning formality and sordid deceits. Sentimentalism, an ethos unconcerned with the law, shaped the attitudes of those charged with the administration of the law in the first decades of the nineteenth century.

The irresponsibility of the heart was born of a withdrawal from moral problems and not an indifference to them. The officials described as the diplomat-sentimentalist type felt the obligations of state service, but had learned to lower their expectations as to what it could achieve. They had experienced in their youth not the hopes of the beginning of Catherine's reign, but a series of calamities that made public and political life appear a nightmare, rather than an arena for the betterment of mankind. The Pugachev uprising, whether experienced as a child or vicariously in the tales of elders, was a traumatic memory for Karamzin, I. I. Dmitriev, Bludov, and other officials of the early decades of the century. Then there followed the brutal despotism of Paul, the French Revolution and the terror, the Napoleonic wars, and the appearance of a community of aristocratic émigrés taking refuge in St. Petersburg. These events introduced a dismaying complexity to the simple enlightenment perspectives.

One response was to seek answers in religion, mysticism, or Freemasonry. But the officials of this type sought secular and aesthetic consolations, though some, like Bludov and Zhukovskii would later also feel a strong attachment to religion. Instead, they withdrew from the public into the personal sphere, and tried to attain personal happiness and purity apart from the imperatives of reason or state service. The sentimental ethos would make it possible for the educated nobleman to abandon his rhetoric of struggle and substitute for it a manner of acquiescence.

The new sentimentalism received its clearest statement in the works of Nicholas Karamzin. Appealing to the nobility, it was far from the sentimentalism of Rousseau or Radishchev. Sensibility came to be identified as the distinguishing mark of nobility; love, friendship, and the home were taken as the principal values of the educated nobleman. The nobleman learned to develop his taste for high feelings from an education centered in literature and language. But though he could adopt the form and themes of sentimentalism without difficulty, the emotional content posed greater problems. The personal feelings dignified by western, mostly bourgeois writers, awakened strange and different echoes in the hearts of the young Russian, who had been taught to seek personal meaning in service to entities greater than himself. Bred to view the elevated as the selfless, he found it difficult to content himself with purely personal happiness or even to comprehend its meaning. The sentimentalism of the early nineteenth century became a futile striving of those conditioned to understand only the eternal, like the hopeless longings of Alexander I — himself the product of sentimentalist education — for a quiet homelife and a close circle of friends. Among the officials who grew up under this influence, the struggle to separate the personal from the public sphere would result in the confusion of the two and the development of affectionate bonds with the symbols of power and authority, expressed in the verse of Vasilii Zhukovskii.

The transition to a sentimentalist mentality is evident in the career of Ivan Ivanovich Dmitriev, Russia's third minister of justice. Dmitriev was a sentimentalist poet and a friend of Karamzin. His career in many ways paralleled Derzhavin's, but his attitudes toward his administrative experience were those of a later generation.

Like Derzhavin, Dmitriev began his career in the military. He served nine years in the Semenovskii guards' regiment. His verse then came to the attention of important figures in the government, and it was Derzhavin himself who was responsible for the initial publication of his poems. Dmitriev was among the first to resign from the guards after Paul's accession. In 1797, by one of Paul's strange whims, he was appointed a chief-procurator in the Senate, a position that he had made no effort to obtain. Dmitriev's attitude to justice was much the same as Derzhavin's. When appointed, he resolved to begin the study of the "science of the administration of the laws" (*nauka zakonovedeniia*). He found the responsibility of reaching legal judgments intimidating, for, like Derzhavin, he understood his task to be the impartial and precise application of existing legislation.

> To protect some laws from intentionally twisted interpretations, others merely to be able to call to mind; to do battle with the passions, not to surrender to temptation, to remain insusceptible to partial views, or slander against the litigants or the accused, or against their protectors and their relatives.[2]

His attempts to follow these principles met with the same difficulties as had Derzhavin's. He learned of "intrigues, egoism, arrogance and obsequiousness before the two ruling passions of our time: grasping greed and ambition." He tried to remain independent in his views, but this resulted in conflicts with many senators—among them Derzhavin—before whom he was supposed to defer. Finding that he had been passed over in the assignment of orders and other rewards, he resigned his post.[3]

Dmitriev returned to service in 1806, when Alexander honored him with an appointment as senator. Alexander was then introducing the institution of senatorial investigations, and like Derzhavin, Dmitriev was one of the few individuals who enjoyed the emperor's confidence to conduct such an investigation impartially. Dmitriev encountered many of the same difficulties as had Derzhavin. His investigation of the liquor concession was fought bitterly by the governor of Riazan province and a chief-secretary of the Senate, both of whom were implicated in the wrongdoings he had exposed. The other senators showed little interest in hearing the case and were about to vote to turn Dmitriev's report over to the threatened chief-secretary, when Dmitriev succeeded in convincing the tsar to intervene. Alexander commanded that the report be published as an example to instill fear in officials who would take liberty with the law. But publication of Dmitriev's findings changed little. The Senate ruled that the report was in error and found only two minor officials guilty.[4] Dmitriev then conducted an investigation of the government of Kostroma province, where he succeeded in securing the removal of several guilty officials.

Dmitriev was appointed minister of justice in 1811. Like Derzhavin, he felt he enjoyed a special, favored relationship with the tsar. But the differences in their personal relationships to the rulers are indicative of a change in style and attitudes. Derzhavin had regarded himself as a schoolmaster, and the ruler as his pupil in both political and ethical questions. Dmitriev regarded himself as a sympathetic human being, and the tsar as a friend. This, of course, was a role that Alexander most enjoyed playing. He shared Dmitriev's tastes, and loved open displays of sensitivity that showed his helpless sorrow before human suffering. "My God," the tsar wept, when Dmitriev brought him a case about the death of a serf due to a landlord's cruelty. "Can we know everything that is done here? How much is concealed from us we cannot even imagine." [5]

Dmitriev thought of his rapport with the tsar as the true source of his authority, and preferred to deal with him directly. When Alexander asked him to refer a proposal to the Committee of Ministers, he felt offended and lept up shouting angrily. Alexander, astonished, gave in. But afterwards, Dmitriev had second thoughts about his conduct before so benign a monarch. He returned and apologized. Alexander forgave him but warned him not to forget the episode. "Look how evil you are!" he teased him. [6]

The autocrat's personal trust was necessary for Dmitriev too, if he was to run the ministry as scrupulously as he wished. Though he had none of Derzhavin's ambition to oversee other branches of government, neither did he wish his ministry to become the instrument of other figures and institutions, as it had been under Lopukhin. He strove to ensure proper procedures in cases under his jurisdiction. But though his approach was entirely defensive, he found it difficult to counter the intervention of powerful figures in cases affecting their interest. Thus, when the wards of Victor Kochubei had lost a case in the Senate, Kochubei succeeded in having the case referred out of the Senate to the Department of Ecclesiastical and Civil Affairs of the State Council, whose chairman was Peter Lopukhin. This violated a specific provision of the statute, establishing the State Council in 1810, which forbade such appeals. Dmitriev, however, had no support in the Committee of Ministers, and Count Saltykov, the powerful chairman of the State Council, convinced the tsar that such appeals should be permitted. Thus the ministry's authority was further weakened and influence over court cases accrued to the State Council, which was supposed to have primarily legislative responsibilities. [7]

Dmitriev's most important setback occurred in one of the numerous attempts made in the early nineteenth century to force liquor concessionaires to pay back taxes. The case went before the Senate, where the many senators in the pay of the concessionaires obstructed its progress. Other powerful people at the court also began intriguing against him. The tsar did not wish to hear of the matter and was clearly irritated at the trouble Dmitriev was causing. Dmitriev knew that he could win a more favorable hearing if he sought the protection of the influential Count Arakcheiev, but he viewed such an appeal as humiliating, for it would mean loss of the direct personal access to the tsar so necessary to the exercise of his authority and so essential to his self-respect. He felt his ministry falling under various intermediary authorities — the State Council, the Committee of Ministers, and the tsar's personal chancellery, headed by Arakcheiev. "It was easier for me to give up my post than to hold it with the loss of my rights and of the possibility to be really useful." [8]

In 1814 Dmitriev submitted his resignation. Alexander's attitude toward him then changed: the warmth and kindness returned. During their final audience, Alexander played fully on his feelings. Dmitriev was touched by the tsar's tender look (*laskovyi vid*). Parting, they embraced in tears. The bureaucrat's loss became personal as well as political. Alexander was now the tsar-coquette, who acted the role of compassionate friend to the functionary struggling against the men who were then in the tsar's favor.[9]

Dmitriev's response to his disappointment in the service was also different from Derzhavin's. He held little hope of improving men or institutions. His attitude toward political life was at best one of squeamish tolerance. When first appointed to the civil service, he regarded the prospect of work in the administration with distaste. He imagined "insufferable misery; waking up on winter mornings in the dark, in order to read petitions written in an ugly, inflated style."[10]

> My entry into the civil service was like entering a new world. Here acquaintanceship and kindness are based mostly on calculations of self-interest; egoism rules in full force; the model of deportment ceaselessly changes in keeping with the positions of each. Comrades are no better than coquettes. Each wants to flatter his superior exclusively, even at the expense of the other. There is no sincerity in responses. Everyone catches, remembers, and repeats every careless word.[11]

Radishchev and Derzhavin had been impressed as young men by the hopes of legality and rational government encouraged by Catherine; Dmitriev had been daunted by the terror of Pugachev. He would always remember the panic he had experienced as a boy at the news of the approach of Pugachev: devastated estates, peasants deserting to the insurgent, the slaying of landlords. He remembered being rushed to Moscow while the fate of the Russian state appeared to hang in the balance. Reality seemed to harbor not the potential for a more humane life, but the menace of chaos and destruction. The French Revolution confirmed this aversion to active political life.

Dmitriev came to regard the unknown as something frightening, whose secrets were not worth penetrating. He avoided the vast philosophical questions that had aroused the imagination of the eighteenth-century writer. The theme of death was too painful for his art. His eulogies, traditional celebrations of dead heroes' valor, contained no speculation about the nature of the hereafter. True grief, he wrote, silenced his lyre. He sang when he wished and not when aggrieved. He found comfort from thoughts of death in nature. When someone dear died, he forgot himself in the fields and on the mountains ("Poslanie k Karamzinu").[12]

Nature and the family were his true consolations. After his struggle with Kochubei and Saltykov, he took a leave to his estate and experienced a sense of liberation. "After the country of egoism, from the great palace chambers I found myself under a low roof, at the foot of mountains covered with oak forests, in an isolated family where there was not one heart alien or cold to me."[13] The old woman's message to the heroine of his tale, "The Crank," stated his sentimentalist faith in the family.

> *That we are always envying another's fate,*
> *And desiring new blessings,*
> *In good will, we leave heaven for hell,*
> *Where is it better to live than in one's*
> *own native family?*[14]

Dmitriev's was a world of private joys and regrets. He preferred the small genres, the song, the elegy, the epistle, and he liked to write about small sorrows, like unrequited or lost love.

> *Without a friend, without my dear,*
> *I wander through the meadows,*
> *I wander with sad heart,*
> *Along the shores,*
> *There I always meet,*
> *Those same little bushes and flowers,*
> *But Oh! Nothing I do,*
> *Can relieve my sadness.*[15]

The pleasures he described were love, friendship, nature, and beauty, which he regarded as the themes of youth. Aside from the family, which appears as more a consolation than a pleasure, there were few mature satisfactions described in his verse, for mature life was spent in government and society fulfilling responsibilities that were largely unpleasant. Rather he took Horatian motifs of the evanescence of youth. In youth, the springtime of life, the personal pleasures seemed the purest. He wrote to Karamzin in 1793,

> *Away from us Cato, Seneca,*
> *Away gloomy Epictetus,*
> *Without delights for man,*
> *We could not endure the world.*
>
> *Youth does not come twice,*
> *He is happy, who as a youth,*
> *Strews his path with flowers,*
> *And doesn't think of stormy days.*

At thirty-three, he lamented his lost youth.

> *The morning of days has darkened,*
> *And will not come again,*
> *My heart has parted with happiness,*
> *And the dreams of my springtime years.*[16]

Karamzin replied with a more consistent and defined statement of the same feelings. At the age of twenty-eight, he looked back wistfully upon his youthful idealism,

> *I loved people with fire,*
> *Like tender brothers and friends,*
> *Longed for their goodwill with all my soul,*
> *I was ready to sacrifice,*
> *My blood for their happiness,*
> *And in my greatest sorrows,*
> *Rejoiced with the sweet hope that,*
> *It is not useless to live for them,*
> *My soul took pride in this thought.*

Time and experience had destroyed his castle of illusions. Karamzin sees he is not Plato, and cannot build a republic. He is not Pittacus, Thales, and Zeno, who could soften cruel hearts. He contemplates the infinite evil on earth. Until the world is transformed,

> *The truth seems a threat,*
> *To some dreary, to others, horrible,*
> *No one wishes to behold it,*
> *And often, poison is the payment,*
> *Of the one who with the voice of wise*
>   *Socrates,*
> *Dares to threaten the violent,*
> *The proud man hates lessons,*
> *The fool enlightenment,*
> *So let us douse the light,*
> *Wishing them a good night.*

He cannot be useful and change people, so rather his lot becomes to mourn their fate. He retreats from the great struggles of the world.

> *And we who love to breathe freely,*
> *Will build ourselves a quiet shelter,*
> *Beyond the gloomy canopy of forest,*
> *Where the evil and the ignorant will*
>   *not find their way*
> *And where without fear and hope,*
> *We could live together in peace,*
> *And loathe vice from afar,*
> *And with a clear and patient gaze,*
> *Regard the clouds, the whirlwind of vanities,*
> *Hiding from the thundrous storm,*
> *And with a pure heart enjoy,*
> *The glimmering of the evening years.*

Personal feelings gave solace in an evil and intractable world.

> *Love and friendship—this is how,*
> *One can console himself under the sun,*
> *Bliss we should not seek,*
> *But learn instead to suffer less.*

The quiet shelter was not to be closed to them because of age. Karamzin refused to relinquish love and friendship to youth, and recalled Othello who, in his declining years,

> *Charmed young Desdemona,*
> *And worked his way into her heart,*
> *By the sublime gift of the kind muses.* [17]

Like Dmitriev, Karamzin had grown up in Simbirsk province, and had experienced the panic over the approach of Pugachev. The bloodshed of the French Revolution, the oppression in Russia during the 1790s, awakened him to the dangers and calamities of history that seemed to defy human understanding. While Radishchev's sentimentalism responded to injustice and tragedy with grief and indignant denunciation, Karamzin's would call for withdrawal into a private sanctum. He wrote to Dmitriev in 1793,

> I am running into the thick gloom of the forest, but the thought of cities destroyed and people perishing aches my heart. Call me Don Quixote but this glorious knight could not love his Dulcinea as passionately as I love humanity. [18]

In the early 1790s, Karamzin revealed the new gentlemanly ethos that he would elaborate in his later writings. The delights of youth were now to become the values of mature men. The talk of justice or the striving after it no longer was to be the mark of cultivation. Rather, it was the awareness that such justice, while beautiful, was unattainable — an awareness of the limits of human nature. Sensitivity was not to appear as sympathy for the suffering, leading to action on their behalf, but as a refined appreciation of the diapason between what was and what ought to be — as sensibility. Karamzin's answer to the problem of theodicy was to have great significance for succeeding generations of educated bureaucrats, for it reconciled enlightenment values with a conservative or impassive political posture. It allowed the expression of enlightened ideals, while inspiring displays of sensibility that would dispense with the obligation to act in their behalf.

Sensibility permitted only a limited spectrum of emotion. The writer was to depict, the reader to enjoy, only the beautiful and elevated feelings that complied with *la belle nature,* as defined by the somewhat relaxed rules of late eighteenth-century French neoclassicism. Tragedy was reduced to misfortune, anguish to elevated pity. Death became something too strong for the poet's delicate taste. In Karamzin's verse, the concern with death is reduced to a wistful, almost playful, dwelling on the virtues of the deceased. Even the consolation is a weak one: "It is our lot too to die," he concluded, in "On the Death of Prince Khovanskii."[19]

Since calamity could arouse only ugly and artless feelings of horror, the author's role became to present symbolic enactments of tragedy, reduced in scale, and described in poignant but muted tones. Karamzin's "Poor Liza," which enjoyed unprecedented popularity and admiration among the Russian nobility, was a fictional acting out of social differences and restrictions by one convinced of his love for mankind. A peasant girl falls in love with a nobleman and is seduced by him. Realizing the impossibility of marriage, he deserts her. Learning of this, she commits suicide. Karamzin turned universal grief into helpless remorse over the misfortunes of a particular individual, and assigned this remorse a tonic effect. The catharsis of tears made the existence of irremediable injustice in a world that was supposed to be good not only tolerable but even pleasureable and uplifting. "Ah," the narrator exclaims, "I love those objects that touch my heart and force me to shed tears of tender grief."[20]

Contemplating the unattainable brought on melancholy, the most subtle feeling for Karamzin and his many followers and imitators. He wrote in "Melancholy," a free translation of Delille's "L'imagination,"

> *The passion of tender gentle souls, oppressed*
> *by fate,*
> *The happiness of the unhappy, the sweetness*
> *of the embittered,*
> *Oh, Melancholy! You are dearer than all*
> *The artificial caprices, the breezy joys.*[21]

The way to this universe of elevated pleasures was through literature. Literature played the role of moral enlightener, which by heightening the aesthetic sense made one sensitive to good and evil and capable of appreciating the feelings of others. Enlightenment thus became equivalent to refinement of the senses. The writer created another world, more beautiful and serene than this one, where the most sensitive could seek refuge — a resplendent shelter. "A poet has two worlds," he wrote to Dmitriev in 1796. "If he is bored in the physical world then he escapes into the land of his imagination and lives there according to his *houris.*"[22]

Karamzin tried to exclude politics from the sphere of personal morality and satisfaction. But he himself found it difficult to resist his strong need for involvement in the country's political life. Indeed, this need grew throughout his life and was the inspiration for his major work, *The History of the Russian State.* He justified this concern, and protected the sphere of personal feelings by creating a separate political sphere, governed by principles completely different from those guiding personal life. Outside the private shelter, cruelty and even bloodshed might be necessary. He posed his example in his "Military Song": the soldier brutally slayed the Turk, but then cleaned the blood from his heart "with tears for his brother and kin."[23] Karamzin's distinction between public and private virtues would provide the model of conduct for the many officials who grew up under the influence of his writings in the subsequent decades.

The political sphere had to deal with reality and reality, unlike the world of the imagination, was terrible and threatening. The fear underlying all of Karamzin's writing was one of disintegration. If the dismemberment of state was no longer to be feared, the breakdown of all authority seemed a real menace to him, and he deemed no measure of force or brutality excessive in preventing that outcome. His writings are haunted by the message of the *Pugachevshchina:* that the existing state order with its culture and enlightenment was fragile, and that however fine reforms might be, the preservation of what had already been achieved was the highest consideration. *The History of the Russian State* taught the reader that the state, whatever its failings, was necessary, and gave him the comfort that it could survive the threats to it. In the introduction to the *History* he cited, as a principal reason for reading history, that history "reconciles the reader with the imperfection of the visible order of things as something that is an ordinary occurrence in all centuries; it consoles him during state catastrophes, attesting that similar and more horrible ones happened before and yet the state did not collapse."[24]

Karamzin brought the notions of historicism to Russia. History for him was not a mere incantation of the glories and progress of the Russian state. It was a narrative description of the political sphere, the realities of Russian governmental life that revealed the truth of Russia's national identity. One discovered this national identity and the needs of state not through speculation about the good and true, which could have meaning only for the individual, but by observing the facts of history and its inexorable course. Thus the republic was the best form of government for Karamzin, but history showed that it was not suited to Russia. In the *History,* he expressed his admiration for the republic of Novgorod, but insisted that it was doomed. "Freedom belongs to the lion not to the lamb, and Novgorod could only choose one of two authorities — Lithuania or Moscow." He then consoled the reader,

> Although the human heart naturally approves of republics based on fundamental rights of freedom so dear to it; although even the [republic's] dangers and disturbances, nurturing magnanimity, charm the mind, especially the young and inexperienced mind; although the Novgorodites, having a popular government and the general commercial spirit and links with the most educated Germans, distinguished them- selves by their noble qualities from other Russians who were humiliated by the Mongol tyranny; nonetheless history in this

130

case must glorify the mind of Ivan [III], for state wisdom moved him to strengthen Russia through the firm unity of its parts into a whole, so that she achieved independence and majesty, i.e., so that she did not perish from the blows of a new Batu or Vitovt.[25]

Karamzin's dualism is most striking in his conception of the ruler. The ruler could be a kind and sensitive person, but that would not affect his political obligations. Thus Karamzin could write of the "tender" Prince Sviatopolk Iziaslavich, and then go on to describe how he murdered three of his brothers. Tsar Alexander, he felt, had let his personal taste impinge on his governmental activity. Karamzin did not care for sentimentality in a tsar. "A sensitive heart, no doubt is averse to severity, but where severity alone can establish order, gentleness is not appropriate. How do painters depict a king? As a warrior brandishing a sword, not as a shepherd with flowers!"[26]

He was sharp in his criticisms of Alexander's attitudes toward justice. Karamzin held the eighteenth-century notion of the monarch as sole creator and interpreter of the law.

> *When not all laws are clear,*
> *You will explain their reason,*
> *But when they conflict in sense,*
> *You will reconcile them.*
> *Law should be like a mirror,*
> *When the sun of truth would shine,*
> *Without gloomy clouds,*
> *The legislator is great like God,*
> *He is founder of peaceful societies,*
> *The benefactor of all times.*[27]

But Karamzin's attitude toward laws, like his attitude toward the entire state order, was one of passive acceptance of the institutions that had kept Russia united. The legislative role he assigned to the ruler, in his ode to Alexander, was clearly subsidiary, being restricted to clarifying and reconciling existing laws. Karamzin put little faith in new laws. "An old nation has no need of new laws," he wrote in criticism of Speranskii's codification efforts of 1809. Codification should consist in the collection and ordering of existing laws, with changes introduced only when necessary.[28] Karamzin's own plan for codification was the approach later prescribed by Nicholas I for the efforts of his Second Section.

But Karamzin was even more concerned with the enforcement of existing laws, and in this he thought Alexander remiss. Effective enforcement demanded frightening the population into obedience, and Alexander's softness only encouraged additional infractions. "One of the worst political evils of our time is the absence of fear. The country is filled with robbers, yet who is punished?" Senatorial investigations accomplished

131

nothing; thieves in service continued to amass fortunes and win medals.[29] "Russia will have no justice if the sovereign, having entrusted it to the courts, fails to keep an eye on the judges. Russia is not England."[30]

Karamzin's views of legal administration were similar to Derzhavin's and Dmitriev's, but he had little of their faith in institutions. He rebelled against the idea of a rule of law in Russia; it was only a fiction that enabled the powerful to rule in the name of the law, while they in fact advanced their own selfish interests. His notion of justice was primitive retribution, his ideal ruler a wrathful father willing to discipline his servants and subjects.

> In Russia the sovereign is the living law. He favors the good and punishes the bad, and wins the love of the former by the fear of the latter. Not to fear the sovereign means not to fear the law! In the Russian monarch concentrate all the powers: our government is fatherly, patriarchal. The father of the family judges and punishes without protocol.[31]

Karamzin's writings expressed a recognition of the role of feeling in government and life. If literature should evoke pity, tenderness, and melancholy, government should evoke fear and reverence. But for Karamzin this was a discovery he was explaining to others, not an expression of his own sensibility. His writings described feelings that he ascribed to others—that seemed unrelated to his own experience. Karamzin's feelings were abstract literary figments created to delight rather than to express, and his characters often seem lifeless constructs introduced to contain or prompt those feelings.

But the young aristocrats at the College of Foreign Affairs, in the first years of the nineteenth century, read literature for far more than a critical approach. They regarded the feelings described by Karamzin and other recent writers as theirs to experience. The sentimentalist ethos was a given standard for them; taste, culture, and sensibility had overshadowed military virtues as signs of noble manhood. Yet they were also Russian noblemen, brought up to serve the state. Most of them would take posts in government, and their early attitudes, though never relinquished, inevitably would undergo a change to suit the society and institutions around them. The change was most effectively expressed in the life and work of their most talented representative, Vasilii Zhukovskii, whose verse told a saga of striving for sentimental purity and personal happiness, a vita for his generation.

Zhukovskii was the leading Russian sentimentalist or preromantic poet of the early nineteenth century, the most illustrious product of the Noble Pension at Moscow University. He is known for his plaintive verse and his translations of contemporary German and English poets into Russian. His literary work, it is agreed, deteriorated in quality after 1815, when he became a tutor to the imperial family and began to play the role of court poet. But Zhukovskii's significance was not merely literary. As he drew closer to the imperial family he became a personal model for the conservative bureaucrats of his era, and particularly for his friend Dmitrii Bludov. He embodied the virtues they esteemed and expressed the weakness and limitations they felt in themselves.

Zhukovskii epitomized the sentimentalist virtues. There was little stoic strength or certainty in him. A mild and quiet man, he had delicate, almost feminine features. His soft wistful eyes, his fine lips, gave him a feminine appearance, and many of his friends described his personality as "maidenlike." A kind and generous person, he abhorred unpleasantness or conflict of any kind. He disliked the military and found the civil service little more to his tastes. Humane in his judgments and in his consideration for others, he tried to shut larger issues out of his mind and avoided political discussion. "I need happiness," he wrote, "A happiness that can be my own, for there is no general happiness."[32]

Zhukovskii was at the center of Moscow's literary and intellectual life. He edited and contributed to the literary journal of the Noble Pension. In 1802, he and a group of young men working at the foreign affairs archive met in a "Friendly Literary Circle." André Turgenev, his closest friend, introduced the group to the early romantic literature from Germany and England. Zhukovskii and Turgenev learned to seek meaning in the beauty of personal feelings rather than in political obligation or commitment. On the flyleaf of a copy of *Werther* he gave to Zhukovskii, Turgenev wrote,

> *Inspired by the free genius of nature,*
> *He painted her with flaming features,*
> *And found his laws only in the feeling*
> *   of the heart,*
> *To no other laws was he subject.*[33]

But the feelings expressed by early romantic writers remained far from these genteel youths. The members of the circle sneered at Karamzin's delicacy and artificiality, but they remained true to his spirit in the expression of their emotions. They too were inhibited by the neoclassical restraints of their aristocratic education, and shied from profound and violent feelings. Their sacred values were sentimental love, and, above all, "the blessed spirit of friendship." Friendship evoked the most sublime of the emotions. "Even a criminal can fall in love," André Turgenev wrote, "But only a virtuous heart can feel friendship."[34]

Another member, F. A. Merzliakov, asserted that friendship would help the individual face the cold world; it would foster the feelings that would endow the arts and sciences with emotion and transform them from "false knowledge" into "human truth." It was clear from their statements that friendship was not a simple feeling of liking and respect between individuals. They conceived of it too as an object of sacrifice.[35] Friendship assumed meaning for them only when removed from everyday experience and elevated to the more solemn realm of death. Zhukovskii's quatrain describes their feelings:

> Tumbling from a mountain top,
> An oak, struck by lightening, lay in the dust,
> Around it a vine of ivy entwined,
> Oh, Friendship, this is you![36]

They became increasingly absorbed with death. They read and translated English and German death poetry. Zhukovskii's beautiful translation of Gray's "Elegy" was among his most successful works from this period. They took long and soulful walks in cemeteries at night. At the age of twenty, André Turgenev declared that he had renounced all hope of being truly happy.[37] Shortly before he died two years later, he wrote in his journal that he found his greatest pleasure in dreaming of death.[38]

Glorification of death was a typical feature of romanticism. Romantic writers sought in death a complete being, "an absorption into the whole," as an escape from the isolation of individual existence.[39] It was a similar impulse that moved Radishchev to seek the ultimate harmony and justice in death. But the members of the Turgenev circle sought a different paradise in death. For them, death was a meeting place of friends. They found immortality in their personal attachments, which in the hereafter became lofty and eternal. Zhukovskii wrote, on André Turgenev's death,

> In this world without you, bereaved,
> Oblivious, I shall wander as in a foreign land,
> And in grief shed tears on your sacred ashes,
> Farewell! Life is not eternal!
> We will see each other again,
> For the grave fate has made our assignation!
> Sweet hope! Pleasant expectation!
> With what joy I will die![40]

They worshipped the idyll of a happy family life they found in German sentimentalist writings. Zhukovskii considered conjugal feelings among the most elevated and sublime. Like Dmitriev, he disdained service, and the two years he spent in the Moscow Custom's House were distasteful to him. Satisfaction and virtue were both private matters, he felt. The public man did not have to be virtuous.

> Not having a good heart, you can, in some respects be a good citizen: be gifted and you will successfully act on a stage which is surrounded by an innumerable mob of judges, who are both curious and strict. Ambition will replace inner goodness for you.[41]

Dmitriev regarded homelife as a quiet retreat from the pressures of service; for Zhukovskii, it became an alternative to service, and the true scene of the virtuous life. "You cannot be a good family man in the full sense of the word, a good husband, father and protector of his servants without a good, tender and sensitive heart." For those so fortunate to enjoy it, a happy home brought the highest pleasure. "If Providence has chosen you to enjoy this blessing, then you may boldly take the title of a happy man." Happiness then would regain its lost meaning: "virtue, enjoyment of oneself, direct enlightenment, true wisdom."[42]

Like his idealization of friendship, Zhukovskii's raptures about the family were the *cri de coeur* of one who found such satisfactions unattainable. The illegitimate son of an aristocratic father and his purchased Turkish captive, Zhukovskii grew up with little attention or affection from his parents. He felt himself excluded from normal human pleasures and he would always pine after parental sympathy.[43] His own love life was equally unfortunate, consisting of a succession of shattering disappointments. His first love, an infatuation for his cousin, a child ten years his junior, wounded him irreparably. He married only in 1841, when, at the age of fifty-eight, he wed a twenty-one-year-old bride. Friendship and the domestic joys became transcendent goals for him, the substance of literature rather than life.

Zhukovskii grew accustomed to his suffering and learned to savor and appreciate it. Grief gave meaning to life. "An invisible chain attaches you to your sorrow; in sorrow is your existence [*bytie*]; once having lost it, you yourself are obliterated, for everything that previously filled your soul has been banished." Dwelling on misfortune produced melancholy, "this incomprehensible enchantment which lends inexplicable charms to suffering itself."[44] These remarks recall Karamzin's taste for melancholy feelings. But Karamzin's sadness came by way of literature; it was a kind of contrived empathy that could be taken in small doses. Zhukovskii's came of profound pains of personal rejection, intolerable to him personally, and too strong to belong to "*la belle nature.*" Karamzin used literature to experience sadness, Zhukovskii to alleviate grief. Art transformed pain into pleasure for Zhukovskii: Melancholy was poeticized sorrow, a muting of anguish.

> *Poetry! with you*
> *Grief, poverty, gloomy exile,*
> *All lose their horror!*[45]

Zhukovskii's poetry was melodic consolation. His verse softened and lyricized the emotions. His translations and free renditions of German romantic poetry were more musical and wistful but less passionate than the originals. He liked the richness of feeling in romantic poetry, but he lacked the romantic's impulse to use art as a means to more profound expression of feeling. His favorites among the German poets were Uhland and Hebel, whose verse was softer and more lyrical than their contemporaries'.[46] Poetry alleviated hopeless longings by giving access to the more beautiful and pleasing world of art.

The literary society, Arzamas, was devoted to creating such a world of magic removed from the realities of public and personal life. Zhukovskii was the central member of Arzamas. He presided over meetings, composed comic invocations and protocols, and conveyed to the meetings their sense of warmth and good will. Members received names from his ballads; appropriately, Zhukovskii's was Svetlana, Bludov's Cassandra. The meetings, held at the homes of Bludov and Uvarov, in Petersburg, were merry and convivial. Rituals satirized the solemn pretentiousness of the ceremonies of the symposium and the Masonic lodges. Upon initiation, members read mock funeral orations over the graves of the Shishkovites, parodying the symposium's stilted eloquence and heavy pseudoclassical pronouncements on death. They invented mock ranks and offices, and created a mock *adres-kalendar'*. Meetings closed with a supper of Arzamas goose, amidst wine and revelry.[47]

The poet, Alexander Viazemskii, wrote to Alexander Turgenev, "Our Russian life is death. I will come to refresh myself in Arzamas and recover from death."[48] Alexander Turgenev, in a talk read by Bludov, declared that his life was divided into two parts:

> To the first belongs everything sublime, everything good, calm and sleep. The other, under Nemeza's influence has received as its share movement without rest, emptiness and error. The blind call only the second part life, but I know its value and often in the first I seek salvation from the sores of the latter — from perfunctory kindness, dull merriment, busy do-nothings. Fortunately, I can control my movement from one to the other. A good book and good work, a wise thought and high feeling — these are the soothing remedies, the transit from evil to good.[49]

For Zhukovskii, poetry created diversion from grief. It also removed grief to the distant past or the future. His works are filled with a "love for the past": a nostalgia and obsessive reminiscence about the two tragedies of his youth, the death of André Turgenev, and the infatuation with his cousin. Poetry sweetened the grief about the past. But even more important for Zhukovskii and his contemporaries, it conjured hope for the future. His verse is suffused with an anodyne optimism, a certainty that fortune would change for the better.

> *Bliss is our goal, when we will reach it,*
> *Providence does not tell,*
> *But sooner or later we will joyfully sigh,*
> *Hope was not given by heaven in vain.*[50]

Art could invert dream and reality and paint a pleasant future free of the unfulfilled longing of the present. Just as Liza's fate symbolized Karamzin's sympathetic fatalism, Zhukovskii's heroine, Svetlana, acted out his simple faith in the future. Svetlana dreams her lover dead, only to awaken to find him before her. The message is set forth clearly at the end.

> Our best friend in life,
> Is faith in Providence,
> The law for one who long awaits blessings,
> Is that unhappiness is the here and now—
>   a false dream,
> Happiness is awakening. [51]

Zhukovskii's faith enabled him to encounter the misfortunes of life with the serene belief that things must surely get better. When he heard pessimistic and gloomy talk, he could remark, "there is incomparably more good than evil in the world." [52] He believed that providence would bring an end to sorrow, and a vague, but certain bliss. But the bliss that providence promised was above personal satisfactions. It had majestic, divine proportions. It could not come from the companionship or domestic warmth that so tempted his imagination. Instead, it came in the excitement of national uplift. The struggle against Napoleon freed him from the bleakness of his private shelter and enabled him to become a part of the greater whole of the nation.

The invasion was like the breaking of a dike for Zhukovskii, releasing his lingering martial and patriotic impulses. His own participation in the struggle was cut short by an attack of typhoid. But he felt the national enthusiasm, and his poetry, like Karamzin's history, renewed his sense of solidarity with the state and people. It created a rapport between him and the military forces, fighting once again for the good of the fatherland. *The Bard in the Camp of the Russian Warriors* celebrated the bond between poet and soldier. Filled with a sense of mission, the poet drinks to victory with the soldiers from a common goblet. The muses inspire the heroes with "cheer, fire of glory, vengeance and the thirst for battle."

> The bards are the leaders' helpers,
> Their songs, the life of victory,
> And grandsons hearkening to their strings,
> Marvel at their grandfathers. [53]

Russia's triumph gave content to his faith in the future. He joined those who saw victory as proof of divine favor, as the manifestation of providence in history. "Providence is on the side of those in the right," the poet cries, and the soldiers echo.

The personal embodiment of the beneficence of providence became the tsar. In the subsequent years, Zhukovskii would try to make of the tsar the apotheosis of both national and personal virtue. He would project the personal virtues onto a figure of superhuman size and, identifying with it, feel himself, for once, a man. The popular religious image that Alexander assumed in 1812 appealed to Zhukovskii.[54] In an epistle of 1814, he expressed the Russian people's thanks to the tsar. Alexander's bearing, he wrote, was not that of the proud conqueror, but of the "humble servant of the will of Providence." No longer distant and cold, the tsar appeared as a great human being, inspiring the poet's love and devotion.

> *Oh marvelous era when the tsar's bard*
> *is no flatterer,*
> *When praise is delight, the voice of the lyre*
> *the voice of the people,*
> *When everything sweet to the heart: honor,*
> *freedom,*
> *Greatness, glory, peace, fatherland, altar,*
> *Everything, everything, has fused in one*
> *divine word: tsar.*[55]

The quiet shelter had proved a hell of unfulfilled personal longings. Now, in the euphoria of victory, the feelings of exalted love and friendship, awakened at the beginning of the century, found an object in the tsar. Derzhavin, in *To Felitsiia,* had portrayed Catherine's exemplary probity; Karamzin had called upon Alexander to serve as "the model of virtue for all." But these, when they were taken seriously at all, were distant and abstract models, classical ideals. Zhukovskii now began to look upon the tsar as a living person evoking admiration and affection — the fulfillment of his sentimental dreams. Zhukovskii found personal meaning and dignity in identification with the ruler. His verse of the postinvasion years proclaimed his affection for the ruler, especially his "Prayer of the Russian People," later to be set to music as the Russian national anthem. He grew closer to the imperial family. In 1815, he became the dowager empress's official reader. In 1817, at Karamzin's suggestion, he was appointed tutor of Russian to the Grand Duke Nicholas's German wife, the future empress, Alexandra Fedorovna. He gained entrée to the court. Zhukovskii's diary in 1817 describes the true personal satisfaction he finally experienced:

> In one word, up to now I feel completely happy, especially be-
> cause I feel myself independent in every way: *outside and*
> *inside the soul.* Ambition is silent; only the desire for the good
> is in my soul. Without any disturbance of desire I look upon the
> future and have surrendered myself completely to the *present.*
> Dear, attractive position! Poetry! Freedom![56]

The family of the Grand Duke Nicholas now became an apotheosis of domestic happiness. In the last years of Alexander's reign, Zhukovskii put his sentimentalist rhetoric at the service of the Romanov house, and helped the tsar to assume the mantle of domestic respectability. In 1818, he greeted the birth of the Grand Duke Alexander Nikolaevich with an epistle to the grand duchess. In 1779, Derzhavin had celebrated the birth of Alexander Pavlovich with an ode that described the rejoicing of nature, and compared the infant to a god. Zhukovskii's epistle described his own feelings and the feelings of the imperial family. The birth revived his faith in providence. He had awaited news apprehensively, but

> *A sweet voice penetrated my soul,*
> *"This is God's world; nothing is accidental*
> *[sluchaino] here,"*
> *And my soul believed without trepidation.*

The people too waited expectantly, and the announcement of the birth brought general rejoicing. The father saw his firstborn.

> *Enter our world, little one, welcome guest.*
> *Beholding you, knees bent,*
> *The young father before the saved mother,*
> *Speechless, sobs in the heat of love.*

Zhukovskii described the joy he sensed the mother felt at the sight of her child.

> *How can one understand, in this incomprehensible hour,*
> *What happened with your soul, young mother?*
> *A new world has been opened for it.*
> *Your child, like a heavenly messenger,*
> *Told your soul of a better life,*
> *Lit the purest hopes within it,*
> *Now your wishes are not for you,*
> *Your joys not for yourself,*
> *Wrapped in diapers,*
> *Still without words, with unseeing eyes,*
> *He finds love in your eyes;*
> *Like silence, his sleep is sublime,*
> *And the news of life has not yet reached him.*[57]

Zhukovskii summoned the newborn to be, above all, a human being. Derzhavin had called upon Alexander Pavlovich, too, to be a human being. But for Derzhavin to be human had meant to exercise reason, to distinguish oneself from the beasts. One of Derzhavin's geniuses said,

> *Be the ruler of your passions,*
> *Be a man on the throne.*[58]

When Zhukovskii used *chelovek*, he meant something more. He envisioned a humble person, who would live for the good of the people, who would put the nation's interest above his own. The tsar had to provide a model of sacrifice for the nation.

Yes, in his exalted sphere he will not forget,
The most sacred of callings; to be a man,
To live for posterity in the nation's
    majesty,
For the good of all, *his own to forget,*
Only in the free voice of the fatherland,
To read his briefs with humility. [59]

By the end of Alexander's reign, Zhukovskii was already beginning to act as court poet. After the Decembrist uprising, he saw his destinies ever more closely entwined with those of the imperial house. The show of violence appalled him, and though he made sincere efforts to intercede in behalf of the condemned revolutionaries, he had no sympathy with their methods or goals. In the late 1820s, his attitudes became more conservative. He began to regard the person of the ruler as the source of all of the forces of good in the nation. The people no longer figured in his patriotic sentiments. No longer did the tsar represent the embodiment of the nation; rather, the nation appeared as an expression of the spiritual state of the tsar. "The soul of the tsar is for the moral life of the country what the climate is for its physical life." "Moral strength is in the soul of the sovereign." [60]

In 1826, Zhukovskii was appointed the tutor of the Grand Duke Alexander, and was given the opportunity to shape the future sovereign's soul. He took his task seriously and worked assiduously to prepare himself, for he had been educated in little besides language and literature. His laborious efforts in behalf of another brought him the ultimate bliss, the complete submergence of his own self and feeling.

> I remain with nothing personal! Every particular thought at its conception has its own special interest. Glory, duty, religion, love of the fatherland, in a word everything intrinsic to the spiritual nature of man already attracts my attention not for my sake but for him in whose soul these exalted thoughts would bring beneficial fruits for mankind. [61]

Zhukovskii conveyed to the grand duke his generation's taste for fine and delicate emotions. He made his own skepticism of the military virtues known. He objected strenuously to the heavy military component in the education of previous tsars, and tried to limit the number of hours devoted to military subjects. He wrote the empress,

> Should he be only a warrior, and be destined to act only within the narrow horizons of a general? When will we have legislators? When will we look with respect upon the true needs of the people, laws, enlightenment, morality? My empress, forgive my exclamation, but the passion for the military trade will crush his soul; he will learn to look upon the people only as a battalion and the fatherland only as a barrack. [62]

Nicholas I's strong military predilections ensured that military subjects and drills would remain a significant part of the grand duke's upbringing. But Zhukovskii did teach Alexander his own notion of the ruler's calling. He emphasized in his lessons on literature and history the Russian ruler's humility and the understanding of the people's needs as the basis of Russia's national greatness. He described Alexander Nevskii to the grand duke, Nevskii's namesake, and taught him to emulate Nevskii's qualities. It was a humble and tender Nevskii that Zhukovskii depicted, a prince who loved nature and was devoted to the Russian people. He stressed Nevskii's "Christian humility" in bringing offerings to the Tatars—the prince's willingness to sacrifice his own interest, his own pride, for the general well-being. The thirteen-year-old Alexander Nikolaevich reproduced this image in his own composition.[63]

Zhukovskii's search for a quiet shelter of personal happiness ended by making the ruler an exemplar of private virtue in whose personality he could live. He thus found release from a personality too weak in its self-respect to find satisfaction in personal endeavors. Zhukovskii, like his many friends and admirers, found a shelter from the ugly realities of administrative life in an absorption and identification with the tsar. Unlike his brother or his forebears, Tsar Nicholas would play the role of the family man and Zhukovskii would help to exalt the dynasty's claims to respectability. "Respect the sacredness of family life, then the sacredness of all state power will be respected," he wrote. At Peterhof, Nicholas built himself a "Cottage," in English style, where he undertook his own, rather ostentatious, "private" homelife. The coat of arms of the Cottage, which hung over the entrance and was used in various motifs in all the rooms, was Zhukovskii's composition. It consisted of a bared sword, rising from a background of a blue shield, through a garland of white roses.[64]

6
COUNT DMITRII NIKOLAEVICH BLUDOV

Gradualness is the dependable spring in the mechanism of community.

Koz'ma Prutkov

The nephew of Gavriil Derzhavin, Dmitrii Nikolaevich Bludov, was marked from birth for a successful career in the service. Derzhavin enrolled him as a child in the Izmailovskii guards' regiment. In 1800 — before he had appeared for service in the regiment — the fifteen-year-old Bludov had the good fortune to be assigned to the Moscow Archive of the College of Foreign Affairs. A year later, he had attained the rank of collegiate assessor, the eighth rank, which many functionaries, even of noble origin, would reach only after long service. Bludov received the best available education at the hands of tutors from the faculty of Moscow University. He learned languages, style, and taste — the ingredients that went into the education of the young initiates in the College of Foreign Affairs. He frequented the literary circles of Moscow and impressed all who met him with the liveliness of his intellect, his brilliant wit, and eloquence.[1] These charms never left him. Squat and homely, he entertained with his gift of speech and an amazing memory, which even in old age could recall vivid anecdotes about the statesmen and writers of the distant past. Memoirs about him invariably remarked on what the poet Batiushkov called the "blinding fireworks" of Bludov's mind.[2]

Dmitrii Bludov was a figure of note in the literary life of the first decades of the century. He was an intimate and confidant of Vasilii Zhukovskii, the friend and protégé of Karamzin, and completed the twelfth volume of *The History of the Russian State* after his mentor's death. The playwright Ozerov and the novelist Pisemskii were his cousins. He knew Madame de Stael and other figures in émigré intellectual circles of the early nineteenth century. The friend of Batiushkov, Viazemskii, Alexander and Nicholas Turgenev, Uvarov, and Dashkov, he founded Arzamas with his friends, and Nicholas Turgenev called him its "mainstay." In later years, he frequently entertained writers and critics, most of them of conservative sympathy.

But Bludov's name is important not in Russian literary history, where he left no mark, but in the history of judicial reform. As chief of the Second Section from 1840 to 1862, he directed the drafting of the reform of Russian legal process, the first such effort since Peter the Great. The initial projects for court reform, submitted to the State Council in the reign of Alexander II, reflected his tastes and values. At that time, an old man in his seventies, he appeared as a bearer of the reform hopes of the beginning of the century, who had maintained his dignity and aspirations for change through the somber last years of Nicholas's regime.

Bludov's rise was swift and without setbacks. He served as ambassador to England, chief of clerical work on the commission investigating the Decembrists, head of the Department of Foreign Confessions, minister of interior, and briefly as minister of justice before being appointed chief of the Second Section. In 1826, Nicholas named him one of his state-secretaries, and frequently called upon him to execute extraordinary commissions, to take charge of the government in his absence, and to serve on secret committees to discuss important legislative problems. Bludov conducted the negotiations for the Concordat of 1847, and for his services received the title of count. Among the gray mass of Nicholaean officialdom, he stood out as an educated and cultured individual, respected by the intellectual community and the officials alike.

Dmitrii Bludov was a product of the culture of expression of the early nineteenth century. He received his early experience in the College of Foreign Affairs and, like his comrades, abandoned the military model of the previous century. Like them, Bludov was never able to find a model of the aristocratic civil servant. He reached ministerial level without experience in government chancelleries, and then found himself in lofty, but largely powerless positions, confronted with demands of compliance. His conception of his own self came not from his service but from the literature he had discovered in his youth, and the sentimental ethos he drew from it. As far removed as he became from the inspiration of his youth, he would remain, during his sixty years in service, a kind of literateur in uniform.

In a letter to Pogodin of 1846, Bludov attributed to Karamzin the qualities he most respected. Besides Karamzin's literary style, he admired "the remarkable qualities of his soul, in which strength [*tverdost'*] is united so impressively with tenderness [*nezhnost'*], and a flaming vitality with a purity that was almost childlike."[3] For Bludov, as for Karamzin, strength came of identification with the state, and tenderness was the sign that one was not corrupted personally by the actual use of that strength. The vitality was in the language, and it was language and literary artifice that would protect his own "childlike purity" from the wearing effects of feeling and experience. Even in his portraits as an old man, he appears with the countenance of a little boy, an aging youngster, obedient, bright, frightened.[4]

Fear haunted Bludov's early memories. The Pugachev uprising cast a shadow over his childhood, and apprehensions of similar cataclysms persisted to darken his view of reality. Born in 1785, he heard frightening tales of Pugachev from his relatives, which inflamed his young imagination. An uncle, with his entire family, had been slaughtered by the rebels. A wet nurse had hidden the baby, but the rebels returned, and before her eyes crushed the infant's head.

Strength came from the established order and from authority, in his family, represented by his mother. His father had died early in his life. There remained only vague memories and tales of a dissolute life that had burdened the family with large debts. His mother, Bludov heard, had repulsed the marauders from the family's Kazan estate with the aid of two small cannons. In his childhood, the cannons were put to use frequently against brigands. Bludov preferred the memories of their estate in a remote area of Vladimir province. There he spent his childhood summers in the midst of large gardens and a dark grove of trees that plunged downward from a hill to a stream. He liked to remember listening to the nightingales singing in the grove until late into the evening, lost in longings and dreams, until a sudden rustle or murmur made his heart contract in terror.[5]

His mother had set right the family fortune. She had repaid his father's debts and left inherited estates with 1,219 souls for her son. Bludov was often praised for his modest tastes and frugality, but such descriptions were conventional and must be judged in terms of the court circles he frequented. Bludov came from the upper one percent of the nobility in wealth. He was a member of the aristocratic elite, and, if he frequently found it impossible to make ends meet, it was because the demands of the Petersburg style of life almost always outran the means of the Russian aristocrat.[6]

His mother also secured the contacts in high circles necessary to pursue his career. She settled in Moscow and established connections in the high aristocracy. Through her efforts, Bludov met the Princess Anna Shcherbatova. Five years younger than Shcherbatova, and unprepossessing in appearance, Bludov was beneath the Shcherbatovs both by ancestry and wealth. Nonetheless, he fell in love with her and pursued her relentlessly. Their courtship lasted eleven years, and they were married in 1813.[7]

By all accounts, Bludov was an adoring and worshipful son. His love for his mother left him bound to her scruples and ambitions. When he became venturesome in his youth, he was given to know that such conduct made him unworthy of her love. At the beginning of Alexander's reign, when reform plans were in the air, he too caught the spirit of self-confidence and criticism. While serving in the College of Foreign Affairs in St. Petersburg, he gathered a group of young men around him to discuss ideas that some of his relatives regarded as bold, though the exact content of the discussions is unknown. A letter to his mother alarmed her greatly, and a reply from her close friend, the Countess Kamenskaia, reproved him for troubling his mother. "Wanting to shine with your knowledge, you have no notion of *yourself,* leading such an idle life as yours. You have called many around me fools and idiots, you think so much of yourself. But you are living not according to reason." She warned him he would incur hatred from all, and concluded by accusing him of egoism. "It is silly to give lessons to others when one does not know his own obligations [*dolzhnosti*]."

At about the same time, he became bored with his sinecure in the College of Foreign Affairs and tried unsuccessfully to transfer to the Ministry of Public Education. He then decided to retire in order to devote himself to literature and write for the journals. Living in Ozerov's home, and seeing Derzhavin on occasion, he seemed to be well connected to enter

the Petersburg literary world. He had already placed several brief translations and critical articles in the journals. He wrote Kamenskaia asking her
to plead for his mother's pardon. "You know the heart and soul of your
priceless mother, and how tenderly she loves you," Kamenskaia replied in
1803, "and so no pardon is necessary. Your confession and your love alone
will console her and the grief will pass. . . ."

The two letters had their intended effect. Bludov abandoned his bold
talk and remained in service. His mother died two years later, leaving him,
at the age of twenty, filled with painful feelings of love, gratitude, and
guilt. His filial devotion fixed forever his dedication to his "obligations,"
and there remained little trace of passion or irreverence in the mature
man.[8] Bludov would live without a masculine model for personal life. He
would take on his mother's anxious and cautious ways, her concern for
appearance and probity.

Bludov shaped his mature persona from the sentimentalist ideas current
in Moscow during the first years of the nineteenth century. Sentimentalism
made his caution and passivity noble virtues. It allowed him to part with
his heroic aspirations while maintaining his self-respect. Heroic aspirations
could give way to sentimentalism's cultivation of tragic resignation. True
exaltation came from the feelings of love and friendship, especially when
these were hopeless and the soul fell into melancholy.

Sentimentalism gave the young Bludov his first understanding of the
pangs of love. Love appeared truer when the beloved was remote, unreal,
close to the sublime. At sixteen, he wrote to Zhukovskii, as he gazed at a
portrait of his beloved, "I am looking at the dear likeness and conversing
with a friend. It seems that I should be happy, but I am unhappy and
very."[9] He wept over a sentimental play he had just read and especially the
words of the heroine in the final scene, "He has died. He has shot himself."
He imagined himself in the hero's role. "Imagine that she said the same to
me in a despairing voice. Then I would feel moved to go to the Sparrow
Hills, and there, amongst the ruins to die. But will she say this? And if so,
How?" He would behold her portrait in the light of the moon,

> I will gaze at her little closed eyes, at her cheeks, where the
> slightest, rosiest blush plays, at her breasts. Oh! Oh! Then I will
> kiss her in my infatuation. Perhaps some day I will kiss her as I
> now kiss only her portrait. She will then awaken, look at me
> with tired eyes, smile, squeeze my hands and I will press myself
> to her breast, feel the beating of her heart. And at the same
> time, the horrible word — *jamais* — will resound in my heart. Oh
> wretch, gaze at the portrait, gaze at her from afar and suffer. I
> look at the portrait some more, kiss it again, and in tears, in
> despair, will fall asleep."[10]

When Bludov married Anna Shcherbatova, he made for himself the
domestic life that remained a dream for Zhukovskii. But even his love for

his wife remained part of his anticipation of death. Personal attachments became perfect only when elevated by death, which promised the only true intimacy. Many years later, when he was already a devoted husband and father, he wrote to his wife:

> It is strange, or perhaps not strange, that every time I think of you, when my eyes are filled with tears of tenderness and gratitude to heaven, the thought of death without fail occurs to me. But this thought neither horrifies nor aggrieves me. On the contrary, I feel that death rather than separating us, unites us more closely; that I will always be allowed in some form to surround you and in a secret voice, only heard by the heart, to repeat: be calm in the waves of life, there is God, there is truth, and virtue, for them it is necessary to live, and for them it is sweet to die.[11]

Bludov's notion of friendship had the same notes of passivity and resignation to life. Sentimentalism made friendship too an appreciation of distance. Friendship could attain true sublimity only when friends were separated by circumstance or death. Bludov found that he liked André Turgenev much more after the latter's death. "I note also," he wrote to Zhukovskii, "that I like you much more when we are apart than when we are together."[12] He defined his friendship for Zhukovskii as the gratitude for the feelings that his friend prompted.[13] What we love most in our friends, one of his aphorisms declares, is "their need for our love."[14]

Zhukovskii's famous "Epistle to Bludov" stressed the theme of death. Written upon Bludov's departure to act as the diplomatic aid of General Kamenskii in the Danube campaign, the poem bids Bludov a sad farewell. The consolation will be their reunion. But friendship could evoke pathos only if saddened by the anticipation of death. Upon his return, Bludov might find his friend gone from this world; and in death, they could establish a warmer, more cordial association than they had in life. The epistle concludes:

> Under the swaying canopy of trees,
> Like an invisible shade,
> Above you, I will
> Fly hand in hand with the lost Philo,
> Then to you, I with a soft sound
> My lyre, left by me
> On the young maple,
> Will announce the arrivals,
> From the mysterious world,
> And above you, quietly,
> Reverie will fly;
> With your hearts, you will see,
> In the invisible distance,
> The longed for fatherland,

The promised shelter,
For wanderers of the earth.[15]

Only art could produce real personal satisfaction. Literature alleviated unhappiness and prompted beautiful feelings. The artist had the special gift of expressing such feelings, and it was taste, the mark of the noble soul that determined which feelings were truly sublime. Bludov was respected for his unerring taste. "Your criticism is law for me," Zhukovskii wrote to him, and he always sought Bludov's opinion about his verse. He declared in "Vadim," a poem dedicated to Bludov,

Your taste was my teacher,
Through my tangled verse,
Like a secret leader-protector,
It paved the way to my goal.[16]

Their delight in the world of literature created the inspiration for the literary society, Arzamas. Bludov was a founder of the society and his parody, "Vision in Arzamas," provided a name and set the tone for the society. Bludov chose a district in Kaluga province to denote distance from official culture. He ridiculed "the gloomy old men," "the youths without freshness," "the young ladies suffering not from shame but from pride" of the symposium. "Wherever I turn my gaze, everywhere I see either rows of trophies or heads burdened with laurels or wounds worthy only of reverence." His vision was a Walpurgisnacht, mocking the Shishkovites' ponderous ceremonies. In contrast, Bludov called upon Arzamas's spirit of youth. "Oh! My youth has passed, vanished in the symposium and the Academy — the serpent of timeless care has gnawed at my heart." It was a summons to his friends to enjoy the delights of youth, and for them these were the only truly human feelings.[17]

But personal pleasures and attachments had to give way when they conflicted with duty. Service overshadowed personal attitudes and preferences: it meant, in the sentimentalist ethic, acting in behalf of government and ruler, whose actions transcended individual judgment. In 1818, Bludov, "the mainstay" of Arzamas, was appointed ambassador to London. He disliked the assignment, but felt no choice about complying. He wrote Zhukovskii,

> To leave for months everything that is valuable, and then not to see the many dear objects of my love — this cannot be called happiness. And as for advantage? Whether there will be any, I don't know and do not wish to know. I would blush if I sacrificed one joy of the heart to personal advantage, only one dear moment of happiness. We can and we must sacrifice, but only to what we consider an obligation. Obligation demands sacrifice.[18]

Obligation required the complete disregard for one's personal feelings, the acceptance of one's lot. Bludov found in the rhetoric of the day a justification for the submergence of individual concerns before the super-ordinate demands of duty. Wisdom for Bludov was the acknowledgment of one's own weakness before events, institutions, and the universe. His aphorisms express this view. "To wish for what does not depend on our efforts is to consider oneself wiser than Providence."[19] He feared change, which might upset the routine of his life and expose him to the dangers lurking in the world. Pride, daring, desire for change were equivalent to folly. "After pride, the greatest sore on humanity is stupidity or ignorance: for stupidity is nothing but all-embracing and incurable ignorance. But isn't pride a kind of stupidity?"[20] "Change of place and situation is the same as turning from side to side in insomnia." "About many people it can be said that they are bold in the manner of that bold fellow who cheerfully walks along the edge of the abyss because he does not see it."[21]

The Decembrist uprising was for Bludov a brief and horrifying glimpse of the abyss. It also gave him the model of active, masculine virtue lacking in his personal life. The new tsar's suppression of the uprising presented an inspiring spectacle of a political leader whom he believed should be ruthless and strong. Bludov regarded Nicholas's stern strength with awe and humble submission. He could not hope to emulate the tsar's qualities, but from him he gained a vicarious confidence, a support before the perils of life. Like Zhukovskii, he found in Nicholas a salvation from his personal weakness. To Zhukovskii, Nicholas represented a friend rescuing him from his loneliness, to Bludov, a protector affording security.

Nicholas appeared as the defender of the national destiny. Bludov thrilled at the coronation ceremonials in 1826. He wrote to his wife, "Yesterday, we saw our monarch, who has succeeded so quickly in stirring so many hopes, arrive in the capital of the fatherland to receive the crown and scepter of his forefathers — to confirm his union with the people." The band played "God Save the King." The melody, mixing with the ringing of the bells of Moscow, exalted him. "The effect was indescribable. It seemed that the words 'God Save the Tsar' resounded in all hearts. I assure you that at least for me, I felt something like a fever running through my heart and nerves — but a pleasant fever of hope. It was as if I more than ever before believed in the blessedness of Providence and the future of the happiness of Russia." The annointment brought tears to his eyes. He was moved by prayers read by the emperor and the metropolitan, and his faith was reconfirmed. "I was again assured of the sweetness and the necessity of Faith, that every passion, even the most noble love of the Fatherland, not purified by religion, leads only to error and misfortune."[22]

The tsar and the Romanov house represented his security before the inimical forces capable of unleashing violence and breakdown. He began to write a history of the Romanovs, meant as a sequel to Karamzin's history, that started where Karamzin had left off, and focused not on the unification of the state, but on the survival of the dynasty. His history detailed the rebuffs the dynasty had dealt to adversaries and pretenders. The sketches Bludov completed describe in bare chronicle form various episodes of lese majesty and insurrection in the eighteenth century, such as Mirovich's attempt to free Ivan Antonovich, and Beniovskii's rebellion on Kamchatka. Bludov presented them as futile, insane efforts that were crushed with ease. His history was a symbolic enactment of his faith in the strength and permanence of the dynasty, a confirmation of its power before threats to authority.[23]

Bludov idolized Nicholas. He saw the tsar as the personification of tenderness and strength. During the Polish Rebellion of 1830, he watched the soldiers shout to their sovereign, "We will die for the honor of the tsar and the unity of the empire." He wrote his wife,

> The crown worn by Nicholas I is not of roses. Fate tests his strength with the worst adversities. But he has the worthy comfort of his heart. In the present situation, he heard with tears of tenderness, and still hears, the voice of his true subjects, his children, for the cries of the zealous warriors, of his guard, are repeated by everyone, everywhere. Russians are incapable of letting down their tsar, especially such a tsar.[24]

But again Bludov felt the full measure of his devotion in the presence of death. In Nicholas's last moments, "the whole treasure of the Christian virtues of the soul of the dying man opened before us." Bludov's single book, *The Last Hours of Nicholas I,* was written to commemorate the tsar's death officially; it appeared in Russian, French, English, and German, and was quickly distributed in Europe. In it Bludov described his own "communing of the spirit with those passing away to another, better life." During his last moments, Nicholas showed his "great soul, strong and tender."[25] He died a true stoic death, "like a worthy grandson of Peter the Great." There was no hint of emotion on Nicholas's face when he learned the end was near.

> The doctor held His hand; not one vein trembled; the pulse did not quicken by even one beat. For the first time since the very beginning of the illness, the thought of his imminent and inevitable end confronted him, and already, His bright, quiet gaze portrayed the state of soul of one relieving himself of the entire burden of griefs, cares and vanities of the earthly world. There was not even a sign of effort in struggling with an attachment to life.[26]

In his last moments, Nicholas's stern devotion to duty became almost godlike to Bludov. Nicholas was the image of self-denial, taking nothing for himself, responding to no inner prompting, but giving himself completely to serve something outside of himself. Bludov felt in Nicholas now "the unshakeable, we dare say, coldblooded strength of the Tsar and Warrior, the thought of the important sometimes so painful obligations of the Monarch which he sacredly fulfilled during his nearly thirty-year-long government of the State."[27] But at the same time, Nicholas became the missing friend and father. Bludov felt in him "the tender love for His brother and for His great family, Russia." He described Nicholas's feelings as he bade farewell to his own family, members of the imperial house, and the court. He showed how Nicholas's testament was concerned for the well-being of his family and Russia. The thought of his obligation and the love of Russia combined in "an all transcending, all embracing and consecrating feeling of Faith. He unflinchingly awaited the approach of death, for he knew that it is only the path to the true life." In Nicholas's chambers, Bludov worshipped the fusion of the political and the personal, an icon of a *podvig,* comprehensible only through faith, performed by the "Tsar-Christian."[28]

In service to his sovereign, personal attachments and morality gave way to the need to submit to the grim morality of the political order. The dualism of sentimentalism allowed Bludov to serve his sovereign without involving his own feelings or injuring his own sensibilities. It enabled him to withdraw from responsibility from the acts he had to perform and attach responsibility to the distant figure of the tsar. In 1826, he proved his ability to subordinate personal loyalty and feelings to state need. As chief of clerical work for the commission investigating the Decembrists, he had the task of composing the sentence, which included the condemnation to death of his friend and fellow Arzamasets, Nicholas Turgenev. Bludov himself did not play a part in determining the sentence, but Nicholas Turgenev, who remained in Europe, and his brother, Alexander, never forgave Bludov. Bludov never overcame his own sense of loss.[29]

Bludov's readiness to do his sovereign's bidding ensured his future success, and he remained the tsar's faithful servant throughout his life. "I am always ready, and especially in the present circumstances, to sacrifice all my pleasures, accounts, hopes and even myself to the service of His Majesty," he wrote to his wife during the Polish Rebellion of 1830.[30] He was at the tsar's call night and day. He tried frantically to please, and was in terror of his master's disapproval. On days he was to report to Nicholas, he was not himself: He listened to no one and could not understand what was said to him. "He jumped about ceaselessly, looked at the clock every minute, and without fail sent someone in the morning to check his watch with the Palace clock." If he was well received, he behaved like a child, prancing through the rooms, ready to kiss anyone he met. Nicholas sensed and exploited his weakness. "This man has never had the courage to be anything," he said of the official who would serve as his minister of interior for eight years and to whom he would occasionally entrust the direction of government in his absence.[31]

Bludov's attitudes typified a civil service that had begun to lose its stigma but had not yet begun to acquire its own esprit. Bludov's service was a submission to a higher order that necessity and the state's welfare prescribed, rather than a pursuit worthy in itself and possessing its own goals. The values remained quasi-military, though Bludov had little of the soldier in him. Nicholas, who had a strong distaste for civil servants, preferred the military manner. In 1826, he declared to Bludov, "You, State-Secretaries, are my civil General-Adjutants; prepare yourself for various assignments."[32] Obedience and discipline were important values to Bludov and he impressed their importance on his sons, both of whom began their careers as guards' officers. He wrote to his son André in 1838,

> You should devote yourself and all your time to another matter, to the study of the *alphabet of service,* which is not taught in the universities, and by this I understand not elementary, so called material knowledge, necessary to military men, but what is needed even more and what is more important, habit, love for precision and subordination. "An officer of the old army," says Guizot in one journal article, "said to me the other day, 'I learned in the regiment what can be learned only there, I learned respect.'" And the Professor Minister — former Rector added, "without respect nothing great can be achieved, nothing durable can be established."[33]

Bludov liked to think of his renunciation as a voluntary act, and emphasized that his submission was a matter of free choice. An official, he asserted, had to have independent means so he would not be dependent on his governmental work. A minister should never become the blind instrument of another. He should act according to his convictions and, if he could not, he should resign. For this it was necessary to be able to live on the income from one's estate and to use salary only for the demands of service. His letters to his children are full of sermons about frugality. He admonished his daughter Antonina in 1846, when she was in her late twenties, "I think that frugality for people who are not well to do is an obligation and naturally is to be preferred to the pleasant things of life."[34] But few Russian aristocrats lived within their incomes, and Bludov was no exception. A certificate of 1815 confirms his ownership of his Smolensk estate for purposes of mortgage; another does the same for his estate in Orenburg province.[35] It is mentioned in his service record that Bludov, in 1856, was forgiven debts to the Loan Bank alone totalling forty-two thousand rubles. These debts exceeded his highest yearly income, that of 1864, when he was receiving large sums as honorary emoluments for his service.[36] The obligation Bludov felt to the autocracy had financial as well as emotional roots.

Independence came only from his own private world. The reward for outward compliance was inner freedom. He concluded his letter to his son, "You also know that respect for authority, that is for the system [*poriadok*], does not prevent the truest most valuable independence, of thought and heart. For our heart is independent as long as it is pure."[37] Happiness came in submitting to external necessity, and enjoying the simple comfort of his own home, which was, by all accounts, relatively modest. There were few luxuries, the only ornaments, the family portraits hanging along the walls in old, tarnished frames. To banquets he preferred dinners at home, attended by three or four interesting guests. He was an attentive and engaging host. In his personal relations he was kind, thoughtful, and generous — almost to the point of irresponsibility. Even when he reached the highest positions in government, the servants had to keep money out of his hands to prevent him from giving it away during his daily walks.[38]

But his service obligations often exhausted his spiritual resources. He found himself without the time to read or think or attend to his personal life. As state secretary, he had to be ready to respond to the tsar's call night or day. He frequently complained that his work seemed endless, especially when combined with semiofficial social events, such as balls, soirées, dinners, and obligatory visits. In one week he attended two balls, one of which he left early, at 2:30 A.M.; meetings of the State Council; sessions of three committees; in addition to working on his routine tasks. After dinner, he often would summon a secretary and return to work. He lamented the loss of time for his "mind and heart,"[39] and on occasion his faith was not enough to sustain him. He would then fear that his inner world did not in fact exist; he would feel a total absence of self, a terrifying emptiness. "Two days I have been suffering from a moral illness, and this moral illness can be called petrifying, because from it all the capacities of soul and mind petrify; it seems to me that I am drowning in a void and seeking myself in it in vain." He described his affliction as "a new kind of tarantula, which does not bring death but takes life away." The mood was dispelled only by recalling some verse of Zhukovskii he had read long ago. "I felt my heart. Enchanting music!"[40]

Bludov's intellectual interests were principally literary and eighteenth-century. His library, according to a list compiled shortly before his trip to England, was almost evenly divided between French and Russian titles, with a few scattered works in German and English. There was a large collection of the critic La Harpe and various works of classical and modern literature. Seventeenth- and eighteenth-century thought was prominent — La Bruyère, Fénelon, Diderot, Mirabeau, Pestalozzi, Swedenborg, Frederick the Great. The library included books by Machiavelli and Montaigne but no work of speculative philosophy. Montesquieu's *Esprit des lois* was the only work at all connected with the law.[41]

Bludov approached government with the manners and values of the literateur. He valued form over content, effect over meaning. Preoccupied with the brilliance of his language, he often remained indifferent to the success or failure of his own opinions. M. A. Dmitriev remarked that Bludov seduced himself with his own language. "In his self-satisfaction his heart melted so much that he gladly surrendered the debate to others, leaving himself with the victory of eloquence."[42] He came to be known as an innocuous debater, but his eloquence and charm could be useful to disarm those who were hostile. In 1832, when minister of interior, he captivated his audience with his reply to a delegation of Poles. "Tears escaped from the eyes of some; others felt sublime emotions ... all like the performance of a melodrama."[43] He never forsook the goals of Arzamas. As minister of interior, he established official newspapers in the provinces of European Russia. He also sent forty subscription blanks for the posthumous edition of Pushkin to each governor for distribution to provincial officials, "knowing how much the creations of good writers assist the perfection of language, education (of the taste and in general), and the elevation of the feeling of the sublime."[44]

Bludov's assignments in government utilized his literary skills. The role of the Karamzinians, it has been mentioned, was to create a style, distinguished by an exceedingly simple, polished presentation of materials and problems. This "ministerial" style was the aristocrats' attempt to make state matters comprehensible, and Bludov was its master. In his administrative work, he would compose clear and graceful papers — the projects that Nicholas used to tighten governmental control, the manifestos that Alexander II would use to announce the era of reform. He concerned himself neither with the goal of his efforts — which he regarded as his sovereign's concern — nor the gathering of factual material, which he left to the chancellery. Chancellery work was repugnant to him, and his one experience working with a chancellery had been unfortunate. As a youth, as head of Count Kamenskii's field chancellery during the Danube campaign, the clerks had jeered at him and his efforts to direct them. It was an experience he never forgot.[45]

Bludov was well suited to compose the reports and the laws that Nicholas would use to strengthen the authority of the central government. His polished exposition smoothed over conflicts of principle and administrative complexity, and created the illusion of change without affecting the basic principles of government. From 1828 to 1832, as director of the Department of Religious Affairs of the Foreign Confessions, he worked to spread the authority of the orthodox church. He introduced a reorganization of the administration of the Lutheran and Uniate churches, and in 1835, when minister of interior, he had Uniate schools placed under the authority of the orthodox church. In 1839, the Uniate church was subordinated to the orthodox hierarchy and made subject to the authority of the holy synod.[46]

As minister of interior, Bludov drafted organizational statutes for the institutions of local government. He worked out the reorganization of the St. Petersburg police, the financial operations of towns, and plans to improve city hospitals. His most important legislation was the General Instruction to Civil Governors of 1837, the first attempt to clarify the tangled lines of authority left by the Provincial Reform of 1775 and the Ministerial Reform of 1802. Bludov's instruction tightened the governor's authority over all branches of local administration. But it also curtailed the governor's discretion by limiting his role to supervision, and concentrating greater authority in the ministries. In this way, Bludov's reform created simple and neat lines of authority with all power concentrated in the center.[47]

The principal part of the instruction was devoted to the reform of clerical work (*deloproizvodstvo*), which would make such concentration of authority possible. Nicholas stated that he had ordered Bludov to "reduce the present forms for clerical work, with all possible aversion to all superfluous correspondence, and to institute the most correct and the most convenient system."[48] But like previous efforts to reduce correspondence, Bludov's instruction failed to achieve its goal, for the fault lay not in the particular rules of procedure but in the entire system of bureaucratic surveillance.[49] His effort, however, seems to have made matters only worse. Bludov had only a distant appreciation of the problems of supervision, and his proposals, due to Nicholas's impatience, were issued as law without the usual discussions in the State Council or the Committee of Ministers. As soon as it was implemented, the instruction provoked complaints from the governors, who found themselves with the responsibility of supervising the most trivial details of chancellery procedure, leaving them with little time for matters of significance. Many of the rules, they claimed, were incomprehensible to local officials and others were simply impossible to execute. One governor wrote, "The majority of its directives are mere fantasies. A case in reality almost never follows the course [the Instruction] prescribes for it and that it ought to follow according to Bludov's speculations." The instruction seems to have produced a sharp increase in the volume of correspondence. Bludov, however, ignored the governors' objections and reported to Nicholas that he had encountered no difficulties in its implementation.[50]

If Bludov's legislative projects aimed at tightening his ministerial control, his daily management of the administration was casual and even amiable. He was confident that the autocratic system was functioning well and possessed the strength of popular support. In his reports, he reassured Nicholas on this score. In 1834, he reported that despite crop failure, the previous year had been marked by "no special moral evil."

> The number of crimes committed has not increased, no important disturbances have taken place and the public tranquil-

lity was neither violated nor threatened. A review of the events of 1834 presents the same comforting conclusion. Thanks to Divine Providence and the vigilance of local authorities and Your Imperial Majesty's untiring care, quiet and order have prevailed everywhere, to the fullest extent.[51]

Bludov's faith in the government was so firm that he found it difficult to believe that serious wrongdoings were taking place. Thus, while he accepted the notion of military discipline from the tsar, he remained a considerate, extremely gentle person who was unwilling to exert discipline himself. He was tolerant of his subordinates' weaknesses and recommended them generously for medals and bonuses, expressing only the highest opinion of them. He found it difficult to suspect them of wrongdoing. When informed of irregularities in his ministry, he responded with disbelief. A. N. Peshchurov, the governor of Pskov province, sent in numerous reports of official abuses, but Bludov questioned their validity and promised only to investigate the situations.[52] When a young nobleman of Vitebsk province, S. A. Ubri, disrupted the gentry assembly with a general critique of the Russian governmental system and proclaimed demands for a constitution and public meetings of the gentry, Bludov reacted forgivingly. He laid the action to youthful folly and recommended a moderate punishment—shifting him to a different office under supervision of the governor, I. M. Bibikov, to learn the obligations of a subject and a nobleman. Bludov did not fear such threats to the stability of the autocracy. He wrote to Bibikov in 1835,

> The principles that the social organization [blagoustroistvo] is based on in Russia, thank God, have need neither of defense nor of defenders. They are known to all and are not open to doubt. The tranquillity and happiness of all estates of His Imperial Highness' subjects are safeguarded from all the catastrophes with which Mr. Ubri threatens us, not by childish, schoolboy eloquence (that so far has saved no one), but by the vigilance and wisdom of the monarch, by the force of laws decreed or perfected by him, by the feeling of reverence and unconditional devotion to the throne that fills and enlivens the heart of every Russian, and which cannot be shaken by a handful of the ill-intentioned or misled.[53]

The system was strong as it existed, a bulwark of confidence. But any substantive change, particularly in the social relations in the countryside, might undermine the entire structure. In a memorandum of 1835, the governor-general of Belorussia, Khovanskii, complained of the terrible condition of the Belorussian peasants. The landlords, Khovanskii claimed, gave the peasants insufficient land, overburdened them with work, and inflicted brutal corporal punishment upon them. He asked for statutory limitations on the landlords' power. Bludov's reply was abrupt and negative. Such limitations would "shake the existing rights of landholders," and set a bad example for the rest of the empire, "where such abuses do not occur or are very rare."[54]

His tolerance, his complacent air made Bludov most unpopular with the Third Section. He once remarked that Benkendorf had received a report accusing him of "extreme liberalism."[55] Benkendorf promised not to submit the report to the tsar, but the Third Section remained antagonistic to Bludov during his tenure as minister of interior. The hostility was partly due to institutional rivalry and conflicting goals. The Third Section was animated by a distrust of the population, and particularly of the administration; its existence was justified by the presence of hostile and inimical elements in Russia. The Ministry of Interior had as its basic purpose the maintenance of tranquillity, and the de-emphasis of elements of dissension and disorder. But in addition, Bludov's disinclination to supervise or direct offended the authoritarian tastes of Benkendorf and the gendarmerie. In any case, the yearly reports of the Third Section on the administration contain a running critique of Bludov's ministry, some of which rings true.

The report of 1833 noted that Bludov was able to win "the most favorable public opinion by his tender and polite manners and his attentiveness to all having business with him." They had expected to find him a serious man (*delovoi chelovek*), expected improvements in his sphere, for they considered him an "intelligent and enlightened individual." But these hopes were not realized, and "public opinion" had lost faith in Bludov. "The Ministry is in a state of somnolence," the report declared. The steps taken to deal with the crop failures during the famine of 1833 appeared feeble. No efforts had been made to correct abuses or replace governors who were incapable or untrustworthy.[56] The report of 1835 claimed that the governor of Vologda province was a notorious drunkard and that Bludov, though aware of this problem, had not attempted to remove him.

> There is no energy in the organization of the Ministry. Governors govern as they are able and many complain that they lack the necessary direction for their work, that in cases when they needed it they did not receive any assistance on the part of the Ministry for the execution of the useful measures they proposed.[57]

The report of 1837 stated that Bludov was moving governors too rapidly from province to province, trying to offset a poor initial selection of candidates. In 1838, reference was made to Bludov's "indiscriminate appointment of governors.... He takes whoever happens to be around or whoever's name is handed to him."[58] In 1839, when Bludov was removed from his post, the attack became ferocious.

Governors arriving in the capital, heads of chancelleries, military governors, unanimously declare that during Bludov's direction of the administration things have reached the stage that his orders are not being executed at all because they are impossible to execute, and, aware of the slowness of correspondence, they have even ceased corresponding with the Minister.[59]

During his subsequent ten-month stay as minister of justice, the Third Section commentators continued to hound Bludov. "Public opinion has viewed Minister Bludov always as a witty person, a good editor of papers, but he has never enjoyed the reputation of a serious person. His character does not have the strength or the patience to penetrate procedural cases." Again the Third Section expected no useful changes from Bludov. "Most of all, the public has feared for his gullibility and weakness of character that allows those around him to direct him according to their own designs. High society and [society] ladies influence him, which was not true under Dashkov, who was known as the 'stone minister.'"[60]

Viazemskii commented about Bludov's administrative skills:

As in the sphere of literature, Bludov is born not a producer but a critic, so in the state sphere he is born for opposition. There he would be a remarkable individual. In the ranks of statesmen, he is a nonentity.[61]

But Bludov was a successful critic only in the sense that he helped to improve verse, like Zhukovskii's, that he regarded as essentially sound. He was apt at making minor alterations in style and form that helped the author. He could not present his own alternative. Similarly in government he was hardly by temperament a member of the opposition. He was talented at finding fault with institutions that he did not wish to alter fundamentally. In his new position as chief director of the Second Section of the chancellery of his imperial majesty, which he assumed at the end of 1840, he would have an opportunity to perform this role. He would return, as the Third Section suggested he ought to, to editing papers. He would direct the supplements and revisions of the *Digest of Laws* and the reforms of the judiciary, but in a manner that would correct rather than change.

Speranskii and Dashkov had concluded in 1836 that a successful reform of the courts would have to be undertaken in accordance with a general design, rather than piecemeal, and Nicholas approved their recommendation. In charge of the reform, Bludov became the custodian of this general design and he fitted specific recommendations into it. The nature of the varying suggestions that came to him was less important than the compromise that he felt called upon to make between change and stability and the use of his design to bring this about. Bludov explained his underlying principles to Alexander in 1859:

> The improvements in legislation as in everything else are only useful and so to say fruitful when they follow one behind the other along the path of civic spirit [*grazhdanstvennost'*] the development of minds and the needs of society; in the drafting of legal statutes, always taking as a basis only the eternal immutable rules of justice and a wise love of humanity, it is necessary to remove oneself in every way from one-sided designs that might obstruct the concordance of various parts of the administration—the closest bond of the different elements and tribes entering into the composition of the Power [*Derzhava*] entrusted to you by God.[62]

"The Eternal, immutable rules of justice" and the "wise love of humanity" were to provide the basis of the reform, and the integrity of the administrative system was to be taken as sacrosanct. This expressed Bludov's conviction that the changes in the courts could be made compatible with the maintenance of the tsar's supreme authority over justice. He professed great respect for the teachings of legal science, but his general scheme had little to do with "science," the expedience or inexpedience of a given change being determined according to his preconceived harmony.

As described in chapter 3, Bludov changed the composition of the Second Section to suit his aristocratic predispositions. Balugianskii and Speranskii had been bureaucrats involved in administrative problems, and they appointed experienced administrators and university teachers, most of whom were non-noble. Bludov preferred men like himself, who had wealth, property, education, refinement, and, especially, literary talent. But such noblemen, like Bludov, had little experience in legal administration. Apart from interim appointments as minister of justice for a few months in 1830 and 1839, Bludov had had no contact with the legal administration. Of Bludov's twenty-three subordinates, nine had served only in the Second Section. Only three members had been in the Senate or the Ministry of Justice, and all briefly—for less than three years.[63]

The high educational qualifications of the Second Section's officials made them valuable assistants, and several were sent abroad to study European systems. But their learning could not affect the basic principles and goals of the projects. The fourteen projects submitted to the State Council presented Bludov's compromise between procedural norms employed in the West and a Russian legal tradition he knew of principally from historical studies.[64] Out of the two, he fashioned a literary unity that presumed a gradual and harmonious change. Actual institutions assumed a value and function it was not clear they possessed; innovations appeared to involve little shock or inconvenience.

The most extensive of Bludov's projects was the reform of civil procedure. He considered the current civil process injurious to gentry economic interests, and thought it could be reformed without compromise of the state authority. The lack of effective remedies from the courts obstructed the flow of credit and undermined the economy of the landholding class.

> How many calamitous results come from this! Public credit declines, enterprises useful to the state stop, and the very motivation for them disappears as well. Private relations are deprived of reliable bases and strength, the tranquillity of many families is violated. Litigation leads to the ruin of fortunes, and it is often more advantageous for a party to lose the most just case than to continue it and hand it down from generation to generation. Finally, what may be most important and woeful of all—there is a weakening and stifling of the feeling of justice in our souls, of the trust in the protective power of the laws, and with that of the necessary, redeeming respect for them.[65]

Bludov's work on the civil reform was eager and swift. He had always been a determined supporter of the adversary process; Panin's diary mentions a debate with him on this subject as early as 1840.[66] In 1843, he requested Panin to collect criticisms from officials under the Ministry of Justice on present civil procedure to be used in the formulation of his project. But serious work began on the reform only when Nicholas learned, in 1848, of the notorious case "concerning the debts and estates of Ivan Balashev." The Balashev case had been stalled in the courts for twenty years and had become impossible to settle or to disentangle. In November 1848, Nicholas declared, "The exposition of the reasons for the inordinate delay with which this well-known case has been processed has exhibited all the inefficiency and shortcomings of our system of procedure."[67] He asked Bludov to report on the changes needed in the system. In January 1849, Bludov presented his "basic principles" for reform, declaring that the system demanded "radical transformations."[68] Nicholas agreed and Bludov swiftly drafted his proposals. Approval was delayed only by the unalterable opposition of Count Panin.

The Bludov reform planned to introduce a limited adversary procedure for civil suits. It endeavored to bring Russian civil procedure closer to European patterns and restore the role of the parties, which had been reduced in the seventeenth and eighteenth centuries. The parties would confront each other but the courts would not be open to the public at large. They could be represented by attorneys who would be state officials. The parties and the attorneys would be responsible for presenting their own evidence and appealing their cases to higher instances; these tasks thus would be removed from the competence of the administrative authorities, and the police would no longer conduct investigations in civil cases. The courts would also be freed of their dependence on the police to enforce court verdicts, which would become the responsibility of a court marshal. The project shortened the periods allowed for defendants to answer a charge and appear in court. It also provided for an abbreviated order for lesser cases that could be mediated by justices of the peace. Administrative surveillance over trials and the practice of written proofs were maintained.[69]

Bludov approached the reform of criminal process with greater diffidence and less enthusiasm. Though work was under way in the late forties, these projects were not completed and submitted until 1861. Throughout the formulation of the criminal projects, Bludov insisted on consistently conservative premises. He did not think Russia was ready to abandon inquisitorial process in criminal trials.

> Despite all the advantages of the accusatorial system, and despite the fact that its principles were not alien to our people in the most distant times, this system is so different from our present one that its sudden introduction, without prior preparation, can easily lead us to clashes and confusion both among the people and in governmental institutions themselves instead of improvements of this branch, and move us away from our desired goal.[70]

In the civil reform, Bludov's principal concern was to further the interests of property by liberalizing the court system; in the criminal reform, it was to improve the system without endangering the interests of property. The abolition of the system of formal written proofs, he feared, would lead inevitably to the advent of the jury system, which, working outside of state tutelage, promised social breakdown and the subversion of the law.

> It is easy to imagine the effect of a jury court when the majority of our people still lack not only judicial, but even primary education, when the concepts of right and obligation are so undeveloped and unclear that the violation of another's rights, particularly infringement upon another's property, is considered by many the most ordinary matter; other crimes are considered daring, and criminals, mere unfortunates. Allowing such people to decide important, sometimes extremely difficult problems of the guilt or innocence of a defendant, threatens not only with inconvenience, but almost outright lawlessness.[71]

Bludov's reform approximated the procedural system common in central Europe in the early nineteenth century, where inquisitorial procedure was applied consistently only in criminal trials.[72] As a result, he proposed only minor changes in Russian criminal process. He wanted to tighten the system of central control over the courts, while introducing a few liberal modifications. Supervisory authority was to be returned to the Senate, and, as in the civil reform, the minister of justice was to lose his right to protest Senate decisions.[73] The courts would assume authority over the preliminary investigation, again limiting the authority of the police. Bludov considered this the most important part of his reform, and his proposals provided a new set of rules to guide the courts in their supervision of the investigations. The reform provided for state defenders for the accused, and in a gesture to the accusatorial system, introduced a hearing after the completion of the investigation, during which the accused could confront the judges accompanied by his defender and one relative. He then could present objections to the investigators' report and his own evidence. But oral testimony continued to be excluded and trials continued to be closed. The judge was still allowed to avoid reaching a decision about guilt, but now the old verdict, "remains under suspicion," was worded more discreetly—"acquitted by the court only due to lack of proofs."[74]

All of Bludov's projects maintained the absolutist reliance on regulation. He even proposed new rules for criminal procedure which, he thought, would enable judges "to find an adequate definition of the characteristics and weights of different kinds of proofs, and the conditions, greater or lesser, of their authenticity." He retained the faith that wisdom and good judgment were to be found in higher instances of the administration. The more backward a country, the more necessary written procedure and specific rules, which could prevent judges from erring.

> In Russia, laws, and particularly the rules of procedure must necessarily be detailed, so that our functionaries, who are in general poorly prepared in juridical science and many of whom are serving by election without the necessary experience in handling cases, can find in the laws a complete guide for their actions in any case awaiting trial or investigation.[75]

However Bludov wished to liberalize procedure, he could not conceive of a judiciary independent of the administrative hierarchy. In 1857, Minister of Interior Lanskoi, endeavoring to lighten the load of tasks burdening the governors, proposed to Bludov that they cease to be responsible for confirming all criminal sentences reached in their provinces. Lanskoi argued that the controls within the judicial administration were adequate to ensure the correctness and justice of the sentences. Bludov replied affirmatively to Lanskoi, but his reservations spoke otherwise. He thought the governor should continue to confirm decisions where the sentences of the provincial chambers would be "final"—the majority of cases in the system he was proposing.[76] He told Alexander,

> It would hardly be appropriate, and in a certain sense even safe, both politically and morally, to allow the dissemination

and the implanting of the idea that the governor, representing in the region entrusted to him the person of the Sovereign Emperor, should give up without contradiction, or at least be deprived of, the means to halt a criminal sentence, that is the punishment of a person who is innocent, in his opinion, according to more or less authentic information. Or to prevent the release of one who is not only stigmatized by public opinion, but also, perhaps, exposed as a criminal, but acquitted by a few special circumstances not recognized as such by the Criminal Chamber. Would this situation be consonant with the significance of one who should be bearing the title of master of the province and acting in the name of his Imperial Highness?[77]

Liberal historians, such as Dzhanshiev, have tried to make of Bludov an official sympathizer of radical transformation of the court system. But however "radical" the changes Bludov proposed might have been, the basic goal of reform and of Bludov's entire career and life ruled out the possibility of judiciary that would enjoy autonomy and dignity. For Bludov, the administrative authority of the autocracy remained the supreme consideration in any institutional reform, for it represented to him the only guarantee of order and security. This consideration was beyond judgment and discussion; it was a matter of a personal belief and trust. At the local level, it meant that the governor's authority had to remain supreme, for otherwise, the governor's police authority to preserve "the public order and tranquillity" would be undermined. Bludov's personal and political orientation made it impossible for him to tolerate a separation of police and judicial authority.[78]

Bludov also opposed innovations such as an independent bar and public trial, which might interfere with state supervision and direction of court proceedings. Alexander II agreed with him and, for a time, viewed Bludov's reform as reaching as far as change could go. He wrote in the margin of one of Bludov's reports of 1857, "I completely share your opinion that we are still not mature enough for the introduction of public justice and lawyers; that is why I do not wish this question to be raised in the State Council."[79]

If Bludov's reforms were aimed at maintaining the system of surveillance, they were equally uncompromising about retaining the second pillar of the old system—class justice. Adversary procedure in civil cases would allow noble judges to hear trials themselves and presumably liberate them from reliance on the secretaries. The new rules contained in the project, it was hoped, would attain that elusive clarity that would enable judges to make decisions without considerable advice from the staff. Bludov's low opinion of the clerks was emphatic and his reform was designed to banish them from the legal process. The chancelleries of the courts, he reported to Alexander in 1859, were "filled with men who have not received even primary education, and what is worse, is that they are immoral, belonging by origin as well as feeling to the lower layers of society."[80]

His reform maintained the system of elective noble judges, which was largely responsible for the low level of knowledge and experience in the courts — and the high property qualifications for electors that had been introduced in 1831. A university degree in the law was to become a requirement, and the salaries would be raised to attract university graduates.[81] But it is clear that Bludov expected his educated judges to come from the nobility. He fully sympathized with the policy of class restrictions on university matriculants and proposed even stricter limits on the number of non-noble students. In 1849, he was named chairman of a committee convened to consider means to exclude all commoners from the university. No member of the committee would support such measures; even such conservatives as Shirinskii-Shikhmatov and Panin argued against them. Bludov submitted the only proposals, which applied the principle of specialization according to class followed by Uvarov, but much more rigorously and consistently than before. His plan had not been acted upon when the new reign brought a reversal of educational policy.[82]

Bludov's reforms strove to bring men of wealth, intelligence, and sensibility into the legal system, and to end the humiliating domination of the clerks. By diminishing the role of the chancellery and excluding the police from the investigation, he endeavored to realize the Nicholaean vision of an autocracy run by educated and experienced members of the landed nobility, working to the autocracy's best interest. His projects appealed to Nicholas and Alexander, as well as to most high figures in the bureaucracy. Nicholas supported Bludov on the reform without reservation. Alexander patiently sat through Bludov's lengthy complaints about his health, then listened to his reports approvingly. At the beginning of Bludov's long summary report of 1859, he noted, "Have read with special interest and pleasure."[83] He assented to all of Bludov's recommendations and approved of all the projects he had submitted. In the State Council, the members of the combined Departments of Law and Civil Affairs began deliberating on the projects in late 1857, under Bludov's chairmanship. They echoed the views of the tsar and raised objections only to the minor points introduced as concessions to Panin. The members of the departments were similar to Bludov in both background and attitudes. None of the nine had received specialized training in the law. They were aristocrats whose chief qualifications for passing on the reforms were their general enlightenment, good taste, and experience in the highest ranks of government.[84]

But while Bludov was conducting agreeable discussions with the tsar, the reform was slipping from his control. Behind the scenes, the younger generation of bureaucrats, who were expert in the law and experienced in its administration, were directing criticisms at his projects. They pointed out that the organization of the reform, consisting of fourteen separate projects, made it all but unrealizable. They were unimpressed with the literary unity Bludov had imposed on the multitude of unrelated proposals. They decried the absence of a unifying scientific principle. The numerous rules he proposed promised to create a new set of formalities that would increase rather than decrease paper work—recalling his ill-starred Instruction to the Governors of 1837.[85] By the time the emancipation was completed and the time came for the consideration of court reform, Bludov's laborious efforts had been discredited. The court reform of 1864 would bear little resemblance to his projects.

In the late fifties and early sixties, Bludov was given numerous administrative assignments, which helped to distract him from the reform. He served as a member of the Chief Committee on the Peasant Question. He was chairman of the Jewish Committee and the Committee on Children's Shelters. In 1856, he was named president of the Academy of Sciences. In 1862, when he was removed as head of the Second Section, Alexander appointed him to the eminent, if largely honorary, position of the chairman of the State Council. In all his capacities, he subordinated himself to the emperor's designs and attempted neither to voice nor advance his own views.

He came to represent the humane and enlightened side of autocracy, a man who, untouched by the crass despotism of Nicholas's reign, remained committed to the values of civilization—a link between the high hopes of the reign of Alexander I and their realization in the reign of Alexander II. "Not only does he speak with intelligence," wrote Nikitenko, "but his conversation is always full of inspiration and sympathy for everything human, for art and for science." At his dinners, he continued to dazzle his guests with his charm and wit. He entertained them with recollections of his past. He dwelled on his early memories of the terrible tales of Pugachev. He recalled the coronation of Alexander I, when the prayers of the metropolitan had cured a deaf mute. A pious man, a friend of his mother's, had exclaimed, "Our faith must be cold and miserly if we need such surprising examples of miracle working." He liked to reminisce about the writers he knew, and to admire what he regarded as the greatest period in Russian literature. He talked of Karamzin and Zhukovskii, his old family circle, and recited verse he recalled from his youth.[86]

Death continued to preoccupy him. He spent much time preparing himself for its onset, the moment when the virtue of the dying man would glow as if a radiant ideal. In his will, written in 1852 when he was sixty-seven, he envisioned his death as bringing an end to a life perfect in its selfless trust in the tsar.

> In this solemn moment, when, as Derzhavin said, I stand at
> the doors of eternity, I think I may be allowed to bring a token

of reverent recognition to my Monarch, to his virtue, to the members of His Imperial House, for the favors which I have had right to only due to my infinite and selfless devotion to service, the weal of the Fatherland, the Glory of the throne.[87]

His testament adjured his children to follow his example, to serve the tsar with loyalty and zeal and "in service as in all the situations of life to act according to the dictates of duty and the pure promptings of conscience, setting aside all personal calculations and designs...."[88]

When he felt death approaching, in 1864, he conveyed the confidence that he had lived his life well. His devoted daughter Antonina left an account of his last hours, just as he had of Nicholas's. The morning of the day he died, he was still receiving state reports, and he spoke of state business a half-hour before his death. Just before death, his thoughts returned to his mother, and he asked to be buried with a golden cross she had given him in childhood. To the end he continued to pray for the tsar and Russia. "I am a sinful man before God, but I die loyal and innocent before You, my sovereign, and Russia. God bless You for your goodness, for your good intentions, for what You wish to do and what You have done for Russia. God bless You for all You have done and are doing for the people. And I will beg God for only one request—that he will vouchsafe me the permission to pray for You and for Russia eternally—*eternally*."[89]

He appeared as a figure in an icon, bringing his life as a sacramental offering to his ruler and God. The poet Tiutchev, a friend of his last years, commemorated his passing.

With last, quiet, steps,
He went to the window. The day was ending,
And with quiet rays, like paradise
It dawned and shone,
And he remembered the year of renewal,
The great day, day of the new testament,
And his face, from tenderness,
Lit up with the shadow of death.
Two images, cherished, kindred,
Which he carried in his heart, like holy relics,
Stood before him: Tsar and Russia
And from the soul he blessed them.
Then his head fell,
The last battle ended,
And the Savior himself released with love,
The obedient and faithful slave.

7
COUNT
VICTOR NIKITICH
PANIN

We do not understand many things not because our ideas are inadequate, but because those things do not enter into the sphere of our ideas.

Koz'ma Prutkov

AFTER THE DEATH OF THE ENERGETIC CHAIRMAN OF THE EDITING COMMISSION, General Ia. I Rostovtsev, at the beginning of 1860, the Russian public was appalled to learn that the emancipation of the serfs would be entrusted to the rigid, conservative minister of justice, Count Victor Nikitich Panin. "He has continually opposed all advances—intellectual, material, judicial, in general every kind," Nikitenko wrote in his diary. "He has come to be viewed as first in the realm of darkness, secrecy, illegality and other similar splendid things." Herzen ran a black border on the first page of *The Bell*, and invited the members of the commission to resign.[1] Constantine Pobedonostev, then serving under Panin as a chief-procurator in the Moscow departments of the Senate, described him as "the shining incarnation of the Nicolaean system," its "zenith, absurdity, madness."

> At the present moment one can say positively that on no single figure is the public hatred concentrated as on Count Panin: the hatred of the nobility, the hatred of the officials of all ministries and particularly of the Ministry of Justice: the hatred of those he persecutes, the hatred of those he protects, the hatred of all the people who have never seen him but have heard about him everywhere, the hatred of all those who, being close to him, have lost practically every feeling of their own worth.[2]

Victor Panin was a bleak and forbidding eminence. Austere and arrogant, he shunned signs of human feeling or sympathy. His appearance, too, repelled. Tall and stooped, with arms "as long as an orangutan's," he seemed both physically and spiritually distant from all those who surrounded him. The disdainful twist of his lips, ready, it seemed, always to break into a sneer, the aloof contempt of his eyes gave him a deathly spinsterish look. His head was too small for his body; his eyes peered out over his spectacles in a cold and dispiriting glare.[3] Valuev wrote of the "ungainly in appearance, spirit and actions, Count Panin."[4]

But the very absence of human qualities that alienated so many from Panin commended him to Tsar Alexander. If Panin lacked warmth, he also lacked other, more troublesome human features. He could be counted upon to execute Alexander's orders without question. Panin's concerns, Alexander remarked, consisted in the precise execution of his commands.[5] Panin, like few other aristocrats, could put himself above intrigue, and Alexander needed a rich aristocrat in the position of chairman to placate the circles of large landholders and neutralize their influence in government. He described Panin, in a letter to M. D. Gorchakov of 16 February 1860, as "an honest and devoted man, who I hope will be able to bring the job to its designated goal without paying attention to all the intrigues and vengeance, of which, unfortunately, there is no lack." A few days later, he wrote to his mother that Panin's appointment had aroused criticism, but that he was used to criticism and it did not disturb him. "Panin, despite his faults, is a loyal person, who understands me and will not deceive me."[6]

Alexander recognized in Panin a rare example of a wealthy aristocrat and serf owner who would put loyalty to his sovereign above personal inclinations. Panin appeared as a relic of tyranny to enlightened society, but to the monarch he represented something new — one of members of the nobility summoned by Nicholas, and heralded by Bulgarin, who could be counted upon to make the autocracy work. Gone was the ease and nonchalance of previous generations of high officials. Panin brought to his service a commitment to the enforcement of statute law. The precise application of the law was a personal and ethical imperative for him. His career represented an attempt of a high aristocrat to assume the role of legal official. That a monster emerged was in part due to the difficulty of assuming such a role, in part to the personal motivations that drove him to try.

Panin was an aberration among the members of his class. At the time of emancipation, he owned over twelve thousand souls located in six provinces. His income reached the sum of over 130,000 rubles yearly, all of which, it was said, he spent.[7] But his obsessive insistence on compliance with law and rule was more characteristic of members of the chancellery class or bureaucratic nobility than of aristocratic officials, who customarily occupied high posts as sinecures and considered technical formalities beneath them. His desire to comply and make others comply exceeded the usual response to the service imperative and became a form of enforced self-denial. Panin was driven to assume the new role by the affliction of his family's past, the burden of a legacy that was at once illustrious and suspect.

The Panin family had risen to prominence in the eighteenth century. Victor Nikitich's great-grandfather, Ivan Panin, had been a successful general in the armies of Peter the Great. Ivan's sons Peter and Nikita had distinguished themselves in the service and were rewarded with generous grants of land and serfs. Peter Ivanovich was a brilliant general. Nikita Ivanovich, after initial service in the guards, rose quickly in the diplomatic corps and joined the clique that helped Catherine seize power in 1762. At the beginning of her reign, he was the empress's most influential and respected advisor. He became the tutor of the tsarevich, Paul.

But the Panins were as arrogant and independent as they were gifted. Peter Ivanovich openly criticized Catherine, who turned against him, banished him to his Moscow estate, and described him as her "first enemy." She was forced to call upon him again, however, to help crush the forces of Pugachev. Nikita Ivanovich drafted his controversial plan to introduce greater legality and regularity into the work of government, and gathered around him writers and intellectuals devoted to the notion of law.

His close connection with the tsarevich made him especially suspect to Catherine.[8] Once the freewheeling spirit of the eighteenth century disappeared, such impudence became intolerable in high spheres, and the victim of this change was Peter Ivanovich's son, Victor Nikitich's father, Nikita Petrovich Panin.

Talented and ambitious, Nikita Petrovich Panin was forever dissatisfied with his lot. He began his service in the military, following his father's example, but yearned for a diplomatic career, and took a position in the College of Foreign Affairs. In 1795, he was assigned to negotiate the demarcation of the Third Partition of Poland with Prussia. In 1797, at the age of twenty-seven, he was appointed ambassador to Berlin. But he considered both positions beneath him. When Paul rejected his pro-English policy, he fell into disfavor, and like his uncle, Nikita Ivanovich, he became involved in a plot to oust the tsar. Nikita Petrovich was personally responsible for enlisting the support of the heir, Alexander Pavlovich, but his involvement did not win him Alexander's favor. The victim of the plot was a father not a husband, and Alexander nurtured a lingering distrust and resentment toward those whom he blamed for his father's death.[9]

Alexander respected Nikita Petrovich's integrity, intelligence, and diplomatic skills. In the first months of his reign, he entrusted him with direction of the foreign affairs of the empire, though he was only third in rank in the College of Foreign Affairs. The triumph was short-lived, however. Staunchly conservative in outlook, Nikita Petrovich agreed with few of Alexander's governmental reforms. His abrasive temperament offended all those he had to deal with. Contemporaries criticized his "dry, imperious character and little affability," his "pride and self-esteem," his unwelcoming, self-righteous manners. He tried to "govern all the ministry himself with no advice from any council or individuals." These were traits which would appear again, almost unchanged, in his son. But they might have been overlooked if he had been more circumspect in asserting his own opinion. Nikita Petrovich was not one to hold his tongue or heed the commands of others. "I regard it as my first duty," he wrote, "not to let myself be intimidated by the fear of displeasing, when it is a question of the glory of my master and the interests of the most sacred cause."[10]

Panin was removed just a half-year after his appointment, and his career came to an end at the age of thirty-one. In the following years, Alexander's suspicions about him grew, probably fed by Nikita Petrovich's critical remarks. In 1805 he was prohibited from entering Petersburg and Moscow, a ban that would remain in effect until his death in 1837. Except for occasional trips to Europe, he would spend the rest of his life on his Smolensk estate at Dugino. But never would he lose hope that his disgrace would be lifted. He plied the authorities, his friends, and his and his wife's (née Orlova) relatives with pleas to intervene on his behalf. He wrote long self-justifications against charges that he had opposed the tsar or advocated constitutional government. But nothing availed him. Even Nicholas's accession did not alter his fate.[11]

Embittered, Nikita Petrovich devoted himself instead to the beautification and organization of his estate. He laid out elaborate English gardens. He created in his estate administration a substitute for the hierarchy he had lost in service. He, like many other noblemen of his station who had spent their life in service, had little sense of his role as farmer. He fashioned the management of his estate on the model of discipline and organization he knew — the state administration — with himself as first in command, and vicariously enacted the drama of authority at Dugino. His detailed instructions created a formal division of responsibilities, hierarchically organized beneath him. His immediate subordinate was the hired estate "director" (*pravitel'*), whose role was "the execution of the orders of the landlord and the preservation of the prescribed order." The director had complete authority over the lower levels of the estate administration, though his subordinates could report his abuses to the landlord. Beneath the director was the head of the commune, the *burmistr,* appointed by Panin and approved by the commune assembly. Lesser officials included *starosty* and *starshiny,* each with a carefully defined area of competence. Panin's estate falls into the category that V. A. Aleksandrov describes as "subordination of the commune to the organs of estate authority." The commune was allowed to meet, but only under the eyes of Panin's representatives, and only to discuss the way to meet state obligations — the distribution of land and taxes — and to elect officials. As Victor Nikitich grew up, he would see his father bearing himself as a potentate on his estate and vesting his personal power with the accouterments of formal authority that existed elsewhere in Russia.[12]

The Panins sought solace for their disappointments in their children. In 1818, Sofia Panin wrote to her husband, "God is more just than are men. He will send you consolations. Those that he gives you in our children, aren't they capable of making amends for other pains?" She bore Nikita Petrovich ten children, but only five survived. The oldest son, Alexander, was a hero of the struggle against Napoleon and later became curator of the Kharkov educational district, but he was not a person of exceptional abilities. The family's hopes fell instead on the second son, Victor. Born in 1801, Victor Nikitich grew up with the consciousness that he was the survivor who would have to restore his family to its past grandeur. His childhood was spent in the shadow of his father's disgrace, and with the knowledge that it would be his destiny to live it down.[13]

The young Panin's intellectual gifts were frequently remarked upon and praised. A talented linguist, he early mastered Latin and Greek as well as

French and German. Educated at Dugino by the best tutors, he passed the examination administered at Moscow University to qualify candidates for the eighth rank in the service. He acquired a strong taste for German culture and style of life, thanks to the influence of an able German tutor. He conducted his correspondence with his family in French, but kept his personal diary in German and spoke German fluently. Later, he would marry the daughter of Senator Paul Tiesenhausen, a member of an old, though landless family of Baltic barons. In 1824, he attended a dinner with Goethe, and it was said that the poet was so impressed with the young Russian who spoke German fluently that he asked that Panin be introduced.[14] He took on a Prussian seriousness, a ponderousness and rigidity that contrasted with Bludov's flightiness and esprit. He would strike the pose of a Prussian junker in the Russian bureaucracy. Such features appealed to Tsar Nicholas.

Panin's progress in service exceeded even his father's expectations. His service record lists an unbroken series of successes. Following his father's example, he entered the Ministry of Foreign Affairs. In 1824, he became second secretary in the Madrid embassy, where he remained until 1826. In 1827, he received the court post of *Kammer-Junker*. A year later, he was assigned to the field chancellery of the College of Foreign Affairs when it accompanied the emperor at the siege of Varna. Nicholas favored those who were close to him on this campaign, and it was clear by the end of the Russo-Turkish War that Panin had been singled out for a distinguished career. He was designated counselor in the Athens embassy in 1829. In 1831, at the age of thirty, he was recalled from Greece to assume the office of state-secretary in the Department of Laws of the State Council and assistant minister of justice. In the first decade of Nicholas's reign, when many ministerial positions were held by aging bureaucrats, the assistant minister was often a powerful figure who played an important role in the ministry. In 1839, Panin was appointed acting minister of justice. In 1841, he was confirmed in the post.[15]

Panin's rise dazzled Petersburg society. One Petersburg lady wrote of his appointment as assistant minister,

> Let us talk about politics! And talk of Panin, for that is the politics of the moment. His nomination as assistant minister of justice must have astonished you my dear George as much as it has astonished everyone, starting with Panin himself. The step is gigantic, but it is consoling that its merit is appreciated. God give the young assistant the strength and the practical talents necessary to traverse the difficult career he has chosen.[16]

"[The public] has responded with especial praise about the Assistant Minister of Justice, Panin," the Third Section report of 1833 stated.

"During the Minister's absence he has merited general approval. His inexperience has been noted, but it is argued that with his intelligence and with the attention he pays to his work, even this failing will be eliminated." The Third Section expressed great satisfaction at Panin's appointment as acting minister in 1839 also. "The public likes the recent appointment of Count Panin and everyone hopes that his intelligence, youth and abilities will enable him to overcome the difficulties awaiting him."[17]

Nikita Petrovich's eyes followed Victor approvingly. He lived in his son. He described his joy at the news of Victor's trip through Europe. "When, in my thoughts, I accompany him on his voyage, I regain the strength to fight my grief." When Victor was appointed assistant minister, Nikita Petrovich wrote him,

> No one can know better than your father the gifts that it has pleased Divine Providence to bestow upon you so liberally and the means that Providence has given you to be useful to the Fatherland. Since I have learned of the indulgent goodness that your August Master honors you with, I could flatter myself that with such support you would one day restore our name to the heights to which your grandfather and great-uncle lifted it.[18]

But favored by providence and the tsar, Victor Nikitich never seemed to enjoy his good fortune. The grief of his family hung over him like a curse. His mother's early letters are filled with talk of *chagrin,* and Victor grew up with the feeling that he bore an irredeemable sin. His brother, Alexander, wrote to him on 28 March 1824, the day of his twenty-third birthday, "I congratulate you on your entry into the world today. Not because of the satisfaction that you can experience in enjoying life, for you have, although young, more than one tribulation to bear." Alexander added that he would not try to make condolences on his "latest sorrows," for he did not think that they would help. "I hope that they will begin to abate, that is all that I ask on this point, and also not to let your regrets degenerate into misanthropy."[19] Alexander Panin's words were prophetic. The nature of the *"derniers chagrins"* is unclear, but morose regrets would continue to haunt Victor Nikitich, and he would express resentment at the wrong done him with the sullen undiscriminating hostility of the misanthrope.

Panin went through life burdened by the sense that he had inherited a disgrace ordained for disobedience. Nikita Petrovich had learned the lesson that willfullness had brought his own downfall, and he made every effort to stress the imperative of obedience. A strong influence upon his son, he impressed upon him the obligation to be as little like his father as possible. Instead of irreverence, Victor Nikitich was to demonstrate total acceptance of the prevalent official viewpoint and order. Yet he too passed through a season of independence when he expressed himself critically about existing institutions. Like Bludov, his season was brought quickly to an end by a show of parental distress and consternation. His efforts to assert himself, like Bludov's, brought only feelings of guilt and renewed efforts to attain the parental goal. Panin's brother Alexander wrote in behalf of Nikita Petrovich, just as Kamenskaia had for Bludov's mother. A letter of 4 December 1824, when Victor Nikitich was serving in the Madrid embassy, indicates that Alexander had found his brother's ideas too liberal. "As for the ideas of our peers and people whom we love, they are good to follow to the extent to which they are in accord with our duty. . . . The more often I reread your letter the less can I conceive that Papa's ideology has made an impression on you, and it seems to have made an impression in a manner completely different than he intended." He then related an anecdote about Suvorov. The great general had been approached by a Prince Shcherbatov with a request for a leave for rest and leisure. Suvorov showed the prince an immense poster with the word *service* inscribed on top in huge letters, *friendship* written on the side in equally large letters, and Suvorov's name written in the corner, almost too small to be read.[20]

To fulfill his father's wish, Victor Nikitich had to prove himself completely devoid of his father's willfullness and even will. He would yield completely to the admonition placed in Suvorov's mouth, and view service as the complete denial of his own wishes, the unthinking acceptance of the imperatives of authority. The noble exploit of service was to be an exploit of subservience, a total abnegation of self. If Zhukovskii and Bludov tried to preserve a separate inner world where they could be noble and humane in the midst of their official obligations, Panin's assumption of obligations meant the submergence of his own noble manhood. The musings about love and death, the tension between the personal and political sphere were foreign to him. His personal aspirations and life were crushed by a Protestant sense of the worthlessness of individual life before the injunctions of the superordinate and everlasting.

"All that is earthly is fleeting, only the eternal remains," he underlined in a diary, printed in Germany, that he kept in the first months of 1840. Other religious commonplaces that he underlined commanded acceptance and obedience. "Go courageously and early to the goal to which God leads you." "Let what must be done always be holy to you. God wills it." ("God wills it" is underlined twice.) "Shun self-will, it is the source of sins." "Ask in the morning, What do I want to do. What should I do? What can I do?" ("What should I do?" is underlined twice.) "Where God places you, stand there with courage and trust." ("Stand there with courage and trust" is underlined twice.)[21]

His initial place of service, the College of Foreign Affairs, was the choice of his father. Shortly after he had assumed his post in Madrid in 1824, he wrote requesting permission to transfer to another branch of the service, probably the judicial. His brother responded angrily that such plans were inopportune. "He [father] wanted to change your mission and then you raise your price and dream of changing your career and you have the heart *to make yourself a clerk,* if I may express myself thus."[22] The letter was in French, but Alexander created a verb out of the root *pod"iachii,* clerk, and underlined it to emphasize his derision.

Victor Nikitich obeyed. But he continued to nurture hopes for a judicial career. In 1830, he requested his father's "eventual consent," to "change a diplomatic career for that of the bar [*barreau*]," according to the reply sent by Nikita Petrovich. The use of the word *bar* by Nikita Petrovich only indicates his distance from Russian realities, which he saw with European eyes. There was no bar in Russia at the time, and Victor Nikitich was scarcely intending to join the class of petty fixers who filled out papers and transferred bribes in the court. More likely, he hoped to obtain an appointment as chief-procurator in the Senate. But Nikita Petrovich withheld his assent, claiming that such a change would be justified only if Victor were intending to marry and live close to him in Moscow. He also thought that his son, when making such a request, could not possibly have known of "the benevolent intentions which the Emperor has deigned to express to your aunt."[23] In any case, Victor Nikitich had made it clear that he viewed his immediate task as obedience. "For the moment," he wrote his father, "I must think above all of fulfilling the duties that the confidence of my chiefs imposes upon me."[24]

In order to prove his subservience, Panin had to find the directives and norms that would show how to act and serve correctly. It was clear that the diplomatic corps was too lax to impose such directives. When serving in the Madrid embassy, Victor Nikitich had been so distressed by the lack of defined assignments that he had put himself on guard duty in the evenings and duly relieved himself of his post in the morning. The legal administration, which so repelled his brother, offered such directives. Nicholas I's conception of legal administration as a precise, unthinking, execution of written positive laws promised Panin the sure structure he needed for life. Specific laws and rules defined his obligations distinctly, rescuing him from the uncertainties of personal impulse. The *Digest of Laws* spelled out his duties briefly and conveniently. After his appointment as assistant minister, he withdrew to his estate to study its contents, and, it was said, learned two of the volumes nearly by heart.[25]

The service to statute law also provided him with a higher goal for his self-denial. In Panin there appeared a devotion, new among noble officials, to the law as an ethical imperative. The law for him was above personal whim. It demanded service and renunciation. Statute law represented the incarnation of authority, to be revered itself. Derzhavin had viewed laws subjectively as means to assert himself in the administration against what he saw as injustice. Panin regarded them as objective truths that showed him how to keep his place and ensure that he would always be in the right.

Panin accepted the existing system as the necessary precondition to the execution of the laws. He firmly believed in inquisitorial procedure, which he defended in a debate against Bludov soon after he became minister.[26] His memoranda of the 1840s stated the case for inquisitorial procedure on many grounds. Adversary procedures, he insisted, could be beneficial only in advanced countries where litigants were able to protect their own interests; if the population was uneducated, individuals could not be trusted to present their own cause. A more original argument referred to the great size of the empire, where distances were so large, the inquisitorial and written system of justice allowed litigants to carry on suits by mail. In this way, it clearly worked to the advantage of those landholders spending most of the year in St. Petersburg.[27] The inquisitorial system dispensed with the need for lawyers, who "try to bias the court, not by law, but by eloquence, and the case is decided not according to justice [*po pravde*], but according to the transports of the moment." But his chief reason was that the written procedure, central to the inquisitorial system, provided the "firm precision" [*tverdaia opredelitel'nost'*] Panin sought in the operations of government.[28]

Panin believed it possible to bring such precision to the haphazard operations of the Russian legal administration. In 1833, as assistant minister of justice, he proved the groundlessness of the conviction of forty-two Jews for ritual murder that had been upheld by a large majority of the Senate in the famous Velizh case. Panin thought such corrective role of high administrative authorities should become general. He sought to intensify the supervision of the courts through the hierarchy of procurators. Judges everywhere were making decisions contrary to or without reference to law, and courts were having their decisions executed without the requisite verification by procurators or *striapchie*. The role of the procurators in preliminary hearings should be extended, he argued, and they should be given greater responsibilities in checking on the legality of arrests. They should also supervise the keeping of court journals. To assist in the task of control, he proposed the establishment of a new office of "public secretary" (*obshchestvennyi sekretar'*), which would oversee the courts' clerical work.[29]

One of Panin's first tasks as minister was to deal with the disorders revealed in the St. Petersburg Aulic Court. In 1837, Nicholas, learning of the enormous backlog of cases in the court, had ordered the officials in both of the two departments of the court to complete all cases within two years, or continue working without salary until the backlog had been eliminated. He established two additional departments to receive new cases. But in 1840, it was clear that the backlog was hardly diminished, even though the officials' salaries had been terminated. The assistant minister, V. A. Sheremet'ev, discovered nearly one thousand unfinished cases and an incalculable number of unexecuted decisions. So lucrative were the payments from parties wishing their interests protected, especially creditors in bankruptcy cases, that the officials in the courts were prospering despite the loss of salary. Court records were in such disarray that all trace had been lost of one property assessed at 650,000 rubles, which turned up under sums belonging to "unknown persons." Nicholas was astonished. "Unheard of shame!—the carelessness of the responsible authorities is incredible, and in no way excusable. I am ashamed and aggrieved that such a disorder could exist almost before my eyes and yet remain unknown to me." He ordered Panin to take appropriate measures to correct the irregularities. Victor Nikitich immediately set out to improve the surveillance of the courts. He took charge of St. Petersburg province; Sheremet'ev of the nine central provinces. Under their direction, procurators and senators were sent out to investigate the size of the backlog in the courts.[30]

Panin became the conscientious agent of Nicholas's efforts to introduce heightened "accountability" in the administration. In the ministry's annual reports, he described his efforts to introduce rigorous surveillance of the courts. The report of 1842 asserted that the ministry was striving for "the preservation of the chancellery and service order, the verification of cases by personal reviews and the gathering of precise information and observation of the movement of cases by precise reports submitted to the Minister."[31] It referred to new rules the ministry was introducing to clarify procedures. The overriding concern of the ministry, the 1844 report indicated, was the completion of cases "with greater dispatch and correctness."[32] Dispatch was vital since it had been the court backlogs that had most distressed Nicholas. Panin made every effort to impress upon his subordinates the importance of reducing these backlogs. His reports of the late forties and early fifties claim that backlogs had been reduced in some courts and eliminated in others.

Embarking on his tasks, Panin appeared as an energetic young administrator determined to bring about compliance with the formal order of state. "One can expect much good from his diligent and vigorous management," Lebedev wrote in his diary after being appointed to a position in the ministry. "The Count is busy from morning till night, he spends all day working." He commented admiringly on Panin's "love for work, his wish to do everything, see everything, and know everything, himself."[33]

Panin's own diary of 1840 confirms Lebedev's impressions of his devotion to work. He threw himself into his obligations, leaving no time for himself. The concerns of state engrossed his life and left him no time for reading or cultural pursuits. The diary makes no distinctions between days of the week or night and day. Evenings and nights were spent attending official functions and toiling over state papers, sometimes as late as six in the morning. He suffered from hemorrhoidal pains, on occasion so severe that he had to put his work aside.[34]

But Panin's dedication could do little to correct the deficiencies of the system or the shortcomings of his subordinates. The investigations may have improved the situation in individual courts but, in the empire as a whole, the number of undecided cases continued to mount.[35] The numbers, moreover, concealed more than they told. The pressure to keep down the number of incomplete cases led to predictable subterfuges. Many officials shifted cases immediately to other instances, or decided cases summarily; others simply falsified their reports.

Like Bludov, Panin could cope with administration only when it was reduced to the order of the printed page. When the legal administration did not comply with his desires or when legal problems eluded his understanding, he created new sets of rules and procedures, and demanded increasingly frequent reports from the procurators. When he could not understand the issue on one case that caused several reversals of verdict in the Senate, he ordered a new kind of report into existence — a list of the cases before each Senate department, which the chief-secretary was to compile and forward to all other departments. The list would not describe the nature of the cases and had no visible purpose. Each secretary complied and compiled his own list, but no one read those sent from other departments.[36] Such reports from procurators and secretaries became so numerous that officials in the ministry could rarely check them, or even ascertain that all were submitted. The innovation resulted in a mounting burden of paper work for lesser officials, which further delayed the processing of cases.

Panin learned that he could not do everything himself. But he also learned that others did not respond precisely to his wishes. Lebedev's delight with his superior was not long-lasting. It came to an end when he noticed Panin becoming "dissatisfied" and "exacting." The change, he thought, occurred because "we are not able to fulfill his wishes, while an independent mind wants everything just right in his own opinion."[37] Panin's answer to his subordinates' failings was to issue rules, which he thought could bring their work in line with his demands.

But the rules Panin introduced were responses to individual infractions; he did not try to penetrate to the general principles involved in specific abuses. The proliferation of meaningless rules burdened and irritated the officials in the ministry. The memoirs about Panin are filled with anecdotes describing his passion for rules. When he learned that a deserter from the army had used false papers to obtain a post in the ministry, Panin ordered that all future candidates for positions had to present not only the usual certificate from their superior, but also a certificate attesting that the first certificate was genuine and that the candidate was actually the person mentioned in it. Needless to say, the rule was not observed. When a group of young officials overstayed their leaves abroad and were reported conducting themselves in a manner Panin thought unseemly, he ordered that no one be granted leaves who had served less than five years in the ministry. Later he lengthened the period to ten years. But the requirements for leaves had already been established by law.[38]

Panin tried to assume the role of civil servant and legal administrator. But law for him carried no inner rationale and brought no general understanding or order to administration. Rather it was a means to subdue refractory impulses, both his own and others'. Like most members of his class, he was accustomed to having things done for him and could find little order in himself. His desk was in continual disarray with papers flying about. Important documents would be lost in his office; one was found after several days behind the pillow of his chair.[39] In his eyes, the system had to work with a mechanical ineluctability that would bar human involvement and thus exclude error.

Above all he feared error, which carried with it the onus of failure and disgrace. Adherence to law spared him from responsibility for his acts, and enabled him to avoid questions of flagrant injustice. When cases of miscarriage of justice were appealed to him, he brushed them aside, claiming that articles 213 and 214 of the first volume of the *Digest of Laws* allowed him to review cases only when they reached him through the established order. He instructed the assistant minister to reply with firm rejections of all such appeals.[40] Actually, he had the right as procurator-general to combat illegality throughout the system, but to do so would have clashed with his conviction that justice was something which he served rather than promoted. He was equally hostile to pleas for intervention of the tsar. Such attitudes aroused the criticism of the Third Section, whose role was the assertion of the tsar's personal role throughout the system. By 1841, the secret police had also become disenchanted with the young count.

> Panin, in his pure soul, and not being completely acquainted with his new duty, cannot imagine to what extent ill-intentioned people, investing their harmful actions in legal form, can bring harm to quiet and good people. He looks upon his sacred office not completely from the right viewpoint. He does not combine moral convictions about the justice or injustice of

a case with the forms of law, and demands that only the latter
be observed in deciding cases.[41]

A year later, the condemnation had become more specific. "Count Panin is
excessively limiting the sphere of his obligations, claiming that they consist
only in the observation of forms and the literal execution of existing legal
statutes." If information came to him about the incorrect actions of a
judicial institution, he would do nothing until the case reached him by
established order. If a protest against an unjust decision reached him,
especially when it was a Senate decision, he would refuse to act "on the
strength of the decision already taken." If a document concealed clear
fraud, he would reply, "it is vested in legal form." "The Minister of
Justice," the report declared, "will not pay heed to moral convictions."

> The advantage of autocratic power consists precisely in the
> fact that the autocratic sovereign has the possibility of acting
> according to conscience and, in certain cases, is even obliged to
> put law aside and complete the case as a father decides a dis-
> pute among his children; for laws are a creation of the human
> mind, and they could not and cannot foresee all of the
> devices of the human heart.[42]

Unwilling to violate the system, Panin found himself, even more than
previous ministers of justice, at the mercy of those authorities of the state
who lacked such inhibitions. This well suited the autocrat's habits and preconceptions. Nicholas, for all his talk about the importance of the
administration of justice, still preferred to exert his own will when he saw
fit. He could cavalierly dismiss regular procedures when necessary, and
allowed his more trusted subordinates and institutions to do so. The Third
Section freely intervened in the working of the courts, even to the point of
ordering gendarmes to decide cases themselves.[43] The Ministry of Interior
also frequently took on judicial functions. The local police in St. Petersburg in the 1840s were ordered to settle all debt cases. Cases involving
important personalities were usually decided through the intervention of
the administrative authorities. When officials in the Ministry of Justice ran
afoul of the administrative authorities under the Ministry of Interior,
Panin assumed his own subordinates were at fault and sacrificed them.[44]
S. S. Lanskoi, when minister of interior, asked him facetiously, "What are
you doing Victor Nikitich with all your judging and bargaining? We will
still ride along in our usual manner." Moving the fingers of his right hand
over his left hand in the manner of a horse, he said with a good-natured
smile, "Look, look how we ride over your justice!"[45]

Panin's relationship to Nicholas had the same stiff and formal air to it.
His submission was total, but it was also cold and mechanical. He
subjected himself completely to Nicholas's approval. Even his marriage,

which took place in 1837, won Nicholas's benediction. "I am extremely happy with the fortunate choice of Count Panin," he declared. "And I wish him the greatest good fortune." Panin always made it clear that he assigned his own opinion no worth. He told Constantine Nikolaevich that when the tsar held views contrary to his, he considered it his duty to fulfill the tsar's will with "even greater energy than if governed by my own convictions." When a member of the Editing Commission refused to sign the final report because it conflicted with his personal views, Panin replied with surprise, "I have spent my life signing things of which I didn't approve."[46] But Panin's worship of his master had none of the personal sentiment for authority that filled Zhukovskii and Bludov. It was an expression of awe, an acquiescence before a force greater than himself. Authority appeared to him as a cold and distant eminence.

Nicholas, while appreciating Panin's subservience, hardly liked it and showed his contempt openly. He received reports from him only once a year, while the other ministers would report frequently. He awarded him few decorations and none in the last nine years of his reign. When asked why he had received so few decorations for a minister, Panin replied, "I do not ask for that. I serve Russia." Nicholas, it is said, exclaimed, "Then let Russia decorate him!" Panin attained the second rank — *deistvitel'nyi tainyi sovetnik* — which most ministers held, only after Nicholas's death.[47]

Panin expected the same conscientious and impersonal subservience from his subordinates, and ascribed the failures of the judicial system to its absence. "I particularly like officials who are modest, like you," he told one young official.[48] He believed that civil service obligations required a denial of personal impulses and a submission to the formal system of law. The word he used to express the official's denial of self and devotion to the system was trustworthiness (*blagonadezhnost'*), and his memoranda dwelled on the importance of this quality. Education and experience were useful insofar as they curbed ill-directed human impulse and inculcated trustworthiness, the signs of which were self-effacement and obedience to authority. It would be those qualities, rather than expertise or ethical standards, that would characterize the professional in his eyes. The distinguishing mark of a good judge was self-denial.

> To be a good judge qualities of mind and heart alone are in-sufficient. A deep awareness of calling is necessary, for the study of law and its practical application is achieved only by the work of many years and by the habit of submitting the prompt-ings of personal justice to the command of law.[49]

Panin used the investigations of the early forties to check on the responsibility of subordinates. Investigators had to submit separate reports on each official in a court.[50] Later in the forties, investigations were specifically directed at replacing erring personnel. In 1846, Nicholas became distressed at the large number of functionaries of the Ministry of Justice who had been tried or were standing trial. In response, Panin dispatched members of the Senate and the Consultation to the ministry's offices at every level. The instructions Panin prepared for the investigators reveal what he meant by "untrustworthiness." They were to seek evidence of abuses in examination of court records, then check on an official's service lists for indication of previous wrongdoing to determine whether he remained "under suspicion" of wrongdoing before a court. If he had been charged with a serious offense, such as extortion, embezzlement, riotous behavior, or unseemly acts, the investigator would undertake a secret inquiry about his moral character. Most important, Panin specified the signs of untrustworthiness the investigators were to seek. Foremost was the concealment of cases or excessive delay in reporting them. Other signs were failure to appear at work or to execute commands. Here too Panin confounded conscientiousness with honesty and loyalty.[51]

Panin appointed his most trusted assistant, the chief of the ministry's department, M. A. Topil'skii, to direct the investigation. In 1847, the first year of the investigations, 173 officials lost their positions.[52] Among them was Michael Dmitriev, then chief-procurator of the Seventh Department of the Senate in Moscow. Dmitriev had regarded his department as a model of procedural order and honesty. To his dismay, he saw the investigation turn into a criminal hearing, involving lengthy interrogations of his subordinates. The investigator sent from St. Petersburg was so menacing that one terrified official hung himself. A special commission, appointed to complete the investigation, found that a large number of cases had not been submitted to the department's archive, a cardinal violation of Panin's procedural order. Dmitriev replied that the Seventh Department of the Senate had processed more cases than any other Senate department, and wrote an angry memorandum in his own defense. But for Panin such defiance was only final confirmation of an official's untrustworthiness, and Dmitriev was dismissed.[53]

Yet for all the energy of his investigations, Panin held little hope that such measures could bring significant improvements in personnel. His appraisal of the human material at his disposal was too pessimistic to permit him to expect more reliable officials, and he was too fearful of sudden changes of any kind, which might only be for the worst. The first of his secret directives warned his investigators not to try to accomplish too much. "The removal from service of all those officials who in the strict sense cannot be considered trustworthy and fully equal to their designation would be extremely inexpedient and would bring the most harmful repercussions for service itself." His report of 1849, on the investigation of Minsk province, asserted that most officials would have to remain in their positions, despite the considerable disorder in the Civil Chamber, because "it will be hard to replace them with more trustworthy and experienced persons." Often when he became aware of an official's dishonesty he concealed it, fearful as he was that it might erupt into a scandal which could disturb the order and respect of his ministry. When a report reached him that one of his provincial procurators had been involved in a scheme to extort money from a Jew by means of a falsified accusation, he simply suppressed the material implicating the procurator.[54]

Panin's hope rather lay in the complete transformation of personnel in the ministry that was the goal of Nicholas's personnel policy. Improvement of the work in the ministry depended upon lifting the social status of those in the ministry. The members of the chancellery class who filled many of the ministry's posts lacked the necessary sense of dignity. They represented "a kind of clerkish rot and ignorance," who pursued their work "like a trade, for advantages to themselves, and because of this, they trade with their rights."[55]

But education was even more important than social origin for Panin. Like Nicholas, he believed that education developed an official's ability to obey. He thought judges should have a university education because "science, developing in these people a love for justice [*pravda*], serves as a guarantee that they will remain faithful to their duty of honor and their civil obligations in service as well."[56]

In the meetings of the Bludov committee of 1849, Panin opposed closing the universities to non-noble students and abolishing the advantages educated officials enjoyed in the service. The spread of education, he argued, had increased the number of officials capable of dispatching their offices, and what advances had been made had been the result of special privileges conferred upon them. "An uneducated official, with experience alone, cannot be truly useful," he claimed. "Graduates of the universities, in general, are distinguished in their service by thorough knowledge," and graduates of the gymnasiums also helped lift the level of administrative work. Rather than eliminate the rights accorded by education, he thought the government should require those who completed the university to remain in service nine years, and the gymnasiums, six years.[57]

Equipped with understanding of law and their obligation, the new officials, Panin believed, would be able to make the formal system he revered work. He conscientiously pursued Nicholas's policy of attracting educated young men to work in the ministry. He visited the School of Jurisprudence frequently and took an active interest in the pupils' progress. He liked to stop them in the hallways and make them do translations of Sallust and Livy. He took part in the final examinations each year. Then, after the graduates entered the ministry, he encouraged them with bonuses and rapid promotions. He assigned several officials in the ministry to check lists of graduating students of the juridical faculties of the universities for promising recruits.[58] He sent educated young officials to work in those provincial courts where flagrant abuses had been reported. As we have seen in chapter 3, he worked to consolidate control of the ministry over provincial chancellery appointments, in effect placing them under the authority of the Judicial Chambers.

Panin was most concerned to attract educated and talented officials to work in the ministry's Consultation, where the ministry's reports were formulated on cases pending before the Senate. Such reports might be heard in the State Council and be read by other ministers. They were composed by consultants and desk chiefs (*stolonachal'niki*) of the ministry. Panin examined reports carefully and completely rewrote those that displeased him. Officials who did good written work won his admiration and were rewarded with bonuses and promotions. Even when he rejected their conclusions, he made use of their analyses and information. He liked to chat with them and deport himself in their midst as a cultivated gentleman, the only familiarity he allowed himself with subordinates.[59]

Like Bludov, Panin had received a literary education and liked governmental problems to be couched clearly and elegantly. His own gifts in this respect were adjudged considerable. His arguments were eloquent, according to some observers, compelling. His language was beautiful; his voice sonorous; his knowledge wide. But his conclusions seemed frequently to be at odds with his arguments. "Count Panin speaks flowingly," Valuev remarked. "His organ is good but his synthetic abilities are weak."[60] "Rarely in his opinions does the end of his speech correspond to the beginning," M. N. Muraviev wrote.[61] In his reports of the early 1840s, his conclusions often contradicted his arguments, making it difficult to persuade even the more docile senators.[62]

Panin's determination to make his views prevail in the Senate and State Council led him to seek help to analyze and present legal questions logically. It was here that Sergei Zarudnyi's extraordinary abilities at lucid, logical exposition made him indispensable to Panin. Panin is said to have remarked, "If I had but once in my life reported a case as well as S. I. Zarudnyi, then my life would not have been lived in vain." By 1851, at the age of twenty-nine, Zarudnyi had been promoted from desk chief to consultant, and began directing the discussions on all cases coming into the Consultation.[63]

Panin's treatment of educated officials in administrative positions, however, was far less congenial. His conception of professional obligation in the dispensation of justice remained a narrow one. He regarded the legal specialist as one trained to follow the law and orders. The notions of dignity of the law or the legal profession did not enter his consideration.

The new officials were worthy of no more trust than the old, but, he thought, could be manipulated more easily. He saw legal specialization as a means to strengthen the exercise of authority.

As a result, Panin exercised his power more freely and despotically over the new officials than the old. He felt able to move them about from position to position at will to carry out his commands in different offices. He was convinced that, given a chance, human weakness and greed would reassert themselves, and this was most likely to happen far from the capital. Officials who held provincial posts for long periods developed "wide local connections, acquaintances, and other personal relations." They began to cater to the passions of "a few of the most powerful people." "They become impudent and insolent and will work only for money, so that the courts are unjust and run only for pay, to the advantage of whoever pays more." He suggested a maximum term of five years for members of district and provincial courts. "This will sever the ill-intentioned contacts, eliminate deceitful clerical work, and remove abuses, because, with the transfer of the officials, their illegal acts can be exposed."[64]

The five-year limit was not approved, but Panin found his own way to move his officials about. He would appoint them only in an acting capacity (*ispravliaiushchii del* or *v dolzhnost'*), and thus avoid the formality of Senate confirmation and the need to present reasons for transfers. Panin easily obtained Nicholas's approval to appoint procurators and assistant chairmen temporarily. But the position of chairman, which was elective, posed problems. Panin had consistently opposed the election of judges, holding it responsible for their low quality. Elected judges were also less subject to central influence and suasion. In a proposal to the State Council of 1843, he asked that he be given the right to appoint chairmen of courts in an acting capacity when he found the elected candidates unsuited to the position. He would then have a trial period "as a means for the decisive certification of the service capabilities and moral characteristics of the designated individuals." It would "open even greater possibilities to improve the composition of provincial government by filling it with people sufficiently tested in their trustworthiness." In his argument, he said little about trustworthiness, however, and, characteristically, dwelled instead on the relatively irrelevant question of the lack of qualifications of officials in other posts — procurators, assistant chairmen, district judges — to become chairmen. The State Council remained unconvinced. The Department of Laws pointed to the illogic of Panin's argument and concluded that it would accomplish little to announce to the population of a province that the government had doubts in the trustworthiness of its principal judge. The department pointed out that there were adequate measures for the removal of untrustworthy officials, and that the new measure was super-fluous. The majority of the State Council voted against the proposal, but Nicholas approved the minority opinion and it became law.[65]

Panin, it is clear, made use of his new authority. Before he took office, acting appointments to provincial judicial offices were made rarely. In 1850, over two-thirds of the assistant chairmen, and about half the procurators were on acting assignments. Through the rights conferred upon him by the tsar, he succeeded in appointing about half of the chairmen of Chambers as well. The practice also accelerated the general trend to shorter terms in provincial offices (see table 3.14). The chief victims were the educated personnel, who most often served in acting capacities.[66]

Panin's distrust of officials affected all ranks. He was as high-handed with senators as with assistant chairmen. In his effort to secure obedience, he would help to obliterate the distinction between positions of power and positions of work that had traditionally characterized the legal administration. All had to follow his orders. He treated senators as if they were ministerial functionaries. Early in his term, he entered into conflict with some of the most elderly and distinguished of the senators who had known him as a child and were reluctant to obey his directives.[67] Later, he was able to have senators appointed who were personally dependent upon him. At the beginning of each year, he would shift a number of senators to different departments without reason or explanation. A senator, who preferred to live in Petersburg for personal reasons and had experience in criminal justice, would find himself assigned to a civil department in Moscow.

Perhaps most offensive to the senators was Panin's practice of appointing ministerial officials rather than nonchalant young aristocrats to serve as chief-procurators and rule over them. Pobedonostev, himself one of the new breed of chief-procurators, considered this innovation an insult to the Senate. To the chief-procurators, Panin made it clear that he considered the Senate an inferior institution. "In an autocracy there can be only the authority of the sovereign," he told them. "And the Senate is not an authority." He had them present their reports on cases only a few hours before the deliberations in the department were to begin, thus making it difficult for the members to formulate their own opinions. When a department opposed the ministerial recommendation, he would summon the senators to his study and command them to comply.[68]

The chief-procurators were also instructed to keep closer observation over the Senate chancellery. They were to conduct a secret surveillance over their subordinates' personal lives as well as their work. Most chief-procurators also held their own positions on a temporary basis. In 1850, only three of ten had been confirmed in office, as compared with nine of thirteen in 1835. The average number of years they spent in office also fell.[69] Panin shifted officials in the offices of the ministry even more frequently. The desk chiefs, who were appointed from among the young graduates of the institutions of higher learning, had spent, in 1849, an average of only 1.6 years in their positions.[70]

But many of the young educated officials had entered the ministry with a new sense of dignity of the law, which, as we shall see in chapter 8, they had acquired in the course of their education. Whereas Panin regarded the law as an objective given, embedded in the published sources of law, they were beginning to look upon it as a subjective creation of the legal intellect, which required the active thought and participation of the individual official. They were oppressed by Panin's pedantic and mechanical formalism and his capricious rules, and became increasingly disenchanted with their work. As Panin realized that education did not produce compliance, he became increasingly bitter, arbitrary, and remote from the workings of the ministry.

They found the frequent and unpredictable reassignments especially demoralizing. The rapid changes of staff disrupted the operation of the courts. The official might not have time to establish local contacts, but at the same time, he could not acquaint himself with his work either. "He looks upon himself as a transient guest, and all his actions take on the character of temporary measures," one subordinate remarked. They were moved as often as eight times in ten years. In moves of less than one thousand kilometers, they had to bear their own expenses. Some preferred to live in hotels, prepared to leave for their next assignment.[71]

The threat of reassignment was especially discouraging to procurators, deterring them from clashing with provincial authorities. Panin disliked such disagreements, and those of his officials who entered into conflict with figures of higher ranks in other branches usually suffered. The procurator of Simbirsk province discovered that the governor had used funds intended for a hospital to build his own home. According to Flerovskii, who reported on the case, Panin believed the procurator to be in the right. But since the procurator had "entered into recriminations," Panin ordered him transferred to the distant town of Viatka.[72]

The young noble officials who began their service did not understand Panin's efforts and believed them a mad despotism. Deprived of security and satisfaction in their work, they sought transfers to other branches. But Panin remained unperturbed by their transfers. He did not believe in the dignity of the individual official and continued to treat personal wishes and interests as illegitimate, to be taken into account only so they could be frustrated. He remained deaf to pleas of sickness and family difficulties. He made few recommendations for decorations or bonuses. "Service is not an almshouse," he was wont to say.[73]

Panin's relationships with his immediate subordinates, the assistant minister and the director of the ministry's Department, could become especially difficult. He found, particularly in his first years, that the officials who held these posts would on occasion venture their own opinions and even contradict him. As he became more entrenched in his position, he replaced them with submissive men, devoid of individual character and will, who could not awaken his insecurity. His misanthropy, held in bounds initially, came out in the late 1840s and 1850s, his resentment at his own subservience being turned against those who did not appear to carry similar burdens.

The chief threat to him in his first years as minister was the office of assistant minister. Panin himself had been able to exercise considerable influence himself in that position, and was concerned lest the second-in-command show too much initiative. His first assistant minister, Sheremet'ev, was not confirmed in his position until 1843. Sheremet'ev was an able official, strict with his subordinates, but without extensive legal knowledge or defined views. He had the genteel education of the early nineteenth century, was deft in his manners and language. Panin disliked him and he was removed in 1847.[74]

Panin replaced Sheremet'ev with the mild-mannered and inoffensive P. D. Illichevskii. Illichevskii had been a protégé of Speranskii, and his career had been spent editing laws for publication until 1842, when he was appointed vice-director of the first Department of the Minister of State Domains.[75] He served as assistant minister conscientiously for eleven years, without leave. But he displayed little desire to exercise authority or to make his presence felt in the ministry. Panin assigned him trivial matters, which involved little more than shuffling papers. Illichevskii issued form directives to procurators, commanding them to finish cases as soon as possible. He responded to appeals with form answers, mostly rejections, prescribed by Panin. Every day he would be brought piles of papers which he would sign and dispatch unthinkingly without seeing Panin. He rarely attended the State Council or the Senate, and when he did, he sat mutely. He sank slowly into insignificance. Meshcherskii, who knew him in the mid-fifties, described him as "nothing in the full sense of the word." Embittered about the absence of work and recognition, he complained that he had been passed over in the awarding of decorations. The loneliness and monotony of his work began to affect his mind. He started to sign his name diagonally rather than horizontally, for the sake of variety. He once exclaimed, "A person whose mind is inert can go mad!" He died in office in 1858 with softening of the brain.[76]

The director of the ministry's Department, who was responsible for all the clerical and administrative work of the ministry, had to be an able and experienced official. Panin was careful about whom he chose for such a post, but he succeeded ultimately in finding a director who was to his taste as well. His first director, B. K. Danzas, was a competent bureaucrat with the broad knowledge conveyed at Tsarskoe Selo. Eager to gain acceptance in St. Petersburg society, Danzas, who owned no land, lacked the means to do so, and efforts led him to the verge of bankruptcy.[77] Danzas did not shrink from questioning Panin's views. Soon after he became acting minister, Panin found this habit of Danzas's disagreeable. "Danzas again wants to teach me a lesson about the nature of my duty," he wrote in his diary on 19 April 1840. Danzas soon learned to manipulate Panin, however. He defended the opposite position on a case to the one he actually held, knowing that Panin, on principle, would reject whatever opinion he recommended and approve the opposite.[78]

Danzas's successor, in 1845, was his bitter rival, M. M. Karniolin-Pinskii. Like Danzas, a nobleman who had risen through the Ministry of Justice, Karniolin-Pinskii was a polished man of the world. A fashionably dressed admirer of women, he was gifted in dissembling and intrigue. A graduate of the Petersburg Pedagogical Institute, he first taught in a gymnasium and was known for a serious interest in natural science and a love of flowers. Pinskii participated actively in the work of recruiting educated officials, and the quality of the ministry's personnel rose noticeably during his tenure. He too was skillful at influencing Panin, but he remained vulnerable during his tenure as director due to his involvement in a scandalous divorce suit, which was pending from 1845 to 1853, and, for much of this period, before the Senate. His wife, a beautiful and tempestuous woman, took revenge by engaging in a series of overt and notorious affairs and bearing several children to her lovers. She absolutely refused her consent to a divorce, and Pinskii was unable to locate her, since she would purchase the protection of local officials wherever she lived. The State Council finally ruled that she should be incarcerated in a monastery. Pinskii became a senator in 1851.[79]

Both Danzas and Pinskii were individuals who could advance views somewhat different from Panin's in the ministry. During the early forties, Panin also occasionally would receive lesser officials in the ministry and hear their opinions. But though he could be deceived in individual matters, Panin was not happy with directors who preserved a degree of independence and were not totally subservient. During the late forties, M. I. Topil'skii, who displayed all the characteristics that Panin sought in an official, began his rise. In 1845, Topil'skii was appointed vice-director of the Department and soon became a rival to Pinskii. In 1850, Panin appointed him director of the Department and, vanishing into his study, used him to run the ministry.[80]

Mikhail Ivanovich Topil'skii was the ideal of the Nicholaean noble bureaucrat. The owner of 240 male souls, he was educated at Moscow

University, where he received the degree of *kandidat* of law in 1830. Learned in classical literature and Russian antiquities, he was a friend and correspondent of the historian Pogodin and other professors at Moscow University. In the 1840s, he learned Swedish, translated a code of Swedish law, and wrote a book on the subject. But for all his learned achievements, Topil'skii saw his mission in life as obedience, and he distinguished himself above all as a conscientious executor of trivial formalities. The image of the gentleman clerk, he was a diligent and selfless worker, expert at managing the petty clerical details of the chancelleries. He began his career in the chancellery of the Moscow military governor-general. In 1835, at the age of twenty-six, he became head of the chancellery of the Tver governor; two years later, he assumed the same position under the military governor of Odessa. In 1840, he was appointed assistant heraldry master. In 1843, he took charge of Panin's chancellery in the ministry, a post he held along with his other responsibilities through the forties and fifties.[81]

But all of Topil'skii's previous experience was mere preparation to serve Count Panin. His father and grandfather had served under the Panins, and Topil'skii, despite his education, felt himself destined to continue his family's tradition. As head of Panin's chancellery, he became a personal retainer fulfilling household as well as ministerial duties. He did the shopping for the count, the countess, and even the children. He saw to the decoration, furnishing, and maintenance of Panin's mansion and apartment in the ministry.[82]

Topil'skii lived for the approval he could win from authority, and dreaded rejection from those with rank and title. At his audiences with Panin, he sat at the edge of his seat trembling, venturing no opinions, replying to everything, "Just so, Your Radiance."[83] When he left, he issued abrupt orders and raging threats, intimidating his subordinates as serfs. When Panin did not make it clear exactly what he wanted, as often was the case, Topil'skii would repeat the order in vague general terms, adding, "And as for how you are to do it, figure it out yourself." Often Panin commanded him to transmit his orders, as if they were from some unknown third person, though everyone realized that they could come only from the minister. Topil'skii then would become frightened and confused and give incomprehensible instructions. But deviation from the prescribed formalities or questioning of the approach taken brought threats of transfer or dismissal. "We don't need people. People need our positions," he would say. He would give terrifying descriptions of Panin's wrath, which he, possessing special access, could describe as he wished. Among the officials in the ministry, he was detested even more than Panin himself.[84]

But with all his strenuous self-abasement, Topil'skii could not please the phlegmatic count. Believing such obedience to be only fitting, Panin treated him as an underling, showering him with contempt. He slighted him openly in recommendations for bonuses and decorations. Among the officials who worked on the Editing Commission, only Topil'skii was not recommended for rewards by Panin, though he worked faithfully as Panin's intermediary and chief clerk.[85] Panin enjoyed subjecting him to special indignities, like forcing him to walk by his carriage, hat removed, while Panin rode wearing his hat. Pobedonostev described him as "an impersonal slave, devoid of rights." Short and squat, with thick gray sideburns, he wore large, round glasses and gave the appearance of a large beetle. Panin towered above him, and looked down upon him as an *untermensch*.[86]

In return, Topil'skii nurtured bitter feelings of resentment and hatred. He watched jealously from the side when Panin associated too closely with other officials, and seized every opportunity to vilify them before him. Once out of Panin's sight, he grumbled openly about him and depicted him in the most pejorative tones. Many of the vindictive personal anecdotes circulated about Panin had their origin in Topil'skii. His heavy work and apprehension about Panin's responses weighed on him. He suffered from severe headaches and would collapse on his bed in sudden fits of exhaustion.[87]

In the 1850s, with Topil'skii as factotum, Panin turned his ministry into a replica of his Dugino estate. The image of Victor Panin, the noble bureaucrat, faded, and there appeared Victor Panin, the potentate of the estate. The strict regulations he issued through his director governed the work of his subordinates. Again, a formal structure was invoked to enhance personal authority and systematize discipline. In the course of the fifties, as he withdrew increasingly from the ministry and left its operations to Topil'skii, his noble personality began to reassert itself. He began to think of himself in the more traditional roles of the nobleman, like those of his father and ancestors. He dreamed of becoming foreign minister, and spent hours reading about diplomatic affairs in Russian and European newspapers. He longed to return to the military. When the Crimean War began, he imagined himself a general, and sat over maps while planning the strategy to drive the enemy from the Crimea. He took it upon himself to inspect the Kronstadt fortifications. He did this without authorization and received an angry rebuke from Tsar Nicholas.[88]

Meanwhile, in the midst of Panin's draconian formalism, the traditional, informal system of favors and bribery continued to function and the pressures of power and wealth continued to influence the dispensation of justice. Panin himself had to bribe an official in his ministry one hundred rubles to have a document completed certifying his daughter's dowry. In his first years as minister, he tried to resist the intervention of powerful figures in the determination of legal cases. But soon, cherishing his position, he learned to please those close to the tsar and do their bidding. His severity then was reserved for those not under the highest protection.[89] While it is difficult to assess the actual effect of his bureaucratic controls on the informal system, they did appear to make corruption more difficult and time-consuming, and to increase the cost of influencing decisions. The working of the judicial administration against such aristocrats as Sukhovo-Kobylin irritated the wealthy nobility and increased their dissatisfaction with the institutions of absolutist justice.

To the end, Panin remained unsure of his grip on his ministry. In his isolation, he sensed that power might slip into the hands of those whose moral promptings were not to his liking. The threat of willfullness, independence, criticism, rebellion, lurked everywhere. His insecurity was even more encompassing than Nicholas's; it could be awakened by the slightest modification of disciplinary order, a perfunctory gesture of an official, an objection to a decision made on the basis of influence. But the single most disturbing threat was the work on reform proceeding in Bludov's Second Section. Bludov's efforts enjoyed Nicholas's backing. Panin could obstruct them, but could not hope to bring them to a halt.

Panin tried to remain aloof from the work on reform, claiming it was not his task to formulate projects. "The Minister of Justice does not compose legislation and does not participate in the original drafting of plans on these matters," he replied to criticism in 1858.[90] His abstention, however, was by choice, and not in obedience to the law, since ministers possessed the right of legislative initiative. His view of the primacy of the executive function expressed his attachment to current practice, which was couched in the rhetoric of official nationality theory. Existing institutions had grown naturally from the national experience, he claimed, and therefore were suited to peculiar national needs. The administrative apparatus was the fruit of historical experience and improvements could come only through the awareness of those involved in the daily practice of adminis-tration. The system, in this way, became its own measure, and foreign ideas, divorced as they were from the needs of the population, were apt to be irrelevant or destructive. Thus Panin, closeted in his study, became the spokesman of practical experience. He agreed with Bludov on the need for reform and for "radical transformation," but in terms that deprived these words of meaning. He wrote in a memorandum of 1849,

> We must eliminate all that hinders or slows the course of cases. Shearing off, so to say, useless forms, we must preserve those procedures which are sanctified by time and the promptings of practice — that sure and unerring guide in the work of legis-lation — which are recognized as useful and necessary for the discussion of a case as fully as necessary.[91]

Consequently, in his work on reform, Panin contended that he had tried to "harmonize the new system with the type of administration [*obraz upravleniia*], the needs, customs and level of education of civil society." The needs and the situation of the state, the practice of the administration, however, meant little more than "the laws of the fatherland," which, together with "the rules taught by theory," would serve as the basis for the reform. "Avoiding as much as possible all principles alien to our legislation, I contend that only when dictated by extreme necessity should we turn to the assistance of foreign laws, and only when procedures, by their apparent inexpedience, and the abuses they bring about or assist, demand radical change." [92]

Without rejecting the Bludov projects in principle, Panin objected to so many petty details that he was able to arrest the progress of court reform effectively. The Bludov proposals, which took a dim view of current administrative practice, could be faulted easily for their lack of respect for existing procedures. Panin followed a similar pattern in each of his objections. He would present a lengthy historical discussion of a procedure, showing how it was an intrinsic part of the nation's institutional developments. He would review existing legislation, then point out its inadequacies. Finally, he would emphasize the backwardness of the Russian population and the protection the traditional procedures afforded, concluding in most cases that change promised no good. Thus, he objected to the adversary system because the population was not sufficiently educated to look after its own interests. They were also too backward to cope with the new public defenders, which Bludov was hoping to introduce. Such defenders would abuse the trust placed in them and, out of self-seeking motives, urge the population to start unproved or invented suits. Bludov had proposed establishing new forms for applications submitted to the courts. Panin argued that the existing form, which had been in effect since the time of Peter the Great, should not be changed. He warned that with the backwardness of the population, and the many languages found in the empire, that the requirements that Bludov set forth for clarity and coherence of applications could not bring beneficial results. "Any requirement concerning the correct and clear presentation of applications would at the present time be more than troublesome by its inopportuneness." [93]

Most threatening was Bludov's intention to abolish the authority of chief-procurators to protest senatorial decisions and refer cases to the State Council. Bludov pointed out that the practice merely created an excuse to add instances in the consideration of a case and prolonged the judicial process. Panin saw Bludov's proposal as an attack on the point of his strongest influence on the judgment of cases. He defended the chief-procurators' power as the only means to enforce adherence to legality in the system. The inadequacies in the laws and the shortcomings of the judges gave rise to many contradictory verdicts, he claimed, and the chief-procurators were responsible for whatever unity could be found in senatorial decisions. Since Russian judges were so incompetent, the weakening of the procurators' influence meant the renunciation of all legal authority; it would "subvert the entire system of our present court organization."[94]

By 1852, Panin's objections brought work on the civil reform to an impasse, and a special committee was instituted to reconcile the differences between "theory" and "practice." Bludov chaired the committee; Illichevskii represented the views of Panin; Zarudnyi served as chief of clerical work. By 1854, compromises had been reached on all but one of the points of contention, but the war and the death of Nicholas prevented further consideration of the reform. The final project was not submitted to the State Council until 1857, and by then it had become outdated.[95] The two sides of Nicholas's policy had thus neutralized each other. Bludov, the theoretician, who had tried to take account of practice, had been too remote from those experienced in the administrative work, and could not speak for them. Panin, the spokesman of practice, knew that the principles proposed would not alter, but undermine irreparably the old system. Panin's views in this way coincided with the reformers; both agreed that a choice rather than a compromise had to be made between two contradictory systems of dispensing justice, and Panin did the reformers the unwitting service of forestalling Bludov's halfway measures.

After the Crimean War, the increasingly open discussion of judicial reform made Panin uneasy. Most disturbing, the leaders of talk of reform included many of those educated officials who had left his ministry. He had begun to become wary of educated officials in the late forties, when, after the revolutions in Europe, university graduates first awakened his suspicion. By the mid-fifties, he had become disenchanted with the *pravovedy* as well, who were showing increasing signs of dissatisfaction and proving difficult to inure to the ministry's routine.[96] He came to the conclusion that education did not in fact inculcate trustworthiness in officials. In 1858, he wrote in reply to criticism from Prince Dmitrii Obolenskii—a *pravoved* serving in the Naval Ministry—"In our time science unfortunately does not have the goals only of acquiring and disseminating knowledge. It strives for the acquisition of power and honor, for the triumph of new theories and for the enslavement of all who possess something by inheritance rather than personal merit. "*'Derrière chaque idée,'* one contemporary democratic writer has said, *'il y a une ambition.'*"[97]

During the preparation of the serf reform, Panin found himself presiding over the very changes he deplored. Alexander treated him as an elder statesman, according him the attention and respect he had never received from Nicholas. But obedience now was in the service of change. Though he remained minister of justice until 1862, effective control of the ministry passed into the hands of the new assistant minister, Dmitrii Zamiatnin, a sympathizer with reform. Panin served on the Chief Committee on the Peasant Question, and the special commission under it that reviewed projects submitted by the landlords. As chairman of the Editing Commission, he showed himself capable of the ultimate devotion to his sovereign, participating in a transformation that was both offensive and incomprehensible to him.

He became the most important spokesman of caution and repression in the administration. He interpreted the vaguest liberal sentiment in the press as a menace to the whole structure in which he had found security and recognition. A memorandum of his to the tsar, concerning an article on public courts in the September 1857 issue of *Russkii Vestnik,* led to a prohibition of further discussion of such questions in the press.[98] In the Council of Ministers, he spoke for the strictest possible curbs on the press. He deplored the influence of publications abroad, which had given rise to a "ferment of minds," which was "appearing everywhere as a new form of salvation or desire for radical transformation of the entire state structure and social life." "One must only recall the state of mind in Russia from 1820 to 1824," he concluded, "to suggest what fruits may come from this ferment." He called upon the government to close all organs that attacked the monarchical form of the government, that ridiculed the "public faults," or that raised questions of fundamental changes suitable for discussion only at the highest echelons of the administration.[99]

He remained to the end a bitter foe of liberal opinion and proved useful whenever Alexander had to deal with oppositional tendencies. In 1862, he was assigned to direct the arrest of the thirteen Tver peace mediators who had called for obligatory redemption of land and a representative assembly. Panin's voice seems to have been decisive in convincing Alexander to punish them.[100] After Karakazov's attempt on the life of the tsar in 1866, he rallied conservative forces in the bureaucracy with talk of a revolutionary threat, and supported harsh repressive measures. He continued to live in his own self-contained world, protected by trustworthiness from the confusing thoughts and phenomena of the new era. His eyesight began to fail, increasing his isolation. On his daily stroll along Nevskii *prospekt,* he presented a strange sight. Staring forward, he recognized few; his expression and glaring stare remained fixed. He acknowledged greetings briefly, then resumed his stiff gait and air of abstraction.[101]

After the emancipation, his poor health and eyesight limited his work in government, and he spent much of his time traveling abroad. In 1864, he was appointed head of the Second Section, where he succeeded in defeating the effort of his predecessor, Baron Modest Korf, to extend the Second Section's legislative responsibilities. He resigned in 1867, but held his seat in the State Council until 1872. In 1869, upon his jubilee in the service, he received a diamond-studded portrait of the tsar from Alexander himself. Topil'skii, who in the meantime had become a senator, continued to run his errands. Topil'skii died in 1873, Panin a few months later in 1874.[102]

A solitary, bookish man, Victor Panin preferred his study to the company of others. Those who knew him considered him educated and well read. One subordinate even thought that his statue should be placed beside those of Plato and Aristotle on the facade of the imperial public library. He owned a large library of historical books, most of them purchased from Count Lobanov-Rostovskii. He was a member of learned societies. In his youth he had belonged to the Free Economic Society. Later he became a member of the Imperial Geographical Society and an honorary member of the Imperial Archive Society and the Imperial Society of History and Russian Antiquities at Moscow University. It was in the *Readings* of the Historical Society that Panin's only published work appeared: a chronicle about the pretendress Tarakanova, who at the time of the Pugachev uprising declared herself the lost daughter of Empress Elizabeth Petrovna. She was caught and died in prison, ostensibly of illness, while still under interrogation. Panin, the title page indicated, "communicated" the work to the society. Bludov's service record, however, lists it among the papers left at his death, which Panin received for disposition. The authors were two Second Section officials, Brevern and Popov.[103]

But though not his own work, the chronicle must have been most appealing to the aging count. It dwelled on the culprit's dishonesty and incorrigible unwillingness to confess, despite conclusive evidence of guilt. Prince A. M. Golitsyn, the St. Petersburg governor-general who directed the interrogation, despaired. "From the testimony of the prisoner," the prince had informed Catherine, "the only thing that is clear is that she is shameless, unconscionable, deceitful and evil in the extreme." All his efforts to exact a confession were in vain. His angry words to the empress could have been written by Victor Nikitich himself:

> Nothing has had an effect upon her: exhortation, strictness, deprivation of food, clothing and other necessities of life, separation from her servant, the continual presence of guards in her chambers. However, perhaps in time these measures will be able to reduce her to confession, since the complete loss of hope of liberation, will not, in all probability, remain without effect.[104]

8
THE EMERGENCE
OF A LEGAL ETHOS

A specialist is like a swollen cheek; his fullness is one-sided.

Koz'ma Prutkov

THE YOUNG RECRUITS TO THE MINISTRY OF JUSTICE REPRESENTED A NEW FORCE in the Russian administration. Middle and lesser noblemen, they came from groups of their class that had traditionally risen through military service. They differed from previous generations of high judicial officials in their social origins, career patterns, and education. As a result they would share the attitudes neither of the elite, who had dominated the system, nor the clerks who had risen painstakingly through the administrative hierarchy.

Their new, civil role also set them apart from the traditions of their forebears, who had served in the military. Filial attachments provided little continuity, since most of them grew up apart from their fathers, and felt remote from their values. The new recruits to the ministry thus felt themselves cut off from institutional, social, and familial traditions. They would seek their guiding ethos in their education and the ideas imparted by their teachers and their reading.

Many of them would find their self-definition in a new conception of the importance of law. They began to conceive of the dispensation of justice as a calling rather than a duty connected with their service obligation. They began to look upon the law as a natural expression of their personalities, and not as a pronouncement of a higher reason demanding self-denial. They began to see themselves as servants of the law, and looked to their work in service for the realization of their own aspirations as noblemen. But once convinced of the integrity of serving the law, they found it difficult to accept a judicial system that demanded the subservience of legal expertise. Feeling the difference between themselves and the other groups in the administration, they began to sense their own special mission and to display the particular "moral identity" that characterizes professional groups.[1]

The older officials recognized and openly deplored the different character of the recruits to the ministry. They had accepted the existing system as a given, adopting rationales of resignation that enabled them to accept what they encountered in the administration. Two of them, Michael Dmitriev and Kastor Lebedev left accounts of their feelings. Though of different generations, social backgrounds, and tastes, both Dmitriev and Lebedev remained attached to the old ways, and the appearance of impudent young officials with unprecedented privileges threatened their rationales and aroused their envy and animosity.

Michael Dmitriev, a poet and nephew of the minister of justice, served as chief-procurator in the Seventh Department of the Senate during the early and mid-1840s. Dmitriev viewed himself as conscientious and dedicated to the law. But he did not think of himself primarily as a legal official, for he believed the administration of the law to be beneath his noble background. From an old noble family, he had inherited about three hundred souls, and liked to style himself an aristocrat with a distinguished family tradition. But he could not remember his father, who had died when he was two years old. Though he took pride in the military exploits of his ancestors, he drew his own guides to life from the sentimentalist literary education he received at the Pension of Moscow University and at the university itself.

At the pension and the university, he learned to appreciate taste and refinement as the supreme noble virtues. His idols became the distinguished graduates of the pension — Dashkov, Alexander Turgenev, the Kaisarovs, and Zhukovskii.[2] Like them, he had participated in a "society of friendship," where he and his friends had discussed their literary works and interests. In his memoirs, Dmitriev made it clear that such pursuits were not merely pleasant diversions. The circle, he claimed, bred in the youths "the notions of morality, friendship, purity of heart and modesty."[3] The broad literary education he received at Moscow University, he thought, befit Russian officials, who might be assigned to any sphere of government. Specialized education, he claimed, did not produce the same refinement and breadth of knowledge.

Dmitriev received his first contact with Russian law in Sandunov's practical courses at the university. But he regarded law as a minor part of his education, and subordinate to his aesthetic pursuits. He also kept in mind that knowledge could be no common denominator among men. He had to rub shoulders with non-nobles in Sandunov's class, but always remained aware that they were beneath him, destined as they were to be clerks or *striapchie*. The commoners liked him, he thought, but he was sure to speak to them as one spoke to chancellery workers. Most of them did not avail themselves of the broader, general education courses and left the university as they had entered, as "*pod"iachie* and blockheads [*bolvany*]."[4]

After leaving the university, Dmitriev followed the path of other aristocratic chief-procurators. He began service in the Moscow Archive of the Ministry of Foreign Affairs, where he undertook light translation assignments. The work suited him, since he was mainly concerned with writing verse and criticism. He then served on special assignments under the Moscow governor-general, D. V. Golitsyn. Golitsyn was endeavoring to improve the courts in Moscow province and fill them with educated individuals from good families. Dmitriev served on the Criminal Committee, which made recommendations to Golitsyn on cases before the courts. When the committee disagreed with a court, Golitsyn simply sent his secretary to have it reverse its decision.[5]

Dmitriev enjoyed the company he was working with in Moscow, "a comradeship of enlightened and well-bred individuals." But the Decembrist revolution upset these easy-going relationships. Several members of

Golitsyn's coterie had associated with the rebels and were implicated. Then Nicholas placed a limit on the "officials on special assignments" (*chinovnik osobennykh poruchenii*), whom governors had used to assemble amiable and loyal coteries in their service. He also limited the awarding of bonuses. There followed tighter controls from the center, and an increase in the number of reports. Then the authority of the political police, his new Third Section, grew and the gendarmes began to intervene in the work of the administration and to supervise private morality. Dmitriev was also offended by the crude bluntness of the new tsar's policies. He resented the way Nicholas asked for quick decisions of criminal cases in order to empty the jails of prisoners long awaiting trial.[6]

But Dmitriev remained in the legal administration. He served as counselor in the Moscow Criminal Chamber, then at the chief-procurator's desk and as chief-procurator in the Senate. He took his tasks seriously, he claimed, reading the briefs written by the secretaries carefully. Yet the work of the legal officials remained unworthy in his eyes; it was something beneath him. The judiciary was a residue of the backwardness of society and did not represent a dignified pursuit.

> If there were no contemptible greed and unrighteous claims, there would be no disputes and suits. If there were no corruption and evil, there would be no criminal courts. We are judges only because it is necessary, because there are inveterate litigants and malefactors! We judges imagine ourselves very important, but we only sweep up the filth of mankind, rummage in the darkness of human souls, and gropingly seek the traces of justice in the murk of falsehood and vice.[7]

Dmitriev's sentimentalist ethos allowed him to serve in the legal administration without feeling defiled. His real dedication was to the world of art, which lifted the individual out of the real world. In his poetry, Dmitriev extolled the glory of the past and contrasted it to the dreary, sordid present. When asked why he sings only of past battles, Dmitriev's blind poet replies:

> *Because the present era,*
> *Wants money, drink and food,*
> *It persecutes the ideal world,*
> *And poetry and honor!*

There was no one to glorify the dying soldier.

> *In the era of greed there is no love,*
> *And no lofty songs.*[8]

During the 1840s, while working in the ministry, he continued to write poetry and contributed numerous philosophical articles in a mystical

Shellingian vein to the journals. He created his own "philosophical system of religion," which conjoined humanity with the deity in the realm of the sublime.[9] He also wrote literary criticism that condemned the tendency of realism among recent writers. The task of the artist, he emphasized, was to depict the sublime, "to elevate everything particular and parochial to the plane of the universal."[10]

Dmitriev maintained his squeamish distaste for his work. He saw the system as corrupt and ineffective. But he believed, like other aristocrats in the administration, that the fault lay not with the institutions, but with the moral quality of the individuals who staffed them. The deficiencies of criminal courts stemmed not from the laws or the system of legal procedure, but from the character of the policemen who conducted the investigation, from the "ignorance of their ideas, the crudeness of feeling."[11] Dmitriev shared Karamzin's faith in the nobility. Only the old nobility had models of virtue to look up to and to praise:

> *Pity the family with no example,*
> *Honorable is the clan with its own ancestors,*
> *Where there is a national faith,*
> *There is also a national honor!*[12]

The first graduates of the School of Jurisprudence appeared in the Ministry of Justice in the early 1840s, and Dmitriev immediately became more fond of the old clerks. The *pravovedy* embodied for him all the defects of specialization. They lacked, he claimed, the cultivation and sensitivity conferred by a general education. They were "lazy and proud schoolboys who were incapable of composing a report, but danced magnificently and sang vaudeville ditties." They regarded their posts as sinecures and were forever groaning about being persecuted. Worst of all, Dmitriev was convinced that the *pravovedy* in his department were informing on him to Panin. When the investigations of 1847 produced evidence of large-scale backlogs and irregularities in his department, he was convinced that it was the work of the *pravovedy*. Rather than behaving as gentlemen, they were reporting on his office to their chiefs in St. Petersburg.[13]

One of the officials sent from Petersburg to investigate the Moscow departments of the Senate was Kastor Nikiforovich Lebedev. Lebedev, who became a Moscow chief-procurator after Dmitriev's dismissal, was appalled at the disorder in chancelleries of the Moscow departments.[14] The nemesis of Sukhovo-Kobylin, Lebedev had little patience with aristocratic carelessness. His father, who died when he was a boy, had been a teacher. Lebedev spent his life in straitened circumstances and felt little respect for the honor that Dmitriev so esteemed. Nor did he feel able to retreat into the world of the sublime to shield himself from the realities of legal service. He had to accept the system as the true source of justice in Russia.

Lebedev was a transitional figure. He had a commitment to the enforcement of the law that Dmitriev lacked. But he had none of the respect for that commitment that underlies a sense of professional dignity. A graduate of Moscow University in the early thirties, he too received a predominantly literary training. Moscow University was his initiation into life. As a child he had lived in penury, kept alive only by the efforts of his mother. "Until 1828, all my past was so bad, so empty, so senseless that it would have been better had it never happened. In Moscow I first learned about the condition of the citizen, the demands of society, the dignity of man." At Moscow University he was a literary figure of note.[15] His satires were widely read, especially his *Tsar Bean,* on the disputes between Podogin and Kachenovskii about Russian history. He also wrote dramas commissioned by members of the aristocracy.[16]

But need forced Lebedev to abandon Moscow intellectual life, with its mode of sensitive expression and dreams of love, to enter service in the St. Petersburg administration. He accepted the bureaucratic order as sacrosanct and worked hard to try to ensure proper enforcement of the law. Filled with romantic feelings derived from his reading, he did not have the sentimentalist nonchalance that could enable him to create a distance between himself and his service experience. Acutely aware of the demands of the administration, he realized that they left little room for personal feeling or literary imagination.[17] In his first assignment in the War Ministry, he found that reducing a case to bureaucratic forms caused him great pain. He could not rid himself of the emotional sense of what he had read.

> The hardest thing was tone. I would lose my way, and, thinking of a case as a person, a state matter as a private one, allowed myself to imagine a person, with feelings, a heart able to become angry and participate in a case, as if in a private matter.... I thought I was doing business with people and ideas. I did not at all believe in things and forms.[18]

He felt service in St. Petersburg was killing his feelings. "I am leading a vegetable life. I serve, eat, relax and sleep. On the other hand there is nothing that I am good for."[19] His feelings gave way to necessity. His ideas cooled and he found himself betraying his gods, Shelling and Herder. He dreamt of writing a book of history, or a novel.[20]

The legal administration appeared to offer Lebedev the possibility of advancing justice by enforcing the administrative regulations he regarded as necessary. Like Panin, he revered written law, and for a short while after his transfer to the Ministry of Justice in 1841 he found his work more rewarding. Panin assigned him to be chief of the Criminal Division of the ministry, a position that was secure and that carried with it a large and responsible role.

Lebedev was still disturbed by his personal feelings of pity but strove to be less trusting. In 1845, he noted that he had learned long ago that "at a certain level of authority goodness [*dobrota*] must not outweigh justice [*spravedlivost'*]." Goodness could have a place in personal sacrifices, but not in the acts of authority. Throughout his career, he had feared lest his love for mankind bring harmful consequences.

> One must be indifferent to poverty and inequality, one must see some necessity in the inequality of men and renounce general improvement by personal efforts. But this seems completely impossible to me. I would like to explode into parts to feed the hungry, or to vanish in ethereal thought with continual concern about the welfare of my brothers, or to do battle to the death with a defender of opposing views. I ascribe this to my weak health and strained nerves.[21]

Compassion was intolerable, but it recurred nonetheless. The system was inhuman, but it had to be endured. He was repeatedly troubled about the condition of the courts. There were too many instances; cases dragged on for years. It would only be improved when everyone lost all faith in the system. But he would accept no alternative and had no hope of improvement. He vented his frustrations in futile fantasies of quitting. "One must serve so as to be beneficial. But here I cannot act beneficially in any way," he wrote in 1843. Completely dependent on service for his income, he continued to suffer from his work.[22]

There took place an inner desiccation in him, a process of embitterment, caught in Sukhovo-Kobylin's picture of the idealistic toady, Tarelkin. An awareness of evil, a hatred of evil, a complete powerlessness to combat it gave rise to a free-floating hostility and misanthropy, a feeling that he was, like Tarelkin, the accursed of fate. He found the life he led in service, following formal rules and suppressing his impulses, utterly degrading. He wrote in 1859,

> With my total dependence, my inability to refuse any task in service, which it has been impossible for me to leave for thirty years, I am ready to stoop to obsequiousness, to blind suffering obedience. But though I tried, I did not succeed. The results have been repellent. I do not like my work, my deeds, or myself.[23]

The graduates of the School of Jurisprudence gave him a fresh cause for discontent. His first tirade against them occurred in 1847, after he had returned from an investigation of several Provincial Chambers. He referred to them as "school boys." "Young people, often under twenty, occupy places which by their importance should belong to those mature people with ripe experience." In 1852, they drove him to think again of resigning.[24] The *pravovedy* upset the very order that he had forced himself to accept. They took over the positions of their seniors, were promoted unfairly over others, and received disproportionate bonuses. They also did not handle cases properly. They disrupted the operation of the ministry and thus caused grumbling among the masses. They approached their work with their own opinions and abstract notions and neglected the established way of doing things. "Ever since the young generation has taken over the positions of Chief-Secretary and Chief-Procurator, the chancellery order has changed in many ways. The old forms have decayed and broken. The old pettifoggery has been replaced by theories of law rarely respecting prior experience."[25]

Lebedev was affronted by the application of theories to practice. Worst of all, the youths' reading had made them converts to the ideas of public justice. "This notion has not been considered by them," he wrote in 1847, "and comes from nothing but laziness, which is always the result of unmerited achievement."[26] Lebedev believed that theories should remain in books. "Nothing is more ruinous for science than the premeditated adaption of its principles to existing social order," he had written in 1835, at the beginning of his service career.[27]

Lebedev was specific about the reason for the failure of the *pravovedy*. These "good-looking, well-bred, and noble" young people did not take their work seriously. "Judicial science is boring to them." He thought they regarded their positions in the Senate as mere stepping stones to higher offices. He considered the upper classes unsuited to dispatch of justice. "Is work compatible with the possibility of getting along without work?"[28]

The feeling of dislike, to be sure, was mutual. One of the courts Lebedev investigated in 1846 was the Kaluga Criminal Chamber, where the twenty-three-year-old *pravoved,* Ivan Aksakov, was serving as assistant chairman. Aksakov wrote to his parents, "The investigator was the typical Petersburg *chinovnik* with the nastiest of faces and wearing white gloves. In his dealing with the officials, even the chairman, he was insolent. Of course, I, as a *pravoved* represented an exception." Aksakov did not take pains to conceal his sense of superiority. When the chairman, embarrassed by one of the investigator's questions, began to lie and speak nonsense, Aksakov interrupted with the declaration that in the court they were not observing the order prescribed by law, but were doing something else. The investigator bit his tongue and remained silent.[29]

The *pravovedy* quickly became a disruptive and unnerving force in the legal administration. The special imperial favor they carried set them apart from the officials of the administration. It enabled them to scoff at usual hierarchical order and to adopt new conceptions of their own role.

The School of Jurisprudence was an elite institution, and the graduates, when they appeared in service, deported themselves and were regarded as young aristocrats. The statute of 1835 limited admissions to members of the hereditary nobility. The permanent statute of 1838 required that candidates for admission be from noble families registered in the sixth section of the genealogy books — those listed in the service before Peter the Great — or be sons of officials of the fifth rank or officers of the sixth rank and above. These requirements appear to have been enforced.[30] The data summarized in table 8.1 suggest that most of the students had parents who were beneath the fifth or sixth ranks. Since many of those holding the highest ranks would belong to the old nobility, it seems reasonable to conclude that most entrants were qualified by ancestry.

But an unwritten service requirement also appears to have influenced the selection. The three pupils whose parents had no rank disappeared from the school in 1837; they would not have had time to finish the course of studies. The proportion of those with parents beneath the eighth rank drops from 22 percent in 1837 to 6 percent in 1846 (see table 8.1). The admissions policy of the school thus worked to encourage the noblemen devoted to state service whom Nicholas saw as a salvation of the state order.

Table 8.1. Ranks Held by Parents of Pupils in Uchilishche Pravovedeniia, 1837-46

Ranks	1837	1839	1842	1845	1846
1-5	41(33)	62(29)	58(28)	91(39)	98(39)
6-8	55(45)	128(60)	138(65)	130(56)	138(55)
9-14	24(20)	22(11)	15(7)	11(5)	15(6)
Without rank	3(2)	...	...	...	...
Totals	123(100)	212(100)	211(100)	232(100)	251(100)

SOURCE: LOA (Otchety Uchilishcha Pravovedeniia), 355-4137-122 (1836); 355-4149-132 (1839); 355-1-4196 (1842); 355-1-4234 (1846).

The aristocratic imprint left by the school came more from its elite spirit and character than the social origin of its pupils. Aristocratic elements lent the school its tone, but they were not representative of the student body as a whole. In the first ten graduating classes, only slightly over 10 percent of the graduates held titles, and just under half of these were barons from the Baltic provinces.[31] Few pupils came from the most eminent families of the elite; such young men, if not bound for the military, would attend the lycee or the university.[32]

The middle or lower layers of the nobility, those families who had traditionally begun their service in the military, provided the majority of the pupils for the school. Most of them held no land, others held medium-sized estates.[33] Some of the titled noblemen, like Prince Dmitrii Obolenskii, the son of a senator, came from scions of their families that no longer held land. The noble entrants were joined by sons of highly placed, non-noble functionaries, and sons of university professors, who carried high rank, such as Constantine Pobedonostev and Alexander Serov.

Half of the pupils were on state support and many of them were poor. Stasov reported that in the early forties it was necessary to pay a tiny sum for breakfast tea, and a good half of the pupils could not afford even this, contenting themselves with a dry sweet roll and nothing to drink for breakfast. But all accounts agree that the wealthy boys avoided extravagance, and social distinctions played no role in the life of the school. "We were all equals and addressed each other with *ty*."[34]

The school provided what was in most respects a secondary education. Those who attended were aware of the invidious distinction between themselves, "pupils" (*vospitanniki*), and university "students" (*studenty*), though they would enter service at ranks higher than university graduates. Their course of study began at ages eleven to fifteen and lasted for seven years. The first three years were devoted to language, history, mathematics, and other general elementary subjects. Most descriptions agree with Arsen'ev's assessment of the elementary classes:

> A poor knowledge of Latin, History, and Geography; a complete ignorance of Mathematics, Physics and Natural History — such were the distinguishing characteristics of our class when we entered the senior specialized classes.[35]

In the last four years of their studies, pupils studied law. They took classes in encyclopedia of law, Roman law, "state law," civil and criminal law and process, local and provincial law, financial and police law, legal medicine, comparative legal practice, and practical law.[36] Several of these subjects were taught in the highest classes by professors from St. Petersburg University, but since all were compulsory, the advanced courses had to be crowded into three years of study, whereas they took up four years of university curriculum. Professor Kalmykov pointed out in 1857 that the pupils had no time to do anything but read and memorize their text and the class notes.[37]

The professors, consequently, simplified their university lectures and presented them carelessly. The pupils responded with a similar indifference. "We were regarded as boys and so studied like boys and not like students [*studenty*]." They spent little time thinking about or discussing what they had heard, and many were depressed by the terrible plodding pedantry of their teachers. The eminent professors seemed to be tangled in a dead scholasticism that held no meaning for them. Stasov wrote of Kalmykov's lectures on criminal law:

> "What kind of higher learning is this?" we asked each other after the lectures. This is nothing but hackneyed administrative claptrap. It astonished us to hear [Kalmykov] shout from the

podium in a voice filled with pathos that "punishment was required by the very idea of divine justice and that "an unpunished crime is a humiliation to the deity."[38]

Professor Palibin, in a course on state law, read the *Digest of Laws* aloud with great emotion. His pupils had to learn by heart the competence of all the departments of the Senate and all provincial and district administrative offices, as well as the detailed rules of clerical procedure.[39] Roman law consisted of recitation of laws and maxims with little attempt to explain their meaning or the relationship between Roman and Russian law. One professor of Roman law did nothing but present the sources.[40] "It seemed to us that Roman Law taught all of the most ordinary things that we knew very well without classical Roman Law, e.g., that one must not build his house on land that belonged to another, or sell apples taken from another's orchard, and other like truths which were extraordinary and new to no one."[41] The great Nevolin merely read from his books, in a soft, almost inaudible monotone.[42]

The popular courses were those furthest removed from the law, like political economy, which introduced them to the views of Say, Ricardo, Malthus, and Smith. Pobedonostev especially liked the course on agriculture. But most successful were the classes on forensic medicine, where the pupils heard of gruesome deaths and watched the dissection of corpses in hospitals.[43]

Despite Oldenburg's original goal for the school, there was little in the curriculum connected with chancellery procedures. Training in criminal and civil procedures took place in the last year. Oldenburg arranged to have records of cases sent to the school from the Senate archives and the archives of provincial and district courts. Using these materials, the pupils were supposed to draw up reports and reach their own decisions about which laws were applicable in particular cases. Many of them enjoyed this experience, but it seems to have produced few positive results. Until 1857, the practical examination in civil process had the pupil compose a report from Senate case extracts (*vypiski*), a mechanical exercise that the teachers in the school concluded did nothing to test knowledge of civil process or law.[44] Stoianovskii, who taught such courses, thought that meaningful training in practical procedure did not begin until the era of reform.[45]

But the influence an educational institution exerts, especially a boarding school like the School of Jurisprudence, is not limited to the content of its classes. The institution's emotional tone, the notions it transmits about the outside world, the ideals it conveys, often mean more in shaping the graduates' personalities and views than the curriculum. The spirit, the way of life, and the goals of the School of Jurisprudence left a deeper mark on the pupils than the teachers' arid lectures. The school, in its early years, created its own ethos that the graduates carried away from it and cherished later in life.

The *pravovedy* learned that it would be their mission to set standards of honesty and reliability in the administration of the law. In 1860, Pobedonostev described the "heritage of the School":

> We were told that there is something called justice [*pravda*] and whoever keeps it in him is an honorable person and a faithful son of the motherland. We were told that justice is not an inspiration and does not come to the individual without effort. It is acquired through strong faith and love; it is acquired through hard work that disdains nothing and through struggle against falsehood in the world, but above all against falsehood in oneself.[46]

They gained the sense that they were a select group dedicated to a particular and exalted cause and this sense of mission strengthened their spirit of unity. "We were graduated hearing the word bond [*soiuz*], and we were told that this bond was for the purpose of work and not for vain pleasures."[47]

Oldenburg himself insisted on the high obligations of the *pravoved*. At the graduation, he exhorted the pupils:

> Preserve the desire burning within you to prove your boundless gratitude for the good deeds of Our Most August Monarch, who has extended to you such great means to prepare yourselves for the service and such great advantages on entering the service.
>
> If at any time you forget the sacred duty of your oath and seek your own self-interest or some other evil goal, you will be the least grateful, the least worthy of men. You will merit the reproof and contempt of contemporaries and of posterity. You will do dishonor to your noble title, to your parents, to the School. For remember the words of the Savior, "From him to whom much is given, much is expected."[48]

Oldenburg made a personal gift to each graduate of a gold thimble, on which was inscribed the school's motto, *respice finem,* adjuring an aspiration to excellence, an aversion to compromise.

Oldenburg's remarks recall usual secondary school rhetoric, but they were reinforced by his own example. He appeared as a person devoted to integrity and justice. He became their benevolent father figure; a model of manliness not martial or despotic in manner. A cultivated member of the European aristocracy thus set a new personal pattern for Russian legal officials.

Oldenburg's own life was filled with personal tragedy. He was the son of Prince George of Oldenburg, who died in Russian service in 1812, and the Grand Duchess Ekaterina Pavlovna. His father died when he was two years old, his mother when he was eight, and Peter grew up in Stuttgart under the guidance of his stepfather, Prince Wilhelm of Württemberg. He was studious and read widely in classical and modern literature. He mastered six modern languages, as well as Latin and Greek. Under the guidance of professors from Stuttgart, he read natural law, civil, criminal, and political law. In 1829, when his brother Nicholas, his only blood relative, died, he returned to Russia at Tsar Nicholas's invitation to build his own family life. He became a devoted family man, whose favorite activity was to gather in the evenings with his wife and eight children for reading and playing music. He often invited the *pravovedy,* and treated them like members of the family. He threw his palace open for parties, where the *pravovedy* found relief from the tedium of their schoolwork in evenings of ice cream and dancing.[49]

Oldenburg provided a measure to guide them in life. "His personal character, his treatment of us and our teachers fostered in us feelings of personal worth, humanity, respect, justice, legality, knowledge and enlightenment," the poet Zhemchuzhnikov wrote.[50] Oldenburg spoke of himself as their father, and emphasized the personal ties between himself and them. At the first graduation, he bade farewell to the pupils, "not as your superior, which I have now ceased to be, but as a human being, loving you with all my soul and truly attached to you."[51]

The pupils felt that the school had less of an official character than other state institutions. There was in it, Stasov recalled, "something recalling the family and home life."[52] Oldenburg selected the students' preceptors himself, and chose men who were humane and intelligent and would not abuse their position. Some of them shared the pupils' interests, discussed literature with them, and took them to the theater. The first director of the school, Poschmann, was typical. Intellectually limited, he demanded respect for authority, but he was a kind and honest person. On Saturdays he held gatherings at his home, where the pupils would assemble, often in the presence of parents and relatives, to chat and dance. The warm atmosphere prevailed until 1849, when Nicholas, suspecting the association of one of the *pravovedy* with the Petrashevtsy group, introduced a severe military regime in the school, as in other institutions. This was lifted after Nicholas's death, but the earlier relationship was never completely restored.[53]

Until 1849, the prince appeared at the school almost daily to supervise its activities. He drew up class schedules, listened to classes, and talked to the pupils. Though Lutheran, he often attended services at one of the school's two chapels. He was a lover of music and actively encouraged concerts at the school. Talented pupils performed at the frequent soirees, which were attended by the prince and other dignitaries, such as Panin, Benkendorf, and Grand Duchess Elena Pavlovna. Other concerts featured the prince himself and visiting celebrities like Clara Schumann. It was perhaps no accident that Peter Tchaikovsky and Alexander Serov were graduates of the school.[54]

The bond the *pravovedy* felt at the school lasted into their service career. It provided them with a different model of human relationships in approaching service.

> The company of youths united for the achievement of a single goal is on the one hand a large family and on the other the state in miniature. Here young people learn about themselves, their merits are judged, all sides of their characters come into the open. Their activity begins with this and competition, ardor and constancy awaken.[55]

This esprit de corps was necessary to sustain them through the difficulties they encountered in trying to improve legal administration. Stoianovskii wrote, "Without [this] bond our isolated efforts would have had no significance."[56] Dmitrii Obolenskii too felt that the comradeship with the *pravovedy* helped him through his struggles in the administration.

> Much spiritual strength was needed for those who wanted to maintain the moral treasure of honor and good without which man loses his dignity. Our close comradely union vigilantly followed the actions of each; it sustained our failing energies with its sympathy, preventing them from ebbing away.[57]

The *pravovedy* felt a strong sense of attachment, particularly to the members of school classes, each of which had its own special corporate spirit.[58] Many of them found a strength of feeling and devotion lacking in their own families. School freed many of them from the prejudices and limitations of their parents and allowed them to shape their own ideals. There was in the school, Stasov wrote, something "infinitely kind, dear and attractive. However much I loved my family, however fine it was to be at home, all my sympathies in a few days went over to the school, to my class." It gave something the family could not: "a life with equals, with comrades in common work and studies, a part in a common cause that was discussed every minute from all sides. . . ."[59] As was common in boarding schools, the boys appear to have found physical as well as intellectual gratification in their comrades.[60]

The eleven-year-old Dmitrii Rovinskii found leaving his home in Moscow for the school an initial step of liberation. His father was a hero of the 1812 war, who, as police chief in Moscow, had made a reputation for his effective organization of the fire brigade. A brash, loud man, he was known as something of a braggart, who "liked to tell of his heroic feats, to put out fires, and to give thrashings with his own hands." When he sent Dmitrii off to Petersburg in 1835, he gave him a list of prohibitions which

included a warning: "You should under no circumstances drink beer."
Rovinskii, who never in his life liked the taste of alcohol, gulped down a
bottle of beer at the first coach stop. The school provided him a relief from
the commands and crudeness of his father, who died when he was
fourteen.[61]

Constantine Pobedonostev's father, a priest's son, was a professor of
literature at Moscow University. He carried his authoritarian pedantry
from the lecture hall into domestic life. "In his faithful commitment to
precise rules and to the observance of established little habits, he must have
been the very model of the neat, diligent and earnest plodder," Robert
Byrnes wrote. He gave his children a good education but apparently
showed them little affection. Constantine Pobedonostev felt little attachment to his family, and when he arrived in Petersburg at the age of
fourteen, the school became his entire life. Two years later his father died.
In the diary he kept at the school, he made no reference to a member of his
family.[62] During vacation, parents of the other pupils would come to take
their children home. But Pobedonostev was left alone in the empty
dormitory, feeling forsaken and envious of his comrades.[63] He placed his
hopes in the ideals and goals of the school, and the bonds it fostered. It was
in the school, he declared in 1860, that the ideals by which he lived were
born. Later, when he rose to eminence, he would favor graduates of
the school. "For him a comrade from the school is something like a
spiritual brother, who on all occasions, including promotion in service,
should be given unquestioned preference before others."[64]

Ivan Aksakov, who came from an aristocratic Moscow family with strong
emotional ties, was less susceptible to such feelings. He felt loneliness at the
school, and a strong need for his parents. He found it hard to get along
with boys his own age, and showed an especial distaste for the provincial
petty noblemen at the school. Nonetheless, even Aksakov, after a time,
overcame his homesickness and felt strong bonds with his classmates,
whom he remained close to in service. When graduated from the school in
June 1842, at the age of nineteen, he felt a curious sense of loss.

> It is sad to part with you,
> And take leave of the fraternity,
> To bid farewell to close friends
> And again wait to meet!
> I am sad! How strange! Is it
> That I love the power of habit,
> Or that I forsake,
> The family of my comrades.
> Of my old lot, my old boredom and constraint![65]

The *pravovedy,* selected as special, privileged figures in the administration, had their own adolescent heroes who represented idealized notions of

211

their mature selves. They liked the romantic literature of the day, the novels of Scott, Bestuzhev-Marlinskii, Hugo, and especially Dumas. Dumas gave them images of dazzling courage, of promethean young noblemen who were at once daring, virtuous, and intelligent, "the type of the gallant young man, the daredevil at all things, the youth from high society, who could do everything, who knew everything, who was handsome, rich, kind, able and brilliantly educated. . . ." [66]

A romantic hero replaced the sentimental hero of the beginning of the century. Rather than the passive figure, whose soul became the vessel for the world's misfortune, they admired the active man, who displayed beauty in action and triumph. The romantic hero was capable not only of great feats; he also knew everything, and understood the world; he was brilliantly educated. The *pravovedy,* in the first decades of the school, worked hard to teach themselves, to make up for the shortcomings of the school's education. Zhemchuzhnikov wrote,

> One can say that we acquired our real education quite apart from the official education and even in spite of its efforts in our behalf. As some may smoke on the sly behind the walls of educational institutions, so others educated themselves on the sly. And for a forbidden book there was in store an incomparably greater punishment than for a poorly hidden cigarette. [67]

The pupils read Pushkin, Lermontov, Gogol, and Belinskii, as well as many foreign writers. Several classes formed libraries, supported by the pupils' dues. They discussed their readings in endless, life-and-death "Russian-style" discussions. In the 1850s, all the classes, even the youngest, formed literary journals. "Literature captivated us all," one graduate wrote. [68]

The *pravovedy* entered the service in their late teens or early twenties with a unique sense of their personal worth and superiority. They believed that they were engaged in a heroic mission in behalf of the law. But once they began their obligatory term—four years for self-supported, six years for state-supported pupils—they found it difficult to endure the burden of dreary paper work, much of which seemed to be without point. "The most onerous and dismal period of my life I consider my entry into service in the Fourth Department of the Senate after graduation from the School of Jurisprudence," Zhemchuzhnikov wrote. His first assignment was to correct the entries under the letter *O* in an old Senate index. [69]

> *The Senate! Where in wearying succession my days,*
> *Went by. There among the papers, the cases,*
> *Where my soul grew cold to poetry,*
> *And like a mouse I dwelled in layers of archival dust.*

Oh, if hell awaits me beyond the grave,
I intone only one prayer,
That my soul not be imprisoned in the Senate,
All other torments I can bear. [70]

Prince Meshcherskii had similar impressions when he began serving in the Senate in the 1850s.

> We undoubtedly left the School alive and felt in ourselves not only a thirst for active work, but also for struggle. We were almost exploding with enthusiasm for the kind of task where both mind and soul could be put to work.
>
> But it was just this that our service did not give us. We suddenly found ourselves in a stifling moral and physical desert, working under people of the purest bureaucratic type. [71]

Serov exclaimed, "Can there be a soul so calloused and dusty to devote himself to tasks in the Senate *con amore?*" [72] Aksakov felt the vital forces of his youth going to waste in the Senate, his spontaneous impulses dying. He found his service simply repugnant.

So in the supreme court—guilty!
I meant to say in the Senate factory—
In the vast stone chambers,
Dirtier than any Provincial Chamber,
I work like a hired laborer.
We have tasted the delights of civil service,
And we see: there is too little sense in it,
To give it the flower of our young days. [73]

They experienced the same oppressiveness as had Lebedev. But they did not need to submit. They carried into service not only a sense that these administrative obligations were beneath them, but also a moral identity, the conscience and sense of moral obligation they had absorbed at the school. They suffered with the boredom but they rebelled at the injustice that they encountered everywhere. The system seemed to work for the guilty and hound the innocent. Aksakov began to manipulate chancellery rules to avoid applying the law. "What good is a law," he wrote, "if observing it results in the highest moral illegality." He managed to acquit a functionary who had left his post for a few minutes to sell something at the market. "Let Panin make merry with him, do the cruelest things for the sake of executing the law—the letter of the law, despite its moral illegality and the fact that it often runs counter to one's convictions." [74] The acquittal of noblemen charged with murder was a frequent occurrence. The Sukhovo-Kobylin case was not an isolated episode, and Aksakov encountered a similar situation, where a powerful aristocrat was charged with murdering a dancer whom he had plied with aphrodisiacs and nearly reduced to insanity. Aksakov, in 1848, as a chief-secretary in the Senate, wrote a brief favoring conviction. But the Senate gave a light sentence — service as a soldier without loss of rights, and assignment to a desk job, due to the convict's poor health. Aksakov discovered a forgotten article in the *Digest of Laws* and, claiming that the sentence was illegal, refused to sign the sentence. This provoked an indignant uproar in the Senate and Aksakov decided to transfer to a position in the Ministry of Interior.[75]

The single assignment the *pravovedy* found gratifying was work on senatorial investigations. Assisting in these investigations suited their temperaments. It placed them above institutions and allowed them to seek out and correct abuses. It gave them their first glimpse of how legal institutions actually worked, and a feeling of what changes were needed.[76] Zhemchuzhnikov was delighted to receive an assignment, which lasted two years, to serve on the investigation of Kaluga and Orel provinces.[77] Aksakov's work on the investigation of Astrakhan province rekindled his interest in service.

> In general I must confess that the investigation, which has aroused in me a great revulsion for chancellery service, has stimulated in me a great concern for state matters (even though in Russia everything can pass for comedy) and if we had a somewhat different order (not in any case the times of Alexei Mikhailovich and the boyars), I would never leave service and would prefer it to all other kinds of work.[78]

But having finished the investigations, they had to return to a dreary accommodation with a system that clashed with their goals. Many of them followed the same path as Aksakov and transferred to other ministries. Dmitrii Obolenskii, a friend of Aksakov, and a cousin of Iurii Samarin, returned from an investigation to serve as assistant chairman in one of the St. Petersburg Civil Chambers. He was a conscientious worker protecting the interests and the rights of the weak, and earned a commendation from the tsar for serving in the St. Petersburg Conscience Court, which handled minor disputes. In his memoirs, Obolenskii described the dissatisfaction with service that he and other *pravovedy* felt at the end of the 1840s. He began to meet with other like-minded young officials to discuss their reading and hopes. A group of *pravovedy* gathered at his apartment, and once a week he visited Nicholas Miliutin's, where there was dinner and discussion. Though there were great differences in the views of these young people, they all shared one feeling, "the wish for a better order."

> Life in the service and important state figures were subjected to bitter and mocking criticism. Everyone came with his own stories about his Minister or Director, and the words of the speaker brought happy laughter.... The youth worked,

studied, read, and regarded the pointless, empty life of high society with contempt. Fear reigned over everything; routine ruled in the administration; in the courts formalism rose to the level of outrage. Life was concealed in the minds and hearts of the youth, and was maintained by them with some incomprehensible, strong hope that the existing order could not last for long and that better days must come soon.[79]

In their circles, they discussed the works of Proudhon, Fourier, Blanc, and others; the revolution of 1848 produced a kind of "platonic animation" among these young officials, none of whom were socialists.[80] Obolenskii became a habitué of the liberal salon of Grand Duchess Elena Pavlovna at the Mikhailov Palace. The grand duchess was interested in the work of the Judicial Chamber, and startled Obolenskii with questions about the court unexpected from a lady. Through the 1850s he continued to attend the meetings of intellectuals and highly placed figures — the morganatic salons — that proved such an important stimulus to the work of reform.[81]

Obolenskii wearied of the meaningless formalism of Panin's regime, and in 1853 went to work under the Grand Duke Constantine Nikolaevich, who was bringing new and energetic leadership to the Naval Ministry. With the debacle of the Crimean War, Constantine Nikolaevich pursued the reform of his ministry, and sought fresh forces to direct this effort. Constantine wrote in his report on the work of the Naval Ministry that many of the old officials were unable to fulfill his demands. "The appointment of two or three new workers, however, would hardly achieve the desired goal, for they would not be able to fight with a whole series of representatives of the old direction." He concluded that to attain meaningful results and enliven the work of the ministry, it was necessary "to introduce a large number of new people, who would understand and help each other." The grand duke mentioned eleven officials whom he recruited specifically for this task. Seven of them, including Obolenskii, were *pravovedy* who had left the Ministry of Justice in search of more fruitful assignments.[82]

The *pravovedy* in the Naval Ministry were among those who repudiated the operation of the existing legal system. But they did not give up their struggle to improve the administration of justice. Rather, they used their position in the Naval Ministry to advance the cause of radical judicial reform. Obolenskii, Glebov, and Varrand and the other *pravovedy* became a force working for the introduction of a new liberal court system in the opening years of the reign of Alexander II. It was Dmitrii Obolenskii who wrote the first memorandum in favor of a public court system to be circulated in the bureaucracy. In it, Obolenskii emphasized the importance of the judiciary. The existing system did not permit the existence of strong judicial authority. The judiciary, Obolenskii insisted, was the vital support of the state structure. "The judicial authority preserving the personal and proprietorial rights of citizens is the base upon which the entire edifice of state administration rests."[83] The class nature of the system, moreover, made it impossible to look upon the judiciary as a calling. "The judge as *judge* should belong to no estate. He is the servant of truth [*istina*], and therefore should be its independent representative."[84]

Within the Ministry of Justice, the Moscow departments of the Senate became something of a haven from the despotism and caprices of Panin. Pobedonostev, serving in the chancellery of the Eighth Department, found his apprenticeship, under the enlightened Chief-Procurator P. A. Zubov, "the best practical school for judicial and administrative activity." Zubov succeeded in effecting a gradual transition from the old to the new officials, training the *pravovedy* in chancellery work before the old clerks were retired. Under Zubov, Pobedonostev developed somewhat more taste for chancellery work than his comrades.[85]

But Pobedonostev, too, felt the irrationality and injustice of the system. He read widely and formulated his own critical approach to explain the abuses he saw around him. He concluded that the problem was the prevalence of the personal principle, the untrammeled bureaucratic authority that did not permit conscientious distinctions between good and evil. "There is no just case that cannot be lost; there is no illegal case that cannot be won; for there are no firm principles that distinguish the legal from the illegal."[86] Pobedonostev increasingly identified the absence of moral sense with Panin, who lacked, he claimed, consciousness of the distinction between good and evil. In 1854, Pobedonostev turned down the opportunity to assume a higher position in Petersburg. He did not care for the damp capital, but also feared for his integrity. "In Moscow I now have very few personal connections in service. I can have my own opinion. There I would have to do business with the personality of one individual, and sometimes subordinate my thoughts and convictions to him."[87]

Pobedonostev's calling required an independence from external influence, the ability to act according to his own convictions of justice. With his resentment of the Petersburg offices and Panin, he strove to insulate himself from the influences of self-interest and administrative pressure. He preserved his integrity by isolation, and asserted his distance from the system by maintaining an austere impersonality in his relationships—a show of strength in suppressing his human weaknesses. He was the type of Egor Kurnatovskii, the cold and righteous chief-secretary of the Senate, rebuffed by the heroine of Turgenev's *On the Eve*.

Dmitrii Rovinskii responded to the system in a similar manner. A nobleman, who inherited 185 souls, Rovinskii struggled to eradicate the excesses of the noble character in him. "He was never what we called a *barin* at the time. He was a man directly concerned with the business of hard work, alien to the pampered way of life, to any sentimentalism." He lived a simple bachelor's life, with few friends, devoting himself to his work and his life's passion—the collection of popular pictures (*liubki*). Shy and withdrawn, "like a blushing young girl," he never learned to dance, never played cards, or uttered elegant niceties in public.[88]

As Moscow provincial procurator in the early 1850s, Rovinskii worked hard to correct the failings of the court and penal systems. He struggled against the formal requirement that let murderers and rapists off with a verdict of "remains under suspicion."[89] He was outraged by the way the police conducted their investigations, observing no rules and often inventing materials themselves or releasing suspects without reason. They would detain and arrest individuals at their own whim.[90] Rovinskii inspected the Moscow jails and discovered atrocities unknown to the noble society of the day—means of torture such as cockroach rooms, tombs— lightless rooms where prisoners languished until they confessed—and the feeding of salted herring.[91] Everything went on in secret. After Nicholas's death, Rovinskii would become a spokesman for publicity and especially for the jury system as a means to keep court personnel honorable.[92] In the early 1860s, the emerging generation of procurators and judges would look to him as a model of the way a legal official should live and work.

Nicholas Stoianovskii, one of the school's most loyal and illustrious graduates, brought the same determination to his work in the administration. The son of a Mogilev nobleman, Stoianovskii inherited an estate of 302 souls with his two brothers. The school gave Stoianovskii the high-minded sense of mission he showed in all his assignments. As chief-procurator in both the Moscow and Petersburg departments of the Senate, he had to struggle to make sense of the investigations concocted by the police. He exposed one case of a state peasant who had been forced to confess to murdering his wife, though his wife was still alive; the charge had been fabricated by a police officer. He taught at the School of Jurisprudence and tried to help the *pravovedy* find their way through the confused articles of the *Digest of Laws* by composing a guide to criminal procedure. Following the current rules, he limited the book to extracts from the *Digest,* allowing himself only the briefest of commentaries. The censors, however, objected even to this display of legal expertise, contending that what one needed to know about the laws was already written in the *Digest,* and more than that was not necessary. Stoianovskii succeeded in having it published only through the intervention of Count Bludov. The guide helped the young graduates free themselves from the influence and practices of the clerks in the Senate.[93]

Pobedonostev, Rovinskii, and Stoianovskii felt an obligation to the law that drove them to reject the existing legal system. In the opening years of Alexander's reign, they would lead the struggle for institutions that would allow legal officials to live up to their calling. Their rigor and commitment were exceptional among the *pravovedy,* but all of the school's graduates, even its detractors agreed, adhered to a high standard of honesty and probity in their service. The school introduced a new moral standard into the administration of justice.

It was less successful, however, in instilling approaches to the law, and ways of legal thinking that would allow graduates to cope with their responsibilities. Here Lebedev's strictures seem justified. While remaining honest, the *pravovedy* proved an alien element disruptive to the work of the legal administration. Contemptuous of the old system, they had nothing to replace it with, and applied their own personal standards. Shifted around rapidly by Panin, many of them could gain only a passing acquaintanceship with work of an office. Some were in fact lazy, and, convinced of their importance, saw no reason to struggle to improve themselves.

V. A. Mukhanov, a rich nobleman, in 1855 commented admiringly about the *pravovedy* with their "noble principles and pure morality," and observed that there were many more honest judges than twenty years before. But the *pravovedy,* moving from place to place, never gained the necessary experience; they were "the pilgrims of our courts, wandering from position to position and therefore no one knows and cannot remember cases presenting analogous circumstances." "Judicial traditions have vanished," he complained. "In the same situation in the exact same conditions judgments should be uniform." The old secretaries, he claimed, could recall similar cases, and this limited the arbitrariness of the judges and created a uniformity, "the violation of which is harmful, for it disturbs the scales of justice and destroys confidence in its servants."[94]

In the 1850s, Pobedonostev deplored the disorder and disarray that the *pravovedy* brought to the ministry. "In general the peripatetic staff of [the Senate] chancellery, especially the Civil Departments, is such that it is surprising that the damaged machine of justice hasn't stopped altogether." The early generations of *pravovedy* had united to work for the general good, but the later generation showed interest only in their careers; they were "idle formalists" who scorned their work. It was true that they did not take bribes, but this was "cheap honesty." The best cadres, moreover, were fleeing from Panin to other ministries.[95]

The flight from the ministry, in fact, grew during the 1850s as more and more *pravovedy* were lured away. The four- or six-year requirement ensured that a certain percentage of the graduates would remain in the ministry. But after the required term elapsed, increasing numbers took the opportunity to leave. The proportion of total graduates remaining in the ministry fell from 1856 to 1865 (see table 8.2). The flight was such that there were fewer *pravovedy* serving in the ministry in 1865 than in

Table 8.2. Graduates of the School of Jurisprudence Remaining in the Ministry of Justice, 1850-70[a]

	1850	1856	1858	1861	1865	1868	1870
Serving in Ministry of Justice	205(88)	292(73)	272(62)	287(56)	283(49)	378(53)	464(58)
Retired or transferred to other ministries	28(12)	107(27)	170(38)	224(44)	301(51)	263(47)[b]	255(42)[c]
Total surviving graduates	233(100)	399(100)	442(100)	511(100)	584(100)	641(100)	719(100)

[a]Data from the annual editions of *Pamiatnaia knizhka Imperatorskogo Uchilishcha Pravovedeniia* (Petersburg).

[b]Of the 263, a total of 152 were serving in other branches, 111 were retired.

[c]Of the 255, a total of 128 were serving in other branches, 127 were retired.

1856, despite the yearly graduation of about twenty-five pupils into its staff.

The ministry took steps to encourage the appointment of *pravovedy*. In 1858, a circular order was issued instructing responsible chiefs of Senate offices to appoint graduates of the School of Jurisprudence, or, failing that, graduates of other higher educational institutions, to chancellery positions. Exceptions were to be made only for lesser posts, for example, assistant secretaries, and then explanations had to be submitted as to why candidates with superior qualifications were not chosen. At the same time, a circular was sent to all governors, instructing them to appoint as provincial *striapchie* graduates of the School of Jurisprudence, or of other higher educational institutions. But these measures did little to attract the *pravovedy* (see tables 8.3 and 8.4).[96] The trend would be reversed only when the court reform made legal office attractive.

The *pravovedy* introduced a notion of honor into Russian legal administration. With them, it became possible to conceive of a high-minded legal official in Russia. Their sense of mission and of superiority destroyed the viability of the old routines and the old approaches to chancellery work. But few of them were suited to finding new approaches and evolving new legal practices. They were limited by their role as knights engaged in a sweeping action to serve general goals. In describing Artsimovich, Koni captured the essence of the *pravovedy*.

> This was a man who couldn't easily keep his feelings within the narrow bounds of a concrete case. He immediately soared from the case to general principles, to the basic principles of social life, to the eternal demands of the human spirit ... the *individual case* oppressed him and hindered his broad flight into the realm of general questions and principled views.[97]

The *pravovedy* led the way. They were followed by graduates of the university. As the proportion of *pravovedy* in the ministry declined, that of university graduates rose (see tables 8.3 and 8.4). Attracted by the freer conditions and higher salaries of the reform era, and the new status attached to positions in the legal administration, university graduates began to enter the ministry in increasing numbers. They still held few posts relative to their numbers, considering that roughly ten times as many students finished the law faculties of the universities as the School of Jurisprudence each year.[98] They enjoyed few advantages in obtaining appointments and bonuses. But, helped by the ranks conferred on them by their degrees and the ministry's policy of recruitment, they rose rapidly to responsible positions. No longer did they have to submit to a dreary, clerical routine, and take their examples, like university graduates earlier in the century, "from people with chancellery [*prikaznye*] notions of service morality."[99]

Table 8.3. Education of Senate Chancellery Officials, 1850-66[a]

	Chief-Secretaries and Secretaries				Assistant Secretaries			
	1850	1856	1860	1866	1850	1856	1860	1866
School of Jurisprudence	43(35)	59(45)	52(43)	26(26)	41(27)	81(47)	54(32)	15(16)
Other higher education[b]	36(29)	47(36)	50(41)	61(62)	30(20)	36(21)	51(30)	57(62)
Total higher education	79(64)	106(81)	102(84)	87(88)	71(47)	117(68)	105(62)	72(78)
Without higher education	44(36)	25(19)	19(16)	12(12)	82(53)	57(33)	63(38)	20(22)
Totals	123(100)	131(100)	121(100)	99(100)	153(100)	174(101)	168(100)	92(100)

[a]Data drawn from the *Spiski Chinam Pravitel'stvuiushchego Senata i Ministerstva Iustitsii.*

[b]Higher education includes university graduates and a handful of graduates from the Aleksandrovskii Lycée.

Table 8.4. Education of Provincial Judicial Officials, 1850-66

	Assistant Chairmen				Procurators				Striapchie			
	1850	1856	1860	1866	1850	1856	1860	1866	1850	1856	1860	1866
School of Jurisprudence	22(26)	25(29)	25(28)	20(22)	14(26)	11(18)	17(29)	22(36)	13(15)	23(24)	7(6)	8(8)
Other higher education	18(21)	21(24)	25(28)	44(46)	11(21)	14(24)	16(27)	24(39)	13(15)	18(18)	29(29)	43(44)
Total higher education	40(48)	46(53)	50(56)	64(68)	25(47)	25(42)	33(56)	46(75)	26(30)	41(42)	36(35)	51(52)
Without higher education	44(52)	41(47)	40(44)	27(32)	28(53)	34(58)	26(44)	15(25)	61(70)	56(58)	65(65)	46(48)
Totals	84(99)	87(100)	90(100)	91(100)	53(100)	59(101)	59(100)	61(100)	87(100)	97(100)	101(100)	97(100)

NOTE: Data are from the *Spiski chinam*. Assistant chairmen and provincial procurators were positions only in the old prereform courts; the 1866 totals therefore include none of the new courts introduced in that year.

The university graduates brought a new element into the administration—a faith in the intellectual dignity of the law. If the *pravovedy* would begin to conceive of justice as a personal ethical ideal, the university graduates would approach it as a science—a discipline of thought and life demanding complete dedication. Many of them looked upon the *pravovedy* scornfully. Koliupanov, who studied at Moscow University, wrote that *pravovedy* "were distinguished by their honesty and brilliant salon education. Few of them had mastered serious judicial knowledge, just as few took their work seriously. Most of them wasted their young forces on social diversions." They were the provincial lions, surrounded by crowds of young ladies eager for their attentions.[100] The university graduates' sense of superiority to the administration was not social but intellectual. They did not enjoy the license of the *pravovedy* to chafe at the unpleasantnesses of work in the administration. They maintained their integrity, rather, by a feeling of their own intellectual preeminence, a confidence that in the long run, their ideas would prevail.

The universities, and especially Moscow University, created a sense of the intellectual stature of the law. They gave the traditional noble disdain for the civil service new content. The students at Moscow University in the 1840s did not "dream of a service career, to take places next to the heroes of Gogol. Anyone who had any means at all did not think of ranks or rewards."[101] The university directed them instead to the service of intellectual ideals. Before the 1830s, Obninskii wrote, the university was little more than a glorified secondary school. "From the 1830s to the 1850s it gradually separated itself from the surrounding world, withdrew into itself, and began to offer a virtual sanctuary, where all persecuted ideals gathered, seeking refuge behind its high walls from the hostile world."[102]

The juridical faculty of Moscow University took the lead in shaping and instilling these ideals. Granovskii told the young Boris Chicherin that it was the only faculty at the university worthy of the name. There taught Redkin, Kavelin, Krylov, and Granovskii himself.[103] These professors introduced a new vital academic commitment to the law. No longer was it a mere dry enumeration of legislation and procedure. It became a science, breathing meaning into thought and life.

The students in the lecture hall, searching for meaningful forms of service, were ripe for new noble ideals, and they saw in their professors new models for their own noble manhood. It was no accident that the three professors with the greatest personal appeal, Redkin, Granovskii, and Kavelin, were noblemen, the first generation of noble professors on the law faculty. The audiences at the juridical faculty responded to the new combination of learning and elegant discourse and presentation. They were attracted by "the force resounding from the *kafedry* of the eternally vibrant, eternally spirit-producing work that led the audience behind the professor-*mentor* out of dismal reality into the bright realm of future civic ideals." [104] The teacher replaced the poet as the model for the noble youth in the lecture halls, and many of them dreamed hopelessly of becoming professors themselves. The teacher stood apart from the irrationality and humiliation of the existing order and attained dignity by dealing with the truths of science. He inhabited the realm of the ideal and called upon them to enter that realm and to bring science to bear upon life.

Peter Redkin stunned the beginning jurists with his passionate and brilliant lectures. For his introductory lecture on the encyclopedia of law, the hall overflowed with expectant students. His appearance was striking. "There was something unusual in his bearing," Koliupanov wrote. [105] He began by asking the students what brought them to his lectures, then answered that it was the search for truth and the desire to become defenders of justice in the fatherland. "You are the high priests of justice, you are jurists," he declared. "The aureole descending on him from God was still there, and he concluded in his booming voice, 'Yes my lords, there is nothing higher than truth and science is its prophet. But like everything sacred and great in the world truth demands selflessness and self-renunciation. Take your cross and come to me.' " The students, against all regulations, would break into applause. Koliupanov rose and went directly to the university offices to transfer to the judicial faculty. [106] Another admirer wrote, "Each student after the lecture felt himself a person capable of everything good." He left the lecture feeling that "there is something higher, universal, that is above everything and that this good should guide life, that 'everything will pass, only justice will remain'" (Redkin's favorite folk saying). From Redkin the students learned the principles of life, that "scientific studies elevate the soul, distract from the petty squabbles of life, and can serve as the guiding star in the attainment of good." [107]

The training of future generations was Redkin's conscious goal. From his years of study in Germany, he had learned to revere the high calling of the jurist. His professors, and particularly Thibaut, had shown him the vital role of the teacher and the need "to carry on a conversation with the living." In his speech of 1846 to the annual assembly of Moscow University, he declared that Russia had entered the third of the phases of history, when the government became a force bringing new ideas into history. During this phase, initiated by Speranskii's *Digest,* the government would put legislation into order and issue new and better laws. This task required an "estate of jurists" to make "customary law and legislation conscious and put them into action; to develop them according to the contemporary demands of science and life, to elevate them to universal principles of law." [108]

The result of this education would be the attainment of the highest stage of law—the "law of jurists," which "represents that level of the development of positive law, when it rises to the philosophical and together with philosophy becomes the object of full consciousness in science and the full realization of that consciousness in life." Jurists would become the organs of "the full consciousness of law." To further this development, Redkin founded the first Russian law journal, *Iuridicheskie Zapiski,* which he envisioned as "the external organ of the joint activity of Russian jurists, where this rising estate can find a point of unity, and where it can use its common forces to help the beneficial goals of government in the work of national jurisprudence, by spreading judicial knowledge in the fatherland and by implanting a conscious feeling of legality and duty."[109] *Iuridicheskie Zapiski* appeared in 1841 and 1842, containing exclusively historical studies of the law. Only the third issue, published in 1859, could deal with problems of contemporary Russian law.

Granovskii, lecturing on European medieval history, exerted a similar power over the minds of the students. His compelling personality made them examine universal trends of history, grasped and made meaningful by the mind of the scholar. "Granovskii's influence came somehow directly and invisibly from his personality. There were people more talented than Granovskii, but no one had so inimitable and unique a charm." He emanated a pure, calming atmosphere, "in which everyone became more moral and good himself."[110] In his lectures, the students found "those guiding principles, those civic feelings, which placed in a young soul, led him and preserved him on the path of life."[111] After Granovskii's premature death, his place was taken by his student, the young and sickly P. N. Kudriavtsev. Kudriavtsev's lectures on ancient history inspired the students until his own death, in 1858, a little more than two years after his teacher's.

N. I. Krylov made Roman law meaningful and vibrant for them. "The basic theses of Roman Law were etched in our memory; Krylov expressed its severe logic in brilliant words."[112] Kavelin aroused a similar enthusiasm, stimulating his students to devote their efforts to the study of the law. His courses on the history of civil law were the first to formulate a philosophical approach to early Russian legal institutions. To the students' delight, he took every opportunity to ridicule the barbarism of old *Rus',* and to make off-handed critiques of serfdom. He gave private lectures on the sources of Russian civil law to the most interested students, and showed an active interest in student problems.[113]

Granovskii, Kavelin, and Redkin held special evening gatherings at their homes, where they discussed problems of law, current issues of the day, and recent literature with their students. They encouraged them to borrow their books and raise questions about the readings. "Every young man showing promise became the object of special attention and care,"

Chicherin wrote.[114] The names of Redkin, Granovskii, and Kavelin spread across Russia, attracting eager young students to Moscow.[115] Science (*nauka*) became their guide to life. Science, they felt, could provide them with the explanations to reshape reality, and that therefore it had to be pursued isolated from reality, among scholars, "in a corporate group that advances and develops the cause."[116]

The impact of the teaching in the juridical faculty was not merely inspirational. The lectures conveyed a whole new way of thinking. In his speech of 1846, Redkin had emphasized that jurists had to be broadly educated. But breadth of education did not suggest to him literary taste and refined feelings. It meant the understanding of philosophy and history as bases for understanding life.[117] He made philosophy, and particularly Hegelian philosophy, the key to the understanding of the law. His course on the encyclopedia of law taught the philosophy of law according to Hegel. Presenting state law, he described the history of political doctrines and left the student to master Russian state law on his own.[118]

If the education at the beginning of the century had a literary cast, irrespective of the subject treated, that of the 1840s took Hegelian idealism as an approach to all the problems of intellect and life. The students came away from Redkin's lectures with "an enthusiastic worship for Hegel and philosophical theories."[119] The advancement of science appeared to them as a universal process of change, of which the individual could become a part. The teacher played the major role in this process, developing ideas and passing them on to the next generation, who would continue the ongoing process of a rising consciousness of ideas. Redkin's lectures changed the students' way of looking at life. "They compelled us to see in the phenomena of this world an inner development, and in this development to recognize a gradualness. They showed us that nothing arises suddenly, that there are laws which are impossible to evade."[120] Even those who recognized the superficiality of the lectures acknowledged their impact. Chicherin, who described Redkin as a person of mediocre intelligence and ordinary talent, wrote,

> We were trained to logical consistency of thought, to under-
> stand the inner bonds of philosophical ideas. Before us arose a
> full sketch of Juridical Science, not as a dead enumeration of
> facts, but as a live organism, penetrated by high principles. We
> learned by heart the teachings of Roman jurists that law
> [*pravo*] comes from justice [*pravda*]. We were told that the
> principle of civil law is freedom; that the principle of criminal
> law is based on vengeance. We learned to see in the state not
> only an external form, a protector of security, but the highest
> goal of juridical development, the realization of the principles
> of freedom and justice in a supreme union, which does not

devour individuality, but gives it sufficient expanse, directing it to the common good.[121]

Redkin, Chicherin found, "gave an impetus to a philosophical movement of thought. We strove to learn the higher principles of existence and burned with love for the eternal ideas of justice and good, which we were preparing to serve with all our being."[122] Hegelianism gave the young noblemen a way to achieve communion with the eternal and the absolute, which previous generations had only been able to find through contemplation of death. The individual's life assumed meaning in a process that linked him to the ultimate. Immortality was guaranteed in an ineluctable historical process and not through impossible individual exploits. The notion of the gradual evolution of the ideal brought to an end the passive acceptance of the existing order, for now change appeared as a struggle unfolding over time, and the individual's efforts were his work for the development, propagation, and passing on of the ideal. However powerful, rigid, and emasculating the autocracy, it still appeared feeble before the overpowering, unremitting progress of the ideal.

Idealism made it possible to conceive of one's life as taking place in the service of a great universal process, working toward good. The individual could participate in this process by acquiring knowledge: once he gained the consciousness offered by science, he could use it for the benefit of mankind. The student's work on his studies and his self-perfection took place not in seclusion but on the stage of world history. He tended to look upon his friendships and his loves in the same way, as possessing the same marvelous transcendent aura. The youth read George Sand and other romantic novelists, and thought of love as an event with metaphysical resonance. Women, like books, were a way to the ideal. "Love at that time rarely ended with serious results. Women appeared in an ideal light, where all earthly thoughts and aims yield to the spiritual unity of the soul."[123]

Constantine Ushinskii, a student preparing for a degree of master of law, felt himself part of this great mission, and resolved to become a teacher of the law. His father had attained hereditary nobility after serving in the military and then the civil service. He played little part in his son's upbringing, serving in Vologda, while Constantine remained with his mother and attended gymnasium in Novgorod-Seversk. After his mother died in 1835, Constantine, at the age of eleven, remained with his younger brother and sister, almost as the head of the family, while his father continued to serve in Vologda. Though he would write many warm descriptions of his mother later in life, he left only one remark that apparently referred to his father. "There is daddy, who having mastered the crude manners of a battalion scribe, worries about the aristocratic manners of his children and picks on his little son because he had played with the janitor's son."[124]

Ushinskii found his own calling at the university. He was inspired by the teaching of Redkin, Kavelin, and other professors. In his diary he described the high cause he felt chosen to serve. "Train minds!" he wrote in November 1844, as he was preparing for his master's examination. "Disseminate ideas! That is our assignment. We do not live in an era when we can act ourselves. Discard egoism, we will work for posterity! As fathers we will give ourselves to our labors and sufferings, which are not fruitful for us, but will be fruitful for our children."[125]

Rather than accepting the role of the obedient son, cowed by an imaginary unyielding father and adopting a melancholy passive attitude, Ushinskii and those of his generation began to see themselves as the start of a new tradition — as forefathers, who themselves would prepare the future. He vowed to sacrifice everything, "the pleasures of the family, honors, glory, wealth." Ushinskii had no hope that the descendants of his generation would remember even their names, though they had sacrificed themselves for the sake of truth, good and the idea. He established a severe work schedule for himself, allowing only six hours of sleep and assigning most of his time to work. But the schedule proved too demanding and he was oppressed by feelings of inadequacy. Only the mind, it seemed, was free. "Only it [mind] should be free from all compulsion, command all, obey nothing but itself; it is completely free. This is not a person with whims and passion. No, it is the basic law — developing out of itself."[126]

Ushinskii struggled to conquer his feelings. His soul summoned him to struggle, to participate in an active movement of faith to change the world. But boredom, ennui, *skuka* overcame him and kept him from acting. Only "mind" could help him escape his egoistic self-indulgence. He suffered fits of despair.[127] Then "thought" (*mysl'*) would arise to rescue him. He wrote in March 1845:

> Thought is a living thing! And we are but its living organs! Even more we are vessels of its soul! Oh, with thought every doubt, every fear, flies away and happiness of being and consciousness engulfs my soul! The feeling of eternity, of conscious eternity — you are the finest feeling of the soul of man. But alas. My weak soul cannot contain it for long.[128]

He read extensively in German history and especially in idealistic philosophy, trying to enter the realm of "thought." In his diary he wrote down numerous quotes from the writings of Hegel and Kant: "The essence of free will is law." "In personality resides the knowledge of self as object, which thought elevates to simple infinity, to the abstract."[129]

In 1846, Ushinskii received an appointment to teach at the Iaroslavl Demidov Lycée. This opened the possibility to realize his dream and become a transmitter of thought to future generations. The Demidov

Lycée had been made a law school in 1833. But this designation had little effect until in 1845, at the instance of Redkin and Granovskii, several young graduates from the law faculty of Moscow University were appointed to its staff. Ushinskii embarked upon his task with great enthusiasm. He planned a new curriculum and introduced a course on the encyclopedia of law, patterned on Redkin's. He convinced the school to order 250 books on law for its meager library. But Ushinskii's indelicate manner and elaborate plans offended the conservative school administration, and with the events of 1848 his position became untenable.[130] Dismissed in 1849, he went to work in the Department of Foreign Confessions. But service did not answer his intellectual and emotional needs, and he gradually turned away from the law to study the education of the young. In the 1850s, he wrote the first of the works on education that would bring him reknown as a pedagogical theorist.

Intellectual ferment centered in Moscow University but, in the 1850s, it spread to other universities as well. Dmitrii Meier and Constantine Kavelin, who taught at St. Petersburg University in the fifties, became the models for the youth there. Meier, who died shortly after his appointment at Petersburg, made major contributions at Kazan University from 1845 to 1855. In the backwater of Kazan society, Meier was a lone figure whose example inspired the youth to become jurists.

The son of a court musician, Meier studied law at Berlin under Puchta, Homeyer, and other followers of the historical school. He returned to teach at Kazan, where in 1848, he defended his doctor's dissertation on ancient Russian security law. So much of Kazan flocked to the defense that a concert had to be cancelled. In the late forties, Meier became increasingly involved with the development of the study of contemporary civil law as a science. He strove to free it from the historical orientation that had dominated the Russian universities, "to show the students the scientific side of civil law, which is often shielded or blocked by its positive nature." He warned against the tendency to quiet one's conscience by accepting existing laws. It was necessary to study the laws of reality, which arose from the spirit of the people and expressed a true natural law. The discovery of this law of reality, however, demanded a "vast knowledge of life, the revealing of the many juridical relationships that are closed to outsiders." His course was the first to focus on the examination of the intricate problems of property law in Russia. Meier endeavored to deal with these problems in a systematic, empirical manner. "I direct the attention of the students to worlds of proprietorial phenomena present in juridical life; and the investigation of these phenomena, the exposing of these laws, I call the problem of civil law as a science like all true sciences."[131]

But Meier tried to do more than study and teach the law. He, too, brought from Germany the notion of the high calling of the judicial official. He strove to emulate the example of his teacher Homeyer, who was both a scholar and a judge. Like Redkin, he saw his role as creating future generations of jurists, but more than Redkin, he emphasized the role of practical experience. The failure of judicial education, he declared, stemmed from the false notion of the historical school that judicial education was an organic part of a nation's development, of a society, all of whose members were naturally equipped at birth to be judges.

Meier stressed the importance of the judicial function and the high demands it placed on judicial personnel. Practical juridical experience provided the legislator with the material he needed to formulate laws. But the jurist could assist the legislator only when he was able to understand "the phenomena of juridical life [*iavleniia iuridicheskogo byta*]" and the way his particular court experiences were related to these phenomena.

> Only by comprehending the principles lying at the base of legislation, can the judge and his assistants apply it properly to cases, many of which are complicated, tortuous, and inaccessible to simple understanding and therefore demanding the intervention of judicial authority. For these cases, the blindfold is the most absurd emblem of justice. What is needed is refined cultivation of the spirit, the use of the most precise technical methods to secure for justice its legitimate rule.

Society needed a "legal estate, whose very education and knowledge are able to inspire respect, [an estate] which has prepared itself through science for its high service." [132] But science was not enough. The members of the legal estate had to gain "educational practice"; otherwise science would be dispelled by the influence of routine. "Educational practice is the duct of science into juridical life." [133]

Meier founded a "juridical clinic" at the university to teach young jurists how to apply principles in their work. He emphasized the combination of theory and practice. The practical courses which were continued by Moroshkin at Moscow University, he thought, were trying to supplant and not supplement juridical education. He had the students do exercises in reaching decisions on old Senate cases, and compose difficult juridical papers and registers of cases. He dreamed of writing a popular "juridical catechism." He met with students at all hours of the day and night, followed their progress, and lent them books on the law, which were hard to come by in Kazan. [134]

Meier made himself an example of the jurist. His writings on civil law were oriented toward present practice and aimed to provide assistance to those working in the courts. After his death, his lectures on Russian civil law and Russian law on bills served as the first guides to civil law for the young generation of law students attracted to service in the courts. He himself went to court and defended the interests of those he thought had just cases. He implored the students to enter service in the Ministry of Justice, and when they pointed to the disagreeable side of work there, he insisted on the obligation of each to serve not for himself, but for the benefit of the state and citizenry. He emphasized the duty of service, and argued that the toleration of bribery, even if many officials were poor, was ruinous to state and society.[135] He lived poorly, giving all his means and all his energies to the cause of the law. When he died in 1856, at the age of thirty-seven, the cortege was made up only of students.[136]

Within the Ministry of Justice, the role of teacher was taken by Sergei Ivanovich Zarudnyi. Zarudnyi came from a poor but old noble family of Kharkov province. His father had inherited little of the family's once vast estates, and Zarudnyi himself lost his own inheritance only a few years after he entered the service. The Zarudnyis had traditionally served in the guards' regiments and the army, and young Sergei had been intended for a career as a naval officer. But by some strange quirk, he was refused admission to the Naval Cadet Corps and instead, at the age of fourteen, he went to Kharkov, where he learned early to fend for himself while he lived alone and prepared for the university. He studied mathematics at Kharkov University and received the degree of candidate. At the same time, he read widely in western literature and philosophy, much of it in the original French, English, German, or Italian. At the university, he became an enthusiast of the idealistic and romantic doctrines of the day.[137]

Zarudnyi was not a jurist by training, but the idealistic outlook he adopted at the university would stay with him and shape his attitude to the law as well. He saw the answers to all questions in the work of thought and science. As a youth, idealism made sense of his personal experiences and gave him a way to cope with his quandaries. His diary of 1834, written when he was eighteen, describes his search for a meaning in life. "Why am I living on earth?" he asked. Looking into the past, he could find no answer in his life. "I don't remember my childhood. I remember only some life that prompts sadness in me." It was "a strange existence that I wandered through, peering into everything, and everything frightened me anew. Even then it seemed to me that I existed because of some strange chance, that I should not exist." The sadness would return from the past. "I remember the weeping, sickness, grief, partings. I remember that I despised myself."[138]

However gloomy the past, the future held out little hope for something better. He would have to meet people, who, he was convinced, would hate him. He felt himself lost in the world, suffering from the disease of unawareness. "Mysteriousness is the emblem of my activity. I think, I act, and I am not aware, am not aware, and cannot be aware." "I! I remain without consciousness. I have become negative and perished." He felt himself striving for goals beyond his reach. "I see only the idea, I chase it." But in the end he gave in to "external forces."

> External forces—they are my enemy. I want to live an inner
> life to fight external forces. I want to think but external forces
> do not permit me.[139]

The external forces were passions, the evidence of his weakness. He
remembered the advice of his mother. Her last words before she died when
he was a child were about the "true activity of the heart." She told him to
"despise, destroy, the actions of passions." Salvation came with the
triumph of thought, as the soul grasped for the idea. The idea, it appears,
increasingly became embodied in a young lady. "The soul exists in
consciousness, consciousness in the idea, the idea in space. The soul is
trying to comprehend all. It hurtles into space and vanishes."[140] The next
day's entry, entitled "The Enchantment of Life Found," described a
momentary liberation.

> Life is opposition to the dictates of fate. When we discard our
> blindfold, tear off the chains of our substance and turn to the
> opposite, only then do we really begin to live. Everything takes
> a new turn, for there appears the Idea! The Idea! The triumph
> of bliss. The Idea! The crown of life, and that Idea should be the
> constant support of our life, the constant goal of our feelings.[141]

Several decades earlier the young Bludov had found the meaning of his
adolescent longings in the manner of sentimentalism and had dreamed of a
beautiful suicide. For Zarudnyi and his generation, romanticism and
idealism provided more active and dynamic ways to respond. They saw
their infatuation as part of an elevating, cosmic struggle. When, a month
later, Zarudnyi's hopes ended in bitter disappointment, he did not content
himself with the taste of melancholy, but resumed his struggle against his
passions. In an entry entitled "Disenchantment," he declared to himself
that life was not a struggle against passions: "the high moment of our life is
the moment of the triumph over passions."[142] Living demanded this
triumph, and the young man, in his initial contacts with reality,
approached it not with the wistful sadness of withdrawal, but with a
determination to assert his will, to fight, and to exist in the realm of
consciousness.

Like others of his generation, Zarudnyi sought consciousness through
science. He hoped to be an astronomer and work in an area appealing to
his taste for the abstract. When he was disappointed and had to go to work
in the Ministry of Justice, he approached the law with the same devotion to
a scientific approach and the preeminence of thought. He was able as a
stolonachal'nik to take advantage of the opportunities provided him by his
daily work. In 1843, Bludov requested materials on practical problems in
applying Russian civil laws. Zarudnyi knew nothing of Russian law at this
time, but the thought of studying their imperfections stimulated his
interest. "From the shortcomings of laws, I began the study of laws

themselves." Instead of merely editing and passing on the reports sent to him, like the typical *chinovnik,* he brought them home and took careful notes. "And the more shortcomings I found in our laws, the more I enjoyed studying them. This was my school." [143] At this point, he resolved to dedicate himself to the cause of improving justice. He began to read in the law, and devote his thought completely to the problem of correcting the deficiencies he had learned of. "Very many people made more of a contribution to [the court reform] than I, but no one, and that I can say emphatically, no one worked for the good of the cause as long, and as constantly." [144]

Zarudnyi showed his methodical and logical talents in composing the reports delivered to the ministry's Consultation. He was appointed *Iuriskonsult* in 1849, and soon after took charge of all cases in the Consultation, with the obligation to sign all proposals of the ministry to the Senate. His intellectual rigor impressed all his associates. "He did not write floridly but precisely and clearly. In his reports there was no eloquence, but strict logical consistency through the entire presentation, from beginning to end." [145]

Zarudnyi began to work out a systematic approach to legal problems in the ministry. He taught young officials how to use legal norms in working out the complex problems of law raised by the cases that came before the Consultation. He would present a historical résumé of the laws bearing on the case, carefully distinguishing those that were outdated from those still in effect. He then strove to understand the laws, not by themselves, which was traditional practice, but in terms of general principles of law. Shubin-Pozdeev, a graduate of the juridical faculty of Moscow University and Zarudnyi's associate throughout the drafting of the court reform, wrote, "The works of Zarudnyi in the Consultation represented an entire epoch." With his guidance, views were worked out that became norms for deciding similar cases. [146]

Under Zarudnyi, the judicial role of the Consultation became a conscious and a respected one. He had the special ability to inspire his associates with his own personal involvement in the process of analysis and decision, in the development of a scientific approach to the law. Senate chief-secretaries and other officials came to him for advice on difficult questions of legal understanding. The young jurists in the ministry looked to him as their teacher. At his "school," which met every week on the evening before the Consultation, he heard their reports, criticized their analyses, and presented his own views. He singled out the most gifted reporters and brought them to the minister's attention. [147]

Zarudnyi, pained by the absence of both a family and a tradition, took on the role of the father and created his own tradition, showing men how to look at problems in a new way. He saw his work as part of a process, the cause of the betterment of the nation through the evolution of law. His approach was active, generative, paternal, far from the perennial son's worship of the values of youth. His willingness to dominate, to be blunt and candid, did not sit well with many traditional bureaucrats, who expected a graceful subservience. But it suited him well to lead the work on reform, and to assume the role of father himself.

Zarudnyi did not limit his concern to the judicial practice of the ministry. He dreamed of a more rational and just order, based upon principles taught by science. An admirer of Jeremy Bentham, he looked toward a social system that would provide the greatest good for the greatest number. In the late forties he took part in the intellectual ferment among the Petersburg officials. He saw the realization of his democratic ideal in the French, "a people possessing a deep consciousness of its right, fully understanding the true meaning of man and his place in the administrative machine . . . a people whose consciousness of true law conquers self-interest, whose freedom is guarded by publicity, whose desire for truth receives full rein." Visiting France in the summer of 1847, he attended the lectures of leading jurists and observed the benefits of a system of public justice.[148]

In 1856, Zarudnyi was appointed assistant state secretary in the State Chancellery, where he directed the work on the technical problems raised by Bludov's project for reform of civil procedure. In the State Chancellery, he would play much the same role as he had in the Consultation, turning a strategic, but largely subordinate organ into a source of intellectual creativity and movement. He gathered around him the most gifted and knowledgeable experts in the administration, instructed and guided them, and enabled them to use their knowledge to fashion a reform that would liberate legal expertise from the bonds of the administrative order.

The new legal officials did not yet comprise a group of professional jurists. They lacked the primary feature of such a group: a power over the interpretation and shaping of the law. But they had already acquired a sense of their own moral identity as jurists. They believed in the moral dignity of their calling: that true jurists should be worthy of trust. They were convinced of its intellectual stature: that the dispensation of justice required minds trained in the methods and doctrines of legal interpretation, and could not be entrusted to every layman in need of an office. They aimed to bring science into life, and looked toward a jurisprudence developing in the practical work of the courts. The preeminence of the executive in the Russian autocracy affronted their own notions of the stature of judiciary. When the era of reforms brought a reevaluation of the traditional attitudes, they would be called upon to formulate a system that could provide a fair and reliable administration of justice. They would lead a fight for a court procedure that would allow the jurist to come into his own—an emancipation of legal expertise.

III
REFORM

INTRODUCTION:
THE OLD JUDICIARY

When finally a misfortune occurs and a suit is inevitable, then it is nearly preferable to sacrifice a few of one's rights in order to avoid it. Life has the goal of the attainment of a certain purpose, and every trial, like a difficult disease, fire, or other unexpected calamity, removes man from his occupations, his goal, and poisons his life. One may say that peace is worth any cost.

L. Denis, *A Practical Dictionary of Russian Civil Law* (1859)[1]

THE CADRES OF OFFICIALS TRAINED IN NICHOLAS'S EDUCATIONAL INSTITU-
tions entered a legal system designed to restrict the discretion of the judiciary
and keep its personnel subordinate to administrative authorities. Governors and governor-generals meddled freely in the courts and saw nothing
sacred in the rulings of judges. Posing as impartial defenders of justice,
they "cancelled or substantially altered promissory notes, annulled court
decisions, initiated investigations in cases where there was not a hint of a
crime, placed the seal of silence and oblivion on morbid criminal cases,
about which it was left to cry to heavenly, but not to earthly justice."[2]

The nascent professional sense of the first generations of Russian legal
officials could not develop in a system geared to safeguard the supremacy
of executive authority. Only in the era of the great reforms, after the
Crimean War, did the autocrat acknowledge the importance of a discrete
judicial branch of government. The Reform of 1864 would endow the
judiciary with a stature and power it never possessed before. It would
assign the responsibility for the legal process to those trained in legal
science and create institutions that embodied modern principles of legal
procedure. Part 3 will describe the circumstances that moved the tsar to
take this step, and the impact of an independent judiciary upon the
workings of autocratic polity.

Despite the ambitious claims and the efforts of the ruler, the absolutist
system of justice was a way of making do with very little. The budget of the
Ministry of Justice in Nicholas's reign indicates the real official priorities.
Increased expenditures went to benefit the military. The Ministry of
Interior received no increase in appropriations from 1839 to 1854 though
the total state budget rose 51 percent and the population 9 percent in this
period.[3] The Ministry of Justice fared no better and it disposed of smaller
funds from the start. A provincial Judicial Chamber received 3,000 to
4,000 rubles a year for support compared with 16,000 to 20,000 rubles for
the Provincial Bureau and 20,000 to 30,000 for the provincial Treasury
Chamber. Salaries were correspondingly lower. The chairman of the
provincial Judicial Chamber received 1,144 rubles a year, as compared
with 4,406 rubles for the chairman of the Treasury Chamber. Officials in
lesser posts in the ministry also received lower salaries than their counterparts in other ministries.[4]

Count Panin tried to secure higher appropriations, but Nicholas found
it easy to disappoint him. In a report of 1855, the minister listed the rebuffs
the ministry had received. In 1834 and 1835 Dashkov had convinced
Nicholas to order increases in the funds available for judicial offices in
the provinces, but the funds were diverted to other governmental
institutions that had shown increased needs. Nicholas again promised
increased funds in 1847, but the armed intervention in Hungary in 1849
drained the treasury, and he again reneged. A project of 1851 to increase

the salaries of judicial officials in the provinces never reached the State Council because the council's Department of Economy was reviewing the budgets of all ministries with the aim of curtailing costs. The members of the department, however, found the ministry's salaries so low that they asked Panin to submit a new increased budget in 1852. This Panin did, but action was postponed until the resolution of the proposed Bludov reform of the courts. By the time the deadlock between Panin and Bludov had been resolved, Russia was in the midst of the fiscal crisis engendered by the Crimean War.[5]

The administration suffered from what Starr has described as problems of "undergovernment" and "underinstitutionalization." The state had few officials to govern its vast territory: a ratio of 1.1 to 1.3 officials per thousand, as compared with 4.1 in Britain and 4.8 in France at that time.[6] The ratios for judicial officials show even more striking discrepancies, reflecting the low standing of the judiciary in the Russian administration at this time. According to a report by Rovinskii, there were 0.04 judicial officials per thousand in Russia (including such officials as noble assessors who really performed no judicial function), as compared with 0.4 per thousand in France. The number of judicial officials had not increased significantly since 1775, a period during which the population had approximately doubled.[7] The system could work only because the landed nobility acted as officials and judges on their estates. But noblemen allowed peasant managers and elders to decide cases according to custom, thus leaving the millions of serfs outside the sphere of formal justice. The emancipation of the serfs would bring the landlords' administrative and judicial roles to an end.

The institutions that resulted from this general neglect earned the condemnation of almost all of educated society. This is not the place to enter into a discussion of the innumerable shortcomings of the old courts, which have been described at length elsewhere,[8] but it is necessary to give a brief account of those characteristics that belied the grandiose claims set forth in the official ideology.

The primary goal of the old courts was to protect the power, interests, and prestige of the administrative authorities rather than the rights of the population. The cloak of chancellery secrecy continued to conceal every stage of the process and all judgments from outside scrutiny. The police, who were responsible to the provincial governors, played an important role in legal cases. The local police chief (*zemskii ispravnik*) was in charge of conducting criminal investigations, gathering evidence in civil suits, and enforcing all court decisions, though judicial responsibilities comprised only part of his assignments. Untrained in the law, he was beholden to the local nobility, who elected him, and to his administrative superiors.[9] The accused had no protection against the actions of the local police. They were allowed no legal defense, and could be kept in jail indefinitely while the police's findings came to the attention of the court and the court reached its verdict. The official review of cases by higher instances and the supervision of the procuracy offered some safeguards, but a case would take years to go through the many instances of the prereform judiciary, and the higher instances had to rely entirely upon materials provided by the police. The defendant had a right to appeal, but only after the punishment was inflicted, and if the appeal failed, the sentence could be increased.

The citizen also lacked ways to defend his rights in civil cases. After a suit was filed, the court officials took full responsibility for conducting it, irrespective of the wishes of the parties. The parties would not see the judge, and were left completely dependent on the whim of the chancellery. Legal representation could be had only from the groups of fixers, usually retired clerks, who frequented the courts and knew its formalities and the methods of bribery. Moving a civil suit forward still required the intervention of powerful patrons and the payment of large bribes.

The cumbersome procedural requirements of the system of written formal proofs appeared to frustrate rather than expedite the dispensation of justice. Proofs were divided into "perfect" and "imperfect." The chief "perfect" proofs were confession and eyewitness testimony of two witnesses, and no combination of lesser or imperfect proofs could influence the verdict if no perfect proof was available. On the one hand this system encouraged use of torture in the interrogation to exact confession; on the other, it was difficult to incriminate those who did not confess.[10] The police, meanwhile, gave undue weight to crude material evidence that they hoped could be used to exact confession.[11] If the formal requirements could not be fulfilled, but doubts lingered, the court could reach a verdict of "remains under suspicion." The accused then left the courtroom free, but spent the rest of his life under the stigma of unproven criminal charges.

It was widespread opinion that the system of formal proofs favored the hardened criminal, who knew how to manipulate the system of proofs and to avoid confession under any circumstances, while the poor innocent could be hectored and intimidated. Though it is impossible to verify such assertions, it is quite clear that these requirements made it difficult to convict. Official statistics indicate that despite the harsh face of Nicholaean justice, the courts had difficulty proving criminal charges. The low percentage of convictions and the horrors inflicted on the arraigned gave rise to a feeling that the criminal courts themselves were a major perpetrator of injustice.[12]

The system appeared no more successful in securing civil remedies. The confusion and inflexibility of inquisitorial procedure here too worked to the advantage of the defendant. Whereas the accused might have to languish in jail while his case was slowly processed, the defendant in a civil suit could, by various stratagems, stall a trial for years; he did not, in fact, have to appear in court but could reply by mail. Locating the defendant was difficult, and if he was abroad, often impossible. If found, the defendant could raise procedural objections that would break the case up into smaller cases, turning the litigation into an inscrutable tangle. Further complications came from the lack of established procedures in legalizing documents; cases involving authenticity of documents filled the courts and often had to be referred as high as the Senate. Civil cases dragged on for years and decades, often not being decided until after the death of the parties. In 1837, Nicholas ordered the courts to conclude a suit against the government undertaken by the merchants Azver and Razovskii, who had supplied food to a military hospital in 1806 and 1807. The case was concluded in 1856.[13] If the plaintiff succeeded in having the case decided in his favor, he then had to induce the police to enforce the decision. Since the police owed no obedience to the court, they could be forced to act only by appeal to the governor.

The formidable difficulties of civil process discouraged litigation and led to a reliance on informal remedies or abstention from the defense of the individual's interests. The minister of justice tried to show a mounting number of civil cases in the years 1840 to 1855. In fact, the number of civil suits processed annually seems to have remained about constant.[14]

The official antagonism to the judicial function gave rise to a general repugnance to the work of courts. Judges swept up "the filth of mankind" or rummaged in "the darkness of human souls," as Dmitriev felt. Litigation was shown as an attractive vice and good people were to avoid the courts. Gogol's judge, Demian Demianovich, sought to end the terrible strife in the defamation suit between the two Ivans in a burst of love and comradely drinking. Legal texts, like L. Denis's, preached silent sustenance of injuries and urged the reader to avoid contention whenever possible. Peace was worth any cost.

But if Nicholas failed to place the dispensation of justice on the sound basis he had hoped for at the beginning of his reign, he did raise expectations of improved enforcement of the law. His high pronouncements held out the hope that the formal system described on paper could be made to work. Given officials of sound education and moral fiber, working under a system of intensified central supervision, institutions, he insisted, could operate lawfully. In the Third Section he created an instrument to oversee the enforcement of the law and the virtue of the citizenry. The supreme power became a "social conscience," whose righteous imperatives would inspire proper conduct, just as personal conscience inspired individual morality. The machinery of supervision and execution grew uncontrollably; the number of officials in the civil service increased by 30 percent from 1847 to 1856 alone. But the hypertrophied administration revealed only "the helplessness of power" to achieve the goal of legality.[15] During the Crimean War, the heightened sense of public morality would turn against the tsarist administration itself.

But even before the war, officials in the administration had begun to sense the disparity between the high goals and the actual performance of absolutist government. At all levels, they were experiencing a growing sense of emptiness and anomie. In 1826, Nikitenko, hearing that the young Tsar Nicholas had forced a great landlord to pay his debts to a private creditor, had remarked: "The legal justice [*pravosudie*] of the monarch should increase credit here." Fifteen years later, Nikitenko did not nourish the same faith. "Enlightened people do not want to be ruled by arbitrariness or chance. They demand law and legal justice. All social disturbances arise from the hidden war of law with authority which does not want to know law, or which applies it poorly."[16]

A year later, in 1842, the loyal Lebedev wrote with disgust of the courts in his diary. Their slowness and incompetence had become unendurable. "Now [the courts] are tolerated in the hope that they will be discarded out of irritation or weariness. This is materially harmful to the state, for it costs enormous sums. It is morally harmful because it deprives the state of trust."[17] He felt himself immersed in lies, unable to determine the truth. A report he wrote on his department in 1853 struck him as complete fabrication. "Should I send in this rubbish, this sickening mess, this falsehood, or make up my mind to write and submit the truth? I would make up my mind to write the truth, but to reach the truth is impossible." The excessive centralization had obscured the truth in a web of formality.[18]

A sense of lawlessness and falsehood pervaded the administration. In 1855, Peter Valuev, the governor-general of Courland and Estland, wrote that "the distinctive features of our governmental system consist in a ubiquitous absence of truth; in the government's lack of faith in its own weapons and the scorn for everything else. The multiplicity of forms crush the meaning of administrative activity, and ensure a universal official falsehood . . . ." It was impossible to distinguish the sense of a case from its paper formalities, to tell "what is real from what is merely apparent, justice from injustice or half-justice . . . . Even the law is often branded with untruthfulness. Taking little care for distinct clarity of expression and practical application of rules, it boldly and consciously demands the impossible." The system was an embodiment of hypocrisy. "On the surface there is glitter, beneath, rot."[19]

The sense of dissatisfaction with the courts was widespread among the population. Dahl's collection of proverbs mentioned none in praise of the courts. Proverbs about the legal system gathered in mid-century conveyed a bleak cynicism about the possibility of judicial remedies. They presented courts as instruments of the rich and powerful. "Justice is strong. Money is stronger." "A court is like a pond, you don't come out dry." "Don't fight with a strong man, don't go to court against a rich man." "Don't go to court, or a sandal will cost you more than a shoe." "In a court with a rich man, a poor wretch, though right, is guilty." Judges were moved exclusively by self-interest. "Do not fear the courts, fear the judges." "What is good for judges is what slips into their pockets." "When you give to the judge, you can defeat anyone." "Where there is a court, there is injustice."[20]

The administrative authorities purported to stand above the morass of the court system. Their claim to superiority was based on their proximity to the tsar in the administrative hierarchy, their prerogatives as the tsar's agents in the province. The tsar, dispensing a paternalistic, personal justice appeared as the incarnation of grace and impartiality. But by the nineteenth century, the charismatic charm of the ruler had lost much of its hold. The tsar was good, but helpless, and gave no hope in balancing the scales of justice. The tsar was too great to concern himself about justice. "God is high and the Tsar is far away." "The sun can't warm everyone and the Tsar can't take care of everyone." "The Tsar is merciful, but his mercy comes through the boyars' sieve."[21]

The widespread peculation and bribery revealed during the Crimean defeat demonstrated finally and incontestably the futility of the absolutist system of justice. The administration was unveiled, riddled with corruption. Authority, which had claimed moral supremacy, now appeared synonymous with deceit and irresponsibility. There spread a sense of the lawlessness of Russian life and an awareness of the costly repercussions of ineffective courts. The decade after the Crimean War would witness justice lifted from its lowly station and extolled as the palladium of the future progress and prosperity of the empire.

9

THE ASPIRATION
TO LEGALITY

With the help of Divine Providence, always beneficent to Russia, may her domestic order be strengthened and perfected; may justice and mercy rule in her courts, and the striving for enlightenment and all useful activity develop everywhere and with renewed strength, and may each, under the canopy of laws equally just for all, equally protective of all, enjoy the fruits of honest labor in peace. Finally, and this is the first and most vital of Our wishes, may the light of saving faith, illuminating minds, preserve and improve more and more public morality, that truest guarantee of order and happiness.

Imperial Manifesto of 19 March 1856,
on the conclusion of the Crimean War

In the words of Count Bludov, Alexander II's manifesto on the signing of the Peace of Paris announced a reversal in the attitudes of the Russian monarch. Previous imperial pronouncements had sought the national well-being in the strengthening, improvement, or expansion of the administrative apparatus. Based on the eighteenth-century notion of the police state, they had presented government overview as the source of rationality and honesty, and its extension as the surest way to uplift the population, morally, culturally, and economically. The debacle of the Crimean War, the scandals it brought to light, proved the futility of such an outlook in the middle of the nineteenth century. It made clear the limits of authoritarian supervision to the autocrat himself, and impelled him to give freer rein to the energies of the population. His manifesto held forth the hope of a creative efflorescence without invoking the intimidating presence of the state.

The image of Alexander Nevskii that Zhukovskii had evoked in the classroom now provided a model of heroism in humility and retreat. Without rejecting the principles of absolute government, Alexander accepted the need to decrease the extent of state responsibility and authority. He attacked the most apparent embodiment of the principle of authoritarian control—the system of serfdom.[1] The decision to embark on the emancipation of the serfs signaled the autocrat's intention to abandon total commitment to the attempt to impose social morality and economic goals from above. He now endeavored to introduce elements of a liberal model that would allow freer social action and encourage the development of a citizenry with a sense of responsibility and economic initiative.

At first, Alexander did not contemplate a fundamental change in the judicial system. Committed to the improvement of justice, he held notions of the judiciary that remained within the traditional conceptions of the Russian autocrat. His knowledge of the law and legal system were derived entirely from the lectures Speranskii had read to him from 1835 to 1837.[2] Speranskii, respecting the established outlook, had barely mentioned the judiciary in his lectures on Russian law. He subsumed all law under state or constitutional law, and described how institutions were divided into legislative and administrative organs.[3] The judiciary was a minor arm of the administration; he dealt with it and the police under the rubric of "means of restoring order," in the event of breaches of the law. As in other legal works of Nicholas's reign, much space was devoted to descriptions of the procedural requirements specified by the *Digest of Laws,* particularly for criminal cases. Speranskii's treatment of procedure amounted to little more than an enumeration of the mechanical steps that would ensure the application of substantive laws to particular cases. Such notions of law continued to dominate the thinking of high circles after Alexander had ascended the throne. When Kavelin, during his brief service as tutor to the heir, asserted that no one should be punished without trial and that no one should punish a person not sentenced by a court, these remarks were taken as impertinent attempts to limit the prerogatives of the supreme power.[4]

But the goal of an active and productive citizenry required a new system of justice, not merely a modified version of the old. The traditional system of "substantive justice" had aimed to facilitate authoritarian control by prescribing laws that would be faithfully enforced by the courts. Its rigid adherence to specific solutions could not fit a society in flux or act as a stimulus to the economic energies of the citizenry. An active, varied economy would raise new and complex legal issues that could not be foreseen by the ruler's decrees. It required the more resilient mechanisms of what Weber describes as "formal justice," where procedural norms, within the framework of an adversary system, provide the flexibility that permits adaptation to new types of cases. Authoritarian controls had to give way to "procedural primacy," whereby the judiciary could "cope with a wide variety of changing circumstances and types of cases without prior commitment to specific solutions."

The system of substantive justice had been irreparably compromised by the events of the previous decades, and the importance of a flexible judicial system to the development of the new society came to be widely recognized both in educated society and in the administration. But neither liberal spokesmen among the nobility, with their numerous suggestions for adopting western judicial institutions, nor traditional burcaucrats were capable of drafting and implementing a reform that would establish a primacy of procedure. Formal justice introduces a new element of abstraction to the legal process, for it demands the observance of legal norms of adjudication rather than the rote application of particular laws.[5] Its introduction meant the ceding of the ruler's power over justice to experts trained in the application of legal norms. But this required a relaxation of the autocrat's traditional suspicion of the judiciary. Both within the administration and among the nobility at large, there took place in these years a struggle for a judiciary, a struggle to grant legal expertise integrity.

The initial plans for reform of civil procedure, drafted in the Second Section under the direction of Count Bludov, reflected Alexander's original notions of judicial reform. These projects, as we have seen in chapter 6, maintained the primacy of the executive over the courts. Bludov's projects left the courts within the framework of the regular administration and under the supervision of the governors. Despite his stated aim to bring radical changes to the system, Bludov offered only modifications, as a limited adversary procedure and state-appointed attorneys. Alexander fully shared Bludov's conception of reform and forbade the discussion of public justice and lawyers in the State Council.[6]

Bludov also directed the discussions of reform in the State Council, which began to consider his projects for reform of civil procedure in 1857. As chairman of the council's Department of Laws, he also chaired its joint meetings with the Department of Civil Affairs, which considered his projects until the spring of 1861. The members of the departments were *sanovniki,* like Bludov, who sympathized with his notions of the judiciary. Only three of the eleven members, Gagarin, Kochubei, and Zamiatnin, the assistant minister of justice, had served in judicial organs. Gagarin and Kochubei, aristocratic officials who entered the service under Alexander I, had risen quickly to high positions without familiarity with the details of procedure or involvement with the study or advancement of the law. Zamiatnin had been educated at Tsarskoe Selo and trained in Speranskii's Second Section. But a polished and refined aristocrat, he was more skilled at detecting the direction of official policy than leading it.

The journals of the departments made only minor criticisms of Bludov's reforms. The members agreed that the old system was ineffectual but defended the system of formal proofs and written procedure. They questioned the existing institutions entirely on the basis of the expedience of this or that particular feature. They enumerated twenty-five discrete faults that they felt the Bludov projects would correct. Police offices were not executing the orders of the courts faithfully or effectively. State lawyers were necessary because the law could not be made clear enough to be understood by laymen. The right of the minister of justice to protest cases delayed justice excessively and undermined the authority of the Senate.[7]

For the reformers to achieve a general reform of the courts and free them from the administration, they had to wrest control of the reform from the Second Section. Their activity began outside of Bludov's purview, under the aegis of the Grand Duke Constantine Nikolaevich. The grand duke, using the Naval Ministry as a base, made possible the statement of a position contrary to the Second Section's. As described in chapter 8, he recruited a group of *pravovedy* to take charge of the reforms in his ministry. To expedite this work, he introduced what he called "artificial publicity" (*iskusstvennaia glasnost'*) — the circulation of reform proposals to all officials in his ministry to stimulate discussion and criticism.[8] He took the same approach to the cause of judicial reform and sent Dmitrii Obolenskii's critique of the Bludov proposals to thirty leading figures in the administration, among them Bludov himself.[9]

Obolenskii objected less to specific recommendations of Bludov than to his general treatment of the judicial power. He declared that the judiciary was the "base upon which the entire structure of state administration rests." The absence of routes of communication prevented the development of the material forces of the country. But the lack of a true court system had even more dire consequences.

> The absence of a court was and still is the insuperable obstacle undermining and vitiating all attempts to advance the internal organization of Russia, to improve the administration, to develop commerce and industry, and finally to define the relationships between peasants and landlords, which will remain unresolved in practice until the authority between the two classes, i.e., a *judiciary*, receives some proper organization.[10]

Arguing that the judge was "the servant of truth [*istina*]" who should be "its independent representative," he showed that the Bludov project merely provided a "system of particulars," an enumeration of the specific defects of the existing courts, but left the system of filling judicial positions untouched. The many new rules the Bludov projects introduced threatened to increase the existing paper work. He called for the introduction of public courts and an adversary system, and urged the adoption of a foreign system, particularly the new system contemplated for Poland, as a model.[11]

The Obolenskii memorandum was widely discussed in the administration and, together with several articles in the press, brought the tsar's emphatic rejection of the principles of open courts and a bar. In 1858, such questions were prohibited from discussion in the State Council and the press. Obolenskii's memorandum, the first suggestion that foreign prototypes be used to determine the outlines of the Russian system, represented a premature and overly radical break with the principles of official nationality. The fact that Obolenskii had written the memorandum in Rome added to suspicions of his motivations. The task of replying fell to Zarudnyi who, as assistant state secretary under the Department of Laws, was subordinate to Count Bludov. Zarudnyi avoided repudiating Obolenskii's individual points, rather insisting on the lack of "practical conclusions" in Obolenskii's proposals. He argued that the Bludov projects were taking the only steps possible toward the introduction of public courts, considering Russia's state of historical development.[12]

Zarudnyi's own approach was quieter, but in the long run more effective. Zarudnyi himself never took an open stand in opposition to the Bludov projects. But he used his position of authority in the State Chancellery to gather a mounting corpus of criticism of the Bludov projects, which he then made available to the aristocrats in the department. Under Zarudnyi's guidance, the State Chancellery became a center of the forces of legal expertise. By means of attacks on particular points of the reform, Zarudnyi made clear the necessity of giving the matter of judicial reform over to judicial experts.

Zarudnyi himself composed eleven memoranda on specific problems of procedure. Technical in nature, they introduced for the first time the notions of a system of justices of the peace and private lawyers into the discussion of reform. One memorandum gave a detailed argument showing the need to distinguish questions of law from those of fact in civil cases. Another criticized the easy annullment of court decisions in the existing system and urged the separation of judicial decisions from the legislative order.[13] Several of his analyses dealt with the so-called voluntary civil procedure, cases of wills and deeds contested by only one party. Here he pointed to the burdening of the courts with semiadministrative responsibilities that he claimed should be the work of notaries. He provided a table of Russian laws on the subject, and then discussed the principal views of foreign jurists on the subject.[14] In all of these memoranda, Zarudnyi strove less to find specific solutions than to reveal judicial problems in all their complexity and to point to the need for a scientific approach within a flexible institutional framework.

Cautious in his reference to foreign models, Zarudnyi nonetheless made an enormous effort to make them available to jurists and officials. In 1858, he traveled abroad to examine European court systems, particularly those of the Italian states, and when he returned he circulated and published translations of procedural codes of Sardinia, Piedmont, and Hungary. In this manner he opened the administration to knowledge of the general liberalization of procedure taking place in central and eastern Europe at this time. In the early 1860s he wrote numerous articles on the English court system, which appeared in *Russkii Vestnik* and *Zhurnal Ministerstva Iustitsii*. But he always warned against uncritical imitation. When he was contemplating publishing his translation of the Sardinian and the Hungarian statutes of civil procedure, he wrote to Aksakov of his fears that official publication would discourage criticism of them.[15]

Zarudnyi established intellectual standards for the work of reform. He made the jurists in the ministry aware of foreign examples, and directed their reading about European theories and institutions. Pobedonostev, now serving in the Moscow Senate and teaching law at the university, turned to Zarudnyi for readings on western procedural systems.[16] Officials drawing up memoranda on one or another aspect of court procedure would submit them to Zarudnyi for his forthright and exacting criticism.[17]

Meanwhile, Zarudnyi was assembling comments from officials in the ministry that would help undermine the confidence of the members of the State Council in the Bludov projects. At Zarudnyi's invitation, Pobedonostev submitted his opinion of the Bludov proposals, with objections to nearly every point. His criticisms were so severe that Zarudnyi found them excessive.[18] In early 1860, Zarudnyi made a digest of all the criticisms, and had it printed and circulated to all members of the council. The initial unsigned remarks in the digest, it is clear, belong to Pobedonostev.[19]

Pobedonostev's attack set the tone for the digest. Like Obolenskii, he complained that the formal controls Bludov proposed would merely make procedure more unwieldy. The project lacked a "vital principle," and without such a principle there could never be a real corps of judges that would create a genuine judiciary. Pobedonostev drew a necessary connection between a system of verbal and open courts and the development of a corps of judges. "Under the rule of written form, with our present closed chancellery court, we will never have an estate of judges, but only judge-functionaries, mechanically observing set ceremonies either in fact or in appearance." Bludov had retained the old attitudes toward judges. "In the project, there is an obvious distrust for the living individual and a faith in dead form. The judge is not a living person but some kind of mute servant of a complex bureaucratic machine." [20]

Other unsigned critiques decried the same lack of system and the reliance on the old written procedure in the Bludov projects. One emphasized that its organization was more complex than the old and demanded more juridical knowledge. Court procedure was unsatisfactory, "not so much from the laws of court procedure as the personal qualities of the members of the lower courts and the lack of means for successful processing of cases in the higher courts." It went on to point to the defective enforcement of debts, which was undermining credit in Russia. The reform, the critique argued, retained the inquisitorial system. The author enumerated nine essential attributes of the adversary system that were absent from the Bludov projects. [21]

The opposition of the experts stalled the work on the civil reform. During most of 1860 the State Council was absorbed with the consideration of the emancipation. When the departments began work on the court reform in the spring of 1861, the influence of the critical attitudes of Zarudnyi and others on members like Gagarin began to tell. [22] The discussion of the Bludov projects in the departments reached an impasse and no recommendations were made to the council as a whole. [23] By March 1861, the members of the departments were expressing the hope that responsibility for the reform be transferred from the Second Section to the State Chancellery, so that work could be quickened by articulating the "general principles" of court procedure. [24]

In June 1860, Bludov submitted the first parts of his long-awaited project on criminal procedure. It was clear that this would receive the same treatment as the civil project. Again the demand for radical reform was announced from the Naval Ministry. Constantine Nikolaevich had initiated work on reform of the outdated criminal procedure in the naval courts. He assigned Pavel Glebov, one of the *pravovedy* he had recruited, to study this problem. Glebov traveled in France where he examined procedure both in naval courts and civil courts. Upon his return, he published his conclusions in a series of articles in *Morskoi Sbornik,* the journal of the Naval Ministry. [25]

Glebov made it clear that naval court procedure in France was conducted on the same principles as general procedure. Accordingly, he embarked on an enthusiastic description of French criminal procedure. The central feature of the system, he stressed, was the independence of the court and the judge, which was safeguarded by a separate judicial system. All other features flowed from this. He emphasized the importance of oral procedure, which allowed the judge to come close to the facts. He also showed the role of publicity of trials and the jury system, which minimized abuses in the courts.[26]

Glebov argued that Russia's backwardness did not rule out the borrowing of more advanced forms. He, like Obolenskii, rejected the principle of national distinctiveness, and asserted the primacy of principle over tradition. He emphasized the apolitical nature of judicial institutions, thus trying to allay the ruler's fears of open court procedure and lawyers as products of the French Revolution. Glebov insisted that open courts had no political direction in themselves, that lawyers could be of any political persuasion, and that it was the administration not the courts that gave a political direction to a nation. Rather, the courts could serve as a school of social morality for the people. Open justice would rid the system of its arbitrary, inscrutable character, and instill a notion of the meaning of crime in the people themselves.[27]

In May 1860, Glebov published his introductory remarks to his project for naval legal procedure. He summarized the points made in his articles on the French system and argued for their application to the Russian naval courts. He also expressed his hope that they be extended to criminal procedure in all courts.[28] In accordance with the practices of "artificial publicity" that Constantine Nikolaevich introduced into the Naval Ministry, comments were solicited from over two hundred officials in the ministry, and outside, including selected senators, governors, and figures in and associated with the State Chancellery. With few exceptions, the responses were favorable. But many of those in the Ministry of Justice and the State Chancellery, while approving of Glebov's principles, believed that they should not be introduced into one type of court but into all courts simultaneously. Consideration of the Naval Statute was in fact postponed until the formulation of the court reform, and by that time new obstacles had arisen which prevented it from being introduced. But it gave a strong stimulus to the cause of radical reform of criminal procedure.[29]

While the difficulties of the reform were proving the importance of legal expertise, the autocrat was showing a new attention to the Ministry of Justice, thus enhancing its stature and morale. The first sign of the changed attitude was a long-awaited increase in the appropriations to the ministry. Despite the dire fiscal difficulties after the war, the budget of the ministry was raised by one million rubles in 1856, and by the same amount in 1858. In 1859, an increase in funds allotted allowed the ministry to raise salaries of officials by 57 percent. The ministry's report of 1859 claimed that these funds were still insufficient, emphasizing that with the hard work and special knowledge required by work in legal institutions, judicial officials' salaries should exceed those paid in other branches. But the increased appropriations had already shown positive effects. "Thus the Chief-Secretaries of the Senate's chancellery have started to move to positions of Chairmen of the Chambers and Provincial-Procurators, while the chancellery of the St. Petersburg Criminal Chamber has been filled with graduates from the School of Jurisprudence." These abler officials could cope with more work, which permitted reductions in the chancellery staff.[30]

The new attitude also brought a change in leadership. Though Panin remained titular head until 1862, he ceased to run the ministry after his appointment to the Secret Committee on the Peasant Question in January 1858. His tasks were assumed by the assistant minister, Dmitrii Nikolaevich Zamiatnin. A product of the first years of the lycée, Zamiatnin combined the qualities of a nobleman able to travel in court circles, and an official of the Ministry of Justice devoted to the law. Zamiatnin was a moderately wealthy nobleman who had inherited 150 souls. His elite education had helped him gain social standing and entrée to the imperial court. By 1840, he had attained the court rank of *kamerger*. In the same year, he assumed the position of heraldry master, and began rooting out the corruption and dealing with the backlog of cases in the Heraldry Department of the Senate. At the lycée he had studied law under Kunitsyn, and when appointed minister of justice in 1862, he would be the first to have received formal legal training. His initial service, in the Codification Commission and the Second Section, also took place under Kunitsyn's direction and gave him a good grounding in the principles of Russian law. In the late 1840s and 1850s, he served as a chief-procurator of the Senate, a member of the ministry's Consultation, and the head of several important investigations of provincial judicial institutions.[31]

An official dedicated to the ordering and execution of the law, Zamiatnin, nonetheless, was not committed to the legal calling. He maintained the attitudes he had adopted at Tsarskoe Selo, where law had been taught as a branch of philosophy, as the creation of the legislator whose wisdom shaped society. As a student, he had learned to revere the legislator's mission to uplift his subjects, and to distrust public opinion which, based on falsehood, could be directed to the good only by the wise monarch. He had written in one of his compositions, "It is in you, Oh Sovereign benefactors, that the power to guide public opinion resides."[32] His career showed his flexibility to the monarch's will. When Alexander II began to turn his attention to justice, it became possible to act both as a loyal servant of his monarch and as a servant of the law.

Though not a legal expert, Zamiatnin felt himself an official of the ministry, and treated his subordinates as if he were one of them. The changeover from Panin to Zamiatnin was startling. Panin's entire mentality had denied the dignity of the official. He had tried to keep his distance from human beings and particularly to avoid falling into dependence upon others. Zamiatnin was known for his "uncommon kindness," his accessibility and consideration. Most important, he openly expressed his desire to study with people more knowledgeable than himself. He turned to the educated officials in the ministry and raised them to high administrative positions.[33] He fought for and won increases in the ministry's budget. As a result of his efforts, the educational level of officials, especially in the provinces, rose even before the drafting of the reform (see table 8.4). With his assumption of authority, the Ministry of Justice became an institution capable of asserting the views and defending the interests of the legal officialdom.

Following Constantine Nikolaevich's example, Zamiatnin encouraged group discussions of legal questions in the ministry. He founded the *Journal of the Ministry of Justice* to provide an organ for the treatment of legal theory and particular legal questions. The *Journal* carried articles by such figures as Ia. G. Esipovich, I. I. Ivanov, and Professor V. D. Spasovich, all of them graduates of the law faculty of Moscow University, and V. Bervi, a graduate of the law faculty of Kazan University. Many of the reformers also contributed. The articles published included treatments of Russian laws on such specific legal matters as debts and mortgages, descriptions of European court systems and practice, translations of the works of European scholars such as Mittermaier, and excerpts from Meier's lectures on civil law. Zamiatnin also succeeded in obtaining the right to publish decisions of the Senate. For the first time, Russian judicial decisions and court process were open to learned discussion. From 1859 to the beginning of 1862, the *Journal* published some two hundred decisions of civil cases and fifty of criminal cases.[34]

The articles submitted for the *Journal* and those that were published became subjects of interest and debate within the ministry and outside. The *Journal* inspired the founding of other law periodicals, the beginnings of a Russian legal press. In 1859, Nikolai Kalachov, an official of the Second Section and former professor of the law faculty of Moscow University, published his *Archive of Historical and Practical Information about Russia*. A student of Redkin's, Kalachov had been limited to study of the historical development of the law, and the first editions of his *Archive* had contained articles only on the history of law. Now contributions by officials and scholars dealt with questions of the interpretation and meaning of contemporary Russian law in the light of legal scholarship. The *Archive* rejected the squeamish attitude toward litigation taken by Denis's text on civil law. One of its reviewers saw justice as a vital part of life, as a means to assert one's interest actively.

> Life is full of doubts and problems. They all demand solution and they find it in the law. And every civil dispute is a doubt, a clash over the law. . . . A doubt arising from a rational principle and rooted in conviction can be satisfied only by a rational solution. Not everyone is capable of extinguishing his doubts and renouncing his rights without being sure that those doubts are groundless. The belief in one's own righteousness, if it is rooted in one's soul, should be dear to everyone. The firmer and more stubborn it is held in the personal consciousness, the more developed the entire notion of law will be in society at large and the stronger the trust in legal justice. One must not scorn this belief. We will go further. It is valuable, it is necessary to society. It is true that one can say that it corresponds to egoism and greed, which blind man. But it has another face too: the pure consciousness of justice must be accepted as the best feature of the man and the citizen.[35]

In 1860, Kalachov turned the *Archive* into the *Legal Messenger* (*Iuridicheskii Vestnik*), the first full-fledged Russian law periodical. In the same year, the novelist Salmanov founded his own, short-lived *Law Journal* (*Iuridicheskii Zhurnal*). The opening issue summoned the public to respond to the government's efforts to improve the dispensation of justice. The journal aimed to teach the public "to master and fully understand the idea of law" and to comprehend the work of reform. "Practice without theory is blind and helpless everywhere; this is especially true in the application of the laws." The editors called for a periodical press devoted to legal problems, for the publication and dissemination of legal guides, and public lectures on political and legal sciences.[36]

The excitement about the law infected the youth. They formed circles in Petersburg and Moscow to discuss cases and legal problems. They looked beyond their courses and read lithographed articles on the law that were passed from hand to hand. "The guiding aim of the circles was exclusively intellectual development, and the explanation of problems about the financial, judicial and social system—the working out of views and directions." They learned to read critically and develop their own judgments. "[The circles] replaced cards, billiards, taverns and carousals for us."[37] In many circles, participants practiced delivering court speeches based on reports of recent Russian or European trials. Some would act as lawyers, others prosecutors, as they prepared themselves to take part in an adversary procedure. "In this way we acquired the habit of speaking impromptu; we overcame our shyness and our fear of criticism." Arsen'ev, at the time assistant editor of the *Journal of the Ministry of Justice,* wrote,

"From our milieu there was practically no one who would not associate himself in one way or another with the work of the new judicial institutions."[38] The number of students registered in the juridical faculties rose, until they constituted over half the students registered at Russian universities by the end of the 1860s.[39]

As the provincial nobility became aware of the terms of the impending emancipation, they too began to turn to the law to define their new civic identity. The withdrawal of political backing from the serf system undermined the position of the landlords and their roles within the autocratic system. Before the emancipation, they had been partners in the wielding of administrative power. They had served as police officials and judges for their serfs, and rarely had to answer for their acts. They shared the official's aversion to legal definitions of his authority and his contempt for judicial institutions as offices beneath the true hierarchy of authority.

With emancipation, the former masters, agents of the authoritarian order in the countryside, had to face the task of becoming citizens responsible for the protection of their own interests, and such prospects brought new attitudes toward justice. Left at the mercy of the vagaries of economic life and bureaucratic arbitrariness, they began to look to the judicial system as a means to safeguard their rights. Courts no longer seemed administrative devices to secure compliance with the law, but necessary means to protect their interests as property owners and citizens. From this vantage point, the old courts, ineffective, slow, and porous to every kind of influence, became a principal grievance of the nobility and their reform a major concern of leading noble publicists.

Graduates of the law faculty of Moscow University, such as A. M. Unkovskii, A. A. Golovachev, and Prince A. V. Obolenskii, brought to the provincial nobility an awareness of the importance of individual rights defended by a strong judiciary to their future status. They looked to independent courts as a way to bring local administrative authorities under effective public control. In 1857, several district assemblies of Tver province, led by Unkovskii and other liberal noblemen, requested that the government establish public courts that could expose abuses in the administration. Such demands spread to other provinces. They were repeated in 1859 by the noble deputies from Riazan and Kharkov provinces. In 1860, the Vladimir nobility called for strict accountability of all officials before the courts. During the next two years, all noble assemblies in European Russia joined the campaign.[40]

The nobility's demand for courts that would control the administration could evoke only a hostile response from higher spheres in the government. It confirmed the fears that a free judiciary would dominate the administration and bring about the end of autocratic government in Russia. Even the reformers in the State Chancellery, all of them noblemen, vigorously opposed such a role for the courts, claiming that it violated the separation of powers. When drafting the section of the court reform on official crimes, they would devise the so-called administrative guarantee provision, whereby an official could be tried by the courts, but only with the consent of his superior.[41]

But the nobility was beginning to see the law as more than a means to prevent administrative abuse. Left without the support of serfdom, they looked to a system of law to provide themselves with the security necessary to allow them to fend for themselves. They began to look upon themselves as citizens, operating in a market economy and needful of the protection and regularity necessary to the work of the entrepreneur. This attitude received a strong stimulus when the government closed the Loan Bank and other credit institutions that had been used to keep the nobility afloat and maintain serfdom. The nobility now saw themselves dependent upon private credit. The courts, geared to protect the debtor, made collection difficult. Faced with the steep rise in interest rates at the close of the fifties, the nobility felt the importance of protecting the creditor and ensuring enforcement. The principal role the courts played for the nobility now shifted from the maintenance of order and the avoidance of disturbing troubles in the countryside to the advancement of equity in civic relations.

The Kharkov nobility gave an emphatic statement of this view in an address of 1858. Their words expressed a new sense of noble dignity and self-reliance. Previously, they claimed, noble assemblies met to beg favors from the government — to ask for extensions or forgiveness for their payments of debts, or additional funds on their mortgages. "To speak the truth, we should be ashamed about these public alms, ruinous to the treasury, unjust in relation to private individuals and humiliating to the honor of the noble estate." They declared they wanted only justice (*spravedlivost'*), and pointed to the judicial process as their chief grievance.[42]

Cases dragged on for years in the court system, the address complained. The police, who were responsible for collecting, refused to act unless threatened with the loss of their positions, and then took no steps to gain evidence that was withheld. "The reason for such a delay is that we have the ability to hide from the rulings of the courts if they are opposed to our interests." Simple debt collection cases continued for years while the debtor managed to transfer his property to another province for safekeeping. "With such obvious slowness and worthlessness of legal process, the creditors do not present their documents for enforcement; they prefer to avoid the loss of time and money this requires. Merchants prefer to take only ten kopeks to the ruble than to start a suit." The merchant then took over a 50 percent profit from his purchasers to make up for his losses.[43]

Estate cases became unbearably complex, requiring investigations that were delayed by individual appeals. They sometimes grew to such proportions that no one could make sense of them, ending only when the estate of one or the other party went to ruin. Trustees bled the estates under their protection, while the courts, able only to check on the observance of formalities, remained helpless to protect the interests of the wards. Paper forms covered the worst types of corruption and crime — the inevitable products of closed procedure — and did little to secure their estates.

> Our capital and our estates are guaranteed by paper documents kept in archives and government offices. But these documents are vague and uncertain; despite the vast number of these paper deeds, held in secret, they cannot protect our property and our persons.[44]

The Kharkov nobility called for open courts to ensure the honesty of officials and the honor of judges. But they also exhorted the public to change its own attitudes. "It is necessary that the estates formulate an idea of the general good, of their obligations, that they become convinced that their interest consists in the faithful observance of the laws — that the tranquillity of life and the security of the property of each and every one consist in an honorable life and legal justice."[45] The Kharkov address was followed by an appeal from the Tula nobility for open courts in cases touching individual and property rights and a jury system. A few months later, the Voronezh noble assembly approved an address demanding publicity of court proceedings and open courts, "upon which depend the prosperity, property, honor and life of all the subjects of Your Imperial Majesty."[46]

During 1859, a commission for the establishment of Land Banks studied the question of new sources of noble credit. The commission's recommendations were not acted upon, but the chairman of the commission, the statistician A. P. Bezobrazov, made clear the nobility's urgent need for credit and the importance of an effective judiciary to create the sources of credit. Bezobrazov traveled through nine provinces of central Russia and found that with the closing of the old credit institutions, loans were hard to come by, carried very high interest rates, and could be gotten only for short terms. Though the need for credit had not reached a dangerous stage, it would increase, he claimed, with the changeover to free labor following the emancipation.[47]

Bezobrazov had reviewed the opinions of noblemen on the question of Land Banks collected in the Ministry of Finances. The great majority of them emphatically insisted on the "difficulties existing for our land credit as a result of the weakness of our *judicial* and *police* protection of property and the person in Russia, and on the necessity of court reform. And thus with all the particular questions about the problem of Land Banks, *it too demands above all the hastening of this reform,* the corner-stone of all governmental reforms without exception." Bezobrazov himself argued that the government was not sufficiently protecting "the inviolability of the right of *private property and private industrial enterprise, both of which create capital.*" It was also not protecting the "*mutual relations between capitalists and debtors,* which create a trust in credit.... Thus even the question of land credit runs up against the problem *of the court*—that primary condition of the prosperity of state and nation." [48]

In these terms, the arguments for a thoroughgoing court reform began to carry a more conservative appeal. Court reform was necessary for the nobility to thrive under conditions of freedom. It was necessary to ensure stability and regularity, to protect the interests of property. The reformers in the Ministry of Justice pressed similar arguments. In the spring of 1861, Pobedonostev stressed the importance of a sound legal basis for credit operations to the state. "The first concern of the law," he wrote, "should be the protection of the *creditor,* for his legal interests are the interests of *property,* and the interests of property are inseparably tied with the internal security and internal prosperity of the state itself." [49]

It was this type of reasoning that ultimately influenced the tsar to abandon his suspicion of an independent judiciary and support a more radical reform of the court system. During the summer of 1861, when the difficulties of the emancipation were arousing discontent among the nobility, many of whom regarded the serf reform as an infringement upon their civil rights, it became necessary to reaffirm the state's protection of the rights of private property. In a report of August 1861, Peter Valuev, the acting minister of interior, gave a disturbing account of the mood among the nobility. Many noblemen were disgruntled, he claimed, simply because they had failed to turn the emancipation to their advantage. But, he conceded, some of their grievances were justified. He acknowledged that the rules of the statute did not sufficiently protect their land rights and that the government had not provided new sources of credit. [50] He urged the tsar to extend a helping hand to the nobility and make credit available to them. Alexander noted in the margin that such measures were of primary importance and that a solution to the credit problem should be expedited. [51]

Valuev advised that to weather the crisis it was necessary "to intensify activity and to encourage enterprise in all branches of industry." Then Valuev, no champion of an independent judiciary, went on to conclude that "the essential obstacle to this has long been recognized in the shortcomings of our court system." He remarked that completion of the work could still not be foreseen, alluding to the standstill of the reform in the State Council. Alexander wrote a note in the margin instructing Butkov, the head of the State Chancellery, to inform him when the projects would be ready. [52]

This report determined the fate of the judicial reform. In a subsequent meeting, the adroit Butkov, always able to scent the direction of official policy, agreed with the tsar that the reform should be turned over to the State Chancellery. Bludov and the members of the combined departments could not cope with the problem of formulating a reform that would answer the demands of the nobility and the standards of the jurists in the ministry. The task had to pass to those on a lower rung of the hierarchy, who had less prestige and power but commanded the skills and knowledge necessary to draft a reform. Similar problems faced the tsar in several of the great reforms. He responded by effecting a shift of responsibility without a shift of authority. Ancillary bodies were utilized, purportedly to provide information and clerical assistance, but in fact to do the substantive work of reform without disturbing the traditional hierarchy. In the preparation of the emancipation, the Editing Commission, which was subordinated to the Chief Committee on the Peasant Question, played this role; in the court reform, it was the State Chancellery.[53]

In January 1861, Zarudnyi, who had been assisting in the work of the emancipation, was promoted to the position of state secretary for the Department of Laws in the State Council, while Stoianovskii was appointed acting state secretary for the Department of Civil Affairs. This placed the two in key positions to direct the work on reform, but they could make little progress while bound by the Bludov proposals. In October 1861, after reading Valuev's memorandum, Alexander approved a plan for further work on the reform composed by Zarudnyi, and officially transferred responsibility to the State Chancellery. To assist in the work, Zarudnyi secured the assignment to the chancellery of six officials distinguished by their specialized knowledge and experience with the law: Rovinskii, Pobedonostev, Nikolai Butskovskii, A. M. Plavskii, A. P. Vilinbakhov, and P. N. Danevskii. P. P. Gagarin then replaced Bludov as chairman of the Department of Laws and, in early 1862, as chairman of the State Council. Under the influence of Zarudnyi, Gagarin became a vocal and influential supporter of an independent judiciary.

The new appointees joined Stoianovskii, Zarudnyi, and his protégé S. P. Shubin-Pozdeev to form the cadre that would draft the basic principles of the reform. They were representative of the new type of legal official who had appeared during Nicholas's reign. All of the nine were hereditary noblemen; seven were from the landed nobility: Zarudnyi, Danevskii, Shubin, Stoianovskii, Rovinskii, Butskovskii, and Plavskii. Their holdings were small or moderate or, like Zarudnyi's, had passed out of the family's hands. All but Butskovskii had received higher education, four at the School of Jurisprudence, four at the universities. Seven had served extensively in the Ministry of Justice; the exceptions were Plavskii and Danevskii, a doctor of law who had been a law teacher.[54]

The specialists in the State Chancellery viewed the judiciary as part of state life that operated according to specific principles of its own, evolved through the study and practice of those versed in the law. Aware of the absence of a Russian legal tradition, they insisted on the need to borrow from western jurisprudence and legal experience. One of the most important examples for them was the Civil Statute introduced in Hanover at the end of the 1840s. The Hanover statute had adopted principles of French procedure and applied them effectively to German courts. In an influential article published in the March 1862 issue of the *Journal of the Ministry of Justice,* Alexander Knirim, a *pravoved* and assistant editor of the *Journal,* described the success of the adoption of verbal and public procedure by the Hanover courts. The Hanover experience, he wrote, showed that there was "no necessity at all to require a gradual transition from a written to a verbal form of the court."[55] He gave a summary of the statute, emphasizing its favorable reception by the old judges and its generally conservative impact.

> One must recognize the chief advantages of public courts in the trust which society feels toward a court conducted publicly, a court that does not conceal its actions in the darkness of secrecy; in the feeling of legality and the respect for law that a public court spreads.[56]

The adoption of foreign examples required a repudiation of the official theory of the distinctiveness of Russian institutions. In January 1862, the officials in the State Chancellery were permitted to use western principles and models. Their comments on the Bludov proposals pointed to the need to turn to western legal science for guides. Prince Gagarin's memorandum in their behalf cited the uselessness of a digest of Bludov's work based on his principles and asserted the necessity of new "considerations" set forth by the experts in the chancellery. These considerations concerned "those general principles recognized by the science and experience of European states and on the basis of which the judicial sphere of the empire should be transformed."[57]

Alexander's approval of the Gagarin mémorandum marked the triumph of a professional legal point of view in the work on the reform. In 1862, the reformers in the State Chancellery drafted *The Basic Principles for the Reform of the Courts,* which outlined the institutional framework necessary for the protection of justice in Russia. The system described in the *Basic Principles* brought the judicial function under the control of professional jurists. It was an independent court system, open to the public, that incorporated adversary procedures, and trusted judges' discretion in the determination of verdicts. It necessitated the creation of a bar of trained and respected lawyers who could make judicial expertise available to the population. Perhaps most controversial was the reformers' prescription of the jury system, an institution that had been considered suited only to more advanced nations with constitutional governments.

The central theme of the *Basic Principles* was the importance of inculcating a sense of law and responsibility in the officials and the population. The mixture of executive and judicial powers in the old system did not permit the application of law, but allowed the full arbitrariness of the administrator. The administrative authorities intervened freely in the courts, "thus weakening the true meaning of the court; they obstruct the correct execution of legal justice." The excessive number of instances weakened the responsibility of the individual judges. It undermined "the judge's firm consciousness of his right and his duty, which is an attribute only of real power and serves as the best stimulus to faithful and conscientious activity, as the best means to the development of a true notion of his dignity, so necessary to the judge." The inquisitorial process, dividing responsibility between the judge and officials of the judicial administration, weakened in the judge "that feeling of moral responsibility which must serve as a stimulus to honesty and caution in all the judge's conclusions and actions."[58]

> In our courts there cannot be a development and strengthening of a consciousness of rights, not a corresponding consciousness of responsibility, if both right and responsibility in judicial cases belongs not exclusively to the judge but to other organs of administration and authority as well.[59]

This theme was expressed most emphatically in the section on the jury system, which emphasized the educational role of the new courts. The judiciary would train the population in respect for law and institutions. A just court "spreads in the people that notion of justice and law, without which there can be no prosperity and order in society." The jury system was especially useful in a backward country, where the uneducated population was distant from the courts and needed institutions they could feel a part of. It would bring the people into the legal system and overcome the sharp distinctions between the classes in Russia.[60] The reformers recommended jury trials in cases of political crimes as well. For the government's side to enjoy the general trust of the population, they argued, it was important that political cases be subject to the same public scrutiny as other criminal cases. If such trials were conducted without jurors, there would be inevitable charges of partiality after all guilty verdicts and the accused would become, in the eyes of society, "unfortunate victims who play the role of martyrs and sufferers for the truth." With the jury, "a government, which does not reject useful reforms for the perfection of state administration and the social order, cannot but find support among the well-intentioned part of the public in its prosecution of ill-intentioned malefactors who strive for the destruction of the existing order in the name of their harmful teachings. . . ."[61]

The combined departments refused to approve jury trials in political cases, but did assign them to the Judicial Chambers, thus leaving them within the jurisdiction of the independent court system. Otherwise, the *Basic Principles* were approved with little change. They won almost universal approval in the press, and a survey of the opinion of officials in the ministry, most of them from the provinces, showed unanimous support on all except secondary points.[62] At the end of 1862, a special commission was constituted to undertake the painstaking work of formulating the new statutes according to the *Basic Principles*. The commission included the reformers and other educated and experienced jurists from the ministry. It also called in consultants from the universities and other branches of the administration to assist on technical questions.[63]

The Court Statutes of 1864 placed Russian justice, for the first time, in the hands of a judicial profession. They created a separate organization of judicial institutions that set the courts apart from the administrative framework of the state. New large judicial regions, "circuits" (*okrugi*), were established that were not coterminous with the provinces. Each circuit included, originally, six to ten circuit courts (*okruzhnye sudy*) and one Judicial Chamber, which heard appeals and served as first instance for official and state crimes. Two cassational departments of the Senate comprised the supreme authority on questions of law. Judges in the Chambers and circuit courts received life tenure and could be removed only in the event of abuses and by ruling of their peers. Justices of the peace, who heard minor criminal cases and civil disputes, were elected by the local *zemstva*. Under certain conditions, they heard minor cases for the peasantry, as did elective peasant *volost'* courts, established by the emancipation to apply peasant customary law. The reform thus aimed to banish administrative authority from the judicial system.[64]

The emancipation of the serfs did not lead ineluctably to a particular system of court procedure or organization. But the emancipation led to an independent judiciary by helping to create political forces that could convince ruling circles and the tsar himself that only independent courts could provide stability in the new social setting. By approving the momentous change to a separate judicial system, Alexander hoped to achieve a stability that could create security and encourage economic enterprise. In his Manifesto of 20 November 1864, enacting the reform, the belated convert presented the statutes as the fulfillment of his original intentions. The projects for the Reform of 1864 "fully correspond to Our wish to introduce to Russia a court that is swift, just, and merciful, to elevate the judicial power for all our subjects, to give it the appropriate independence, and in general to strengthen in the people that respect for law, without which public prosperity is impossible and which should be the constant guide of each and everyone from the highest to the lowest."[65]

The reform met with general acclaim. The press responded enthusiastically. The only dissent came from radicals like Herzen and Ogarev who insisted that court reform was meaningless when introduced apart from institutions of representative government. It was one of those enraptured moments when hopes were suddenly realized, and beckoning, if illusory perspectives opened into the future. In Voronezh, at banquets held to honor the reform, guests delivered toasts to the new statutes. In Kharkov, people kissed each other for joy. The Odessa authorities received petitions from "private persons" requesting the right to meet to discuss the statutes. Merchant guilds petitioned to have circuit courts placed in their towns, offering to donate the funds for the premises. It was, as Koni described it, the era of first love, when blemishes faded in the glow of infatuation.[66]

Zamiatnin and Stoianovskii took charge of the difficult tasks of organizing the new courts and recruiting their staffs. The State Council ruled that the new courts should be opened immediately, rather than in gradual stages. However, financial and administrative difficulties delayed implementation. Nonetheless, by the early seventies the new courts had opened in all the provinces of European Russia.[67] A law sponsored by Zamiatnin, issued on 11 October 1865, introduced public and oral procedure to all the old courts, preparing their personnel for the transition.[68] Zamiatnin then sent out special emissaries to the provinces awaiting reform to clear up the backlogs in the old courts. He traveled through the provinces, meeting the members of the old courts and determining which of them were worthy to enter the new system. Trusted subordinates informed him about the abilities and reputation of those in the courts.[69] Zamiatnin examined both their achievements in service and their "moral qualities." He found that a large number of former officials of the Ministry of Justice were returning to work in the new courts. The old system, he informed the tsar, provided very much of a base for the new. "Among the Chief-Procurators, Chairmen, Assistant-Chairmen, Procurators and Chief-Secretaries, there are already many individuals with legal knowledge and moral qualities that give reason to expect that their participation in the judicial reform will proceed successfully."[70]

There was no lack of candidates for positions in the new courts. Material considerations were set aside, as officials as high as governors and vice-governors applied to be judges. Old Prince Vladimir Odoevskii, a senator in the Moscow departments, felt hurt that he had not been appointed a judge in the Moscow Chamber. "In the first years, no one looked upon the new positions as usual service in the ranks. This was work that gripped the soul, a task, a calling."[71]

The composition of the new courts is difficult to ascertain in the detail that is possible for the old. The reform brought a decentralization of service records, which are now dispersed in local Soviet archives. But from the printed and archival sources that are available, we can discern the same trends as those at work during previous decades, now accelerated by the effects of the reform. The reform spurred the movement to an educated legal officialdom drawn predominantly from the nobility.

Educational qualifications rose sharply after 1866, when the first of the new courts opened. In 1866, assistant chairmen of the Provincial Chambers had the highest percentage of any legal office — 56 percent — completing higher educational institutions (the universities, the School of Jurisprudence, the Alexandrine lycée). In 1870, nearly 80 percent of all judges in the new courts had completed higher education in the four new circuits listed: St. Petersburg, Moscow, Kharkov, Odessa (see table 9.1). Court procurators, who acted as prosecutors in the new adversary process, show about the same proportions (see table 9.2). The Judicial Chambers were concentrations of *pravovedy,* who made up over half of their judges and procurators.[72] The sources do not permit precise statements about social composition of the courts. But the high proportion of *pravovedy* and graduates from the universities, who were preponderantly noble in this period, leaves little doubt about continued predominance of the nobility.[73]

The changed character of the judiciary was most evident in the composition of the cassational departments of the Senate in 1870 (table 9.3). For the first time, trained legal officials staffed the supreme instance of the Russian court system. Four were graduates of the School of Jurisprudence, eight of the universities, one of the Alexandrine lycée, one of an engineering school. Due to their education, they had entered the service late (at an age of close to 20, compared with an age of 12.8 for senators of 1846 who had begun in civil service). Six of the fifteen had begun their careers in the legal administration and all but one had served in high posts in the Senate chancellery or the Ministry of Justice for extended periods. Their average age was low for senators, yet they had accumulated considerably more civil service experience than senators during Nicholas's reign. Their service had been predominantly in central organs; only five had served in provincial offices, two of them for less than two years. But though there were marked changes in educational qualifications and career patterns, social composition remained close to the old Senate's. Thirteen of the fifteen senators were noblemen, seven of them with estates. The proportion of landholders and large landholding was somewhat below the proportion for the Senate in 1855. Chief-procurators came from much the same layers of the nobility. Seven of the eight were noblemen; three had held serfs, a proportion somewhat above that for 1856. Three of the eight chief-procurators were university graduates, four

Table 9.1. Education of Judges in New Courts in 1870

Educational Background	Chambers	Circuit Courts	Totals
Universities	23(44)	153(50)	176(49)
School of Jurisprudence	27(52)	65(21)	92(26)
Alexandrine Lycée	1(2)	9(3)	10(3)
Other	1(2)	80(26)	81(22)
Totals	52(100)	307(100)	359(100)

NOTE: Drawn from data in *Spisok chinam Pravitel'stvuiushchego Senata, Departamenta Ministerstva Iustitsii i sudebnykh mest, obrazovannykh na osnovanii sudebnykh ustavov 20ogo noiabria 1864 goda* (St. Petersburg, 1870).

Table 9.2. Education of Procurators in New Courts in 1870

Educational Background	Chambers	Circuit Courts	Totals
Universities	3(23)	108(60)	111(58)
School of Jurisprudence	8(62)	23(13)	31(16)
Alexandrine Lycée	2(15)	6(3)	8(4)
Other	...	42(24)	42(22)
Totals	13(100)	179(100)	192(100)

NOTE: Data drawn from same source as in table 9.1.

Table 9.3. Service Experience of Officials in Cassation Departments of the Senate, 1870[a]

Mean	Senators	Chief-Procurators and Assistant Chief-Procurators[b]
Age	53.1(15)	40.1(8)
Years civil service	33.1(15)	19.3(8)
Years in provincial offices	2.5(15)	4.1(8)
Years in central offices	31.6(15)	15.2(8)
Years of previous civil service	27.7(15)	16.3(8)
Age entry to civil service (all)	19.8(15)	21.1(8)
Age entry to civil service (lifetime civil servants)	19.2(13)	21.1(8)
Years in office	5.4(15)	3.0(8)

[a]Materials are from *fonds* 1363,1365, of TsGIA. They cover all senators, chief-procurators, and assistant chief-procurators of the civil and criminal cassation departments of the Senate in 1870.

[b]The office of assistant chief-procurator was introduced with the reforms.

were *pravovedy,* one a graduate of the lycée. Their age of entry to the service continues the upward trend observed during the reign of Nicholas I.[74]

The historical literature has often conveyed the impression that the new cadres were the product of the judicial reform. A majority of the judges in the new courts in 1870, it is true, were recruits of the reform era, who had begun service in the Ministry of Justice after 1855 (see table 9.4). But older judicial officials who had received their education and initial experience in the reign of Nicholas I dominated the higher positions in the system. Most of the officials in the Chambers and all of the senators in the cassational departments of the Senate had begun service before 1855. As we shall see in the next chapter, it was the older officials who proved the most vociferous of the initial defenders of the independent judiciary.

Table 9.4. Years of Entry into Ministry of Justice of Judges in Reformed Courts, 1870

Year of Entry into Ministry of Justice	Chambers	Circuit Courts (*okruzhnye sudy*)	Totals
1850 or earlier	31(60)	46(15)	77(21)
1851-55	13(25)	55(18)	68(19)
1856-60	7(13)	47(15)	54(15)
1861-65	1(2)	96(31)	97(27)
1866-70	...	63(21)	63(18)
Totals	52(100)	307(100)	359(100)

NOTE: Data drawn from same source as in table 9.1.

Most important, the older officials took the lead in establishing new patterns of conduct for the judiciary. *Pravovedy* like G. N. Motovilov, Dmitrii Rovinskii, and A. N. Burnashev became exemplars of the new judge and prosecutor, setting high standards of knowledge and devotion to their calling. Motovilov, the first chairman of the St. Petersburg Circuit Court, labored to introduce the new procedures, working indefatigably and resisting pressures from the Ministry of Interior.[75] Rovinskii attracted around him a group of young procurators in the Moscow Chamber. He participated in the sittings of the Chamber, the work of the Prosecutors' Chamber, and generously gave of his time to explain the new laws. The new procurators found him eager to help them with his vast practical knowledge and saw how he was completely free from the stiff formality characteristic of Russian official life. Chairmen and procurators from the entire circuit came to Moscow to seek his advice.[76] Burnashev, the assistant chairman, then chairman of the Kharkov Circuit Court, won the respect and love of the town's population for his unimpeachable honesty and his great learning. He guided the court with complete explanations of the legal basis of his verdicts and the procedural formalities of cases he tried.[77]

Belonging to the judiciary provided a new means of self-definition and source of dignity for the nobleman abandoning the persona of officer and master. The independent courts opened vast opportunities for creative constructive work. The first contingents of judges had to devise their own examples and precedents for the new court system. The old texts gave them little help. Before 1866, "one could not find a single guide to the civil law in effect, not a single monograph or study of positive law, nothing that the Germans would call *eine juristische Abhandlung*." Under the leadership of the educated officials who had worked for reform over the previous decade, the new judges would create the judicial practice—the consideration of actual legal problems on the basis of the principles of legal science—that Dmitrii Meier had envisioned.[78]

The reform introduced the type of honorable and high-minded noble judge, who could claim impartiality and justice in his decisions, "the judge-man, not the indifferent machine who signed decisions prepared by the chancellery." A new feeling of professional dignity appeared that manifested itself in the wonderful sense of solidarity among the court personnel in the years of the "first love" of the court reform. It was based on what Gromnitskii called "a selfless faith in the infallibility of the court." As procurator in Voronezh and Moscow in the 1860s, Gromnitskii experienced a spirit of comradeship and common goals that united all levels of the procuracy and the court investigators. They would meet on Saturday evenings to discuss the problems that arose in their daily work. The court became Gromnitskii's whole life; he thought of nothing else; his self was his profession.[79] It was this sense of solidarity and professional purpose that would make the ebullient new judiciary anathema to those who ruled the Russian state.

10
EPILOGUE
AND CONCLUSION

Oh why, oh why, is Count Pahlen,
So parallel to the jurors!
Were he more vertical,
Their judgment would be more sensible!

A kind justice is the command of the tsar,
But the jurors' justice is a woeful one,
All because Count Pahlen,
Is too parallel to them!

Now the killer is impudent,
The court a charitable institution,
All because our Count Pahlen,
Is parallel with our jurors.

Everyone fears to be shot down,
To be knifed or set aflame,
Because there is such a parallel,
Between the jurors and Count Pahlen.

Herr, erbarm' dich unserer Seelen!
Habe Mitleid mit uns allen,
And let Count Pahlen,
Not be parallel to jurors!

   Alexei Konstantinovich Tolstoi, *Rondo*

THE REFORM OF 1864 CREATED A MODERN JUDICIAL SYSTEM AND INTRODUCED the necessary preconditions to a rule of law in Russia. The new courts enjoyed complete discretion in civil suits, bringing to an end the intervention of administrative authorities in disputes between individuals. Protecting property rights and the interests of creditors, they provided elements of legal security in Russian life. Though the guarantees for the accused in criminal prosecution were far from complete, the statutes established rules against arbitrary arrest and other denials of personal liberty. They made legal defense a regular part of criminal trials. The police continued to enjoy rights of preliminary detention and immunities from official responsibility, but they usually observed the rules of the statutes in nonpolitical cases. It is clear that whatever their deficiencies, the independent courts made available remedies and means to safeguard personal rights that were unattainable in the past.[1]

The judges in the new courts developed a sense of the competence and the integrity of the judicial system. While the *Digest of Laws* continued to be the law of the land, they evolved their own body of legal norms and precedents that relied increasingly on western principles of jurisprudence. They created the beginnings of a Russian common law.[2] Those who attained high governmental office fought attempts to abridge the independence of the judiciary. In the last two decades of the nineteenth century the large number of former legal officials in the State Council resisted attempts to cripple or eliminate the jury system and to restore the "unity" of state institutions by reinstating administrative control of the courts.[3] With the reform, a Russian bar arose with high professional standards and established itself during the next half-century as a group working to defend and extend the rights of the individual in Russia.[4]

The officials in the new judiciary assumed authority over areas of the law that had previously been within the purview of the administration. They enjoyed the authority that accrues to technical expertise, what Talcott Parsons describes as "the specificity of function," which allows the professional to enjoy authority, but only in his special field. Such authority disregards the hierarchical principles upon which authoritarian government is based. The professional man "often exercises his authority over ~~~~l~ who are, or are reputed to be his superiors in social status, in

tual attainments or in moral character."[5] This specialization gives rise not only to new authority, but to an ethos that endows the professional with a sense of his own responsibilities, goals, and importance. In Russia, where legal professionals were faced with a general sense of lawlessness and an incomprehension of the law, this ethos grew into a sense of mission. They regarded the dispensation of justice as their own special responsibility, thus claiming an authority that had been viewed as the monarch's prerogative.

Specialization, it is likely, proceeded in other branches of the administration as well after the great reforms. Undoubtedly, in other ministries the level of education of personnel continued to rise during the second half of the nineteenth century, and specialized expertise became more common. But until we have detailed monographic studies on other institutions, we cannot assess the extent of these tendencies and the nature of their impact on the operation of autocracy. It appears, however, that nowhere did it proceed as far as in the judiciary during the decades after the reform. As Alfred Rieber has suggested, Alexander II's notion of unlimited power, as a "tangible personal possession," placed a limit on the rationalizing tendencies the tsar would allow.[6] The concessions to judicial expertise, as we have seen, were a result of the economic exigencies of the reform era, and the particularly grievous state of the courts. Thus, while it is probable that professional competence rose generally in the administration, nowhere would the sense of professional consciousness be as articulate as it was in the judiciary.

But the specialized authority of the new judiciary fit uncomfortably into the traditional patterns of autocratic attitudes. The sacrifice of part of sovereign authority might lead to the loss of supreme prerogatives. The ruler feared that legal interpretation could not be kept within bounds, that once a judiciary began to interpret the law, interpretation could pass imperceptibly into rulings on law that would have the semblance of legislative enactment. It was this misgiving that had made Catherine the Great and Alexander I so wary in their dealings with the Senate, and that underlaid Nicholas I's general attitudes toward judicial authority.

The new judiciary introduced an element of disruption into Russian institutions that would split the Russian polity into mutually antagonistic and uncomprehending parts. The clashes took place at a high level— where the officials responsible for the defense of the interests of administration and judiciary confronted each other, and often proved incapable of fathoming each other's mentalities or goals. On the one side were the administrators, beholden to the power of the executive as the instrument of the autocratic will; on the other, the legal officials who regarded the judiciary as the only guarantor of justice. The administrators feared legal expertise, which seemed to introduce doubts and the snares of legal reasoning when forceful action was called for. The legal officials feared the government, which seemed, as always, to regard the judiciary as a nuisance thwarting its political designs.

The traditional fears of the autocrat were immediately given substance by the efforts of Minister of Justice Zamiatnin. Hardly was the ink dry on the statutes of 1864, when Zamiatnin sought to aggrandize the Ministry of Justice at the expense of the other branches of the administration. There took place a reenactment of the drama performed at the beginning of the century, but with new players. The acerbic Valuev now played the role of minister of interior taken by the phlegmatic Kochubei, and the mild-mannered Zamiatnin, the part of the abrasive Derzhavin. The occasion was the need to redefine the functions of the first, the administrative department of the Senate after the reform. Zamiatnin seized the opportunity to enhance "the important significance of this, the oldest of all existing institutions."[7]

Zamiatnin's proposals, submitted in March 1865, were in effect aimed at reviving the Senate's supervisory role over the ministries, which it had possessed on paper, but never effectively exercised. He tried to insinuate the Senate's authority into the ministries by requiring that all circulars that ministers sent to their subordinates explaining the meaning of particular laws for the purposes of execution be sent to the Senate and be published in *Senatskie Vedomosti*. More important circulars that related to "general laws" would require Senate approval. Zamiatnin even suggested that the Senate pass on legislative proposals involving administrative reforms before they reached the State Council.[8]

Zamiatnin also sought to diminish the competence of the Committee of Ministers. Since the ministers were supposed to attend the sessions of the First Department of the Senate, he suggested that those cases of administrative law that could be decided there be excluded from the competence of the Committee of Ministers. All cases that exceeded the authority of individual ministers and required imperial confirmation, he argued, should be presented for Senate ruling, for only this procedure could preserve an orderly allotment of cases between branches. The proposals also would have restored the Senate's right, withdrawn in 1816, to exact fines from governors and issue reprimands to them.[9]

The project evoked hostile opposition from the other ministers. Valuev replied that Zamiatnin's proposals should be concerned with the internal reform of the Senate and "should not touch on the objects of competence and the degree of authority of other state institutions, particularly because the Judicial Statutes, fulfilling the chief tasks of judicial reform, separated judicial from executive and legislative authority without at all affecting the relations between different administrative organs." Dmitrii Miliutin, the minister of war, responded with similar arguments. All the ministers objected to the increased role of the Senate and, by implication, the Ministry of Justice in the decisions of the administration. Even Zamiatnin's attempt to mollify them with more moderate proposals failed to dispel their misgivings.[10] Zamiatnin also initiated a move to restore to the procurators their prereform authority to supervise the legality of the acts of administration. Valuev succeeded in blocking this attempt, arguing that it would allow the judiciary to meddle in the administration, and thus violate the separation of powers.[11] Zamiatnin's project was stillborn, and the drama, with a new cast, ended as before.

The minister of interior represented the forces of self-defense within the autocracy. While an independent judiciary encouraged the flourishing of autonomous and dynamic forces in society, the autocracy had traditionally been suspicious of all independent groups as bearers of opposition and sedition. The suspicion persisted through the reforms, and would seek the first signs of threat to burst forth once again, now in new circumstances, when increased social activity raised untold possibilities of loss of autocratic control. Karakazov's attempt on the life of the tsar and the articles in liberal journals were immediate sources of distress. But any disturbance of the placidity of the system, inevitable in the postreform conditions, would have been enough to reawaken the feelings of insecurity and direct the tsar to his primary concern, the preservation of the autocratic system.

Valuev stepped forth as the chief harbinger of danger. Shortly after the Karakazov shooting, he asserted that the interests of the treasury and administration — *interesy kazny, interesy administratsii* — had not been taken into consideration sufficiently in the drafting of the provisions of the judicial reform on suits against the state. Though at first Valuev objected only to the procedure regulating civil suits against the state, this was only the first step in an offensive he led to strengthen the administrative authorities in their relations with the independent judiciary. No major system of European law, he declared, placed the administration in such a "defenseless position" as did the new court statutes.[12] The battle rhetoric set the tone for a campaign he organized at the highest level of government. In 1866, together with the chief of police, Count Shuvalov, and the minister of state domains, the adjutant-general Zelenoi, he introduced a special memorandum into the Committee of Ministers pointing to the need to strengthen the power of the governors' supervision in the provinces and giving them authority to summon and demand explanations from officials of all branches, including the judiciary, on matters concerning the state order and security.[13]

Valuev's proposal brought prompt rejoinders from both Zamiatnin and Reutern, the minister of finance. It was then referred to a special commission, chaired by Prince Gagarin, who strongly opposed any measure that would violate the principles of the Judicial Reform, and objected to many of Valuev's proposals. Gagarin found himself in the minority, however, and Alexander approved the majority position, because, the tsar explained, "all the information, reaching me from the inner provinces confirms the necessity to take the proposed measures without further delay."[14] The new rules, issued through the Committee of Ministers, gave the governor the right to summon members of the judiciary, as other branches of the administration, to him. They were obliged to appear and to show him the proper respect. He also could pass on all special awards and express his opinions on all appointments of functionaries in his province.[15]

The new judiciary was most troublesome to Valuev in his effort to direct the execution of the new press law. Press crimes were under the jurisdiction of the Chief Press Administration, a division of the Ministry of Interior. But they were supposed to be prosecuted in the courts by the procurators. From the start, this division of responsibilities was an unhappy one. The procurators tried the cases according to their notions of law, and ignored the commands of the Chief Press Administration. Valuev complained in a message to Stoianovskii, then assistant minister of justice, that the procurators, "if they do not share the view of the Chief Press Administration, are obliged to adopt it."[16]

Valuev was personally embroiled in the problems of the press. The journal, *Vest'*, in which he collaborated, took a conservative line and published attacks on the independent judiciary, some of which were written to his order. In late 1866, a procurator initiated a suit against *Vest'*, but Valuev succeeded in having it quashed by making a deal with Gagarin and Zamiatnin to keep some other matters quiet. Then Valuev ordered the Moscow procurator, Lange, to initiate a suit against the newspaper *Moskovskie Vedomosti,* but Lange, a veteran of nineteen years in the ministry, refused for lack of grounds. As a result, Lange was removed and assigned to the Moscow Judicial Chamber. In the same year, the St. Petersburg Circuit Court acquitted A. N. Pypin and Iu. G. Zhukovskii, editors of the journal *Sovremennik,* of violations of the press law, which sent Valuev to the tsar with a report demanding the removal of the chairman, Motovilov. Only Zamiatnin's opposition prevented Alexander from following Valuev's recommendation. When the case was appealed to the Petersburg Chamber, a stronghold of the *pravovedy,* the editors were acquitted of the charge — and found guilty of a minor offense — using swear words.[17]

Considerations of law rather than immediate state interest governed the courts' judgment of press cases, and, naturally, the procurators' cases for the prosecution. Press violations had never before been subject to judicial discretion, and the procurators had the difficult task of working out the legal basis for condemning excessive liberties of the printed word. Here their loyalty to the law conflicted directly with their loyalty to the government they represented. Their strained, involved reasoning and references to principles of law tried the patience of those like Valuev, who saw only dangerous statements threatening to the state order. The speech delivered on the *Sovremennik* case by Tiesenhausen, the assistant procurator of the St. Petersburg Chamber, was almost a statement for the defense. A *pravoved,* Tiesenhausen was very concerned with the legal grounds of his argument. "The chief peculiarity of crimes of the press," he asserted, "consists in the fact that the prosecution and court have before them not an act subject to the force of law, as this is expressed in other cases, but thought and word." He went on to argue that the external side of the fact, the expression of thought by means of illicit statements, "does not in itself represent something criminal." Criminality was involved only when the thoughts expressed in words were made illegal by specific legislation. But the thought of an individual could not be subject to external evaluation. It could be evaluated only by "the moral law etched in the heart of man and expressed in the sentences pronounced by his conscience." Tiesenhausen tried to salvage the government's case by presenting a rather tenuous argument, that crimes of the press depended on "the circumstances of the time," which the lawyer for the defense, Arsen'ev, easily rebutted.[18]

To rid himself of these irritations, Valuev moved to have press crimes taken out of the jurisdiction of the courts. Zamiatnin presented a powerful reply, which, Valuev remarked sneeringly, had been written by someone else. Zamiatnin's memorandum of October 1866 held that the procurator's role was to serve as a defender of the law, who had to be able to understand both sides of the case. The law forbade the procurator from presenting the case in a one-sided manner and exaggerating the value of the evidence or the crime. "On the other hand, he is required by law, when announcing his conclusion to judicial offices, to act solely on the bases of his convictions and existing laws; and in those cases where he finds acquittal of the accused worthy, to inform the court of that by command of his conscience, without defending accusations overthrown by the court investigation." The censorship bureau, as a specialized organ, had to look upon the case with a one-sided concern for violations of the press statutes, and therefore could not be considered an impartial defender of the law. The members of the Chief Press Administration were prone to hold personal animosities against certain authors and to be swayed by events of the moment. Only the procurators could prosecute cases "without fear of recriminations about the injustice of their recommendations, or even ridicule."[19]

On 30 September 1866, Valuev wrote in his diary that this memorandum "undercuts [Zamiatnin] finally."[20] In December, the tsar ordered that cases were to be initiated by the procurators only in the event of libel against officials. In all other cases, they had to use the briefs provided by the Chief Censorship Administration. By the end of the sixties, the Chief Press Administration was beginning to close journals by administrative order, without troubling with court prosecution. In response, a group of senators of the First Department, in 1869, declared that the court had upheld the press laws from 1866 to 1868, and that press cases would not remain unpunished in the courts. In the General Assembly, nine senators, among them Zarudnyi and Kalachov, repeated these claims, then went on to give a legal definition of "harmful tendency," when administrative

274

direction could be used against harmful teaching that involved no clear violation of the law. All other cases should be tried in the courts. Their pleas went unheeded, however, and the Chief Press Administration continued to deal with most violations without recourse to the courts. It replied to the Senate that court trial of press cases could take place 3½ years before, but "a whole series of trials made clear those attitudes of the court toward press cases which have led to a review of existing legislation."[21]

In their first years, the new courts threatened lower levels of the administration as well. Independent courts placed a limit on administrative authority that neither governors nor police officials were accustomed to, and both complained loudly. Police chiefs felt it humiliating to appear before court investigators at court hearings. The Kazan governor complained to Koni, then procurator of the Circuit Court, that the procurators had the right to issue warnings to the police and even to drag them into court. "That means they have two superiors? They won't think me worth a cent. What kind of head of the province am I after this?" The Orel governor found that the police were refraining from preparing reports to avoid the chagrin of appearing in court. They felt especially humiliated by the authority justices of the peace enjoyed to issue warnings to them, and the procurators to initiate disciplinary procedures against them. Prince Odoevskii wrote in September 1866 that the Moscow police were complaining that the courts hindered their work: "They don't let them hit or yell at people, or, even worse, let them take money from anyone and everyone."[22]

The governors, too, felt humiliated by the new practices. They objected to the prohibition against their official visits to the courts. They regretted the loss of authority to supervise the lower ranks of judicial personnel and their inability to influence appointments of justices of the peace. The Riazan and Orel governors wanted the right to receive information on criminal investigations, from which they were now excluded. Judicial officials like Gromnitskii refused to yield to pressures to appoint governors' protégés.[23]

Many aspects of the new system affronted the governors. At special commissions, they were distressed to find themselves only second in rank to the chairmen of the Judicial Chambers. There was a great stir in Moscow when the chairman of the Circuit Court asked a *tainyi sovetnik* (the third rank) to rise. Many judicial officials refused to appear before governors when summoned, even after Alexander approved Valuev's rules. In 1870, a crisis developed in Kherson province, when the entire judicial corps defied an order by a newly appointed governor to appear before him. In retaliation, the governor ordered the police not to cooperate with the courts. The police chief began composing reports accusing an assistant-procurator of drunken conduct. That assistant-procurator, it turned out, was in charge of a case involving illegal actions by a police officer. The police chief also accused a judge in the Circuit Court of robbery and abduction.[24]

Filled with pride in their new station, some judical officials felt emboldened to make open shows of disrespect. The chairman of the Orel Circuit Court returned a notice from the governor that invited the members of the judiciary to prayers for forthcoming holidays. The chairman informed him that "members of the court, by the force of law itself are placed beyond dependence on the Governor." The Olonets governor submitted a list of impertinences committed by members of the courts. A court investigator had appeared before him in a sheepskin coat (*polushubok*), claiming that he did not have to wear a uniform. Other court investigators sent careless reports to him written on scraps of paper. Judges appeared at committee meetings in casual jackets rather than uniforms. The uncertainty of the relations allowed the members of the judiciary to "make direct ridicule of the administration."[25]

The courts seemed hostile to the needs of the administration. In 1866, a jury trying a minor official of the Ministry of Interior for offending his superior acquitted him on grounds that he had been seized by a fit of "mental frenzy." Valuev, who had wanted the official removed as an example, carried the struggle to the press, his newspaper *Vest'*, attacking the courts for revolutionary designs. The acquittal, together with Zamiatnin's position on press cases, made it appear that the Ministry of Justice needed a chief more sympathetic to the goals of administration. On 1 January 1867, the governor of Pskov, Count Constantine Ivanovich Pahlen, who had never served in a judicial office, was appointed assistant minister of justice, replacing Stoianovskii, who was promoted to senator. The tsar told Zamiatnin that he was preparing Pahlen to be minister. One of Zamiatnin's subordinates asked him why he did not resign. But Zamiatnin had been chosen well. Not a professional jurist, he still retained the old administrative ethic. A servant of the law, he was even more a servant of his sovereign. Zamiatnin replied, "I was brought up by the old rules and will serve my sovereign as long as it pleases him. But don't worry, Pahlen will be prepared by Easter."[26]

Between New Year's Day and Easter 1867, Zamiatnin's position became untenable. The tsar felt himself increasingly uncomfortable with the independent courts, and Zamiatnin would not let him forget the new limits to his authority. The most serious clash occurred when Alexander tried to remove Liuboshchinskii, one of the authors of the Judicial Reform, from the Civil Cassational Department of the Senate. Liuboshchinskii, a representative in the Petersburg *zemstvo,* had taken part in a session of 1867, when the members called for a central *zemstvo* assembly. Zamiatnin advised the tsar that judges were irremovable. "But not for me," Alexander answered. Nonetheless, he relented and left Liuboshchinskii in office.[27]

In April 1867, Zamiatnin was relieved as minister. His passing went unlamented in the upper ranks of the administration. His commitment to the judiciary lost him, as it had Gagarin, imperial favor. He remained in the State Council, but the respect he received was formal and cursory. On the anniversary of his fiftieth year in the imperial administration in 1873, the government witheld the customary recognitions for long service. Congratulations came only from the judiciary. A delegation arrived from the Moscow courts, and he received thirty telegrams from various officials in courts across Russia.[28]

The fall of Zamiatnin brought to an end the brief period of assertive leadership by a minister committed to the judiciary. Prince Sergei Urosov served as acting minister for six months, then Count Constantine Ivanovich Pahlen became minister of justice. Pahlen, while not opposed to the independence of the judiciary, worked to ensure that it would not arrogate to itself a position above its station in the Russian state system. A candidate of Petersburg University, the thirty-four-year-old Pahlen was the first minister of justice to hold a law degree. But his rapid rise had occurred entirely through the Ministry of Interior. The heir to an estate of three thousand *desiatiny,* he had associated himself with the conservative group of large landowners in the government and was a protégé of its leaders, Valuev and Shuvalov. He had served as vice-director of the Department of Police, then as governor of Pskov province. In these positions, he had openly defended the interests of the police and administration against the threat of a new judiciary. When Zamiatnin had visited Pskov to select officials for the new courts, Pahlen had made a point to be out of town on a tour of the province.[29] His appointment struck the judicial cadres as an openly hostile act.[30]

Pahlen early was apprehensive of the menace posed by the judiciary to administrative hegemony. He shared the sense that judicial authority could not be limited unless subordinated. Even before the new courts had appeared in Pskov, he warned, in 1865, that "the influence of the police will weaken as a result of the full dependence of the political authority on the judicial."[31] As minister, he became a defender of the governors and the police in their squabbles with the independent judiciary. He supported a project, sponsored by Petersburg Police Chief Trepov, which would have allowed the police to issue their own administrative rulings, making them responsible only to the governor. This plan, which Gradovskii described as signifying "the police has ordered, the court sentenced," was forestalled by strong opposition in the State Council. But during the 1870s Pahlen was able to secure approval for individual measures enhancing the role of the police.[32]

The chief aim of Pahlen's policy in his first years as minister was to make the agencies of prosecution an effective arm of the government. The procurators of the 1860s regarded themselves as impartial defenders of the law, and were not, in Pahlen's mind, sufficiently concerned with securing convictions. He had in common with Zamiatnin a friendliness and ability to associate with subordinates, and tried to win them over to his point of view by persuasion. But when this did not work, he could use more direct methods. Most prominent of these in the late sixties was his effort to end the independence of the court investigators. The new investigators, introduced in 1860, had developed before the reform into a cadre with high morale that worked together with the procurators and felt a common esprit with them. Pahlen changed all investigators' appointments to acting investigators, and made them completely dependent on the whim of their superiors and the ministry. The effect on their morale was devastating: They lost the standing and independence they enjoyed as members of the judiciary, and became petty *chinovniki* holding inferior, insecure positions. Pahlen succeeded in destroying the spirit uniting procurators and investigators that had helped to promote an independent, professional view of the role of prosecution.[33]

Pahlen's appointment also brought to an end the influence of Sergei Zarudnyi. After the reform, Zarudnyi had continued working in the State Chancellery, drafting supplemental projects. But his dominating irreverent personality could not be tolerated in the upper ranks of the administration. After Zamiatnin's removal, he found himself increasingly isolated in the State Chancellery. Pahlen then ensured that Zarudnyi did not succeed to a position that would allow him to exert his leadership in behalf of the new courts. He had Zarudnyi appointed to the Second Department, which as part of the old Senate, now had no importance in the shaping or application of the law. "You worked more than anyone on the destruction of the old Senate and ended up amongst its ruins," Prince Gagarin remarked to Zarudnyi. Serving in the Second and the Cadastral departments of the Senate, Zarudnyi was cut off from creative work on the law at the height of his powers. He spent his remaining years writing on the law and translating Beccaria's *Crimes and Punishments* and Dante's *Hell* into Russian. He increasingly retreated into his own personal life, playing the role of the old and kind paterfamilias for his family of eight children. They would later remember how he would read French romantic novels and begin to weep at the end, when good triumphed over evil.[34]

Once reliable and loyal leadership was ensured for the new judiciary, the government attempted to make use of the courts to answer the challenge presented by the revolutionary movement. The tsar and his advisors had expected the new sense of legality engendered by the reform to promote the respect for law in the population and to align the interests of the population more closely with those of the regime. Pahlen was the chief proponent of the view that court prosecution could stigmatize the revolutionaries as outlaws and neutralize their appeal. He tried to use the courts to dispense political justice. The courts were called upon to play the role that Otto Kircheimer has shown has always devolved upon them when hearing political cases: to "eliminate a political foe of the regime according to some prearranged rules."[35]

Rather than try the revolutionaries summarily in secret, as had been the previous practice, the government now allowed the "judicial space" for proper legal deliberation and judgment, hoping to use the repute of the experts to enhance the condemnation.[36] Pahlen had come away from his training in the law with a sense of the political usefulness of the legal process. Accordingly, he insisted that the trials in the early seventies be made known to the public. He called for full publicity of the stenographic accounts of the trial of the Nechaev group in 1871, stating that "the most candid and full presentation of the facts should deal the greatest blow to the party sympathizing with the accused."[37]

But the political justice of the 1870s did not achieve its appointed goals. The trials proved serious miscalculations that only revealed the gulf between the principles animating the autocracy and its judiciary. The public would watch the prosecution clumsily fumbling to bring in convictions, often on weak or nonexistent grounds. Conservatives, like Aleksei Tolstoi and Pobedonostev, would see in the trials a dangerous concession of the autocracy's power of punishment to popular judgment. By 1878, Pahlen's brash self-confidence appeared a tragicomic self-delusion that pointed to the need for a more ruthless policy toward the judiciary.

The refusal of the courts to deal harshly with the revolutionaries was in part the result of the sharp division that had grown up between state and society in Russia. The reformers, when prescribing public jury trials in 1862, had presumed a government "not rejecting any useful transformations for the perfection of the state administration and the social order." They had predicated their recommendation of the jury system upon "a certain degree of harmony between the strivings of the government and society."[38] Then the momentum of reform gradually diminished, and the censorship and police continued to be active in suppressing free thought, all of which left aspirations unsatisfied and created bitter resentments toward the government.

Judges in political trials, despite their image of Olympian impartiality, often are influenced by their social sympathies and opinions. But many of the judges who dismayed the government with their impartiality or leniency were not sympathetic to the revolutionaries, and in the trial of the 193, specially chosen members of the Senate reached the decision. The verdicts and sentences were at least in part the result of the way the government approached the problems of prosecution. The administration's contempt for the legal process ensured an ignorance of the problems of dealing with the courts. Pahlen, carrying the administrative mentality into the judicial system, treated the organization of the prosecution with nonchalance and even apathy. He tried to remain above demeaning clashes in the legal arena, where the state had to play the role of equal adversary. He scorned issues of jurisprudence. "Akh, all of that is theory," was his customary reply to opinions on legal questions.[39] But this fashionable *hauteur* would leave the government at the mercy of those who could exercise legal expertise.

The most extraordinary feature of the trials of the 1870s was not the government's cynical use of the courts for political purposes, which is the usual function of the political justice, but its unwillingness to comprehend what was involved in prosecuting these cases. In the trial of the participants in the Nechaev conspiracy, so confident was Pahlen that the judges would respond sympathetically to the government's case, that he took no care to have the prosecution conducted effectively. But the St. Petersburg Judicial Chamber did not share the ministry's certainty about the outcome. The senior chairman of the chamber, A. S. Liubimov, a highly respected *pravoved* who had been a member of the Consultation of the Ministry of Justice, conducted the trial with an impartiality unanticipated by the government. He allowed the accused and their lawyers full freedom to state their views. The lawyers for the defense, V. D. Spasovich, A. I. Urusov, and K. K. Arsen'ev, used all their brilliance to show the lack of grounds for the government's case. An agent of the Third Section remarked, "without exaggeration one can say that Spasovich has more intelligence and scientific knowledge than the whole court and Procuracy. Can one place up against Spasovich, Polovtsov, whose speech clearly proves an absolute lack of talent and absence of juridical knowledge?" The response of the press was unanimously on the side of the defendants; not one newspaper printed an article attacking the theories of the Nechaevtsy.[40]

But most disturbing of all was the final verdict. The St. Petersburg Judicial Chamber reached its judgment on legal grounds and did not slavishly submit to the government's determination to condemn the revolutionaries. The judges, to the anger of higher circles, chose to apply the law against illegal societies rather than the more severe conspiracy law. Of eighty-seven brought to trial, fifty-four were acquitted for absence of proofs, twenty-seven were imprisoned, four were sent to penal labor, and two into exile for life.[41] The Third Section agents reported that "many are saying that the Judicial Chamber decided the fate of the accused too sympathetically and that it was necessary without fail to punish them as an example to others...." Particularly objectionable were the words uttered by the chairman to a group of those absolved: "You are free from the court and from penal detention. My lords, from now on your place is not the bench of shame but among the public, among all of us." This made the police agent doubt the chairman's political loyalty. Nikitenko wrote in his diary, "our justice is in disgrace."[42]

Yet the St. Petersburg Chamber was not composed of frantic liberals of the reform era. Thirteen of the fifteen members were *pravovedy*. Twelve of the fifteen had entered the service during the reign of Nicholas I. Their verdict was not an act of sympathy with the revolutionaries but a demonstration of the integrity and impartiality of justice and an unwillingness to submit legal judgment to political ends.[43]

The tsar was exceedingly unhappy with the outcome.[44] Pahlen responded by having political trials assigned to more reliable, higher, instances. He sponsored a law that removed important political trials from the Chambers to a special session of the Senate, with class representatives, or, by decree of the tsar, to a specially constituted Supreme Criminal Court.[45] Yet the government did not abandon the practice of public trials. The Committee of Ministers, in a session of 1874, reasserted its faith in publicity and the use of the courts to expose the revolutionaries. Indeed the ministers hoped to use publicity to an unprecedented extent "for the full clarification in our society of the outrageous teaching of the agitators." The committee concluded that "the natural and most direct route for such beneficial publicity is presented by the court, where in a court investigation all the noxiousness of the clarified teachings and the dangers of their threats can be exposed."[46] Through the successive trials—the Dolgushintsy, the Kazan square demonstration, the fifty—the government held to its policy of publicity. In the first political trials following the Nechaev case, the special session of the Senate turned in a better record than the Petersburg Chamber, acquitting only 39 of 110 defendants.[47]

But the great trial of the participants in the going-to-the-people movement, the 193, staged in 1877, threatened to produce a stream of propaganda from the courtroom that the government could not tolerate. As a result, though stenographic accounts were permitted, they were destroyed upon completion. Nonetheless, the proceedings took place in public, and lawyers like Spasovich and Utin used the opportunity to attack the government's case. Pahlen again treated the mounting of the prosecution with perfunctory disdain. He and his subordinates allowed the accused to languish in prison for three years during the desultory course of the prior investigations; during this period, seventy-five revolutionaries perished or lost their sanity. By the time the case reached court, it had gained the reputation of an atrocity. The prosecution was then conducted carelessly and ineptly. Again the defense was brilliant and took the initiative as if the state officials were on trial rather than the revolutionaries. In their fumbling attempts to put together a case, the prosecution herded peasants into the courtroom to testify against the revolutionaries, only to hear the majority of them testify in their favor. There was no evidence against most of the revolutionaries. Koni, backed by Constantine Nikolaevich and E. V. Frisch, tried unavailingly to convince Pahlen to terminate the proceedings.[48]

The results were shocking to the authorities. Even the senators chosen for their special loyalty felt obliged to make their decisions on the grounds of law and to take into consideration time spent in custody. Of the 193, they acquitted 90, and gave only 64 additional sentences; the senators recommended mercy in 27 of these. The government then showed its own lack of faith in the judicial process by immediately arresting many of the acquitted and subjecting them to administrative punishment.[49]

The combination of all the separate cases into one gigantic show trial magnified all the blunders into a stunning spectacle of incompetence. Assembling all the defendants in one courtroom created a feeling of solidarity and unity among the revolutionaries that they had never before experienced. "They represented," Koni wrote, "an entire political party dangerous in their own eyes to the state."[50] Constantine Pobedonostev, meanwhile, was wringing his hands in the wings. As a jurist, Pobedonostev knew well the dangers of playing irresponsible games with the courts. He wrote to his pupil, the heir, Alexander Aleksandrovich:

> Only a completely blinded or insane and inept government can start a trial like this at a time like this. But the misfortune is that the pride of Count Pahlen is tied to this trial.... If you only knew what kind of senseless impossible manner this trial has been conducted in from the very beginning! Two sensible minds have conducted it—Count Pahlen and Potapov! To our greatest misfortune, Count Pahlen has reached such absurd self-confidence that allows for no common sense. No respectable, intelligent, or experienced people can have any influence on him.... How many incompetents has that person raised, who now surround and direct him.[51]

Yet the failure of his approach did not change Pahlen's mind. Rather it drove him to try harder to win approval for the government's struggle against the revolutionaries. His last attempt to use the courts as an instrument of autocratic policy was the trial of Vera Zasulich. Zasulich had shot and wounded Trepov, the Petersburg governor-general, in retaliation for his striking a revolutionary prisoner, Bogoliubov. There was no doubt about the shooting; Zasulich herself openly admitted it. Pahlen now committed what was perhaps his greatest miscalculation. Since there was no doubt about the act, he decided to turn the case into a jury trial, hoping, as the reformers had promised, to use the jury as a means of branding the revolutionaries for what they were. Accordingly, he decided to try the case not as a political trial but as a simple attempted murder, requiring a jury, and he had evidence of Zasulich's revolutionary associations withheld.[52]

Pahlen again assumed an attitude of indifference toward the prosecution. After two procurators refused to take the case, and resigned their position, the ministry settled for Kessel, a mediocrity who had only recently been promoted to his position. Pahlen's own efforts were limited to a clumsy attempt to influence Koni, the presiding judge in the Petersburg Circuit Court. He repeatedly asked Koni to guarantee him a verdict of guilty. When Koni refused, he threatened to tell the tsar or remove the case from the jurisdiction of the jury. "The prosecutor is not so important," he told Koni. "We are relying more on you.... What's a prosecutor?" When informed that Kessel was a poor prosecutor, Pahlen replied, according to Perets, "It doesn't matter, it is such an open and shut case."[53]

The verdict of not guilty sent the audience into a tumult. "Cries of uninhibited joy, hysterical sobbing, desperate applause, the stamping of feet, cries: *Bravo! Ura! Molodtsy! Vera! Verochka! Verochka!*" Many crossed themselves, many in the upper "more democratic section" embraced each other. But enthusiastic applause also came from the section reserved for judges. The press greeted the decision with a similar acclaim. It was seen as the triumph of public opinion, an open protest of "public conscience" against the oppression of autocracy, the sign of an awakening of the forces of society.[54] But the Zasulich verdict taught other lessons as well, and, as has been so often the case, the voice of the future proved to be the voice of the past. Pobedonostev wrote to his pupil, in horror, that the response of the audience was "just like at the end of a drama in the Mikhailovskii theatre."

> Most important, how can this attempt be regarded as not political! And these people resolved out of a faint-hearted fear to offend public opinion, out of a wish to strut before the intelligentsia and even Europe, to show respect for the jury system. The state interest connected with this case was so great and important that it should have been defended at all costs, with full certainty, without the slightest thought of the possibility of excusing the crime.[55]

The jury's acquittal of Zasulich dealt the final blow to Pahlen's policy. The judgment, taken in what appeared as flagrant disregard of the facts, merely confirmed the lingering fear that, rather than impartial tribunals, the courts represented a political element, a forum for antigovernment sentiments menacing to the autocratic power. Pahlen shortly submitted his resignation. His sucessors, Nabokov, Manasein, Murav'ev, were officials who had come out of the judicial system and could speak for its interests. But the judicial system itself had shown its unreliability and their influence in the government was small.

After the Zasulich trial, the government gave up its pretense of legality in its struggle against the revolutionaries. It dealt with them through the administrative order — direct police punishment or by summary military justice.[56] This tendency culminated in the law of 14 August 1881, which provided for siege conditions with broad executive authority for summary justice in political crimes. The strained tolerance the autocracy had shown toward its judiciary now turned into open animosity. Official publicists issued vitriolic attacks on the independent judiciary and the jury system. Legislative efforts were launched to cripple or eliminate the jury system and to restore the "unity" of state institutions by reinstating administrative control of the courts. The result was a state at war with its own court system, a fatal rift between the traditional and the legal bases of the autocrat's authority.

The inability to deal with the judicial process cost the government dearly not only in the political arena. The government, indeed, was defenseless in confronting the courts on their terrain, as Valuev suggested, though not merely because of the court statutes. The state proved clumsy and incompetent in the defense of its interests in civil cases against the treasury as well. The plaintiffs would hire the best lawyers, while the fiscal interests received at best perfunctory and weak defenses. Nor did the government appear concerned to protect its legal position. Rather, it held to the old conceptions of power, even when they no longer worked. Thus the form of official contracts and agreements, often of enormous length, did little to secure the state's interest, but the officials of the treasury administration retained the old view. They regarded themselves "not as contracting parties, obliged to observe the conditions of agreements, but an authority [*vlast'*] whose commands must be obediently accepted."[57]

A separate judiciary raised difficulties for the Russian autocracy that it did not for other states that had followed absolutist patterns. The Prussian administration—Russia's model of institutional effectiveness, order, and power—possessed a tradition of working with jurists and officials who had an understanding of the law, and was able to adapt to an independent court system. In the face of threats from revolutionaries, the courts and the administration shared common goals in striving to protect the regime against its enemies. This basic agreement continued under the empire, so that while the courts did not always act according to the government's plans, they were not thought to harbor an alien system of law.[58]

The experience of Japan, which borrowed the Prussian judicial system in the last decades of the nineteenth century, is also in striking contrast to Russia's. In Japan, too, the judiciary had traditionally been held in low regard and had no existence separate from the administration; litigation was viewed as an evil. But the reforms of the second half of the nineteenth century that established separate courts in Japan did not create a conflict between courts and monarchy. The judiciary did not raise threats to the emperor's supremacy. The greater security of the ruler's authority, the greater harmony between administration and society, permitted a separate judiciary to be introduced without the conflict and trauma that accompanied it in Russia.[59]

For the Russian autocracy to accept an independent judiciary required that it betray its essence and cease to be the Russian autocracy. The judicial function had received little homage in the political culture of Russian autocracy. The exertion of untrammeled executive power had been the flair of autocracy, providing its magnetic appeal and making possible its greatest triumphs. Through forceful direct action, it had achieved the consolidation of a centralized state authority and the conquests that had first united the Russian lands and then made the Muscovite prince an emperor.

The chief virtues in such a state were military. The Russian nobility was preponderantly a class of military servitors and lacked both the feudal rights and the traditions of service in local judicial institutions inherited by most European nobilities. When they became owners of the serfs, they shared their sovereign's executive predispositions and regarded themselves as little potentates in the image of the tsar. A sense of the importance of their legal rights came only in the late eighteenth century, and then as a result of the efforts of the autocracy itself to emulate western political systems.

The image of a patriarchal tsar dispensing a personal justice maintained its hold in the eighteenth and early nineteenth century and fed a distrust of formal institutions that might dilute the monarch's power to extend personal grace, benefits, and privilege. Personal connections, access to high individuals close to the tsar, gave the Russian nobility a way to avoid submitting themselves to the demeaning rule of petty officials. Though noblemen staffed judicial institutions in the eighteenth century, they left the technical work to clerks, who carried on their work in secret and almost without responsibility. As a result of these attitudes, an awareness of the need for judicial understanding, legal literature, and education came late to the Russian nobility.

It was in this setting that the Russian autocracy took on the aspirations of European absolutist monarchies. It buttressed its traditional appeals of legitimacy with new claims to be the guarantor of the well-being of the nation and the rights of the population. The means it used were those of the European police states of the seventeenth and eighteenth centuries: the rational will of the sovereign legislator would be enforced by well-organized institutions, closely supervised by special organs to minimize error and dishonesty. A rationalized administrative structure could induce lesser officials, including the judges, to apply laws precisely, according to their letter. The antilegalist bias of western absolutism, with its faith in the supreme wisdom of the legislator, fit in well with the traditional Russian suspicion of the judiciary. It was this absolutist vision, in one or another form, that guided Russian statecraft down to the great reforms.

By the early nineteenth century, the experience of absolutist government, as well as the challenge posed by liberal and revolutionary doctrines, made the leaders of the autocracy increasingly aware of the need for expertise in applying and understanding the law. The attempts to centralize and rationalize the bureaucracy, undertaken by Alexander I and Nicholas I, led to the creation of specialized, functional branches of the administration, which in turn demanded a greater training and specialization of personnel. An expansion of higher education accompanied the administrative reforms, as the government endeavored to prepare officials capable of understanding the law. The goal was to produce officials trained in the law who would be loyal and technically proficient servants of the executive.

But the new officials differed from the old not only in the extent of their knowledge about the laws. Introducing men knowledgeable in the law involved the end of the hegemony of eminent noblemen, whether retired officers or aristocrats enjoying sinecures, over the legal system. They were replaced by members of the middle or lower nobility, who used the advantages conferred by education to rise quickly to important positions. For the first time, high judicial posts were filled by men who had spent most or all of their service in the judicial administration. They formed a group of legal officials with common social characteristics, education, and career experiences. They worked in an official world that assigned a great, though ill-defined importance to their expertise and ability.

The new contingent also brought different attitudes and goals into the administration. Educational and cultural currents exerted a decisive influence on the outlook of Russian officials, providing them with an ethos that would govern their relationship to their peers and their work. Many officials barely knew their fathers, and carried little in the nature of social commitment or goals away from their homes. They found their values in the intellectual world and institutions they entered as youths. When these values changed, the mentalities of officials changed as well, permitting significant discontinuities of viewpoint between succeeding generations of officials. In Nicholas I's reign, cadres of officials trained to respect the law and the universal norms of legal science entered an administration geared to subordinate the judicial function and exclude legal expertise.

Thus in the first half of the nineteenth century, the Russian autocracy, following the model of the absolutist state, introduced a new element into its officialdom. The judicial experts came from a stratum of the nobility that had previously sought to rise through the military. Its members had little in common with either the military traditions of their families or the institutional traditions of the earlier officialdom. Unguided by traditional values, they sought their own way. Abandoning the separation between personal and public lives sought by their sentimentalist predecessors, they found personal meaning in their work and cherished a genuine professional commitment to the law. They regarded the law as their own province and not the monopoly of the autocrat and his favorites. For the first time a sense of the calling of the legal official appeared in the Russian state.

As we have seen, the circumstances of the reform era allowed the legal experts to triumph and embody their ideas in new judicial institutions that vested authority over the interpretation and application of the law in a professional judiciary. But the members of this judiciary, imbued with an idealist sense of the mission of the law and a romantic sense of personal commitment, remained a world apart from the Russian state system. More traditional bureaucrats, who had learned to see all authority emanating from the tsar, regarded alternative sources of law with growing qualms. Two mutually hostile intellectual universes thus existed side by side in the Russian state. When issues of conflict arose, the traditional antagonism to the judiciary resurfaced, creating an atmosphere that was antipathetic to the basic values of the new courts and breeding conditions that would stunt their further development.

The new judicial system expanded in the decades after the reform. It was extended to the western Ukraine, the Baltic provinces, Siberia, and the Caucasus. The number of officials in the new courts increased threefold from 1870 to 1900 and continued to rise in the first years of the twentieth century. The budget of the ministry also grew, increasing about threefold from 1869 to 1894 and almost twofold again by 1914.[60] Despite this expansion, hereditary noblemen continued to play a dominant, if diminishing, role in the system. In 1900 all the members of the Senate's Criminal Cassation Department, 70 percent of all the members of the Chambers, and 58 percent of the members of the Circuit Courts were hereditary noblemen. By 1913, the proportions had fallen to 58 percent of the chamber members and 42 percent of the circuit court members.[61]

The growth of the system, however, indicated no change in the basic antipathy that administrative authorities felt toward it. Unable to abolish the independence of the courts, the government acted in insidious and demoralizing ways that were injurious to their development. It favored politically loyal and submissive officials for appointment to high judicial positions. During the 1870s and 1880s, the School of Jurisprudence turned into a training ground for elite mediocrities, attentive to the needs of the executive authority. Their preeminence was a constant grievance to university graduates.[62] Judges' salaries were raised little after the 1860s, and with the rise in the cost of living, complaints were heard again that judges were receiving salaries that were low and even inadequate.[63]

The government showed itself hostile or indifferent to the basic principles and concerns of the court system. It introduced minor but troublesome abridgments of the independence of judges. It strove to undermine public confidence in the jury system and curtail its competence.[64] It proved inattentive to the legislative needs of the new judiciary. In postreform Russia, the old *Digests of Law* became increasingly cumbersome and outdated, but the government again pursued the goal of codification desultorily, like some kind of necessary but distasteful charade. Corps of legal experts completed a criminal code in 1903 and a civil code in 1913, but except for parts of the criminal code, they remained on paper in 1917. Reform of the police, a precondition to the proper operation of criminal justice, was never undertaken seriously after the 1860s.[65] The government remained averse to the reforms in credit and commercial law necessitated by the new industrial economy. The autocracy thus kept itself apart from the forces of change it had stimulated and, as the Russian economy developed and expanded, ensured its own obsolescence.

As before the reform, the dominant attitudes in society came to mirror official attitudes. The intelligentsia shared the government's absorption with political goals and contempt for the judicial process, Kistiakovskii lamented in 1909. This had led to a general debasement of legal institutions. "Here 'judge' is not an honorable calling that attests to impartiality, selflessness, and high service to the law alone, as it does among other peoples." Only in the first decades after the reform, he claimed, had there been high-minded and distinguished judges.[66] Writers like Leo Tolstoy and Dostoevsky expressed a common distaste for members of the judicial profession as officials cold and un-Russian in their rational adherence to legal science. The intelligentsia saw true justice as emanating from a just political, social, or ethical order—the creations of better legislators—and not from a legal process guided by principles of jurisprudence.

Legal modernization did not bring an element of stability to Russia. Imbued with a consciousness of its own worth and mission, the new legal profession had impugned the autocrat's claim to be the source and protector of legality. It represented an alien system that did not share the preoccupations and fears of the ruler and his entourage. As such, it only added to the inimical forces the government found beyond its power to direct or curb.

The independent courts defended standards of legality that the autocrat, in the midst of bitter political struggle, could not observe. The tsarist government resorted to increasingly brutal and extralegal methods to deal with the revolutionary movement at the close of the nineteenth and the beginning of the twentieth century. In such circumstances, it was difficult for the ruler to maintain his former image as champion of the law. Shedding the guise of absolute ruler, guardian of the rights and welfare of the population, the last two tsars tried instead to resume the role of patriarch, personal and religious leader of the nation. They appealed to national feeling and tried to appear close to the common people. But these products of the international culture of royalty were poor candidates for personal or charismatic leadership. Rather, their reactions to threats were defensive and retaliatory. Embattled, the Russian autocracy in sure and fatal steps took leave of its legal system and relied increasingly on force. Elevating itself beyond legality, it subverted the claims to obedience upon which its power ultimately rested.

NOTES

NOTES TO GENERAL INTRODUCTION

1. Some examples of the copious liberal literature on the reform are N. V. Davydov and N. N. Polianskii, eds., *Sudebnaia Reforma,* 2 vols. (Moscow, 1915); I. V. Gessen, *Sudebnaia Reforma* (St. Petersburg, 1905); G. Dzhanshiev, *Epokha velikikh reform* (Moscow, 1896).

2. V. A. Shuvalova, "Podgotovka sudebnoi reformy" (diss. for degree of *kandidat iuridicheskikh nauk,* Moscow University, 1965); B. V. Vilenskii, *Sudebnaia reforma i kontrreforma v Rossii* (Saratov, 1969).

3. See *Sudebnye ustavy 20 noiabria 1864 goda za piat'desiat' let,* 2 vols. and apps. (St. Petersburg, 1914).

4. Friedhelm Berthold Kaiser, *Die russische Justizreform von 1864: Zur Geschichte der russischen Justiz von Katherina II bis 1917* (Leiden, 1972).

5. See Dzhanshiev, *Epokha,* p. 383; Samuel Kucherov, *Courts, Lawyers, and Trials under the Last Three Tsars* (New York, 1953), p. 21; *Sudebnye ustavy,* 1:288.

6. Kaiser, pp. 420-23.

7. A. F. Koni, *Ottsy i deti sudebnoi reformy* (Moscow, 1914); K. K. Arsen'ev, *Glavnye deiateli i predshestvenniki sudebnoi reformy* (St. Petersburg, 1904); Dzhanshiev, pp. 582-601, 657-71; idem, "S. I. Zarudnyi i Sudebnaia Reforma," *Sbornik statei* (Moscow, 1914), pp. 341-436.

8. S. N. Eisenstadt, "Post-traditional Societies and the Continuity and Reconstruction of Tradition," *Daedalus,* Winter 1973, pp. 8-10; Zbigniew K. Brzezinski, "The Patterns of Autocracy," in Cyril E. Black (ed.), *The Transformation of Russian Society* (Cambridge, Mass., 1960), pp. 93-97.

9. See, for example, William J. Bouwsma, "Lawyers and Early Modern Culture," *American Historical Review,* April 1973, pp. 303-27; Wolfram Fischer and Peter Lundgren, "The Recruitment and Training of Administrative and Technical Personnel," ed. Charles Tilly, *The Formation of National States in Western Europe* (Princeton, 1975), pp. 516-17.

10. Hans-Joachim Torke, *Das russische Beamtentum in der ersten Hälfte des 19. Jahrhunderts* (Berlin, 1967). (*Forschungen zur osteuropäischen Geschichte,* no. 13), pp. 158-59; Marc Raeff, "The Russian Autocracy and Its Officials," *Harvard Slavic Studies* 4:77-91.

11. S. M. Troitskii, *Russkii absoliutizm i dvorianstvo v XVIII v; Formirovanie biurokratii* (Moscow, 1974); P. A. Zaionchkovskii, "Vysshaia biurokratiia nakanune krymskoi voiny,"

NOTES TO CHAPTER 1

Istoriia S.S.S.R., July-August 1974, pp. 154-64; idem, "Gubernskaia administratsiia nakanune krymskoi voiny," *Voprosy Istorii,* September 1975, pp. 33-51; Walter Pintner, "The Social Characteristics of the Early Nineteenth-Century Bureaucracy," *Slavic Review,* September 1970, pp. 429-43.

12. Walter Pintner, "The Russian Civil Service on the Eve of the Great Reforms," *Journal of Social History,* Spring 1975, pp. 55-68.

13. Bruce Lincoln, "The Genesis of an 'Enlightened' Bureaucracy in Russia, 1826-1856," *Jahrbücher für Geschichte Osteuropas* 3, no. 20 (September 1972): 321-30.

14. Daniel Field, "The End of Serfdom: Nobility and Bureaucracy in Russia, 1855-1861"; S. Frederick Starr, *Decentralization and Self-Government in Russia, 1830-1870* (Princeton, 1972), pp. 122-38.

15. George L. Yaney, *The Systematization of Russian Government* (Urbana, Ill., 1973).

NOTES TO CHAPTER ONE

1. Michel Foucault, *Madness and Civilization* (New York and Toronto, 1967), p. 49.

2. N. I. Pavlenko, "Idei absoliutizma v zakonodatel'stve XVIII v," *Absoliutizm v Rossii (XVII-XVIIIvv)* (Moscow, 1964), pp. 398-403.

3. Georgii Gurvich, *"Pravda voli monarshei" Feofana Prokopovicha i eia zapadnoevropeiskie istochniki* (Iur'iev, 1915), pp. 14-15.

4. Henry E. Strakosch, *State Absolutism and the Rule of Law* (Sydney, 1967), p. 118.

5. *PSZ (IP),* 1572, 21 February 1697.

6. Cesare Beccaria, *Crimes and Punishments* (London, 1880), p. 128; W. F. Reddaway, *Documents of Catherine the Great* (Cambridge, England, 1931), pp. 228, 236; N. D. Chechulin, "Ob istochnikakh Nakaza," *Zhurnal Ministerstva Narodnogo Prosveshcheniia* 340 (April 1902): 282, 308-9.

7. *PSZ (IP),* 14392, 7 November 1775, art. 184.

8. I. V. Gessen, ed., *Istoriia russkoi advokatury* (St. Petersburg, 1914-16), 1:1-10.

9. William J. Bouwsma, "Lawyers and Early Modern Culture," *American Historical Review,* April 1973, pp. 303-27.

10. *PSZ (IP),* 3006, 30 March 1716, pp. 2-5.

11. Gessen, *Istoriia,* 1:26.

12. Yaney, p. 64.

13. *PSZ (IP),* 3261, 22 December 1718.

14. *PSZ (IP),* 3969, 17 April 1722; S. M. Soloviev, *Istoriia Rossii s drevneishikh vremen* (Moscow, 1959-66), 9:465-66.

15. *PSZ (IP),* 3979, 27 April 1722.

16. P. Ivanov, *Opyt biografii general-prokurorov i ministrov iustitsii* (St. Petersburg, 1863).

17. M. M. Bogoslovskii, *Oblastnaia reforma Petra Velikogo* (Moscow, 1903), pp. 173-233, 256.

18. The Provincial Reform also created second instance courts beneath the Chambers. These were abolished by Paul I. For a complete description of the judicial institutions introduced by the reform, see John P. LeDonne, "The Judicial Reform of 1775 in Central Russia," *Jahrbücher für Geschichte Osteuropas* 1 (1973): 29-46.

19. *PSZ (IP),* 12448, 21 April 1764; 14392, 7 November 1775, art. 81-83.

20. V. M. Gribovskii, *Vysshii sud i nadzor v Rossii v pervuiu polovinu tsarstvovaniia Imperatritsy Ekateriny II* (St. Petersburg, 1901), pp. 73, 288-89, 330.

21. P. P. Bobrovskii, *Proiskhozhdenie voinskikh artikulov i izobrazheniia protsessov Petra Velikogo po ustavu voinskomu 1716 goda* (St. Petersburg, 1881), pp. 1-25; *PSZ (IP),* 3006, 30 March 1716; 3010, 10 April 1716.

22. *PSZ (IP),* 3006, 30 March 1716, "Kratkoe izobrazhenie protsessov ili sudebnykh tiazhb," glava I, 10.

23. Ibid., pt. 2, gl. 1-5.

24. Ibid., gl. 6.

25. A. G. Man'kov, "Ispol'zovanie v Rossii shvedskogo zakonodatel'stva pri sostavlenii proekta ulozheniia 1720-1725 gg," in AK Nauk SSSR, Institut Istorii SSSR, Leningradskoe Otdelenie, *Trudy*, vyp. 11 (1970), (*Istoricheskie sviazi Skandinavii i Rossii IX-XX vv. Sbornik statei*), pp. 120-22.

26. M. Bogoslovskii, *Oblastnaia reforma*, p. 191.

27. Richard Wortman, "Peter the Great and Court Procedure," *Canadian-American Slavic Studies*, Summer 1974, pp. 303-10; *PSZ (IP)*, 4344, 5 November 1723.

28. For a discussion of this issue, see Marc Szeftel, "The Form of Government of the Russian Empire Prior to the Constitutional Reforms of 1905-06," ed. John Sheldon Curtiss, *Essays in Russian and Soviet History* (New York, 1965), pp. 105-9.

29. See Strakosch for a description of the problems intrinsic to the eighteenth-century notion of codification in Austria.

30. *Istoriia Pravitel'stvuiushchego Senata*, 2: 221-28, 232-51.

31. Marc Raeff, "The Domestic Policies of Peter III and His Overthrow," *American Historical Review* 75, no. 5 (June 1970): 1307; "Sobstvennoruchnoe nastavlenie Ekateriny II Kniaziu Viazemskomu pri vstuplenie im v dolzhnost' general-prokurora," *Sbornik Russkogo Istoricheskogo Obshchestva* 7 (February 1864): 345-47.

32. M. M. Speranskii, *Obozrenie istoricheskikh svedenii o Svode Zakonov* (St. Petersburg, 1833), pp. 55-56.

33. See *Svodnyi katalog russkoi knigi grazhdanskoi pechati XVIII veka* (Moscow, 1962-67); *Pis'movnik soderzhashchii raznye pis'ma, prosheniia, zapiski po delu, kontraktu, atestaty, odobreniia, rospiski, propuski i pis'mennoi vid krepostnym liudiam, prikaz staroste, formu kupecheskikh assignatsii, kvitantsii, rospiski, pis'ma posylochnye i kreditnye* (St. Petersburg, 1789). Later editions carried the title *Vseobshchii sekretar' ili novyi i polnyi pis'movnik.*

34. M. Speranskii, *Obozrenie*, p. 132.

35. Graf E. A. Salias, "Poet Derzhavin: Pravitel' namestnichestva, (1785-1788)," *Russkii Vestnik*, September 1876, p. 95.

36. A. Romanovich-Slavatinskii, *Dvorianstvo v Rossii* (St. Petersburg, 1870), pp. 134-35.

37. P. Bobrovskii, *Razvitie sposobov i sredstv dlia obrazovania iuristov voennogo i morskogo vedomstv v Rossii* (St. Petersburg, 1879), 1: 152-53; N. F. Demidova, "Biurokratizatsiia gosudarstvennogo apparata absoliutizma v XVII-XVIII vv.," *Absoliutizm v Rossii (XVII-XVIII vv.)*, pp. 233-35. Ninety percent of the membership of colleges was comprised of hereditary noblemen. Of the approximately 10 percent of the membership that was non-noble, the majority were from the chancellery class. Of the lists for officials of 1755 in the top five ranks — senators, presidents and some members of colleges, and so on — in the Central Institutions, Troitskii, pp. 214-16, found sixty-three hereditary noblemen, two foreigners, and nine non-nobles.

38. Bogoslovskii, *Oblastnaia reforma*, p. 187; Demidova, pp. 227-28, 234. Demidova notes that of forty-one *voevody* appointed in 1738, twenty-seven were retired officers; Troitskii, p. 284; I. I. Vasil'ev, *Dela pskovskoi provintsial'noi kantseliarii* (Pskov, 1884), pp. iii-viii; Robert Givens, "Seigneurs or Servitors: The Nobility and the Eighteenth-Century State," manuscript, chapter 6; figures for the beginning of the nineteenth century are assembled from lists in TsGIA, *fond* 1349.

39. Troitskii, pp. 217-18; Arcadius Kahan, "The Costs of 'Westernization' in Russia: The Gentry and the Economy in the Eighteenth Century," ed. Michael Cherniavsky, *The Structure of Russian History* (New York, 1970), pp. 241-42; John LeDonne, "Appointments to the Russian Senate, 1762-1796," *Cahiers du monde russe et sovietique*, January-March 1975, pp. 27-56. Brenda Meehan-Waters found that 78 percent of the officials she studied in the *generalitet*, the highest four ranks, came from the Muscovite nobility or old *generalitet*

families, from 1740 to 1770. See "The Russian Aristocracy and the Reforms of Peter the Great," *Canadian-American Slavic Studies,* Summer 1974, p. 291.

40. Kn. Iakov Petrovich Shakhovskoi, *Zapiski* (St. Petersburg, 1872), pp. 125-71.

41. Gribovskii, pp. 108-11, 119-21.

42. Wilson R. Augustine, "Notes toward a Portrait of the Eighteenth-Century Russian Nobility," *Canadian Slavic Studies,* Fall 1970, pp. 384-86.

43. David Ransel, "Bureaucracy and Patronage: The View from an Eighteenth-Century Letter Writer," ed. Fred Jaher, *The Rich, the Well-Born and the Powerful: Studies of Elites and Upper Classes in History* (Urbana, Ill., 1973), pp. 162-63, 169-76.

44. M. M. Bogoslovskii, *Istoriia Rossii XVIII veka (1725-1796),* (Moscow, 1915), pp. 230-32.

45. Pobedonostev describes one case in which a clerk sent to summon a landlord to appear in court in a civil suit was beaten, bound, and abducted by the landlord's men. Apparently there were no drastic repercussions for the landlord. K. P. Pobedonostev, "Iz dalekogo proshlogo," *Sudebnoe Obozrenie,* 10 August 1903, p. 597. Also see Ransel, pp. 175-76; N. F. Dubrovin, "Russkaia zhizn' v nachale XIX veka," *Russkaia Starina,* no. 1 (1899), pp. 4-5.

46. Robert E. Jones, *The Emancipation of the Russian Nobility, 1762-1785* (Princeton, 1973), p. 80.

47. Augustine, pp. 381-82.

48. Jones, pp. 62, 80-81.

49. Augustine, p. 385.

50. A. V. Bezrodnyi, "O podgotovlenii opytnykh i obrazovannykh deiatelei dlia gosudarst-vennoi sluzhby," *Zhurnal Ministerstva Iustitsii,* no. 9 (1903), pp. 250-53.

51. Iu. Got'e, *Istoriia oblastnogo upravleniia v Rossii ot Petra I do Ekateriny II* (Moscow, 1913), 1:263, 272-73. Got'e provides the following data on three chancelleries of *voevody*.

Social Origins

Year	Town	Clerks (*pod'iachie*)	Clergy	Nobles	Others	Totals
1740	Dmitrov	8	2	0	2	12
1775	Valiuiki	13	2	0	1	16
1779	Klin	4	4	1	0	9

52. Got'e, 1:260-63.

53. Ibid., pp. 264-65.

54. Gavriil Dobrynin, "Istinnoe povestvovanie ili zhizn' Gavriila Dobrynina im samim pisannaia, 1752-1823," *Russkaia Starina,* no. 4 (1871), p. 184.

55. Francois Bluche, *Les magistrats du parlement de Paris au XVIII siècle, 1715-1771* (Paris, 1960), pp. 78-80, 236-37.

56. N. A. Voskresenskii, ed., *Zakonodatel'nye akty Petra Velikogo* (Moscow and Leningrad, 1945), p. 383.

57. Erik Amburger, *Geschichte der Behördenorganisation Russlands von Peter dem grossen bis 1917* (Leiden, 1966), p. 171; P. Ivanov, *Opyt biografii general-prokurorov i ministrov iustitsii* (St. Petersburg, 1863); LeDonne, "Appointments to the Russian Senate"; Troitskii.

58. Raeff, "The Domestic Policies of Peter III and His Overthrow."

59. *PSZ (IP),* 4449, 31 January 1724.

60. M. V. Kozhevnikov, "Kratkii ocherk istorii iuridicheskogo fakul'teta Moskovskogo Universiteta," Moskovskii Universitet, *Uchenye Zapiski; trudy Iuridicheskogo Fakul'teta,* vyp. 180, p. 7.

61. Fridrich Genrich Shtrube, *Programma v kotoroi ravnuiu pol'zu voennoi i sudebnoi nauki pokazyvaet: I kupno zhelaiushchikh uprazhniat'sia v osnovatel'neishem uchenii na*

svoi lektsii prizyvaet Fridrikh Genrikh Shtrube Akademii nauk professor (St. Petersburg, 1748), pp. 2-3.

62. For discussions of Catherine's relations with the nobility, see Augustine and Jones, as well as Paul Dukes, *Catherine the Great and the Russian Nobility* (Cambridge, England, 1967).

63. Jones, pp. 281-82.

64. N. Sushkov, *Moskovskii Universitetskii Blagorodnyi Pension* (Moscow, 1858), pp. 5, 41.

65. At the end of the eighteenth century there were not more than one hundred students at Moscow University, of whom somewhat less than half were noble. M. N. Tikhomirov, ed., *Istoriia Moskovskogo Universiteta* (Moscow, 1955), pp. 84-85. In 1765, there was only one undergraduate in the law faculty, which graduated its first two students in 1770. Patrick L. Alston, *Education and the State in Tsarist Russia* (Stanford, 1969), p. 10.

66. S. A. Pokrovskii, ed., *Iuridicheskie proizvedeniia progressivnykh russkikh myslitelei* (Moscow, 1959), pp. 143-46, 150-54.

67. Ibid., p. 227.

68. Ibid., pp. 229-30.

69. Ibid., p. 230.

70. Ibid., pp. 230-31.

71. Vasilii Novikov, *Rech' sochinennaia na sluchai sobraniia Kaluzhskogo dvorianstva dlia vybora sudei na 1786 g.* (St. Petersburg, 1786).

72. Vasilii Novikov, *Teatr sudovedeniia ili chtenie dlia sudei i vsekh liubitelei iurisprudentsii, soderzhashchee dostoprimechatel'nye i liubopytnye sudebnye dela, iuridicheskiia izsledovaniia znamenitnykh pravoiskusstnikov i prochiia sego roda proizshestviia, udobnye prosveshchat', trogat', vozbuzhdat' k dobrodeteli i sostavliat' poleznoe i priiatnoe vremiaprovozhdenie* (St. Petersburg, 1790), vol. 1.

73. Ibid., 1:5-6, 13; 4:3.

74. A. P. Sumarokov, *Polnoe sobranie sochinenii v stikhakh i proze* (Moscow, 1781), 7:356-58; for a discussion of notions of nobility and Sumarokov and the Fonvizin group, see Walter Gleason, *Changes in Values among Certain Russian Writers of the 1760s* (diss. for Ph.D., University of Chicago, 1973).

75. Sumarokov, 7:362-63.

76. Harold B. Segel, *The Literature of Eighteenth-Century Russia* (New York, 1967), 2:352-53.

77. Ibid., pp. 335.

78. G. Makogonenko, ed., *Russkaia proza XVIII veka* (Moscow, 1971), p. 367.

79. M. V. Khrapovitskii, *Razgovor uezdnykh dvorian o vybore v sud'i* (St. Petersburg, 1790).

80. V. Ikonnikov, "Russkie universitety v sviazi s khodom obshchestvennogo obrazovaniia," *Vestnik Evropy*, no. 9 (1876), pp. 202-3; A. N. Antonov, *Pervyi kadetskii korpus* (St. Petersburg, 1907), p. 9. In 1750, according to Ikonnikov, of 328 cadets, all took military subjects. The enrollment in other courses was as follows: German, 258; dance, 160; French, 101; history, 60; geography, 40; Latin, 38; and jurisprudence, 28.

81. Vladimir Zolotnitskii, *Sokrashchenie estestvennogo prava, vybrannoe iz raznykh avtorov dlia pol'zy Rossiiskogo obshchestva* (St. Petersburg, 1764), p. 2.

82. F. H. Strube de Piermont, *Ébauche des lois naturelles et du droit primitif* (Amsterdam, 1744), pp. 40-48, 53-55, 65-86, 108-12.

83. Pokrovskii, pp. 235-36.

84. Fillippa Gendrikh Diltei, *Izsledovanie iuridicheskoe o prinadlezhashchem dlia suda meste, o sudebnoi vlasti, o dolzhnosti sudeiskoi, o chelobitnoi i dokazatel'stve sudebnom* (Moscow, 1779).

85. Ibid.

86. N. N. Polianskii, "Zakharii Goriushkin — zachinatel' russkoi nauke o sude," *Vestnik*

Moskovskogo Universiteta, no. 7 (1951), pp. 145-52; N. M. Korkunov, *Istoriia filosofii prava* (St. Petersburg, 1903), pp. 296-329.

87. Mikhail Chulkov, *Slovar' iuridicheskii ili svod rossiiskikh uzakonenii, vremennykh uchrezhdenii suda, i razpravy* (Moscow, 1788).

88. TsGIA, 1349-4-9 (1803).

89. Speranskii, *Obozrenie,* pp. 132-35.

90. O. A. Przheslavskii, "Vospominaniia, 1818-1831," *Russkaia Starina,* November 1874, pp. 455-57.

NOTES TO CHAPTER TWO

1. *PSZ (IP),* 19,989, 25 August 1801.

2. M. M. Speranskii, *Proekty i zapiski* (Moscow and Leningrad, 1961), pp. 123, 125.

3. Marc Raeff, *Michael Speranskii: Statesman of Imperial Russia, 1772-1839* (The Hague, 1969), pp. 66-70.

4. Marc Raeff, ed., *Plans for Political Reform in Imperial Russia, 1730-1905* (Englewood Cliffs, N.J., 1966), pp. 89-90.

5. *PSZ (IP),* 20406, 8 September 1802; On the separation of the functions of internal well-being and finances in Europe, see Hans Hausherr, *Verwaltungseinheit und Ressorttrennung vom Ende des 17 bis zum Beginn des 19 Jahrhunderts* (Berlin, 1953).

6. *Istoriia Senata,* 3:518, 461.

7. See chapter 4, pp. 115-17.

8. Yaney, pp. 194-96.

9. Ibid., p. 197.

10. S. M. Seredonin, *Istoricheskii obzor deiatel'nosti Komiteta Ministrov* (St. Petersburg, 1902), 2 (pt. 1): 3-5; I. I. Dmitriev, *Vzgliad na moiu zhizn'* (Moscow, 1866), pp. 207-10.

11. Torke, p. 139.

12. *PSZ (IP),* 20597, 24 January 1803.

13. E. M. Kosachevskaia, *M. A. Balug'ianskii i Peterburgskii Universitet* (Leningrad, 1971), p. 5.

14. *PSZ (IP),* 23771, 6 August 1809.

15. P. Miliukov, *Ocherki po istorii russkoi kul'tury* (Paris, 1931), 2 (pt. 2): 775-76.

16. S. V. Rozhdestvenskii, *Sankt-Peterburgskii Universitet, 1819-1919* (Petrograd, 1919), 1:xciv, 25, 33; Kosachevskaia, pp. 76-90, 135-51.

17. D. N. Sverbeev, "Vospominaniia," in V. O. Kliuchevskii, P. M. Obninskii, D. N. Sverbeev, eds., *Vospominaniia o Moskovskom Universitete* (Moscow, 1899), pp. 86-87, 91-94; N. Sushkov, *Moskovskii Universitetskii Blagorodnyi Pansion* (Moscow, 1858), p. 42; A. Blagoveshchenskii, "Istoriia metod nauki zakonovedeniia v XVIII i XIX vekax," *Zhurnal Ministerstva Narodnogo Prosveshcheniia,* July 1835, p. 49.

18. Bezrodnyi, pp. 264-80.

19. James T. Flynn, "The Universities, the Gentry, and the Russian Imperial Service, 1815-1825," *Canadian Slavic Studies,* Winter 1968, pp. 493-94; Ikonnikov, pp. 546-47.

20. M. N. Tikhomirov, *Istoriia Moskovskogo Universiteta* (Moscow, 1955), 1:84-85, 113-14.

21. Flynn, passim.

22. Ibid., pp. 502-3.

23. A. N. Fateev, "K istorii iuridicheskoi obrazovannosti v Rossii," *Uchenye Zapiski osnovannye russkoi uchebnoi kollegiei v Prage,* vyp. 3 (Prague, 1924), 1:219.

24. Richard Pipes, ed., *Karamzin's Memoir on Ancient and Modern Russia* (New York, 1969), p. 149.

25. Ibid., p. 201.

26. Flynn, p. 500.

27. N. K. Nelidov, "Nauka o gosudarstve kak predmet vysshego spetsial'nogo obrazo-vaniia," *Vremennik Iaroslavskogo Demidovskogo Litseiia,* no. 3 (1872), pp. 169-70.

28. A. N. Kulomzin, "Dmitrii Nikolaevich Zamiatnin," *Zhurnal Ministerstva Iustitsii,* November 1914, p. 255.

29. I. Seleznev, *Istoricheskii obzor Imperatorskogo byvshego tsarskosel'skogo nyne Alek-sandrovskogo Litseia za pervoe ego piatidesiatiletie 1811-1861* (St. Petersburg, 1861), p. 166.

30. See chapter 3.

31. P. Baranov, *Mikhail Andreevich Balug'ianskii, 1769-1847* (St. Petersburg, 1882), p. 23.

32. *Gosudarstvennyi Sovet, 1801-1901* (St. Petersburg, 1901), p. 56.

33. G. Tel'berg. "Uchastie Imperatora Nikolaia I v kodifikatsionnoi rabote ego tsarstvo-vaniia," *Zhurnal Ministerstva Iustitsii* 22 (Janurary-March 1916): 233-44; see Raeff, *Michael Speranskii,* pp. 320-44, for a discussion of the work of codification.

34. *SZ,* 1832, vol. 10, no. 1875; vol. 15, no. 1062, 1064.

35. Seredonin, vol. 2, pt. 1, p. 2.

36. *Ministerstvo Vnutrennikh Del, 1802-1902* (St. Petersburg, 1901), p. 63; V. V. Bervi [N. Flerovskii], *Tri politicheskie sistemy* (n.p., 1897), pp. 49-50.

37. E. Anuchin, *Istoricheskii obzor razvitiia administrativno-politseiskikh uchrezhdenii v Rossii s Uchrezhdeniia o gubernïiakh do poslednego vremeni* (St. Petersburg, 1872), p. 52; *Ministerstvo Vnutrennikh Del, 1802-1902,* pp. 61-62; *PSZ (IV),* 10303, 3 June 1837; see the discussion of the question of the increase of the size of the bureaucracy and paper work in Starr, pp. 9-14, 26-35.

38. Ia. Barshev, *Istoricheskaia zapiska o sodeistvii Vtorogo Otdeleniia sobstvennoi ego I. V. Kantseliarii razvitii iuridicheskikh nauk v Rossii* (St. Petersburg, 1876), p. 8.

39. Kosachevskaia, p. 151; Barshev, pp. 8-12, 20-22; P. M. Maikov, "Speranskii i studenty zakonovedeniia," *Russkii Vestnik,* August 1899, pp. 609-26; September 1899, pp. 239-56; October 1899, pp. 673-82.

40. The chairs established were encyclopedia, or general system of legal method (*zakon-ovedenua*), including the study of Russian state laws; Roman law and its history; civil laws; laws of order and decorum (*blagochinie*); laws on taxes and finances; police and criminal laws; principles of international jurisprudence (*pravovedeniia*). *PSZ (IV),* 8337, 26 July 1835; Nicholas ordered that the teaching of natural law in abbreviated form be assigned to the chair of moral philosophy, "to give this subject a completely different direction and ensure its usefulness." *PSZ (IV),* 8492, 17 October 1835.

41. N. P. Iasnopol'skii, *Spetsializatsiia uchebnykh planov prepodavaniia i zaniatii naukami iuridicheskimi, gosudarstvennymi i economicheskimi v universitetakh Rossii* (Kiev, 1907), p. 16; Torke, pp. 141-42.

42. N. K. Shil'der, *Imperator Nikolai Pervyi: Ego zhizn' i tsarstvovanie* (St. Petersburg, 1903), 1:705.

43. F. Bulgarin, *Petr Ivanovich Vyzhigin* (St. Petersburg, 1834), pp. 1-5.

44. Bulgarin, *Sochineniia* (St. Petersburg, 1830), 8:10.

45. Ibid., p. 24.

46. S. Uvarov, *Desiatiletie Ministerstva Narodnogo Proveshcheniia, 1833-1843* (St. Peters-burg, 1864), p. 32.

47. Miliukov, 2 (pt. 2): 785.

48. Ibid., pp. 789-90.

49. Torke, p. 89; previously, students after their graduations had received the fourteenth rank, and candidates, the twelfth. *PSZ (IP),* 20,597, 24 January 1803.

50. Harold A. McFarlin, "The Extension of the Imperial Russian Civil Service to the Lowest Office Workers: The Creation of the Chancery Clerkship, 1827-1833," *Russian History* 1 (pt.

1, 1974): 7-9.

51. N. Ozhe-de-Rankur, "V dvukh universitetakh," *Russkaia Starina* (June 1896), p. 571; Leonid Grossman, *Prestuplenie Sukhovo-Kobylina* (Leningrad, 1928), pp. 57-58; N. Koliupanov, "Iz proshlogo," *Russkoe Obozrenie,* no. 3 (1895), p. 17.

52. The number of students in all Russian universities rose from 1,326 in 1824, to 1,444 in 1836, to 3,373 in 1848; then, after the revolution of 1848, it dropped to 3,141. Of these, an almost constant two-thirds of the students were designated nobles' or officers' sons. The only university for which separate figures are available for hereditary nobles was Moscow University. There, noblemen made up about 40 percent and never more than half of the total enrollment during Nicholas's reign — about the same proportions that prevailed under Alexander. Iu. N. Egorov, "Reaktsionnaia politika tsarizma v voprosakh universitetskogo obrazovaniia v 30-kh-50-kh gg. XIX v.," *Nauchnye doklady vysshei shkoly: istoricheskie nauki,* no. 3 (1960), p. 61; Tikhomirov, pp. 113, 117; Miliukov, 2 (pt. 2): 778.

53. Georgii Siuzor, *Ko dniu LXXV iubileia imperatorskogo uchilishcha pravovedeniia 1835-1910* (St. Petersburg, 1910), pp. 20-21.

54. M. M. Speranskii, "Imperatorskoe Uchilishche Pravovedenie," *Russkaia Starina,* December 1885, pp. i-iii.

55. Siuzor, pp. 21-22.

56. Ibid., pp. 117, 121.

57. Ibid., pp. 122-23.

58. T. Koniuchenko, *Statisticheskie svedeniia o lichnom sostave vospitannikakh i khoziast-vennoi chasti Imperatorskogo Uchilishcha Pravovedeniia za 50 let ego sushchestvovaniia* (St. Petersburg, 1886), pp. 114-16.

59. Siuzor, pp. 125-26.

60. IM, 117-78, pp. 15-16; Bezrodnyi, p. 264.

1. The judiciary at the beginning of the century fits the general description of the administration given by Marc Raeff in "The Russian Autocracy and Its Officials," *Harvard Slavic Studies* 4 (1957): 77-91; also see Torke, p. 171.

2. GBL, 178- Muzeinoe sobranie-8184 (M. A. Dmitriev, *Glavy iz vospominanii o moei zhizni*) (hereafter cited as *Glavy*), 1:238.

3. Pintner, "The Social Characteristics," pp. 437-40, 442.

4. The service lists (*formuliarnye spiski*) of the Ministry of Justice, which are the chief source for this chapter, required listing of landed wealth in terms of the number of "revision souls," or male serfs, the official owned. Factories are also mentioned on the lists, but rarely. Commercial wealth is, of course, not indicated, but since the officialdom came preponderantly from nobility, officials' sons, and clergy, it does not seem to be a significant variable. As explained in the note to table 3.2, I have felt that it was not meaningful to distinguish between hereditary and acquired property.

5. Kahan, pp. 240-42; Jerome Blum, *Lord and Peasant in Russia* (New York, 1964), pp. 368-69. It is true that the total number of noble serfholders declined from 1834 to 1858, but this is due to the elimination of serfholders without land, as a result of the prohibition of holding serfs without land. These were servants of the officials and the change is reflected in the virtual disappearance of the category of officials owning one to ten souls.

6. S. Uvarov, *Desiatiletie Ministerstva Narodnogo Prosveshcheniia 1833-1843,* p. 33; the appearance of educated noble officials in high positions seems to be a general feature of the administration at the end of Nicholas's reign. See Pintner, "The Russian Civil Service."

7. Zaionchkovskii, "Vysshaia biurokratiia," p. 160; Zaionchkovskii's sample is different from that used here. *Ministerstvo Iustitsii za sto let,* p. 36.

8. On Derzhavin, see chapter 4; on Panin, chapter 7.

9. This change is in line with the decline in landholding of high officials that Zaionchkov-

skii has noted for the second half of the century. P. A. Zaionchkovskii, *Rossiĭskoe samoderzhavie v kontse XIX stoletiia* (Moscow, 1970), pp. 112-17.

10. TsGIA, 1349-3-1212, 1600-73, 2390-8, 1870-21, 1340-7, 1797-5.

11. A. A. Kizevetter, "Vnutrenniaia politika v tsarstvovanie Nikolaia Pavlovicha," in M. Pokrovskii, ed., *Istoriia Rossii v XIX veke* (St. Petersburg, 1907), 1:180.

12. TsGIA, 1349-5-8845, 4501.

13. L. V. Vinogradova, "Osnovnye vidy dokumentov Senata i organizatsiia ego deloproizvodstva," Glavnoe Arkhivnoe Pravlenie, *Nekotorye voprosy izucheniia istoricheskikh dokumentov XIX—nachala XX veka* (Leningrad, 1967), pp. 121-22.

14. I. I. Dmitriev, *Vzgliad na moiu zhizn'*, pp. 145-46, 184.

15. Przheslavskii, pp. 458, 462-64.

16. Torke, p. 126 n.

17. M. A. Dmitriev, *Glavy*, 2:62.

18. Educational data for these chief-procurators are drawn from various editions of the *Spiski chinam Pravitel'stvuiushchego Senata i Ministerstva Iustitsii;* Pintner, "The Russian Higher Civil Service," pp. 63-65.

19. TsGIA, 1349-3-478-50, 1136; M. A. Dmitriev, *Glavy*, 1:211; Iv. Aksakov, *Ivan Sergeevich Aksakov v ego pis'makh* (Moscow, 1888), 1:77, 108-9, 164.

20. Lebedev, *Russkaia Starina*, no. 1 (1888), pp. 481-82.

21. TsGIA, 1364-15-694.

22. Ibid., 1364-15-781.

23. *Russkii Biograficheskii Slovar'*, 10:107-8.

24. PD, 28850/C2, ix-b-45.

25. Leonid Grossman, *Prestuplenie Sukhovo-Kobylina* (Leningrad, 1928); GBL, Stoian-11-3 (Vypiska iz otcheta i doneseniia ober prokurora 2ogo otdeleniia 5ogo departmenta predstavlenna Ministerstvu pri raporte 30ogo dekabria 1855 goda).

26. Grossman, pp. 176-77 n.

27. A. B. Sukhovo-Kobylin, *Trilogiia* (Moscow, 1955), pp. 87-88; Grossman, p. 177.

28. Vinogradova, pp. 120-21.

29. Przheslavskii, p. 458.

30. G. Dzhanshiev, *Stranitsa iz istorii sudebnoi reformy: D. N. Zamiatnin* (Moscow, 1883), p. 122.

31. *Spisok chinam Pravitel'stvuiushchego Senata i Ministerstva Iustitsii za 1856 god* (St. Petersburg, 1856).

32. TsGIA, 1349-3-2340, 1349-5-734, p. 209.

33. TsGIA, 1349-5-734, p. 207.

34. TsGIA, 1349-3-1881-14.

35. TsGIA, 1349-5-734, p. 208.

36. *PSZ (IV)*, 539, 22 August 1826.

37. TsGIA, 1349-4-1855.

38. *Spisok chinam*, p. 120.

39. TsGIA, 1363-3-775.

40. TsGIA, 1349-5-4501.

41. TsGIA, 1349-5-467, 1405-528-83; D. P. Shubin-Pozdeev, "Nekrolog Zarudnogo," *Russkaia Starina*, no. 2 (1888), p. 479; Gr. Dzhanshiev, *Epokha velikikh reform*, pp. 583-85, 587.

42. Of the remaining seven, three came from the clergy, one was the son of a court servant, one of a merchant, one was from free estate, and one was a foreigner.

43. On Koz'ma Prutkov, see Barbara Heldt Monter, *Koz'ma Prutkov: The Art of Parody* (The Hague, 1972).

44. See chapter 1, pp. 13-14, 19.

45. *PSZ (IV)*, 4989, 6 December 1831; for Panin's approach to appointments, see chapter

7, pp. 184–86.

46. The percentage of noble chairmen declines from 90 percent at the beginning to 87 percent at the quarter and 77 percent at mid-century. Assistant chairmen decline from 68 percent to 52 percent then rise to 63 percent noble. Procurators decline from 100 percent to 55 percent, then rise to 75 percent noble. Zaionchkovskii shows a somewhat smaller proportion of hereditary noblemen in chairmen and procurators' positions — about two-thirds, or the same as my findings at the end of the first quarter, suggesting no further decline. See his "Gubernskaia administratsiia," pp. 47–50.

47. Zaionchkovskii's figures on chairmen's landholding are about the same as my own; he does not give specific figures for procurators. See "Gubernskaia administratsiia," pp. 48–50. The decline in the landholding of appointed officials was assisted by governmental measures aimed at discouraging officials from accumulating landholdings in the provinces where they served and from becoming powers in the provincial assemblies. It had been common for procurators to own extensive lands in the provinces where they worked and to use their influence to determine the outcome of local elections. A law of 1811 forbade procurators from participating in elections in provinces where they held office. S. A. Korf, *Dvorianstvo i ego soslovnoe upravlenie za stoletie 1762–1861* (St. Petersburg, 1906), p. 340.

48. The number of those who have worked in central institutions rises from sixteen of seventy-six (21 percent) at the beginning to twenty-five of fifty-seven (43.9 percent) at the quarter to thirty-five of sixty-five (53.8 percent) at mid-century.

49. *Spisok chinam Pravitel'stvuiushchego Senata i Ministerstva Iustitsii za 1850 god* (St. Petersburg, 1850).

50. N. Koliupanov, "Iz proshlogo," *Russkoe Obozrenie,* no. 5 (1895), p. 7.

51. Dzhanshiev, *Stranitsa,* p. 121.

52. TsGIA, 1349-4-53 (1805).

53. Ibid., 1349-4-62 (1804).

54. Ibid., 1349-4-179 (1825).

55. Ibid., op. 5, 1349-4-7770 (1851).

56. Ibid., 1349-4-1635 (1850).

57. *PSZ (IV),* 20618, 18 November 1846; *Otchet Ministra Iustitsii za 1847 g.,* p. lxv.

58. *PSZ (IV),* 25944, 28 January 1852; SZ (1857 ed.), vol. 2, chap. 1, p. 477; GBL, Stoian-53-5 (*Materialy po voprosu o naime i uvol'nenie sudebnykh chinovnikov—zakliuchenie*).

59. For a description of the powers, jurisdiction, and structure of district courts, see LeDonne, "The Judicial Reform of 1775 in Central Russia," pp. 34, 37–38. Courts served the nobility, the magistracies, the townsmen. I have selected district courts for examination because the magistracies preserved numerous nonjudicial functions, even after the reform of 1775. Staffed by townsmen who did not enjoy the right to state service, the magistracies had even greater difficulty attracting able personnel and in many towns barely functioned.

60. Bulgarin, "Sud po vyboru," p. 14.

61. S. Korf, pp. 132–33.

62. Koliupanov, no. 6 (1895), pp. 600–1.

63. *PSZ (IP),* 16197, 21 April 1785, art. 62–64; *PSZ (IV),* 4989, 6 December 1831.

64. Koliupanov, no. 6 (1895), pp. 601–2; S. Korf, p. 642.

65. S. Korf, pp. 700–1.

66. *PSZ, (IV),* 4989, 6 December 1831.

67. Staffing of the district courts was governed by different principles in areas where there were few or no members of the landed nobility. In provinces like Arkhangelsk, Vologda, Perm, and Tobolsk, which had no noble corporations to elect members of the courts, the judges were appointed by the governors. I will therefore deal separately with the noble and non-noble provinces. In order to ensure a similar geographical area, I have narrowed my

sample for noble courts to five provinces (Kostróma, Novgorod, Kursk, Orel, and Tambov), where nobles' serfs comprised at least 40 percent of the population.

68. S. Korf, pp. 601–2.

69. Service lists for Tver are in *fond* 1349, op. 4, d. 94, and op. 5, d. 1827; for Tambov *fond* 1349, op. 4, d. 30 and 178, and op. 5, d. 4648.

70. For Vologda, *fond* 1349, op. 4, d. 41 and 207; op. 5, d. 4616; for Arkhangelsk *fond* 1349, op. 4, d. 37; op. 5, d. 7646.

71. 1349, op. 5, d. 1308 (Perm); d. 1278, Tobolsk.

72. B. G. Koriagin, "Iz istorii provedeniia sudebnoi reformy v zapadnoi Sibiri," *Trudy Tomskogo Gosudarstvennogo Universiteta* 159 (1965): 155.

NOTES TO INTRODUCTION TO PART TWO

1. On the absent father and the role of education in the eighteenth century see Marc Raeff, *Origins of the Russian Intelligentsia: The Eighteenth-Century Nobility* (New York, 1966), pp. 122–47.

2. F. F. Vigel', *Vospominaniia* (Moscow, 1864), 1:172–73; Romanovich-Slavatinskii, pp. 140–41; Dmitriev, *Glavy*, 1:51.

3. Dmitriev, *Glavy*, 1:127.

4. Vigel', 1:173.

5. *Istoriia Senata*, 3:171.

6. E. Karnovich, *Russkie chinovniki v byloe i nastoiashchee vremia* (St. Petersburg, 1897), pp. 83–94.

7. Konstantin Nevolin, *Entsiklopediia zakonovedeniia* (Kiev, 1839), p. 54.

NOTES TO CHAPTER FOUR

1. *Svodnyi katalog russkoi knigi grazhdanskoi pechati XVIII v.*, 1:49; Marc Raeff, *Origins of the Russian Intelligentsia: The Eighteenth-Century Nobility*, pp. 232–33.

2. Alexander Radishchev, *A Voyage from St. Petersburg to Moscow*, p. 123.

3. James Edie, James Scanlan, and Mary-Barbara Zelden, eds., *Russian Philosophy* (Chicago, 1965), 1:80; see Hugh Honour, *Neo-Classicism* (Hammondsworth, 1968), pp. 148–50, for a useful discussion of "the eighteenth-century way of death."

4. G. R. Derzhavin, *Sochineniia* (St. Petersburg, 1864), 1:668, 486. Good translations of these poems may be found in Harold L. Segel, *The Literature of Eighteenth-Century Russia*, 2:254, 317, which also contains discussions of the background and themes.

5. A. N. Radishchev, *Polnoe sobranie sochinenii* (Moscow and Leningrad, 1952), 3:145.

6. Ibid., p. 146.

7. Iurii Tynianov, *Arkhaisty i novatory* (Leningrad, 1929), p. 21; Segel, 2:265.

8. Derzhavin, 1:83–90; Segel, 2:262–79; G. R. Derzhavin, "Zapiski, 1743–1812" (hereafter cited as *Zapiski*), in *Sochineniia*, 6 (1871): 621.

9. *Zapiski*, pp. 414, 542, 545–46.

10. Ibid., pp. 417–18.

11. Khodasevich, p. 195.

12. In 1769, while still in the guards, Derzhavin was a member of one of the special commissions connected with work of codification, that "on various establishments [*o raznykh ustanovleniiakh*]." It is not clear, however, whether he actually participated in the commission's work. V. S. Ikonnikov, *Gavriil Romanovich Derzhavin v svoei gosudarstvennoi i obshchestvennoi deiatel'nosti* (Petrograd and Kiev, 1917), p. 5.

13. Derzhavin, *Sochineniia*, 1 (1864): 265–67; 2 (1865): 172–75.

14. Khodasevich, pp. 114–15; Ia. Grot, "Zhizn' Derzhavina," *Sochineniia*, 8 (1880): 720; Ikonnikov, pp. 57–58.

15. On Derzhavin's capriciousness in interpreting the law, see Yaney, p. 98.

16. *Zapiski,* p. 413.

17. B. M. Eikhenbaum, *Skvoz' literaturu* (Leningrad, 1924), p. 11; Khodasevich, p. 116.

18. Derzhavin, *Sochineniia,* 1 (1864): 109-15; Segel, 2:260-61.

19. Derzhavin, *Sochineniia,* 1 (1864): 93.

20. *Zapiski,* pp. 550-53.

21. Ibid., pp. 553-56.

22. A. D. Gradovskii, "Istoricheskii ocherk uchrezhdeniia general-gubernatorstv v Rossii," *Sochineniia* (St. Petersburg, 1899), 1:312-13.

23. *Zapiski,* p. 563.

24. Derzhavin, *Sochineniia,* 7 (1878): 108-10. The 1878 edition has more complete versions of Derzhavin's responses than earlier ones.

25. Ibid., 7:111-13.

26. E. Anuchin, *Istoricheskii obzor razvitiia administrativno-politseiskikh uchrezhdenii v Rossii* (St. Petersburg, 1872), pp. 7-11; Grot, pp. 363-64.

27. Derzhavin, *Sochineniia,* 7 (1878): 116-17.

28. V. I. Semevskii, *Krestiane v tsarstvovanie Ekateriny II* (St. Petersburg, 1901), 2: 633-48; *Istoriia pravitel'stvuiushchego Senata,* 2: 513-14.

29. Khodasevich, pp. 143-44.

30. Graf E. A. Salias, "Poet Derzhavin: Pravitel' namestnichestva (1785-1788)," *Russkii Vestnik,* September 1876, p. 89.

31. Ibid., pp. 99-103.

32. Ibid., p. 95.

33. Ibid., p. 93; *Russkii Vestnik,* October 1876, p. 600.

34. *Russkii Vestnik,* October 1876, pp. 602-19.

35. *Zapiski,* pp. 604-6; see Arcadius Kahan, "The Costs of Westernization in Russia: The Gentry and the Economy in the Eighteenth Century," for a description of debts among the wealthiest nobility.

36. Salias, *Russkii Vestnik,* October 1876, pp. 619-23.

37. Khrapovitskii, *Dnevnik* (Moscow, 1901), p. 175.

38. *Zapiski,* pp. 627-31.

39. Ibid., pp. 631-32; Khrapovitskii, p. 339.

40. *Zapiski,* pp. 654, 664, 685-92.

41. Ibid., pp. 667-68.

42. Grot, pp. 620-21.

43. *Zapiski,* pp. 764-65.

44. Ibid., pp. 765-76; N. F. Dubrovin, "Russkaia zhizn' v nachale XIX veka," *Russkaia Starina,* no. 6 (1899), pp. 500-4; Parusov, p. 177.

45. *Zapiski,* p. 758.

46. A recent treatment of Alexander's attitude toward senatorial constitutionalism is Allen McConnell, "Alexander I's Hundred Days: The Politics of a Paternalist Reformer," *Slavic Review,* September 1969, pp. 373-93.

47. Derzhavin, "Mnenie Senatora Derzhavina o pravakh, preimushchestvakh i sushchestvennoi dolzhnosti Senata," *Chteniia obshchestva istorii i drevnostei rossiiskikh,* no. 3 (1858), p. 124; N. M. Korkunov, "Proekt ustroistva Senata G. R. Derzhavina," *Zhurnal Ministerstva Iustitsii,* no. 10 (1896), p. 13; *Zapiski,* pp. 760-65; Clardy even claims that Alexander solicited Derzhavin's project to offset the liberal demands of the other senators. Jesse Clardy, *G. R. Derzhavin: A Political Biography* (The Hague and Paris, 1967), p. 191.

48. Marc Raeff, *Michael Speranskii* (The Hague, 1969), pp. 44-45.

49. *PSZ (IP),* 20405, 8 September 1802.

50. A. Kornilov, *Kurs istorii Rossii XIX veka* (Moscow, 1918), 1:106-8; *Zapiski,* pp. 786-97; G. Tel'berg, *Pravitel'stvuiushchii Senat i samoderzhavnaia vlast' v nachale XIX veka* (Moscow, 1914).

51. *PSZ* (*IP*), 20406, 8 September 1802.
52. *Zapiski,* p. 780.
53. Ibid., pp. 780-83.
54. *Arkhiv Kniazia Vorontsova* (Moscow, 1880), 18:289-90.
55. *PSZ* (*IP*), 20406, 8 September 1802.
56. *Zapiski,* pp. 798-99.
57. Raeff, *Speranskii,* p. 51.
58. *Zapiski,* pp. 810-11.
59. Ibid., pp. 824-25; *Ministerstvo Iustitsii za sto let* (St. Petersburg, 1902), p. 22.
60. *Zapiski,* p. 806.
61. V. I. Semevskii, *Krest'ianskii vopros v Rossii v XVIII i pervoi polovine XIX veka* (St. Petersburg, 1888), 1:254-55.
62. Derzhavin, *Sochineniia,* 2 (1865): 457-58.
63. Derzhavin, *Sochineniia,* 3 (1866): 525.
64. See the excellent discussion of the changes in Derzhavin's verse in Jane Gary Harris, "The Creative Imagination in Evolution: A Stylistic Analysis of G. R. Derzhavin's Panegyric and Meditative Odes" (diss., Columbia University, 1969).
65. Derzhavin, *Sochineniia,* 3 (1866): 233-34.

NOTES TO CHAPTER FIVE

1. Prot. Georgii Florovskii, *Puti russkogo bogosloviia* (Paris, 1937), pp. 128-29.
2. I. I. Dmitriev, *Vzgliad na moiu zhizn',* p. 134.
3. Ibid., pp. 145-46.
4. Ibid., pp. 159-62.
5. M. A. Dmitriev, *Melochi iz zapasa moei pamiati* (Moscow, 1869), pp. 137-38.
6. Ibid., pp. 138-39.
7. Ibid., pp. 145-47; Dmitriev, *Vzgliad,* pp. 207-17.
8. Dmitriev, *Vzgliad,* pp. 226-30.
9. Ibid., pp. 232-37.
10. Ibid., p. 131.
11. Ibid., p. 144.
12. I. I. Dmitriev, *Polnoe sobranie stikhotvorenii* (Leningrad, 1967), pp. 120-23.
13. Dmitriev, *Vzgliad,* p. 220.
14. Dmitriev, *Polnoe,* p. 185.
15. Ibid., pp. 290-91.
16. Ibid., pp. 123-35.
17. N. M. Karamzin, *Polnoe sobranie stikhotvorenii* (Moscow and Leningrad, 1966), pp. 136-40.
18. N. I. Mordovchenko, *Russkaia kritika pervoi chetverti XIX veka* (Moscow and Leningrad, 1959), pp. 37-38.
19. Karamzin, *Polnoe,* p. 192.
20. N. M. Karamzin, *Izbrannye proizvedeniia* (Moscow, 1966), pp. 35-54.
21. N. M. Karamzin, *Polnoe,* pp. 260-61.
22. Henry M. Nebel, *N. M. Karamzin: A Russian Sentimentalist* (The Hague, 1967), p. 174.
23. Karamzin, *Polnoe,* pp. 67-68.
24. N. M. Karamzin, *Istoriia gosudarstva rossiiskogo* (Moscow, 1903), 1:13.
25. Ibid., 6:67.
26. Richard Pipes, *Karamzin's Memoir on Ancient and Modern Russia* (New York, 1969), pp. 196-97; N. L. Rubinshtein, *Russkaia istoriografiia* (Moscow, 1941), p. 178.
27. Karamzin, *Polnoe,* p. 263.
28. Pipes, pp. 185-90.

29. Ibid., p. 196.

30. Ibid., pp. 196-97.

31. Ibid., p. 197.

32. V. A. Zhukovskii, *Polnoe sobranie sochinenii* (St. Petersburg, 1902), 12:143.

33. V. Zhirmunskii, *Gete v russkoi literature* (Leningrad, 1937), p. 76.

34. M. Raeff, "La jeunesse russe a l'aube du XIX siecle: André Turgenev et ses amis," *Cahiers du monde russe et sovietique,* 8 (October-December 1967): 570 n.

35. Ibid., pp. 568-70, 577.

36. Zhukovskii, *Polnoe,* 1:24.

37. Marcelle Ehrhard, *V. A. Joukovskii et le préromantisme russe* (Paris, 1938), p. 56.

38. PD, 21-823/S21b6, p. 16.

39. Jacques Choron, *Death and Western Thought* (New York, 1963), pp. 156-57.

40. Zhukovskii, *Polnoe,* 1:18.

41. Ibid., 9:31.

42. Ibid., pp. 31-32.

43. A. N. Veselovskii, *V. A. Zhukovskii: Poeziia chuvstva i "serdechnogo voobrazheniia"* (Petrograd, 1918), p. 43.

44. Ibid., pp. 111-12.

45. Zhukovskii, *Polnoe,* 1:21.

46. Zhirmunskii, pp. 97-111; A. S. Arkhangel'skii, "V. A. Zhukovskii: Biograficheskii ocherk"; V. A. Zhukovskii, *Polnoe sobranie sochinenii,* 1:17-18.

47. M. S. Borovkova-Maikova, ed., *Arzamas i arzamaskie protokoly* (Leningrad, 1933), pp. 26-28, 116-27; "Parnasskii adres-kalendar'," *Russkii Arkhiv* 4 (1866): 760-66.

48. Borovkova-Maikova, p. 59.

49. Ibid., p. 221.

50. Zhukovskii, *Polnoe,* 1:18.

51. Ibid., p. 71.

52. L. N. Maikov, *Batiushkov, ego zhizn' i sochineniia* (St. Petersburg, 1887), p. 131.

53. Zhukovskii, *Polnoe,* 2:8.

54. Michael Cherniavsky, *Tsar and People* (New Haven and London, 1961), pp. 128-36.

55. Zhukovskii, *Polnoe,* 2:70-77.

56. Ibid., 12:150.

57. Ibid., 2:124-26.

58. Derzhavin, *Sochineniia,* 1 (1864): 81-86.

59. Zhukovskii, *Polnoe,* 2:126.

60. A. N. Veselovskii, p. 347.

61. S. S. Tatishchev, *Imperator Aleksandr II: Ego zhizn' i tsarstvovanie* (St. Petersburg, 1903), 1:13.

62. Ibid., p. 18.

63. *Sbornik russkogo istoricheskogo obshchestva,* 3:167-68.

64. A. Shemanskii and S. Geichenko, *Krizis samoderzhaviia: Petergofskii Kottedzh Nikolaia I* (Moscow and Leningrad, 1932), pp. 28, 18 n.

NOTES TO CHAPTER SIX

1. E. P. Kovalevskii, *Graf Bludov i ego vremia* (St. Petersburg, 1871), pp. 1-24.

2. K. N. Batiushkov, *Sochineniia* (St. Petersburg, 1886-87), 3: 468; see also *Russkii Arkhiv* 2 (1902): 115, for letter of A. O. Smirnov to Zhukovskii; "Iz zapisok Ippolita Ozhe," *Russkii Arkhiv* (1877), 1:252, and many others.

3. N. Barsukov, *Zhizn' i trudy M. P. Pogodina* (St. Petersburg, 1888-1910), 8:214-15.

4. See, for example, N. V. Davydov and N. N. Polianskii, *Sudebnaia Reforma,* vol. 1.

5. Kovalevskii, pp. 4-5.

6. TsGIA, 1162-6-42 (Delo Bludova), p. 36; on the economic problems of wealthy members of the gentry, see Kahan, "The Costs of Westernization," and Michael Confino, *Domaines et seigneurs en russie vers la fin du XVIII siecle* (Paris, 1963).

7. Kovalevskii, pp. 20-22.

8. Ibid., pp. 31-33, 37.

9. The name of the girl is illegible and neither I nor those giving me assistance at Pushkinskii Dom were able to determine whether it was a term of affection for Shcherbatova or whether it referred to someone else.

10. PD, 21-823/S21b6, pp. 1-2.

11. Kovalevskii, p. 269.

12. PD, 21-832/S21b6, p. 13.

13. A. N. Veselovskii, p. 265.

14. Kovalevskii, p. 264.

15. Zhukovskii, 1:66-67.

16. Ibid., 1:81; Zhukovskii, "Neizdannoe pis'mo k D. N. Bludovu," *Raduga* (St. Petersburg, 1922), pp. 19-20.

17. "Materialy k istorii Arzamasa: Rech' chlena Kassandry," *Otchet Imperatorskoi publichnoi biblioteki za 1888 god* (St. Petersburg, 1891), app. III.

18. PD, 21-823/S21b6, p. 32.

19. D. N. Bludov, *Mysli i zamechaniia* (St. Petersburg, 1866), p. 26.

20. Kovalevskii, p. 275; Bludov, pp. 26, 28.

21. Bludov, *Mysli,* pp. 26, 28.

22. "Dva pis'ma gr. D. N. Bludova k supruge ego," *Russkii Arkhiv* 5 (1867): 1046-47.

23. Kovalevskii, pp. 191-244.

24. A. D. Bludova, "Zapiski," *Russkii Arkhiv* 10 (1872): 1046-47.

25. D. N. Bludov, *Poslednie chasy zhizni Imperatora Nikolaia Pervogo* (St. Petersburg, 1855), pp. 4, 39.

26. Ibid., pp. 14-15.

27. Ibid., p. 5.

28. Ibid., pp 5, 11.

29. Kovalevskii, pp. 123-25, 132-34; A. O. Smirnova-Rosset, *Avtobiografiia* (Moscow, 1931), pp. 174-75.

30. Bludova, 12 (1874) : 760.

31. A. I. Koshelev, *Zapiski* (Berlin, 1884), p. 23; K. S. Veselovskii, "Vospominaniia," *Russkaia Starina* 148 (1901): 528.

32. Bludova, 11 (1873): 2068 n.

33. PD, 21-821/S1b66.

34. PD, 21-818/SZ1b5, p. 1.

35. GPB, 78-B-13, 78-B-73.

36. TsGIA, 1162-6-42 (*Delo Bludova*), pp. 170, 199, 240-41.

37. PD, 21-821/S1b6.

38. K. S. Veselovskii, pp. 508, 527; "Iz bumag V. A. Zhukovskogo," *Russkii Arkhiv,* no. 3 (1875), p. 342 n.

39. Bludova, 13 (1875): 367-68; 11 (1873): 2068 n; K. S. Veselovskii, pp. 508-9.

40. Kovalevskii, 1:268.

41. GPB, 78-B-12.

42. M. A. Dmitriev, *Glavy,* 2:26.

43. GBL, Venev-64-17 (Anna Venevetinova, letter to E. E. and S. V. Koramovskii, 3 May 1832).

44. "Literatura o Pushkine," *Istoricheskii vestnik* 77 (1899): 606-7.

45. N. I. Grech, *Zapiski o moei zhizni* (St. Petersburg, 1886), pp. 73-74.

46. Erik Amburger, *Geschichte der Behördensorganisation Russlands von Peter dem Grossen bis 1917*, pp. 184-85; TsGIA, 1284-20-III otd. II st. ch. I (*Otchet Ministerstva Vnutrennikh Del za 1834 god*), pp. 50-51.

47. Anuchin, p. 52.

48. *PSZ (IV)*, 10303, 3 June 1837.

49. Starr, pp. 26-32.

50. TsGAOR, *Otchet III otdeleniia E.I.V.K. za 1837 god*, pp. 97-98; Anuchin, pp. 53-54; TsGIA, 1284-23-8 (*Otchet Ministerstva Vnutrennikh Del za 1837 god*), p. 205; A.M. Fadeev, "Vospominaniia," *Russkii Arkhiv*, no. 2 (1891), p. 21.

51. TsGIA, 1284-20-III otd., II st. (*Otchet Ministerstva Vnutrennikh Del za 1834 god*), pp. 11-12.

52. PD, 25784/SXXXVIIb20.

53. GBL, Polt-9-21.

54. V. I. Semevskii, *Krestianskii vopros,* 2:487.

55. Nikitenko, 1:448.

56. TsGAOR, *Otchet III otdeleniia E.I.V.K. za 1833 god*, pp. 206-8.

57. *Otchet III otd. za 1835 g.*, pp. 74-75.

58. *Otchet III otd. za 1838 g.*, pp. 164-65.

59. *Otchet III otd. za 1839 g.*, p. 121.

60. Ibid., p. 119.

61. Kn. P. A. Viazamskii, *Zapisnye knizki* (Moscow, 1963), p. 283.

62. TsGIA, 1261-14-16 (*Vsepoddanneishii otchet glavnoupravliaiushchego II otdeleniia za 1859 god*), pp. 6327-28.

63. TsGIA, 1349-5-7753 (*Chinovniki II otd. za 1847 god*).

64. Two recent studies have stressed the importance of practical reports from officials in the Ministry of Justice in providing the substance of the Bludov reforms (Shuvalova, pp. 145-47; Kaiser, pp. 156-57). Bludov, it is true, examined these reports closely and expressed the necessary obeisance before the Ministry of Justice to give the appearance that the reform had not come from the Second Section alone. But in reading through these reports, I find it difficult to find any connection between them and the Bludov projects. The overwhelming majority called for tightening procuratorial supervision through minor provisions that were in keeping with Panin's notions of the administration of justice. An occasional report emphasized the need for defense of the accused; one even called for open courts. Several argued for court control over preliminary investigations. But these hardly represented a ground swell of support within the administration for basic changes. The liberal suggestions provided Bludov with few new ideas, since they were, for the most part, well-known critiques of the system. Bludov had proposed court control over investigations as early as 1826, and he admitted privately that he had learned little from the materials submitted by the minister of justice, which he described as distinguished, for the most part, "neither by thorough knowledge nor clear and logical conclusions" (TsGIA, 1261-1-128a, pp. 153-54; Shuvalova, p. 181).

65. *Obshchaia ob"iasnitel'naia zapiska k proektu novogo ustava sudoproizvodstva grazhdanskogo* (*Materialy*, no. 2), pp. 100-1.

66. GPB, KP-1936-130 (*Dnevnik V. N. Panina*), p. 69.

67. TsGIA, 1261-1-162 (*Po vysochaishemu poveleniiu ob ispravlenii nedostatok nashego grazhdanskogo sudoproizvodstva: Po delu ob imenii i dolgakh kollezhskogo registratora Ivana Balasheva*), (hereafter cited as *Delo Balasheva*), pp. 1-6.

68. *Obshchaia zap . . . sudoproizvodstva grazhdanskogo,* pp. 194-95.

69. Ibid., passim; for a thorough description of the Bludov projects, see Kaiser, pp. 155-268.

70. *Obshchaia ob"iasnitel'naia zapiska k proektu novogo ustava sudoproizvodstva po prestupleniiam i prostupkam*, pp. 70-72.

71. Ibid., pp. 131-32.

72. Most prerevolutionary descriptions of Bludov's reforms tend to focus on one or the other reform and categorize Bludov accordingly. Dzhanshiev (*Epokha,* pp. 374-75) stresses Bludov's extensive intentions in the civil reform and concludes that he was planning radical changes. Kucherov follows this interpretation in *Courts, Lawyers, and Trials* (p. 17). V. Pletnev, on the other hand, focuses exclusively on the criminal reform and concludes that Bludov's intention was to leave the system largely intact. (V. Pletnev, "Raboty po sostavleniiu proektov sudebnykh preobrazovanii do 1861," in Davydov et al., *Sudebnaia Reforma,* 1:287-96.) V. A. Shuvalova ("Podgotovka sudebnoi reformy 1864 goda v Rossii," pp. 241-42) claims that the criminal reform was in response to the threat of the revolutionary stirrings of the late fifties. Bludov's consistency on this question, however, makes such an explanation difficult to accept. Bludov's reports to Alexander also argued for retention of inquisitorial procedure in criminal cases.

73. *Obshch. zap* ... *po prestupleniiam i prostupkam,* p. 75.

74. Ibid., pp. 73-75, 84-85, 110-17, 140-41.

75. TsGIA, *O polozhenii del II otd* ... *za 1847 god,* p. 30.

76. TsGIA, 1261-2-86 (*Ob uchastii nachal'nikov gubernii v utverzhdenie ugolovnykh prigovorov*).

77. TsGIA, 1261-4-16 (*Vsepoddanneishii otchet glavnoupravliaushchego II otdeleniia za 1859 god*), pp. 6571-72.

78. Ibid., pp. 6574-75.

79. TsGIA, 851-1-4 (*Doklad Bludova, 7 noiabria 1857 g.*), p. 324.

80. TsGIA, 1261-2-135a (*Ob ustroistve sudebnykh mest*), pp. 42-43.

81. Ibid., pp. 45-47, 51-52, 56; Prilozhenie, 2:1-4, 6-7.

82. S. Rozhdestvenskii, "Poslednaia stranitsa iz istorii politiki narodnogo proveshcheniia Imperatora Nikolaia Iogo (Komitet grafa Bludova, 1849-1856)," *Russkii Istoricheskii Zhurnal* 3-4 (1917): 55-56.

83. TsGIA, *Vsepod. otch* ... *II otd. za 1859 g.,* p. 6245.

84. *Zhurnal soedinennykh departamentov grazhdanskogo i zakonov Gosudarstvennogo Soveta o glavnykh nachalakh priniatykh imi pri razsmotrenii proekta novogo ustava grazhdanskogo sudoproizvodstva 1857-1859: Zhurnal soedinennykh departamentov Gosudarstvennogo Soveta Mai. Okt. 1860.* Members of the combined departments who signed the journals of 1860 supporting the Bludov projects were as follows: Bludov, P. Gagarin, Admiral F. Litke. L. Seniavin, General Baron P. Rokasovskii, General P. Gorchakov, Alexander Kochubei, N. Bakhtin, D. Zamiatnin. Only two had attended institutions of higher learning—Zamiatnin, the lycée, and Bakhtin, St. Petersburg University in the early 1820s. Only three—Gagarin, Zamiatnin, and Alexander Kochubei—had served in the judicial branch, and all only in high positions: chief-procurator of the Senate or senator. Biographical materials are from service lists, *Russkii biograficheskii slovar'* and *Entsiklopedicheskii slovar', Brokgauz-Efron.*

85. "Obshchie zamechaniia," in *Svod obshchikh zamechanii na proekt i na glavnye nachala sudoproizvodstva grazhdanskogo priniatye soedinennymi departamentami (Materialy,* no. 11), pp. 7-9.

86. Nikitenko, 2:182; Kovalevskii, 1:4-11; Bludov, *Mysli i zamechaniia,* p. 58.

87. TsGIA (*Delo Bludova*), p. 255.

88. Ibid.

89. Bludov, *Mysli i zamechaniia,* pp. 59-61.

1. Nikitenko, 2:108; A. Kornilov, 2:174.

2. [Constantine Pobedonostev], [no title], *Golosa iz Rossii,* book 7 (1859), pp. 37-39 (hereafter cited as Panin).

3. A. K. Dzhivelegov, "Graf V. N. Panin," *Velikaia Reforma* 5 (1911): 151-52.

4. P. Valuev, "Dnevnik, 1847-1860," *Russkaia Starina* 72 (1891): 141.

5. Dzhivelegov, p. 148.

6. TsGAOR, 728-1-2456, p. 128; 728-1-2496, p. 147.

7. TsGIA, 1162-6-399 (*Delo Panina*), p. 8; Nikolai Semenov, "Graf Viktor Nikitich Panin," *Russkii Arkhiv*, no. 3 (1887), p. 542.

8. *Russkii Biograficheskii Slovar'*, 13:212-48; on Nikita Ivanovich Panin, see David Ransel, "Nikita Panin's Imperial Council Project and the Struggle of Hierarchy Groups at the Court of Catherine II," *Canadian Slavic Studies*, Fall 1970, pp. 443-63.

9. Grimsted, pp. 69-70.

10. Ibid., pp. 73, 78.

11. A. Brikner [Bruekner], *Materialy dlia zhizneopisaniia Grafa Nikity Petrovicha Panina* (St. Petersburg, 1892), 7:223; *Russkii Biograficheskii Slovar'*, 13:210-11.

12. V. A. Aleksandrov, "Sel'skaia obshchina i votchina v Rossii (XVII-nachalo XIX v.)," *Istoricheskie zapiski* (Moscow, 1972), 89: 271-73. Nikita Panin's instructions date from 1820, but describe an order in effect from the beginning of the century, according to Aleksandrov; see Michael Confino, *Domaines et seigneurs en russie vers la fin du XVIIIe siècle* (Paris, 1963), pp. 260-61, for a general discussion of this type of mentality; Brikner, 7:233-34.

13. Brikner, 7:227.

14. Ibid., pp. 245-46; S. Durylin, "Russkie pisateli i Goethe v Veimare," *Literaturnoe Nasledstvo* (Moscow, 1932), 4-6:253-54.

15. TsGIA, 1162-6-399; *Russkii Biograficheskii Slovar'*, 13:179-80.

16. GBL, Venev-64-17 (Anna Venevetinova, letter to E. E. and S. V. Koramovskii, 3 May 1832).

17. TsGAOR, *Otchet III otdeleniia E.I.V.K. za 1833*, p. 209; *Otchet ... za 1839*, p. 117.

18. Brikner, 7:246, 266.

19. GBL, 22-19-2 (letter of 28 March 1824).

20. GBL, 22-19-4 (letter of 4 December 1825).

21. GPB, KP, 1936, 130 (*Dnevnik V. N. Panina*), pp. 14, 19, 43, 64, 83, 94.

22. Letter of 4 December 1825.

23. Brikner, 7:262-63.

24. Ibid., p. 262.

25. Semenov, pp. 538, 544.

26. *Dnevnik Panina*, p. 69.

27. *Delo Balasheva*, pp. 188-93.

28. Ibid., p. 190.

29. TsGIA, 1261-1-70a (*O sostavlenii proekta novogo ustava o sudoproizvodstve ugolovnom i po proektu polozheniia o sledstviakh*), 1:6-7, 17-20.

30. *Ministerstvo Iustitsii za sto let*, pp. 69-71.

31. *Otchet Ministerstva Iustitsii za 1842 g.*, p. lx.

32. *Otchet Ministerstva Iustitsii za 1844 g.*, pp. liv-lv.

33. Lebedev, "Iz zapisok," *Russkii Arkhiv*, no. 7 (1910), pp. 406-7.

34. *Dnevnik Panina*, pp. 40, 54, 57, 112.

35. Figures from the *Otchety* of the Ministry of Justice for 1841, 1850, and 1855 indicate little improvement. From 1841 to 1850 the number of criminal cases left undecided rose from 19,213 to 38,150, while the total number of new cases rose only from 80,740 to 105,792. The number of defendants in custody increased over the same period from 464 to 2,863. Undecided civil cases rose from 16,526 in 1841 to 24,152 in 1855; this was roughly proportional to the increase in civil cases, from 45,503 to 66,607.

36. Pobedonostev, "Panin," pp. 49-50.

37. Lebedev, "Iz zapisok," *Russkii Arkhiv*, no. 8 (1910), p. 470.

38. Pobedonostev, "Panin," pp. 52-56.

39. Semenov, pp. 544-46.

40. Kolmakov, "Panin," p. 328.

41. TsGAOR, *Otchet III otd* . . . *za 1841 g.,* pp. 144-45.

42. TsGAOR, *Otchett III otd* . . . *za 1842 g.,* pp. 201-2.

43. N. M. Kolmakov, "Staryi sud," *Russkaia Starina* 52 (1886): 528-29.

44. Semenov, p. 542.

45. Kolmakov, "Staryi sud," pp. 529-30.

46. *Russkii Biograficheskii Slovar',* 13:180; Dzhivelegov, p. 148; Valuev, "Dnevnik, 1847-1860," *Russkaia Starina* (1891), 72:153.

47. PD, 265-2-1960 (M. N. Liuboshchinskii, V. D. Filosofov, *Rasskazy o grafe Viktore Nikitiche Panine*), p. 6; N. M. Kolmakov, "Graf Panin," *Russkaia Starina* 56 (1887): 316-17; K. Lebedev, "Iz zapisok," *Russkii Arkhiv,* no. 2 (1888), p. 233.

48. GBL, 455-1-10 (*Zapis' obrashcheniia Panina (V. N.) k Shakovskomu, kn. Mikhailu Nikolaevichu*).

49. *Delo Balasheva,* pp. 521-22.

50. Dmitriev, *Glavy,* 2:125-26.

51. G. K. Repinskii (*soobshchil*), "Mery protiv neblagonadezhnykh chinovnikov," *Zhurnal Ministerstva Iustitsii,* February 1897, pp. 277-81.

52. *Otchet Ministerstva Iustitsii za 1847 g.,* p. lxvi.

53. Dmitriev, *Glavy,* 2:175-78.

54. Repinskii, p. 278; TsGIA, 1405-47-7751, p. 132; Bervi, pp. 56-58.

55. *O sost. novogo proekta o sudoproiz. ugol.,* pp. 21, 23.

56. *Delo Balasheva,* p. 323.

57. Rozhdestvenskii, "Poslednaia stranitsa," p. 49.

58. N. M. Kolmakov, "Ocherki i vospominaniia," *Russkaia Starina* 71 (1891): 128.

59. Kolmakov, "Graf Panin," pp. 323-24; V. V. Bervi [N. Flerovskii], pp. 85-87.

60. P. A. Valuev, *Dnevnik P. A. Valueva, Ministra vnutrennikh del* (Moscow, 1961), 1:57.

61. Gr. M. N. Muraviev, "Zapiski o miatezhe v Zapadnoi Rossii," *Russkaia Starina,* no. 1 (1883), p. 151. Semenov, p. 543, expressed the same opinion.

> [Panin], with his stunning gift of speech, masterfully extracted the essence of all different viewpoints stated by others, developed his thought clearly and consistently, but sometimes reached such an unexpected conclusion that it was impossible to connect it with what his speech was tending toward, and still less to put his proposal into action.

62. M. Dmitriev, *Glavy,* 2:137.

63. Kolmakov, "Graf Panin," p. 24; Shubin-Pozdeev, "Nekrolog Zarudnogo," *Russkaia Starina* 57 (1888): 480.

64. *O sost. novogo proekta o sudoproizvodstve ugolovnom,* pp. 7-9.

65. TsGIA, 1149-3-16 (1843), (*O predostavlenii Ministru Iustitsii prava poruchat' ispravlenie dolzhnostei Predsedatelei Sudebnykh Palat po ego porucheniiu*).

66. In 1850, of fifty procurators of Provincial Chambers, twenty-six were in an acting capacity. Of ninety assistant chairmen, sixty-one were acting. Of eighty-five chairmen, Panin succeeded in appointing at least forty-two, sixteen of whom were acting, the remainder in provinces where the electoral law did not yet reach.

The preponderance of educated officials among those in acting capacities is clear. Of twenty-six acting procurators in 1851, seventeen had finished institutions of higher education, while only three of the twenty-four confirmed in office had. Of the sixty-one acting assistant chairmen, who actually ran the Chambers, thirty-eight had completed higher education, while only one of the thirty-one confirmed in the position had. Figures are calculated from data in *Spisok chinam Pravitel'stvuiushchego Senata i Ministerstva Iustitsii za 1850* (St. Petersburg, 1850), and the same source for 1851.

67. K. Lebedev, "Iz zapisok," *Russkii Arkhiv,* no. 8 (1910), p. 493.

68. Dmitriev, *Glavy*, 2:138; Pobedonostev, "Panin," pp. 99-101, 108-9; A. D. Borovkov, "Zapiski," *Russkaia Starina* 96 (1898): 608; Bervi, pp. 61-62.

69. Dmitriev, *Glavy*, 2:130; *Spisok chinam . . . za 1853 g.; Spisok chinam . . . za 1850 g.*

70. TsGIA, 1349-5-4501.

71. IM, 117-78 (anonymous, *Zapiska o sudoproizvodstve*), pp. 19-20.

72. Semenov, pp. 541-42; Bervi, pp. 54-55.

73. Pobedonostev, "Panin," pp. 125-30; Semenov, p. 548.

74. Kolmakov, "Ocherki," pp. 120-22.

75. TsGIA, 1405-56-6994 (*Formuliarnyi spisok P. D. Illichevskogo*).

76. Kolmakov, "Ocherki," pp. 122-24; Kn. V. P. Meshcherskii, *Moi vospominaniia* (St. Petersburg, 1897), pt. 1, p. 96; Bervi, pp. 50-52.

77. It was rumored that Danzas was an illegitimate son of D. V. Golitsyn; Lebedev, "Iz zapisok," *Russkii Arkhiv* 2 (1910): 497-98; 3 (1911): 94-95.

78. *Dnevnik Panina*, p. 122; Dmitriev, *Glavy*, 2:132.

79. Kolmakov, "Ocherki," pp. 125-27; Pobedonostev, "Panin," p. 43; Dmitriev, *Glavy*, 2:passim; N. Khristoforov, "Matvei Mikhailovich Karniolin-Pinskii," *Russkii Arkhiv*, no. 8 (1876), pp. 454-59.

80. TsGIA, 1349-3-2256 (*Formuliarnyi spisok M. I. Topil'skogo*), pp. 70-73.

81. Ibid., pp. 50-51, 65-67; Kolmakov, "Graf Panin," p. 782; *Formuliarnyi spisok Topil'skogo*, pp. 50-70.

82. Semenov, p. 347.

83. Kolmakov, "Graf Panin," p. 779; Meshcherskii, p. 96.

84. Semenov, p. 551; Pobedonostev, "Panin," pp. 78-79, 118; Kolmakov, "Graf Panin," p. 778.

85. Barsukov, 17:179-80.

86. Kolmakov, "Graf Panin," pp. 763-64; Meshcherskii, p. 96; Pobedonostev, "Panin," p. 81.

87. Pobedonostev, "Panin," pp. 80-81; Kolmakov, "Graf Panin," pp. 763, 781.

88. Pobedonostev, "Panin," p. 44.

89. Kolmakov, "Staryi sud," p. 523; Dmitriev, *Glavy*, 2:116-17; Pobedonostev, "Panin," pp. 76-77.

90. IM, 117-78 (*Doklad Ministra Iustitsii Panina Aleksandru II, February 1858*) (hereafter cited as *Doklad Panina . . . February 1858*), p. 4.

91. *Delo Balasheva*, pp. 185-86.

92. Ibid., p. 186.

93. Ibid., pp. 198-99.

94. Ibid., pp. 236-65; *Osobye po nekotorym voprosam zapiski predstavlennye komitetu vysochaishe uchrezhdennomu dlia razsmotreniia proekta novogo ustava sudoproizvodstva grazhdanskogo* (bound in *Materialy*, no. 2), pp. 95-115.

95. *Obshch. zap . . . sudoproizvodstva grazhdanskogo*, pp. 74, 77-78.

96. Pobedonostev, "Graf Panin," pp. 124-25.

97. *Doklad Panina . . . February 1858*, p. 10.

98. Pobedonostev, "Panin," pp. 61-62.

99. TsGIA, 1275-1-3a, 1858 (*Zhurnal Soveta Ministrov*, Meeting 11 December 1858, *Po delu o napravlenii nashei literatury*), pp. 160-64.

100. Terence Emmons, *The Russian Landed Gentry and the Peasant Emancipation of 1861* (Cambridge, England, 1968), pp. 345-46; Semenov, pp. 551-54.

101. Meshcherskii, pp. 94-95.

102. *Russkii Biograficheskii Slovar'*, 13:186-87; Semenov, p. 554.

103. *Delo Bludova*, pp. 271-72.

104. Gr. V. N. Panin (*soobshchil*), "O samozvanke, vydavavshei sebia za doch' Im-

peratritsy Elizavety Petrovny," *Chtenia v Imperatorskom Obshchestve Istorii i drevnostei rossiiskikh pri Moskovskom Universitete,* January 1867, book 1, p. 88.

NOTES TO CHAPTER EIGHT

1. For the concept of the "moral identity" of specific occupational groups, see Suzanne Keller, *Beyond the Ruling Class* (New York, 1963), pp. 135, 141. The notion that professions create their own specific moral sense was developed by Durkheim. "Functional diversity induces a moral diversity that nothing can prevent, and it is inevitable that one should grow as the other does." *The Division of Labor in Society* (New York, 1964), p. 361.

2. This section is based on the manuscript of Dmitriev's memoirs: Mikhail Aleksandrovich Dmitriev, *Glavy iz vospominanii o moiei zhizni,* GBL, 178, Muzeinoe sobranie 8184-1. Brief sections of this pertaining to his literary encounters are contained in his *Melochi iz zapasa moei pamiati* (Moscow, 1869); for Dmitriev's service list, see TsGIA, 1349-5-8556.

3. Dmitriev, *Glavy,* 1:39-40, 43.

4. Ibid., pp. 83-86.

5. Ibid., pp. 177, 181-83.

6. Ibid., pp. 183-84, 209-13.

7. Ibid., 2:29.

8. M. A. Dmitriev, *Stikhotvoreniia* (Moscow, 1865), 1:4-6.

9. Dmitriev, *Glavy,* 2:29, 101.

10. M. A. Dmitriev, *O natural'noi shkole i narodnosti* (Moscow, 1848), p. 28.

11. Dmitriev, *Glavy,* 1:240-41, 247; 2:1-2.

12. Ibid., 1:8.

13. Ibid., 2:134-35, 178.

14. Lebedev, "Iz zapisok," *Russkii Arkhiv,* no. 10 (1910), p. 199.

15. Ibid., no. 7 (1910), p. 381; V. O. Kliuchevskii et al., *Vospominaniia o studencheskoi zhizni,* pp. 172-73.

16. *Russkii Biograficheskii Slovar',* 7:333.

17. Lebedev, "Iz zapisok," *Russkii Arkhiv,* no. 7 (1910), pp. 345-46.

18. Ibid., p. 345.

19. Ibid., p. 353.

20. Ibid., pp. 393, 402-3.

21. Ibid., no. 8 (1910), pp. 511-12.

22. Ibid., pp. 516, 478-79, 487.

23. Ibid., no. 10 (1900), p. 261.

24. Ibid., no. 10 (1910), p. 203; no. 1 (1888), p. 620.

25. Ibid., no. 2 (1888), p. 352.

26. Ibid., no. 10 (1910), p. 204.

27. Ibid., no. 7 (1910), p. 352.

28. Ibid., no. 2 (1888), pp. 137, 140.

29. Ivan Aksakov, *Ivan Sergeevich Aksakov v ego pis'makh,* pp. 401-2.

30. Siuzor, pp. 121-22. Siuzor indicates (p. 128) that exceptions were made for Baltic nobles who were able to prove noble title for at least one hundred years, Caucasian nobles, and descendants of Wallachian boyars. After 1868, children of officials high in the court system were also accepted. In the *Journals of the School Council* I consulted, there is only one example of an exception. This was in response to the petition of the widow of an official who died with only two years remaining until he would reach the fifth rank. The official's family had been in Austrian service since 1689 and Russian since 1751. The council in this case made an exception and admitted her son (LOA, 355-1-4233a [*Zhurnal Zasedanii soveta uchilishcha, 1845 g.*], p. 2).

31. *Pamiatnaia Knizhka Imperatorskogo Uchilishcha Pravovedeniia* (St. Petersburg, 1871).

32. Modest Chaikovskii, who like his brother Peter was a pupil at the school, wrote that

most of the pupils were average types of noblemen (*srednego kruga*). Only a very small number came from the upper layers of the nobility "whose names were on everyone's lips." Modest Chaikovskii, *Zhizn' Petra Il'icha Chaikovskogo* (Moscow and Leipzig, 1900), 1:86.

33. Data from the service lists of *pravovedy* working in central and provincial institutions at mid-century confirm Chaikovskii's impression. The thirty lists used in the mid-century sample for chapter 4 show the following distribution of serfholding.

Souls	
0	19
1-10	0
11-100	1
101-500	9
501-1,000	1
Total	30

34. V. V. Stasov, "Uchilishche pravovedeniia sorok let tomu nazad, 1836-1842," *Russkaia Starina*, no. 2 (1881), pp. 394-95; Meshcherskii, *Moi vospominaniia*, 1:80; I. A. Tiutchev, "V Uchilishche Pravovedeniia v 1847-1852 gg.," *Russkaia Starina*, no. 11 (1885), p. 370; K. K. Arsen'ev, "Vospominaniia ob Uchilishche Pravovedeniia," *Russkaia Starina*, no. 4 (1886), p. 219.

35. Siuzor, pp. 122-23; Arsen'ev, "Vospominaniia," p. 207.

36. I have translated *gosudarstvennoe pravo* as "state law" *faute de mieux*. It is a literal translation of the German *staatsrecht*, which is usually translated as public or constitutional law. *Publichnoe pravo*, however, was considered a separate discipline, while *konstitutsionnoe pravo* only dealt with the state law of representative government. Since *gosudarstvennoe pravo* dealt preponderantly with the laws governing the Russian state, state law seems to be the best approximation.

37. Siuzor, pp. 122-23; LOA, 355-1-4268 (*Zhurnal zasedanii soveta*, 1852 g.), pp. 2-4.

38. Arsen'ev, "Vospominaniia," p. 208; Stasov, "Uchilishche," *Russkaia Starina*, no. 2 (1881), p. 249.

39. Stasov, "Uchilishche," p. 249; Arsen'ev, "Vospominaniia," pp. 210-11; Tiutchev, *Russkaia Starina*, no. 12 (1885), p. 670.

40. Tiutchev, *Russkaia Starina*, no. 12 (1885), p. 670.

41. Stasov, "Uchilishche," *Russkaia Starina*, no. 2 (1881), p. 250.

42. Tiutchev, *Russkaia Starina*, no. 12 (1885), p. 669; Arsen'ev, "Vospominaniia," p. 210.

43. K. P. Pobedonostev, *Dlia nemnogikh—otryvki iz shkol'nogo dnevnika* (St. Petersburg, 1885), p. 106; Stasov, "Uchilishche," *Russkaia Starina*, no. 2 (1881), p. 253; Arsen'ev, "Vospominaniia," p. 213; Tiutchev, *Russkaia Starina*, no. 12 (1885), p. 670.

44. [M. M. Molchanov], *Pol-veka nazad: Pervye gody Uchilishcha Pravovedeniia v Peterburge* (St. Petersburg, 1892), p. 29; Siuzor, p. 189; LOA, 355-1-4309 (*Zhurnal zasedanii soveta, 1857 g.*), p. 1.

45. N. I. Stoianovskii, *Kratkii ocherk ob osnovanii i razvitii Imperatorskogo Uchilishcha Pravovedeniia* (St. Petersburg, 1885), p. 3.

46. Molchanov, *Pol-veka nazad*, p. 33.

47. Ibid.

48. Siuzor, p. 35.

49. A. Pankov, *Zhizn' i trudy printsa Petra Georgievicha Ol'denburgskogo* (St. Petersburg, 1885), pp. 50-58, 68, 117-19; M. M. Molchanov, "Aleksandr Nikolaevich Serov v vospominaniiakh starogo pravoveda," *Russkaia Starina*, no. 8 (1883), p. 341; Pobedonostev, *Dlia nemnogikh*, p. 53.

50. A. M. Zhemchuzhnikov, *Izbrannye proizvedeniia* (Moscow and Leningrad, 1963), p. 63.

51. Pankov, p. 121.

52. Stasov, "Uchilishche," *Russkaia Starina,* no. 12 (1880), p. 1023.

53. Ibid., pp. 1023-24; Siuzor, pp. 141-45, 150.

54. Stasov, "Uchilishche," *Russkaia Starina,* no. 3 (1881), pp. 577-81; Molchanov, "Aleksandr Nikolaevich Serov," p. 341; Siuzor, pp. 216-22.

55. Fedor Biuler, *Dve rechi proiznesennye v Imperatorskom Uchilishche Pravovedeniia* (St. Petersburg, 1860), p. 6.

56. N. I. Stoianovskii, *Vospominanie o 5-m i 7-m dekabria 1860 goda* (St. Petersburg, 1860), p. 8.

57. Ibid., p. 30.

58. Molchanov, *Pol-veka nazad,* pp. 38, 46.

59. Stasov, *Russkaia Starina,* no. 12 (1880), p. 1036.

60. The common practices were described in the beautiful "Pravoved's Song," which was popular in the school during the forties and fifties.

> Tovarishchi sami,
> Daiut i ebut,
> Priatnoe delo
> Drug drugu davat'
> I zhonkoiu smelo
> Pred khuem viliat'.

See *Russkii erot. Ne dlia dam* (n.p., 1879), p. 89.

61. V. V. Stasov, *Vospominaniia tovarishcha o D. A. Rovinskom* (St. Petersburg, 1896), p. 34; Koni, *Ottsy,* p. 2.

62. Robert F. Byrnes, *Pobedonostev: His Life and Thought* (Bloomington, Ind., 1968), pp. 13-14.

63. Pobedonostev, *Dlia nemnogikh,* pp. 14, 50.

64. Stoianovskii, *Vospominanie,* pp. 27-28; A. A. Polovtsov, "Iz dnevnika A. A. Polovtsova," *Krasnyi Arkhiv,* 33 (1929): 194.

65. Aksakov, *Ivan Sergeevich Aksakov,* 1: 29-30, 110, 134; idem, *Stikhotvoreniia i poemy* (Leningrad, 1960), pp. 40-41.

66. Stasov, "Uchilishche," *Russkaia Starina,* no. 2 (1881), pp. 420-21.

67. Zhemchuzhnikov, p. 14.

68. Stasov, "Uchilishche," *Russkaia Starina,* no. 2 (1881), pp. 408-11; no. 12 (1880): p. 1037; Molchanov, *Pol-veka nazad,* p. 19; Pobedonostev, pp. 17-18; Chaikovskii, 1:96.

69. Zhemchuzhnikov, pp. 63-64.

70. Ibid., p. 12.

71. Meshcherskii, 1:92.

72. Stasov, "Aleksandr Nikolaevich Serov," *Russkaia Starina,* no. 8 (1875): p. 592.

73. Aksakov, *Ivan Sergeevich Aksakov,* 1: 38; Aksakov, *Stikhotvoreniia,* p. 42.

74. Aksakov, *Ivan Sergeevich Aksakov,* 1:259.

75. K. K. Arsen'ev, *Glavnye deiateli i predshestvenniki sudebnoi reformy* (St. Petersburg, 1904), p. 54.

76. *Viktor Antonovich Artsimovich: Vospominaniia-Kharakteristika* (St. Petersburg, 1904), p. 4.

77. Zhemchuzhnikov, p. 61.

78. Aksakov, *Ivan Sergeevich Aksakov,* 1:109.

79. Kniaz' Dm. A. Obolenskii, *Moi vospominaniia o Velikoi Kniazhne Elene Pavlovne* (St. Petersburg, 1909), pp. 5-6.

80. Ibid., p. 6.

81. For an analysis of the interrelations between the bureaucracy and the intelligentsia, see Lincoln, pp. 321-30.

82. GBL, 169-42-27 (Vel. Kn. Konstantin Nikolaevich, Kratkii ocherk deistvii Velikogo

Kniazia Konstantina Nikolaevicha po morskomu vedomstvu so vremeni vstupleniia v upravlenie onym po ianvar' 1858), p. 5.

83. TsGAOR, 828-1-1345 (Kn. D. A. Obolenskii, Zamechaniia na proekt novogo ustava sudoproizvodstva v Rossii), p. 2.

84. Ibid., p. 3.

85. K. P. Pobedonostev, "Vasilii Petrovich Zubkov," *Russkii Arkhiv,* February 1904, p. 302.

86. Pobedonostev, "Panin," pp. 137-38.

87. IM, 445-231, p. 28.

88. TsGIA, 1349-3-1899, p. 9; I. A. Zabelin, *Vospominanie o D. A. Rovinskom* (St. Petersburg, 1896), pp. 3-4; Stasov, *Vospominaniia . . . o Rovinskom,* pp. 6-7.

89. Koni, *Ottsy,* pp. 5-6.

90. D. A. Rovinskii, "K sudebnym sledovatel'iam," *Vek,* no. 16 (1861).

91. Dzhanshiev, *Epokha,* pp. 659-60.

92. Rovinskii, p. 547.

93. TsGIA, 1363-8-805; G. Dzhanshiev, *Stranitsa iz istorii sudebnoi reformy: D. N. Zamiatnin,* pp. 122-23; Koni, *Ottsy,* pp. 97-98.

94. V. A. Mukhanov, "Iz dnevnykh zapisok," *Russkii Arkhiv,* no. 2 (1897), p. 93.

95. Pobedonostev, "Panin," pp. 114-15, 120-22, 136.

96. *Otchet Ministerstva Iustitsii za 1858 g.,* pp. 61-62. In the decade 1850 to 1860, the number of provincial *striapchie* from the school dropped from twenty-three to seven. In 1858, appointment of the provincial *striapchie* was assigned to the minister of interior, but this appears to have had little positive effect in lifting the number of educated officials in that position.

97. *Viktor Antonovich Artsimovich,* p. 6.

98. Iu. N. Egorov, "Studenchestvo Sankt-Peterburgskogo Universiteta v 30-50kh godakh XIXv, ego sotsial'nyi sostav i raspredelenie po fakul'tetam," *Vestnik Leningradskogo Universiteta,* no. 14 (1957), p. 15.

99. Pobedonostev, "Panin," p. 113.

100. N. Koliupanov, "Iz proshlogo," *Russkoe Obozenie,* no. 3 (1895), p. 10.

101. Ia. P. Polonskii, "Moi studencheskie vospominaniia," *Niva: Ezhemesiachnye litera-turnye prilozheniia,* p. 669.

102. V. O. Kliuchevskii et al., *Vospominaniia o studencheskoi zhizni,* p. 46.

103. B. A. Chicherin, *Vospominaniia Borisa Nikolaevicha Chicherina: Moskva sorokovykh godov* (Moscow, 1929), pp. 10-11.

104. P. N. Obninskii, *Sbornik Statei* (Moscow, 1914), pp. 20-21.

105. Koliupanov, *Russkoe Obozrenie,* no. 3 (1895), p. 7.

106. Ibid; M. V. Shimanovskii, *Petr Ivanovich Redkin* (Odessa, 1891), pp. 9-10; R. A. Kovnatov, ed., *Moskovskii Universitet v vospominaniiakh sovremennikov* (Moscow, 1956), p. 231.

107. Shimanovskii, pp. 19, 22.

108. Ibid., pp. 29-31; P. Redkin, *Kakoe obshchee obrazovanie trebuetsia sovremennostiu ot russkogo pravovedtsa* (Moscow, 1846), p. 10.

109. Redkin, *Kakoe,* p. 10; *Iuridicheskie Zapiski izd. Petrom Redkinym,* no. 1 (1841), p. iii.

110. Koliupanov, *Russkee Obozrenie,* no. 3 (1895), p. 15.

111. Kliuchevskii et al., p. 28.

112. Ibid., p. 50; Kovnatov, p. 160; *Kniaz' Vladimir Aleksandrovich Cherkasskii, ego stat'i, ego rechi i vospominaniia o nem* (Moscow, 1870), p. ix.

113. Koliupanov, *Russkoe Obozrenie,* no. 4 (1895), pp. 535-36.

114. Chicherin, p. 31.

115. Kliuchevskii et al., p. 191.

116. Ibid., p. 54-55.

117. Redkin, *Kakoe,* pp. 23-24, 27-30, 30-37.

118. Koliupanov, *Russkoe Obozrenie,* no. 3 (1895), pp. 7-8.

119. A. K[aznachcev], "Mezhdu strokami odnogo formuliarnogo spiska: Ocherk iz zapisok odnogo Senatora, 1823-1881," *Russkaia Starina,* no. 12 (1881), pp. 819-20.

120. Kovnatov, p. 155.

121. Chicherin, pp. 37-38.

122. Ibid., p. 38.

123. Koliupanov, *Russkoe Obozrenie,* no. 5 (1895), pp. 18-19.

124. K. D. Ushinskii, *Sobranie sochinenii* (Moscow and Leningrad, 1952), 11:241-44; V. Ia. Struminskii, *Ocherki zhizni i pedagogicheskoi deiatel'nosti K. D. Ushinskogo* (Moscow, 1960), pp. 34-35.

125. Ushinskii, 11:11-12.

126. Ibid., pp. 12, 15.

127. Ibid., pp. 19-20.

128. Ibid., pp. 33-34.

129. Ibid., pp. 23, 40.

130. S. P. Pokrovskii, *Demidovskii litsei v g. Iaroslavle v ego proshlom i nastoiashchem* (Iaroslavl', 1914), pp. 143-45; S. P. Pokrovskii, "Stranitsa iz professorskoi deiatel'nosti K. D. Ushinskogo v Demidovskom litsee," *Vestnik Vospitaniia,* no. 9 (1911).

131. P. P. Pekarskii, "Studencheskiia vospominaniia o Dmitrie Ivanoviche Meiere," *Bratchina* (St. Petersburg, 1859), p. 211; D. I. Meier, *Russkoe Grazhdanskoe Pravo* (St. Petersburg, 1897), p. 8; M. K. Korbut, *Kazanskii Gosudarstvennyi Universitet imeni Lenina za 125 let, 1904/5-1929/30* (Kazan, 1930), 1:55.

132. Dmitrii Meier, *O znachenii praktiki v sisteme sovremennogo iuridicheskogo obrazovaniia* (Kazan, 1855), pp. 3-4.

133. Ibid., pp. 12-14.

134. Ibid., pp. 42, 46-47; Pekarskii, pp. 213, 216-18; A. Gol'msten, "Dmitrii Ivanovich Meier, ego zhizn' i deiatel'nost'," Meier, *Russkoe Grazhdanskoe Pravo,* p. viii.

135. Pekarskii, pp. 224, 232.

136. Ibid., p. 242.

137. Dzhanshiev, *Epokha,* pp. 584-85.

138. PD, 445-528, p. 2 (Zarudnyi, *Dnevnik).* This fragment appears to be the only extant diary of Zarudnyi's.

139. Ibid., pp. 3-4.

140. Ibid., pp. 4-5.

141. Ibid., pp. 8-9.

142. Ibid., pp. 10-11.

143. S. I. Zarudnyi, "Iz vospominanii S. I. Zarudnogo," *Sbornik Pravovedeniia,* no. 3 (1894), pp. 2-3.

144. Ibid., p. 4.

145. D. P. Shubin-Pozdeev, "K kharakteristike lichnosti i sluzhebnoi deiatel'nosti S. I. Zarudnogo," *Russkaia Starina,* no. 2 (1888), p. 480.

146. Ibid., p. 481; G. A. Dzhanshiev, *Sbornik Statei* (Moscow, 1914), p. 350.

147. N. M. Kolmakov, "Ocherki i vospominaniia," *Russkaia Starina,* no. 7 (1891), p. 130; Shubin-Pozdeev, p. 481.

148. *Russkii Biograficheskii Slovar',* 7:242.

NOTES TO INTRODUCTION TO PART THREE

1. Quoted in *Arkhiv istoricheskikh i prakticheskikh svedenii otnosiashchikhsia do Rossii izd. Nikolaem Kalachovym* (1859), 2, pt. 3, p. 51.

2. A. F. Koni, *Ottsy i deti,* p. ii.

3. Starr, pp. 14-15.

4. *Ministerstvo Iustitsii za sto let,* pp. 74-75.

5. TsGIA, 1261-1-162 (*Po vysochaishemu poveleniiu ob ispravlenii nedostatok nashego grazhdanskogo sudoproizvodstva*), pp. 488-90.

6. Starr, pp. 46, 48.

7. D. Rovinskii, "Ustroistvo grazhdanskogo suda," p. 7 n, in *Materialy,* no. 17, pt. 19; Ia. E. Vodarskii, *Naselenie Rossii za 400 let (XVI-nachalo XX vv)* (Moscow, 1973), p. 54. According to Rovinskii, the French judicial administration numbered 13,100 officials, not counting justices of the peace or police judges, for a population of 37 million. In European Russia at the same time, there were 2,530 judicial officials excluding the chancellery and peasant assessors, for a population of about 60 million.

8. For descriptions of the old courts, see Kucherov, *Courts, Lawyers, and Trials,* pp. 1-17; idem, "Administration of Justice under Nicholas I of Russia," *American Slavic and East European Review* 7, no. 2 (1948): 125-38; Kaiser, pp. 1-89; Gessen, *Sudebnaia Reforma,* pp. 1-30; N. M. Kolmakov, "Staryi sud," *Russkaia Starina,* no. 12 (1886), pp. 511-44; V. Bochkarev, "Doreformennyi sud," Davydov, ed., *Sudebnaia Reforma,* pp. 205-41.

9. John P. LeDonne, "Criminal Investigations before the Great Reforms," *Russian History* 1 (pt. 2, 1974): 106.

10. Gessen, *Sudebnaia Reforma,* pp. 6-7.

11. LeDonne, "Criminal Investigations," p. 108.

12. Gessen cites figures that full convictions were obtained in only 12.5 percent of criminal cases! My figures from 1840 to 1854, from the annual *Otchet Ministerstva Iustitsii,* show a decline in the percentage of convictions from 36 percent in 1840 (34,748 of 96,780) to 27 percent in 1854 (32,718 of 121,799). In these years, "remains under suspicion" verdicts comprised between 10 and 13 percent of criminal verdicts. In either case, it appears that the system involved considerable wasted suffering and effort.

13. N. P. Eroshkin, *Ocherki istorii gosudarstvennykh ucherzhdenii dorevoliutsionnoi Rossii* (Moscow, 1960), p. 233.

14. The number of civil disputes heard in Civil Chambers was 15,932 in 1841 and 14,380 in 1855, according to the *Otchety Ministerstva Iustitsii.* In the same period, the number of so-called undisputed (*besspornye*) cases, involving only one party, rose from 28,248 to 46,641, allowing the minister to show an increase in civil cases. In fact, many of these cases involved the completion of documents, a largely notarial function, which was then under the courts. Also included were cases that resulted from the investigation of the reports of Noble Trust Councils and Orphan Courts. See S. Zarudnyi, *O podavaemykh vne appeliatsionnogo poriadka zhalobakh (O delakh okhranitel'nogo poriadka)* (n.p., 1859).

15. A. E. Presniakov, *Apogei samoderzhaviia: Nikolai I* (Leningrad, 1925), p. 13; Zaionchkovskii, "Vysshaia biurokratiia," p. 155.

16. Nikitenko, 1:34-35, 236.

17. Lebedev, "Iz zapisok," *Russkii Arkhiv,* no. 7 (1910), p. 479.

18. Ibid., no. 2 (1888), p. 141.

19. P. Valuev, "Duma Russkogo," *Russkaia Starina,* no. 5 (1891), p. 354.

20. I. Illiustrov, *Iuridicheskie poslovitsy i pogovorki russkogo naroda* (Moscow, 1885), pp. 2, 3-5, 14-15, 71.

21. Ibid., pp. 12-13.

NOTES TO CHAPTER NINE

1. Daniel Field, "The End of Serfdom: Nobility and Bureaucracy in Russia, 1855-1861," chap. 2, pp. 147-53.

2. Kaiser, pp. 429-31.

3. M. M. Speranskii, "O zakonakh. Besedy s Ego Imperatorskim Vysochestvom Gosudarem Velikim Kniazem Naslednikom Tsesarevichem Aleksandrom Nikolaevichem," *Gody ucheniia*

ego Imperatorskogo Vysochestva Naslednika Tsesarevicha Aleksandra Nikolaevicha (*Sbornik Russkogo Istoricheskogo Obshchestva. T. 30*) (St. Petersburg, 1880), pp. 382-83.

4. Ibid., pp. 348, 426-32, 483-91; F. A. Oom, "Vospominaniia," *Russkiï Arkhiv* 2 (1896): 248.

5. Max Weber, *On Law in Economy and Society* (New York, 1967), pp. 228-29; Talcott Parsons, *Societies: Evolutionary and Comparative Perspectives* (Englewood Cliffs, N.J., 1966), p. 27.

6. TsGIA, 1261-14-16 (Vsepoddanneishii otchet glavnoupravliaiushchego II otdeleniia za 1859 god), pp. 6327-28; Kaiser, pp. 149-268.

7. *Zhurnal soedinennykh departmentov grazhdanskogo i zakonov Gosudarstvennogo Soveta o glavnykh nachalakh priniatykh imi pri razsmotrenii proekta novogo ustava grazhdanskogo sudoproizvodstva 1857-1859* (*Materialy,* no. 10); *Zhurnal soedinennykh departamentov zakonov i grazhdanskogo po proektu ustava sudoproizvodstva grazhdanskogo* (15 November 1857-23 September 1859 g.), (*Materialy,* no. 10), pp. 65, 105.

8. GBL, 169-42-27 (Vel. Kn. Konstantin Nikolaevich, *Kratkiï ocherk deistvii Vel. Kn. Konstantina Nikolaevicha po morskomu vedomstvu so vremeni vstupleniia v upravlenie onym po ianvar' 1858 g.*), p. 2.

9. TsGAOR, 722-1-460, p. 1.

10. TsGAOR, 828-1-1345 (Kn. D. A. Obolenskii, *Zamechaniia na proekt novogo ustava sudoproizvodstva v Rossii*), p. 2.

11. Ibid., pp. 3, 7-9, 11, 18-19.

12. TsGAOR, 722-1-515 (S. Zarudnyi, *Zapiska o zamechaniiakh na proekt novogo poriadka sudoproizvodstva v Rossii*).

13. G. A. Dzhanshiev, "S. I. Zarudnyi i sudebnaia reforma," *Sbornik Statei* (Moscow, 1914), pp. 367-82.

14. S. I. Zarudnyi, *Okhranitel'nye zakony chastnogo grazhdanskogo prava* (St. Petersburg, 1859).

15. PD, 3-4-255 (Zarudnyi, letter to Ivan Aksakov, 17 October 1858), p. 4.

16. A. E. Nol'de, *K. P. Pobedonostev i sudebnaia reforma* (Petrograd, 1915), p. 12.

17. GBL, Stoian-160 19 (N. Kolomoitsev, letter to Stoianovskii, 25 November 1859).

18. Nol'de, pp. 10-11.

19. The opening section of the digest of criticisms appears to be taken from parts of Pobedonostev's "Zapiska o grazhdanskom sudoproizvodstve," which was later printed in December 1861, when Pobedonostev was working in the State Chancellery.

20. *Svod obshchikh zamechanii na proekt i na glavnye nachala sudoproizvodstva grazhdanskogo priniatye soedinennymi departamentami.* (*Materialy,* no. 11), pp. 7-8.

21. Ibid., pp. 19, 33, 141-43.

22. Shubin-Pozdeev, p. 482.

23. Kaiser, p. 270.

24. Dzhanshiev, "S. I. Zarudnyi," p. 393.

25. On the reform of procedure in naval courts, see E. D. Dneprov, "Proekt ustava morskogo suda i ego rol' v podgotovke sudebnoi reformy (aprel' 1860 g.)," *Revoliutsionnaia Situatsiia v Rossii v 1859-1861 gg.* (Moscow, 1970), pp. 57-70; Kaiser, pp. 237-41.

26. P. N. Glebov, "Morskoe sudoproizvodstvo vo Frantsii," *Morskoi Sbornik,* no. 11 pt. 3 (1859), pp. 108-10.

27. Ibid., pp. 103-7; no. 12, pt. 3 (1860), pp. 347-58; no. 1, pt. 3 (1860), pp. 76-78.

28. P. N. Glebov, "Vvedeniie ili ob"iasnitel'naia zapiska k proektu ustava morskogo sudoustroistva i sudoproizvodstva," *Morskoi Sbornik,* no. 5, pt. 3 (1860), pp. 1-54.

29. *Otzyvy i zamechaniia raznykh lits na proekt ustava o voennomorskom sude* (St. Petersburg, 1861).

30. *Otchet Ministerstva Iustitsii za 1858 god,* p. 62; *Otchet Ministerstva Iustitsii za 1859 god,* pp. 40, 41, 49.

31. Kulomzin, passim; TsGIA, 1349-5-450.

32. Kulomzin, pp. 263-64.

33. Dzhanshiev, *Stranitsa,* pp. 23-28.

34. TsGIA, 1275-1-52 (Sovet ministrov, Doklad D. N. Zamiatnina, 17 sentiabria, 1863 g.), p. 16.

35. *Arkhiv istoricheskikh i prakticheskikh svedenii otnosiashchikhsia do Rossii izd. Nikolaem Kalachovym,* bk. 2, pt. 3 (1859), p. 53.

36. N. V. Davydov, N. N. Polianskii, eds., *Sudebnaia Reforma,* 1:359.

37. Obninskii, *Sbornik statei,* pp. 56-57.

38. K. Arsen'ev, "Iz vospominanii," *Golos Minuvshego,* no. 2 (1915), pp. 118-19.

39. V. R. Leikina-Svirskaia, *Intelligentsiia v Rossii vo vtoroi polovine XIX veka* (Moscow, 1971), p. 77.

40. Emmons, pp. 80, 83, 154, 255-57, 291, 354.

41. *Soobrazheniia gosudarstvennoi kantseliarii ob osnovnykh nachalakh osobennykh rodov sudoproizvodstva ugolovnogo po proektu sostavlennomu II otdeleniem S. E. I. V. Kantseliarii.* (*Materialy,* no. 18), p. 19.

42. TsGIA, 1405-57-1903 (1859 g.) (*Po otnosheniiu Ministra Vnutrennikh Del za 270 i 465 po predmetu sostoiavshiesia v obshchikh Gubernskikh Sobraniiakh Khar'kovskogo, Tul'skogo, i Voronezhskogo Dvorianstva postanovleniia o neobkhodimosti glasnogo sudoproizvodstva),* pp. 5-6, 12. This address has been described in "Istoricheskie materialy izvlechennye iz Senatskogo arkhiva: Dokumenty otnosiashchiesia do sudebnoi reformy 1864 goda," *Zhurnal Ministerstva Iustitsii,* no. 8 (1914), pp. 260-64.

43. TsGIA, 1405-57-1903 (1859 g.), pp. 7-8.

44. Ibid., pp. 8-12.

45. Ibid., pp. 12-13.

46. Ibid., pp. 19-23; "Istoricheskie materialy," pp. 264-66.

47. V. P. Bezobrazov, *Otchet o deistviakh Kommissii vysochaishe uchrezhdennei dlia ustroistva zemskikh bankov* (St. Petersburg, 1861), pp. 40-43.

48. Ibid., pp. 109-10. (Italics in original.)

49. K. Pobedonostev, "Veshnyi kredit i zakladnoe pravo," *Russkii Vestnik,* 33 (June 1861) : 440.

50. P. A. Valuev, "Zapiska Aleksandru II: O polozhenii krest'ianskogo dela v nachale sentiabria 1861 g.," *Istoricheskii Arkhiv,* January-February 1861, p. 74.

51. Ibid., pp. 77-78.

52. Ibid., p. 79.

53. On the role and operation of the Editing Commission, see Field, chaps. 3-5.

54. *Gosudarstvennaia Kantseliariia 1810-1910,* pp. 223-26, primechaniia, xii-xiii.

55. A. Knirim, "O Gannoverskom grazhdanskom sudoproizvodstve," *Zhurnal Ministerstva Iustitsii,* March 1862, pp. 545-47.

56. Ibid., p. 548.

57. *Zhurnal soedinennykh departamentov zakonov i grazhdanskikh del Gosudarstvennogo Soveta o preobrazovanii sudebnoi chasti v Rossii* (*Materialy,* no. 19), p. 10.

58. Ibid., pp. 14, 16, 50.

59. Ibid., p. 53.

60. Ibid., pp. 183-84.

61. *Soobrazheniia gosudarstvennoi kantseliarii ob osnovnykh nachalakh osobennykh rodov sudoproizvodstva ugolovnogo po proektu sostavlennomu II otdeleniem S. E. I. V. Kantseliarii* (*Materialy,* no. 18, pt. 2), pp. 8-9, 12.

62. *Zamechaniia o razvitii osnovnykh polozhenii preobrazovaniia sudebnoi chasti v Rossii* (*Materialy,* nos. 21-26); I. V. Gessen, *Sudebnaia Reforma* (St. Petersburg, 1905), pp. 78-86.

63. Of the twenty-six members of the commission, twenty-four had higher degrees. In one case, I have not been able to find information. Twelve had completed the School of

Jurisprudence, twelve the universities, five of them the juridical faculty of Moscow University, Material on education comes from *Gosudarstvennaia Kantseliariia,* and various editions of the *Spisok chinam Pravitel'stvuiushchego Senata i Ministerstva Iustitsii.*

64. For complete descriptions of the statutes, see Kaiser, pp. 340-407; Samuel Kucherov, *Courts, Lawyers and Trials under the Last Three Tsars,* pp. 26-97.

65. *PSV (IV),* 41473, 20 November 1864.

66. M. F. Gromnitskii, "Iz proshlogo," *Russkaia Mysl',* February 1899, pt. 2, p. 62; A. L. Levenstin, *Khar'kovskii Sudebnyi Okrug 1867-1902* (Kharkov, 1903), pp. 5-6; "Istoricheskie materialy izvlechennykh iz Senatskogo archiva: Dokumenty otnosiashchiesia do sudebnoi reformy 1865 goda," *Zhurnal Ministerstva Iustitsii,* December 1914, pp. 286-99.

67. Some areas, such as the Baltic provinces, Siberia, and the Caucasus, did not receive the reform until the end of the nineteenth or the first years of the twentieth century. By the end of Alexander's reign, new courts were at work in thirty-three provinces (Kaiser, pp. 466-67).

68. G. Dzhanshiev, *Epokha velikikh reform,* pp. 404-5.

69. Kulomzin, pp. 314-16; Dzhanshiev, *Stranitsa,* p. 79.

70. TsGIA, 1275-1-52 (Sovet ministrov, *Doklad D. N. Zamiatnina, 17, sentiabria, 1863 g.*), pp. 10-11.

71. A. Koni, "Novyi sud," *Zhurnal Ministerstva Iustitsii,* April 1916, p. 10; V. K. Sluchevskii, "Iz pervykh let zhizni sudebnykh ustavov," *Zhurnal Ministerstva Iustitsii,* November 1914, p. 196; "Tekushchaia Khronika i osobye proishchestviia: Dnevnik V. F. Odoevskogo, 1859-1869 gg.," *Literaturnoe Nasledstvo,* nos. 22-24 (1935), p. 206.

72. The sources do not distinguish faculties at the university for legal personnel. The first materials to do so that I have been able to find are for 1888, when 88 percent of legal officials had specialized legal education. See *Vedomost' ob obrazovatel'nom tsenze lits sudebnogo vedomstva* (St. Petersburg, 1889), p. 324.

73. The *Spiski chinam* for the ministry do not carry information on social origin until the last decade of the century. On the social composition of the student bodies of Russian universities, see Leikina-Svirskaia, pp. 61-65.

74. Serfs that officials in the cassational departments held before emancipation are as follows (one senator, not included below, listed estates of one thousand *desiatiny*):

Serfs	Senators	Chief-Procurators
0	8	5
1-10	0	0
11-100	0	1
101-500	3	2
501-1,000	1	0
1,001-	2	0
Totals	14	8

75. Koni, *Ottsy,* pp. 181-84.

76. Ibid., p. 37; idem, "Novyi sud," pp. 23-24; Gromnitskii, "Iz proshlogo," *Russkaia Mysl',* June 1899, p. 9 n.

77. Levenstin, p. 116.

78. Davydov and Polianskii, 1:365-66; Sluchevskii, p. 196.

79. Koni, "Novyi sud," p. 14; M. F. Gromnitskii, "Rol' prokurora na sude po delam ugolovnym," *Zhurnal Ministerstva Iustitsii,* February 1896, p. 63; Gromnitskii, "Iz proshlogo," *Russkaia Mysl',* February 1899, pp. 63-64; September 1899, pp. 214-15.

NOTES TO CHAPTER TEN

1. Marc Szeftel, "The Form of Government of the Russian Empire Prior to the Constitutional Reforms of 1905-06," pp. 114-16; idem, "Personal Inviolability in the

Legislation of the Russian Absolute Monarchy," *American Slavic and East European Review* 17 (1958) : 1, 23-24. There is almost no scholarly literature on the operation of the new courts. Both comprehensive studies and monographs are lacking on the courts in all areas except the Russian bar and the courts' clashes with the administration.

2. Szeftel, "The Form of Government," p. 115.

3. See Heide Wolker Whelan, "Alexander III and the State Council: The Politics of Equilibrium" (diss. for Ph.D., University of Chicago, 1973).

4. Kucherov, pp. 302-16.

5. Talcott Parsons, "The Professions and Social Structure," *Essays in Sociological Theory* (Glencoe, 1964), p. 38.

6. Alfred J. Rieber, *The Politics of Autocracy: Letters of Alexander II to Prince A. I. Bariatinskii, 1857-1864* (Paris and The Hague, 1966), p. 55.

7. Baron A. M. Nol'ken, "Sudebnaia reforma 1864 goda i pervyi departament Pravitel' stvuiushchego Senata," *Zhurnal Ministerstva Iustitsii,* February 1905), pp. 113-14.

8. Ibid., pp. 115-16, 120-21.

9. Ibid., pp. 123-25.

10. Ibid., pp. 126-42.

11. *Sudebnye Ustavy 20 noiabria 1864 goda za piat'desiat' let,* 1:374.

12. Ibid., pp. 384-85.

13. Seredonin, 3 (pt. 1) : 130-35.

14. Ibid., 3 (pt. 1) : 139; *Sudebnye Ustavy . . . za piat'desiat' let,* 2: 562 n.

15. Seredonin, 3 (pt. 1) : 141-43.

16. TsGIA, 1149-6n-1866, no. 107 (Delo Gosudarstvennogo Soveta, Departament Zakonov, *O proekte iziatii iz obshchego poriadka ugolovnogo sudoproizvodstva dlia del pechati i dopolnenii k pravilam 11-ogo oktiabria 1865-ogo goda o poriadke sudoproizvodstva v sudebnykh ustanovleniiakh prezhnego ustroistva*), p. 15.

17. Nikitenko, 3: 48-49; Gessen, *Sudebnaia Reforma,* pp. 134-47; Valuev, *Dnevnik,* 2: 164.

18. *Sudebnye Ustavy . . . za piat'desiat' let,* 1:323-25.

19. TsGIA, 1149-6n-1866, no. 107, p. 28.

20. Valuev, *Dnevnik,* 2:153.

21. Charles Ruud, "The Russian Empire's New Censorship Law of 1865," *Canadian Slavic Studies,* Summer 1969, p. 243; *Sudebnye Ustavy . . . za piat'desiat' let,* 1:328-29.

22. *Sudebnye Ustavy . . . za piat'desiat' let,* 2:499-500, 502-3; Odoevskii, p. 220.

23. *Sudebnye Ustavy . . . za piat'desiat' let,* 2:492-97; Gromnitskii, *Russkaia Mysl',* September 1899, p. 226.

24. *Sudebnye Ustavy . . . za piat'desiat' let,* 2:492-93, 507-8; Odoevskii, p. 217.

25. *Sudebnye Ustavy . . . za piat'desiat' let,* 2:508.

26. Kulomzin, pp. 329-30; Gessen, pp. 139-40.

27. Kulomzin, p. 330.

28. Nikitenko, 3:294.

29. Dzhanshiev, *Stranitsa,* p. 76.

30. Gromnitskii, "Iz proshlogo," June 1899, pt. 2, p. 28.

31. *Sudebnye Ustavy . . . za piat'desiat' let,* 2:504-5.

32. Ibid., 1:356-62.

33. Gromnitskii, "Iz proshlogo," *Russkaia Mysl',* June 1899, pt. 2, p. 30; December 1899, pt. 2, pp. 59-60.

34. Dzhanshiev, *Sbornik statei,* pp. 426-27; Zarudnyi, *Iz vospominanii,* p. 6; TsGIA, 1405-528-83; personal communication from Katerina Zarudnaia Singleton, 1975.

35. Otto Kirchheimer, *Political Justice: The Use of Legal Procedure for Political Ends* (Princeton, 1961), p. 6.

36. Ibid., pp. 421-25.

37. B. V. Vilenskii, *Sudebnaia Reforma i Kontrreforma v Rossii* (Saratov, 1969), p. 234; it was a common view in the administration at this time that secrecy of political trials was against state interest. See Ia. G. Esipovich, "Zapiski Senatora Esipovicha," *Russkaia Starina,* January 1909, p. 133.

38. *Soobrazheniia gosudarstvennoi kantseliarii ob osnovnykh nachalakh osobennykh rodov sudoproizvodstva ugolovnogo po proektu sostavlennomu II otdeleniem S. E. I. V. Kantseliarii* (*Materialy*, no. 17), p. 12.

39. A. F. Koni, *Sobranie sochinenii* (Moscow, 1966), 2: 74.

40. Vilenskii, pp. 236-37.

41. *Sudebnye Ustavy* . . . *za piat'desiat' let,* 2 : 600; S. S. Tatishchev, *Imperator Aleksandr II, ego zhizn' i tsarstvovanie* (St. Petersburg, 1903), 2:587.

42. Vilenskii, pp. 238-41.

43. *Spisok chinam Pravitel'stvuiushchego Senata, Departamenta Ministerstva Iustitsii i Sudebnykh Mest, obrazovannykh na osnovanii Sudebnykh Ustavov 20-ogo noiabria 1864 goda* (St. Petersburg, 1870).

44. Baron A. I. Del'vig, *Moi vospominaniia* (Moscow, 1913), 2:482-83.

45. Vilenskii, pp. 317-18.

46. Tatishchev, 2:595-96.

47. Ibid., p. 596.

48. Koni, *Sobranie sochinenii,* 2:59-64.

49. Ibid., pp. 64, 462.

50. Ibid., p. 63.

51. Vilenskii, pp. 257-58.

52. Koni, *Sobranie sochinenii,* 2: 66-67.

53. Ibid., pp. 72-74, 87-88, 450-51; Polovtsov, "Iz dnevnika," p. 190.

54. Ibid., pp. 171-72, 180-81.

55. Vilenskii, p. 262.

56. Of seventy-three trials of members of the People's Will in the 1880s, forty-two were heard by military courts, seven by a special session of the Senate. Only the least significant cases were left to the regular court system (N. A. Troitskii, *"Narodnaia Volia" pered tsarskim sudom, 1880-1891 gg.*[Saratov, 1971], p. 25).

57. N. G. Prints, "Sluchainosti vliavshiesia na sudebnoe preobrazovanie 1864 goda," *Zhurnal Ministerstva Iustitsii,* December 1894, pp. 17-18.

58. John R. Gillis, *The Prussian Bureaucracy in Crisis, 1840-1860: The Origins of an Administrative Ethos* (Stanford, 1971), pp. 159-60; Kirchheimer, pp. 128-29.

59. Takaaki Hattori, "The Legal Profession in Japan: Its Historical Development and Present State," in Arthur Taylor von Mehren, ed., *Law in Japan: The Legal Order in a Changing Society,* pp. 111-20; Kohji Tanabe, "The Processes of Litigation: An Experiment with the Adversary System," in von Mehren, ed., pp. 73-78.

60. Leikina-Svirskaia gives the following figures for court personnel including members of the courts, procurators, and court investigators, but not justices of the peace in the new courts.

	Circuits	Judicial Officials
1870	5	854
1880	7	2,386
1890	9	2,900

Leikina-Svirskaia, pp. 85-86. The *Spiski chinam* for 1890 and 1913 show an increase of about 250 percent in the number of officials in the St. Petersburg and Moscow Circuits alone. The expenditures on the Ministry of Justice were 9,030,952 rubles in 1869, 25,963,000 in 1894, and 45,478,986 in 1911, excluding the costs of the prison administration. See *Ministerstvo finansov* 1802-1902 (St. Petersburg, 1902), *Ezhegodnik Ministerstva finansov na 1869 god* (St. Petersburg, 1869), *Gosudarsvennaia rospis' dokhodov i raskhodov na 1911 god.* (St. Petersburg, 1911).

61. My figures for 1890 from the *Spiski chinam* correspond exactly with those in *Entsiklopedicheskii slovar' Granat* 36 (pt. 5): 618, though I have no figures for the senators. Percentages for 1913 are calculated on the basis of figures from *Spiski chinam* for that year tabulated by Richard Horowitz.

62. N. Rennenkampf, *Sud'by privillegirovannykh i neprivillegirovannykh iuristov* (n.p., n.d.). This pamphlet appears to have been written about 1880.

63. Gessen, *Sudebnaia Reforma*, pp. 180-219; Levenstin, pp. 66-71.

64. There are many summaries of the changes in the court statutes. See for example, Gessen, *Sudebnaia Reforma*, pp. 142-79; Vilenskii, pp. 305-69; Davydov, ed., 2:41-80.

65. Szeftel, "Personal Inviolability," p. 23.

66. B. A. Kistiakovskii, "V zashchitu prava," *Vekhi* (Moscow, 1909), p. 152.

BIBLIOGRAPHY

ARCHIVAL AND OTHER UNPUBLISHED SOURCES

See abbreviation list for full titles

I. LENINGRAD ARCHIVES

		Fond	
TsGIA	851	A. V. Golovnin
	1149	Department of Laws of State Council
	1169	State Chancellery
	1190	Commission for the Completion of the Work on the Reform of the Judicial Branch
	1250	Materials of the Chairman and Members of the State Council
	1261	The Second Section of His Majesty's Personal Chancellery
	1275	Council of Ministers
	1281	Council of the Ministry of Interior
	1349	Service Lists
	1389	Senator Kapger's Investigation of Kaluga and Vladimir provinces
	1405	The Ministry of Justice
LOA	355	The School of Jurisprudence
GPB		Miscellaneous personal materials on Bludov and Panin
PD		Miscellaneous personal materials on Bludov, Panin, Zarudnyi, and Lebedev

II. MOSCOW ARCHIVES

TsGAOR	109	The Third Section of His Majesty's Personal Chancellery
	564	A. F. Koni
	647	Grand Duchess Elena Pavlovna
	678	Alexander II
	722	The Marble Palace
	728	The Winter Palace
	828	A. M. Gorchakov
GBL		Stoianovskii *fond* and materials on M. A. Dmitriev, Bludov, Panin, Constantine Nikolaevich
IM	117	N. A. Mukhanov
TsGADA	1274	Bludov-Panin

III. MATERIALY

Materialy or *Delo po preobrazovaniiu sudebnoi chasti* is a collection of the materials printed and circulated within the government during the preparation of the reform, according to Constantine Nikolaevich's principle of "artificial publicity." There are such collections in GBL, GPB, and TsGIA. Listings of the contents are contained in Dzhanshiev, *Osnovy,* pp. 3–52, and Kaiser, pp. 501–14. The numbering of the three varies slightly. I have listed below only those materials cited in the present volume.

Materialy ...	No. 2, pt. 1, *Obshchaia ob"iasnitel'naia zapiska k proektu novogo ustava sudoproizvodstva grazhdanskogo*

No. 2, pt. 2, *Osobye po nekotorym voprosam zapiski predstavlennye komitetu vysochaishe uchrezhdennomu dlia razsmotreniia novogo ustava sudoproizvodstva grazhdanskogo*

No. 7, pt. 1, *Obshchaia ob"iasnitel'naia zapiska k proektu novogo ustava sudoproizvodstva po prestupleniiam i prostupkam*

No. 10, pt. 1, *Zhurnal soedinennykh departamentov grazhdanskogo i zakonov Gosudarstvennogo Soveta o glavnykh nachalakh priniatykh imi pri razsmotrenii proekta novogo ustava grazhdanskogo sudoproizvodstva* (1857–59)

No. 10, pt. 3, *Zhurnal soedinennykh departamentov zakonov i grazhdanskogo po proektu ustava sudoproizvodstva grazhdanskogo* (15 November 1857–23 September 1859)

No. 11 or No. 12, pt. 1, *Svod obshchikh zamechanii na proekt i na glavnye nachala sudoproiz-*

vodstva grazhdanskogo priniatye soedinennymi departamentami
No. 18, pt. 2, *Soobrazheniia gosudarstvennoi kantseliarii ob osnovnykh nachalakh osobennykh rodov sudoproizvodstva ugolovnogo po proektu sostavlennomu II otdeleniem S. E. I. V. Kantseliarii*
No. 19, *Zhurnal soedinennykh departamentov zakonov i grazhdanskikh del Gosudarstvennogo Soveta o preobrazovanii sudebnoi chasti v Rossii* (April-July 1862)
Nos. 21-26, *Zamechaniia o razvitii osnovnykh polozhenii preobrazovaniia sudebnoi chasti v Rossii*

PUBLISHED SOURCES

Aksakov, I. S. *Ivan Sergeevich Aksakov v ego pis'makh.* 2 vols. Moscow, 1888.
— — —. *Stikhotvoreniia i poemy.* Leningrad, 1960.
Aleksandrov, V. A. "Sel'skaia obshchina v Rossii (XVII-nachalo XIXv)." *Istoricheskie Zapiski* 89 (1972): 231-94.
Alston, Patrick L. *Education and the State in Tsarist Russia.* Stanford, 1969.
Amburger, Erik. *Geschichte der Behördenorganisation Russlands von Peter dem grossen bis 1917.* Leiden, 1966.
Antonov, A. N. *Pervyi kadetskii korpus.* St. Petersburg, 1907.
Anuchin, E. *Istoricheskii obzor razvitiia administrativno-politseiskikh uchrezhdenii v Rossi s uchrezhdeniia o guberniiakh do poslednego vremeni.* St. Petersburg, 1872.
Arkhangel'skii, A. S. "V. A. Zhukovskii: Biograficheskii ocherk." In V. A. Zhukovskii, *Polnoe sobranie sochinenii.* St. Petersburg, 1902, 1:v-xxx.
Arkhiv Kniazia Vorontsova, vol. 38. Moscow, 1892.
Arsen'ev, K. K. *Glavnye deiateli i predshestvenniki sudebnoi reformy.* St. Petersburg, 1904.
— — —. "Iz vospominanii." *Golos Minuvshchego,* no. 2 (1915), pp. 117-29.
— — —. "Vospominaniia ob Uchilishche Pravovedeniia." *Russkaia Starina,* no. 4 (1886), pp. 199-220.
Augustine, Wilson. "Notes toward a Portrait of the Eighteenth-Century Russian Nobility." *Canadian Slavic Studies,* Fall 1970, pp. 374-425.
Baranov, P. *Mikhail Andreevich Balug'ianskii, 1769-1847.* St. Petersburg, 1882.
Barshev, Ia. *Istoricheskaia zapiska o sodeistvii Vtorogo Otdeleniia sobstvennoi ego I. V. Kantseliarii razvitiiu iuridicheskikh nauk v Rossii.* St. Petersburg, 1876.
Barsukov, N. *Zhizn' i trudy M. P. Pogodina.* 22 vols. St. Petersburg, 1888-1910.
Batiushkov, K. N. *Sochineniia.* 3 vols. St. Petersburg, 1886-87.
Beccaria, Cesare. *Crimes and Punishments.* London, 1880.
Bervi, V. V. [N. Flerovskii]. *Tri politicheskie sistemy.* n.p., 1897.
Bezobrazov, B. P. *Otchet o deistviakh kommissii vysochaishchei uchrezhdennoi dlia ustroistva zemskikh bankov.* St. Petersburg, 1861.
Bezrodnyi, A. V. "O podgotovlenii opytnykh i obrazovannykh deiatelei dlia gosudarstvennoi sluzhby." *Zhurnal Ministerstva Iustitsii,* no. 9 (1903), pp. 249-85.
Biuler, Baron Fedor. *Dve rechi proiznesennye v Imperatorskom Uchilishche Pravovedeniia.* St. Petersburg, 1860.

Blagoveshchenskii, A. "Istoriia metod nauki zakonovedeniia v XVIII i XIX v." *Zhurnal Ministerstva Narodnogo Prosveshcheniia,* no. 6 (1835), pp. 375-441; no. 7, pp. 42-52.

Bluche, Francois. *Les magistrats du parlement de Paris au XVIII siècle: 1715-1771.* Paris, 1960.

Bludov, D. N. "Dva pis'ma gr. D. N. Bludova k supruge ego." *Russkii Arkhiv* 5 (1867): 1046-48.

——. "Materialy k istorii Arzamasa: Rech' chlena Kassandry." *Otchet Imperatorskoi Publichnoi Biblioteki za 1888 god.* St. Petersburg, 1891, app. 3.

——. *Mysli i zamechaniia.* St. Petersburg, 1866.

——. *Poslednie chasy zhizni Imperatora Nikolaia Pervogo.* St. Petersburg, 1855.

Bludova, A. D. "Zapiski." *Russkii Arkhiv* 10 (1872): 1217-1310; 11 (1873): 2049-2138.

Blum, Jerome. *Lord and Peasant in Russia from the Ninth to the Nineteenth Century.* New York, 1964.

Bobrovskii, P. P. *Proiskhozhdenie voinskikh artikulov i izobrazheniia protsessov Petra Velikogo po ustavu voinskomu 1716 goda.* St. Petersburg, 1881.

——. *Razvitie sposobov i sredstv dlia obrazovania iuristov voennogo i morskogo vedomstv v Rossii.* St. Petersburg, 1879.

Bogoslovskii, M. M. *Istoriia Rossii XVIII veka (1725-1796).* Moscow, 1915.

——. *Oblastnaia reforma Petra Velikogo.* Moscow, 1903.

Borovkov, A. D. "Aleksandr Dmitrievich Borovkov i ego avtobiograficheskie zapiski." *Russkaia Starina,* no. 9 (1898), pp. 533-64; no. 10, pp. 41-63; no. 11, pp. 331-62; no. 12, pp. 591-616.

Borovkova-Maikova, M. S., ed. *Arzamas i arzamaskie protokoly.* Leningrad, 1933.

Bouwsma, William J. "Lawyers and Early Modern Culture." *American Historical Review,* April 1973, pp. 303-27.

Brikner, A. *Materialy dlia zhizneopisaniia Grafa Nikity Petrovicha Panina,* vol. 7. St. Petersburg, 1892.

Brzezinski, Zbigniew K. "The Patterns of Autocracy." In *The Transformation of Russian Society.* Edited by Cyril E. Black. Cambridge, Mass., 1960, pp. 93-109.

Bulgarin, Faddei. *Petr Ivanovich Vyzhigin.* St. Petersburg, 1834.

——. *Sochineniia.* 12 vols. St. Petersburg, 1829-30.

Byrnes, Robert F. *Pobedonostev: His Life and Thought.* Bloomington, Ind., 1968.

Chaikovskii, Modest. *Zhizn' Petra Il'icha Chaikovskogo.* 3 vols. Moscow and Leipzig, 1900.

Chechulin, N. D. "Ob istochinikakh Nakaza." *Zhurnal Ministerstva Narodnogo Prosveshcheniia,* April 1902, pp. 279-320.

Cherniavsky, Michael. *Tsar and People: Studies in Russian Myths.* New Haven and London, 1961.

Chicherin, B. N. *Vospominaniia Borisa Nikolaevicha Chicherina: Moskva sorokovykh godov.* Moscow, 1929.

Choron, Jacques. *Death and Western Thought.* New York, 1963.

Chulkov, Mikhail. *Slovar' iuridicheskii ili svod rossiiskikh uzakonenii, vremennykh uchrezhdenii suda i raspravy.* Moscow, 1793.

Clardy, Jesse. G. R. *Derzhavin: A Political Biography.* The Hague and Paris, 1967.

Confino, Michael. *Domaines et seigneurs en russie vers la fin du XVIIIe siècle.* Paris, 1963.

Davydov, N. V. *Iz proshlogo.* Moscow, 1913.

Davydov, N. V., and Polianskii, N. N., eds. *Sudebnaia Reforma.* 2 vols. Moscow, 1915.

Del'vig, Baron A. I. *Moi vospominaniia.* 4 vols. Moscow, 1913.

Demidova, N. F. "Biurokratizatsiia gosudarstvennogo apparata absoliutizma v XVII-XVIII vv." In *Absoliutizm v Rossii XVII-XVIII vv.* Moscow, 1964, pp. 206-42.

Derzhavin, G. R. "Mnenie Senatora Derzhavina o pravakh, preimushchestvakh i sushchestvennoi dolzhnosti Senata." *Chteniia v Imperatorskom Obshchestve istorii i drevnostei rossiiskikh pri Moskovskom Universitete,* no. 3 (1858), pp. 122-27.

— — —. *Sochineniia.* 9 vols. St. Petersburg, 1864-83.

Dilthei, Phillippe Henrich. *Izledovanie iuridicheskoe o prinadlezhashchem dlia suda meste, o sudebnoi vlasti, o dolzhnosti sudeiskoi, o chelobitnoi i dokazatel'stve sudebnom.* Moscow, 1779.

Dmitriev, I. I. *Polnoe sobranie stikhotvorenii.* Leningrad, 1967.

— — —. *Vzgliad na moiu zhizn'.* Moscow, 1866.

Dmitriev, M. A. *Melochi iz zapasa moei pamiati.* Moscow, 1869.

— — —. *O natural'noi shkole i narodnosti.* Moscow, 1848.

— — —. *Stikhotvoreniia.* 2 vols. Moscow, 1865.

Dneprov, E. D. "Proekt ustava morskogo suda i ego rol' v podgotovke sudebnoi reformy (aprel', 1860 g.)." In *Revoliutsionnaia Situatsiia v Rossii v 1859-1861 gg.* Moscow, 1970, pp. 57-70.

Dobrynin, Gavrill. "Istinnoe povestvovanie ili zhizn' Gavriila Dobrynina im samim pisannaia, 1752-1823." *Russkaia Starina,* no. 4 (1871), pp. 395-420.

Dubrovin, N. "Neskol'ko slov v pamiat' Imperatora Nikolaia I." *Russkaia Starina,* no. 6 (1896), pp. 449-70.

— — —. "Russkaia zhizn' v nachale XIX veka." *Russkaia Starina,* no. 12 (1898), pp. 479-516; no. 1 (1899), pp. 3-65; no. 3, pp. 539-69; no. 4, pp. 53-75; no. 6, pp. 481-508.

Dukes, Paul. *Catherine the Great and the Russian Nobility.* Cambridge, England, 1967.

Durkheim, Emile. *The Division of Labor in Society.* New York, 1964.

Durylin, S. "Russkie pisateli i Goethe v Veimare." *Literaturnoe Nasledstvo.* 4-6 (1932): 83-504.

Dzhanshiev, G. A. *Epokha velikikh reform.* Moscow, 1896.

— — —. *Osnovy sudebnoi reformy.* Moscow, 1891.

— — —. *Sbornik statei.* Moscow, 1914.

— — —. *Stranitsa iz istorii sudebnoi reformy: D. N. Zamiatnin.* Moscow, 1883.

Dzhivelegov, A. D. "Graf V. N. Panin." In *Velikaia Reform,* Moscow, 1911, 5:68-87.

Egorov, Iu. N. "Reaktsionnaia politika tsarizma v voprosakh universitetskogo obrazovaniia v 30-kh-50-kh gg. XIX v." *Nauchnye doklady vysshei shkoly: Istoricheskie nauki,* no. 3 (1960), pp. 60-75.

— — —. "Studenchestvo Sankt-Peterburgskogo Universiteta v 30-50kh godakh XIX v., ego sotsial'nyi sostav i raspredelenie po fakul'tetam." *Vestnik Leningradskogo Universiteta,* no. 14 (1957), pp. 5-19.

Ehrhard, Marcelle. *V. A. Joukovskii et le préromantisme russe.* Paris, 1938.

Eikhenbaum, B. M. *Skvoz' literaturu.* Leningrad, 1924.

Eisenstadt, S. N. "Post-traditional Societies and the Continuity and Reconstruction of Tradition." *Daedalus,* Winter 1973, pp. 1-27.

Ekaterina II. "Sobstvennoruchnoe nastavlenie Ekateriny II Kniaziu Viazemskomu pri vstuplenie im v dolzhnost' generalprokurora." *Sbornik Russkogo Istoricheskogo Obshchestva* 7 (1864): 345-48.

Elanin, E. "Iubileinaia literatura o Pushkine." *Istoricheskii Vestnik* 77 (1899): 264-82, 592-613.

Emmons, Terence. *The Russian Landed Gentry and the Peasant Emancipation of 1861.* Cambridge, England, 1968.

Eroshkin, N. P. *Ocherki istorii gosudarstvennykh uchrezhdenii dorevoliutsionnoi Rossii.* Moscow, 1960.

Esipovich, Ia. G. "Zapiski Senatora Esipovicha." *Russkaia Starina,* no. 1 (1909), pp. 123-44.

Fadeev, A. M. "Vospominaniia." *Russkii Arkhiv,* no. 2 (1891), pp. 14-60.

Fateev, A. N. "K istorii iuridicheskoi obrazovannosti v Rossii (Zametki o zapadnom vlianii)." *Uchenye zapiski osnovannye russkoi uchebnoi kollegiei v Prage* 1 (vyp. 3, 1924): 129-256.

Field, Daniel. *The End of Serfdom: Nobility and Bureaucracy in Russia, 1855-1861.* Cambridge, Mass., forthcoming.

Fischer, Wolfram, and Lundgren, Peter. "The Recruitment and Training of Administrative and Technical Personnel." In *The Formation of National States in Western Europe.* Edited by Charles Tilly. Princeton, 1975, pp. 456-561.

Florovskii, Prot. Georgii. *Puti russkogo bogosloviia.* Paris, 1937.

Flynn, James T. "The Universities, the Gentry, and the Russian Service, 1815-1825." *Canadian Slavic Studies,* Winter 1968, pp. 486-503.

Foucault, Michel. *Madness and Civilization.* New York and Toronto, 1967.

Gessen, I. V. *Istoriia russkoi advokatury,* vol. 1. Moscow, 1914.

— — —. *Sudebnaia Reforma.* St. Petersburg, 1905.

Gillis, John R. *The Prussian Bureaucracy in Crisis, 1840-1860: The Origins of an Administrative Ethos.* Stanford, 1971.

Givens, Robert. "Seigneurs or Servitors: The Nobility and the Eighteenth-Century State." In preparation.

Gleason, Walter. "Changes in Values among Certain Russian Writers of the 1760s." Ph.D. dissertation, University of Chicago, 1973.

Glebov, P. N. "Morskoe sudoproizvodstvo vo Frantsii." *Morskoi Sbornik,* no. 11 (1859), pt. 3, pp. 101-11; no. 12, pt. 3, pp. 344-69; no. 1 (1860), pp. 47-63; no. 4, pp. 318-52.

— — —. "Vvedenie ili ob"iasnitel'naia zapiska k proektu ustava morskogo sudoustroistva i sudoproizvodstva." *Morskoi Sbornik,* no. 5 (1860), pt. 3, pp. 1-54.

— — —. "Gody ucheniia ego Imperatorskogo Vysochestva Naslednika Tsesarevicha Aleksandra Nikolaevicha." *Sbornik Russkogo Istoricheskogo Obshchestva,* vol. 30. 1880.

Gol'sten, A. "Dmitrii Ivanovich Meier, ego zhizn' i deiatel'nost'." In D. I. Meier, *Russkoe grazhdanskoe pravo.* St. Petersburg, 1897, pp. i-xvi.

Gosudarstvennaia Kantseliariia, 1810-1910. St. Petersburg, 1910.

Gosudarstvennyi Sovet, 1801-1901. St. Petersburg, 1901.

Got'e, Iu. *Istoriia oblastnogo upravleniia v Rossii ot Petra I do Ekateriny II.* 2 vols. Moscow, 1913, 1941.

Gradovskii, A. D. "Istoricheskii ocherk uchrezhdeniia general-gubernatorstv v Rossii." In Gradovskii, A. D., *Sochineniia,* vol. 1. St. Petersburg, 1899, pp. 299-338.

Grech, N. I. *Zapiski o moei zhizni.* St. Petersburg, 1886.

Gribovskii, V. M. *Vysshii sud i nadzor v Rossii v pervuiu polovinu tsarstvovaniia Imperatritsy Ekateriny II.* St. Petersburg, 1901.

Grimsted, Patricia Kennedy. *The Foreign Ministers of Alexander I.* Berkeley, 1969.

Gromnitskii, M. F. "Iz proshlogo." *Russkaia Mysl',* no. 2 (1899), pt. 2, pp. 49-71; no. 6, pt. 2, pp. 1-33; no. 9, pt. 2, pp. 210-50.

— — —. "Rol' prokurora na sude po delam ugolovnym." *Zhurnal Ministerstva Iustitsii,* no. 2 (1896), pt. 2, pp. 1-65.

Grossman, Leonid. *Prestuplenie Sukhovo-Kobylina.* Leningrad, 1928.

Grot, Ia. "Zhizn' Derzhavina." In G. R. Derzhavin, *Sochineniia,* vol. 8. St. Petersburg, 1880.

Gurvich, Georgii. *"Pravda voli monarshei" Feofana Prokopovicha i eia zapadnoevropeiskie istochniki.* Iur'iev, 1915.

Harris, Jane Gary. "The Creative Imagination in Evolution: A Stylistic Analysis of G. R. Derzhavin's Panegyric and Meditative Odes." Ph.D. dissertation, Columbia University, 1969.

Hattori, Takaaki. "The Legal Profession in Japan: Its Historical Development and Present State." In *Law in Japan: The Legal Order in a Changing Society.* Edited by Arthur T. von Mehren. Cambridge, Mass., 1963, pp. 111-52.

Hausherr, Hans. *Verwaltungseinheit und Ressorttrennung vom Ende des 17 bis zum Beginn des 19 Jahrhunderts.* Berlin, 1953.

Iasnopol'skii, N. P. *Spetsializatsiia uchebnykh planov prepodavaniia i zaniatii naukami iuridicheskimi, gosudarstvennymi i ekonomicheskimi v universitetakh Rossii.* Kiev, 1907.

Ikonnikov, V. *Gavriil Romanovich Derzhavin v svoei gosudarstvennoi i obshchestvennoi deiatel'nosti.* Petrograd, 1917.

— — —. "Russkie universitety v sviazi s khodom obshchestvennogo obrazovaniia." *Vestnik Evropy,* no. 9 (1876), pp. 161-206.

Illiustrov, I. *Iuridicheskie poslovitsy i pogovorki russkogo naroda.* Moscow, 1885.

Istoriia Pravitel'stvuiushchego Senata za 200 let. St. Petersburg, 1911.

"Istoricheskie materialy izvlechennykh iz Senatskogo arhkiva: Dokumenty otnosiashchiesia do sudebnoi reformy 1864 goda." *Zhurnal Ministerstva Iustitsii,* no. 10 (1914), pp. 286-99.

Ivanov, P. *Opyt biografii general-prokurorov i ministrov iustitsii.* St. Petersburg, 1863.

Jones, Robert E. *The Emancipation of the Russian Nobility, 1762-1785.* Princeton, 1973.

Kabuzan, V. M. *Izmeneniia v razmeshchenii naseleniia Rossii v XVIII—pervoi polovine XIX v.* Moscow, 1971.

Kahan, Arcadius. "The Costs of 'Westernization' in Russia: The Gentry and the Economy in the Eighteenth Century." In *The Structure of Russian History.* Edited by Michael Cherniavsky. New York, 1970, pp. 224-50.

Kaiser, Friedhelm Berthold. *Die russische Justizreform von 1864: Zur Geschichte der russischen Justiz von Katherina II bis 1917.* Leiden, 1972.

Karamzin, N. M. *Istoriia gosudarstva rossiiskogo.* 12 vols. Moscow, 1903.

— — —. *Izbrannye proizvedeniia.* Moscow, 1966.

— — —. *Karamzin's Memoir on Ancient and Modern Russia.* Edited by Richard Pipes. New York, 1969.

— — —. *Polnoe sobranie stikhotvorenii.* Moscow and Leningrad, 1966.

Karnovich, E. *Russkie chinovniki v byloe i nastoiashchee vremia.* St. Petersburg, 1897.

Kaznacheev, A. "Mezhdu strokami odnogo formuliarnogo spiska: Ocherk iz zapisok odnogo Senatora, 1823-1881." *Russkaia Starina,* no. 12 (1881), pp. 817-80.

Keller, Suzanne. *Beyond the Ruling Class.* New York, 1963.

Khodasevich, V. F. *Derzhavin.* Paris, 1931.

Khrapovitskii, A. V. "Pamiatnye zapiski." *Chteniia v Imperatorskom Obshchestve istorii i drevnostei rossiiskikh pri Moskovskom Universitete,* no. 3 (1862), pp. 177-294.

Khrapovitskii, M. V. *Razgovor uezdnykh dvorian o vybore v sud'i.* St. Petersburg, 1790.

Khristoforov, N., and Tomashevskii, A. "Matvei Mikhailovich Karniolin-Pinskii." *Russkii Arkhiv,* no. 8 (1876), pp. 454-60.

Kirchheimer, Otto. *Political Justice: The Uses of Legal Procedure for Political Ends.* Princeton, 1961.

Kistiakovskii. B. A. "V zashchitu prava." *Vekhi.* Moscow, 1909, pp. 125-55.

Kniaz' Vladimir Aleksandrovich Cherkasskii, ego stat'i, ego rechi i vospominaniia o nem. Moscow, 1879.

Knirim, A. "O Gannoverskom grazhdanskom sudoproizvodstve." *Zhurnal Ministerstva Iustitsii,* no. 3 (1862), pt. 2, pp. 545-608.

Koliupanov, N. "Iz proshlogo." *Russkoe Obozrenie,* no. 1 (1895), pp. 247-55; no. 2, pp. 480-94; no. 3, pp. 5-24; no. 4, pp. 527-47; no. 5, pp. 5-28; no. 6, pp. 596-615.

Kolmakov, N. M. "Graf Panin." *Russkaia Starina,* no. 11 (1887), pp. 297-332.

— — —. "Ocherki i vospominaniia." *Russkaia Starina,* no. 4 (1891), pp. 23-43; no. 5, pp. 449-69; no. 6, pp. 657-79; no. 7, pp. 119-48.

— — —. "Staryi sud." *Russkaia Starina,* no. 12 (1886), pp. 511-44.

Kommissiia dlia ustroistva zemskikh bankov. *Trudy,* 4 vols. St. Petersburg, 1860-63.

Koni, A. F.. "Novyi sud." *Zhurnal Ministerstva Iustitsii,* no. 4 (1916), pp. 1-33.

— — —. *Ottsy i deti sudebnoi reformy.* Moscow, 1914.

— — —. *Sobranie sochinenii.* 8 vols. Moscow, 1966-69.

Koniuchenko, T. *Statisticheskie svedeniia o lichnom sostave vospitannikakh i khoziastvennoi chasti, Imperatorskogo Uchilishcha Pravovedeniia za 50 let ego sushchestvovaniia.* St. Petersburg, 1886.

Korbut, M. D. *Kazanskii gosudarstvennyi universitet imeni Lenina za 125 let, 1804/5-1929/ 30.* Kazan, 1930.

Korf, S. A. *Dvorianstvo i ego soslovnoe upravlenie za stoletie 1762-1861.* St. Petersburg, 1906.

Koriagin, B. G. "Iz istorii provedeniia sudebnoi reformy v zapadnoi Sibiri." *Trudy Tomskogo Gosudarstvennogo Universiteta* 159 (1965): 154-63.

Korkunov, N. M. *Istoriia filosofii prava.* St. Petersburg, 1903.

— — —. "Proekt ustroistva Senata G. R. Derzhavina." *Zhurnal Ministerstva Iustitsii,* no. 10 (1896), pp. 1-14.

Kornilov, A. *Kurs istorii Rossii XIX veka.* 3 vols. Moscow, 1918.

Kosachevskaia, E. M. *M. A. Balug'ianskii i Peterburgskii Universitet.* Leningrad, 1971.

Koshelev, A. I. *Zapiski Aleksandra Ivanovicha Kosheleva.* Berlin, 1884.

Kovalevskii, E. P. *Graf Bludov i ego vremia.* St. Petersburg, 1871.

Kovnatov, R. A., ed. *Moskovskii Universitet v vospominaniiakh sovremennikov.* Moscow, 1956.

Kozhevnikov, M. V. "Kratkii ocherk istorii iuridicheskogo fakul'teta Moskovskogo Universiteta." *Uchenye Zapiski Moskovskogo Universiteta. Vypusk 180: Trudy iuridicheskogo fakul'teta,* 1956, pp. 5-40.

Kozlinin, E. *Za polveka: 1862-1912.* Moscow, 1912.

Kucherov, Samuel. *Courts, Lawyers, and Trials under the Last Three Tsars.* New York, 1953.

Kulomzin, A. N. "Dmitrii Nikolaevich Zamiatnin." *Zhurnal Ministerstva Iustitsii,* no. 9 (1914), pp. 233-322.

Lebedev, K. N. "Iz zapisok." *Russkii Arkhiv* 1 (1888): 481-88, 617-28; 2:0133-0144, 0232-43, 0345-56; 3:249-70, 455-67; 1 (1893): 284-97, 337-99; 2 (1897): 633-55; 3 (1900): 55-70, 244-80; 2 (1910): 333-408, 465-524; 3:183-253, 353-76; 1 (1911): 87-128, 216-34, 375-422, 534-66; 2:132-60, 224-60, 343-94, 465-511; 3:53-107, 191-216, 321-52.

LeDonne, John. "Appointments to the Russian Senate, 1762-1796." *Cahiers du monde russe et sovietique,* January-March 1975, pp. 27-56.

— — —. "Criminal Investigations before the Great Reforms." *Russian History* 1 (pt. 2, 1974): 101-18.

— — —. "The Judicial Reform of 1775 in Central Russia." *Jahrbücher für Geschichte Osteuropas* 1 (1973): 29-46.

Leikina-Svirskaia, V. R. *Intelligentsiia v Rossii vo vtoroi polovine XIX veka.* Moscow, 1971.

Levenstin, A. L. *Khar'kovskii Sudebnyi Okrug, 1867-1902.* Kharkov, 1903.

Lincoln, Bruce. "The Genesis of an 'Enlightened' Bureaucracy in Russia, 1826-1856." *Jahrbücher für Geschichte Osteuropas* 3 (1972): 321-30.

Liubavskii, Aleksandr. *Iuridicheskiia monografii i issledovaniia.* St. Petersburg, 1875.

Maikov, L. N. *Batiushkov: Ego zhizn' i sochineniia.* St Petersburg, 1887.

Maikov, P. M. "Speranskii i studenty zakonovedeniia." *Russkii Vestnik,* no. 8 (1899): pp. 609-26; no. 9, pp. 239-56; no. 10, pp. 674-82.

— — —. *Vtoroe otdelenie sobstvennoi ego Imperatorskogo Velichestva kantseliarii, 1826-1882.* St. Petersburg, 1906.

Makogonenko, G., ed. *Russkaia proza XVIII veka.* Moscow, 1971.

Man'kov, A. G. "Ispol'zovanie v Rossii shvedskogo zakonodatel'stva pri sostavlenii proekta ulozheniia 1720-1725 gg." In Akademiia Nauk SSSR. Institut Istorii SSSR. Leningradskoe

BIBLIOGRAPHY

Otdelenie. *Trudy,* vyp. 11, 1970. *Istoricheskie sviazi Skandinavii i Rossii, IX-XX vv. Sbornik statei,* pp. 112-26.

McFarlin, Harold A. "The Extension of the Imperial Russian Civil Service to the Lowest Office Workers: The Creation of the Chancery Clerkship, 1827-1833." *Russian History* 1 (pt. 1, 1974): 1-17.

Meier, Dmitrii. *O znachenii praktiki v sisteme sovremennogo iuridicheskogo obrazovaniia.* Kazan, 1855.

Meshcherskii, Kn. V. P. *Moi vospominaniia.* 2 vols. St. Petersburg, 1897.

Miliukov, P. *Ocherki po istorii russkoi kul'tury,* vol. 2. Paris, 1931.

Ministerstvo Iustitsii. *Otchet Ministerstva Iustitsii.* St. Petersburg, published annually from 1834.

— — —. *Spisok chinam Pravitel'stvuiushchego Senata i Ministerstva Iustitsii.* St. Petersburg, published annually from 1842.

Ministerstvo Iustitsii za sto let: 1802-1902. St. Petersburg, 1902.

Ministerstvo Vnutrennikh Del: 1802-1902. St. Petersburg, 1902.

Molchanov, M. M. "Aleksandr Nikolaevich Serov v vospominaniakh starogo pravoveda." *Russkaia Starina,* no. 8 (1883), pp. 331-60.

— — —. *Pol-veka nazad: Pervye gody Uchilishcha Pravovedeniia v Sankt-Peterburge.* St. Petersburg, 1892.

Monter, Barbara Heldt. *Koz'ma Prutkov. The Art of Parody.* The Hague, 1972.

Mordovchenko, N. I. *Russkaia kritika pervoi chertverti XIX veka.* Moscow and Leningrad, 1959.

Mukhanov, V. A. "Iz dnevnykh zapisok." *Russkii Arkhiv* 1 (1897): 45-109; 2:75-94.

Muraviev, Gr. M. N. "Zapiski o miatezhe v Zapadnoi Rossii." *Russkaia Starina,* no. 1 (1883), pp. 131-66.

Nebel, Henry M. *N. M. Karamzin: A Russian Sentimentalist.* The Hague, 1967.

Nelidov, N. K. "Nauka o gosudarstve, kak predmet vysshego spetsial'nogo obrazovaniia." *Vremennik Iaroslavskogo Demidovskogo Iuridicheskogo Litseiia,* no. 3 (1872), pp. 115-219.

Nevolin, C. A. *Entsiklopediia zakonovedeniia.* Kiev, 1839.

— — —. *Polnoe sobranie sochinenii.* 6 vols. St. Petersburg, 1857-59.

Nikitenko, A. V. *Dnevnik.* 3 vols. Leningrad, 1955-56.

Nol'de, A. E. *K. P. Pobedonostev i sudebnaia reforma.* Petrograd, 1915.

Nol'ken, Baron A. M. "Sudebnaia reforma 1864 goda i pervyi departament Pravitel' stvuiushchego Senata." *Zhurnal Ministerstva Iustitsii,* no. 2 (1905), pp. 107-43.

Novikov, Vasilii. *Rech'sochinennaia na sluchai sobraniia Kaluzhskogo dvorianstva dlia vybora sudei na 1786 g.* St. Petersburg, 1786.

— — —. *Teatr sudovedeniia ili chtenie dlia sudei i vsekh liubitelei iurisprudentsii, soderzhashchee dostoprimechatel'nye i liubopytnye sudebnye dela, iuridicheskie izsledovaniia znamenitnykh pravoiskusstnikov i prochiia sego roda proizshestviia, udobnye prosveshchat' trogat', vozbuzhdat' k dobrodeteli i sostavliat' poleznoe i priatnoe vremiaprovozhdenie.* 4 vols. St. Petersburg, 1790.

Obninskii, P. N. *Sbornik statei.* Moscow, 1914.

Obolenskii, D. A. *Moi vospominaniia o Velikoi Kniazhne Elene Pavlone.* St. Petersburg, 1909.

Odoevskii, Kn. V. F. "Tekushchaia khronika i osobye proishestviia: Dnevnik V. F. Odoevskogo, 1859-1869 gg." *Literaturnoe Nasledstvo,* nos. 22-24 (1935): pp. 79-308.

Oom, F. A. "Vospominaniia." *Russkii Arkhiv* 2 (1896): 217-72.

Otzyvy i zamechaniia raznykh lits na proekt ustava o voenno-morskom sude. St. Petersburg, 1861.

Ozhe, Ippolit. "Iz zapisok." *Russkii Arkhiv* 1 (1877): 51-75, 240-61, 519-41.

Ozhe-de-Rankur, N. "V dvukh universitetakh." *Russkaia Starina,* no. 6 (1896), pp. 571-82.

Pamiatnaia Knizhka Imperatorskogo Uchilishcha Pravovedeniia. St. Petersburg. Published annually with breaks from 1850.

Panin, Gr. V. N. (*soobshchil*). "O samozvanke, vydavavshei sebia za doch' Imperatritsy Elizavety Petrovny." *Chteniia v Imperatorskom Obshchestve istorii i drevnostei rossiiskikh pri Moskovskom Universitete* 1 (1867): 3-91.

Pankov, A. *Zhizn' i trudy printsa Petra Georgievich Ol'denburgskogo.* St. Petersburg, 1885.

"Parnasskii adres-kalendar'." *Russkii Arkhiv* 4 (1866) : 760-66.

Parsons, Talcott. "The Professions and Social Structure." In *Essays in Sociological Theory.* Glencoe, Ill., 1964, pp. 34-49.

— — —. *Societies: Evolutionary and Comparative Perspectives.* Englewood Cliffs, N.J., 1966.

Parusov, A. V. "K istorii mestnogo upravleniia v Rossii pervoi chetverti XIX veka." In Gor'kovskii Gosudarstvennyi Universitet, *Uchenye zapiski: Seriia istoriko-filologicheskaia* 72 (1968): 155-226.

Pavlenko, N. I. "Idei absoliutizma v zakonodatel'stve XVIII v." *Absoliutizm v Rossii (XVII-XVIIIvv).* Moscow, 1964, pp. 389-427.

Pekarskii, P. P. "Studencheskiia vospominaniia o Dmitrie Ivanoviche Meiere." In *Bratchina.* St. Petersburg, 1859, pp. 209-42.

Pintner, Walter. "The Russian Civil Service on the Eve of the Great Reforms." *Journal of Social History,* Spring 1975, pp. 55-68.

— — —. "The Social Characteristics of the Early Nineteenth-century Russian Bureaucracy." *Slavic Review,* September 1970, pp. 429-43.

Pis'movnik, soderzhashchii raznye pis'ma, prosheniia, zapiski po delu, kontraktu, atestaty, odobreniia, rospiski, propuski i pis'mennoi vid krepostnym liudiam, prikaz staroste, formu kupecheskikh assignatsii, kvitantsii, rospiski, pis'ma posylochnye i kreditynye. St. Petersburg, 1789.

Pobedonostev, C. P. *Dlia nemnogikh: Otryvki iz shkol'nogo dnevnika.* St. Petersburg, 1885.

— — —. "[Panin]." *Golosa iz Rossii,* no. 7 (1859), pp. 1-142.

— — —. "O reformakh v grazhdanskom sudoproizvodstve." *Russkii Vestnik* 21 (1859): 541-80; 22 (1859): 5-34, 153-90.

— — —. "Vasilii Petrovich Zubkov." *Russkii Arkhiv* 1 (1904): 301-5.

— — —. "Veshnyi kredit i zakladnoe pravo." *Russkii Vestnik* 33 (1861): 409-51.

— — —. "Zapiska o grazhdanskom sudoproizvodstve." Unpublished manuscript, dated December 1861, available in the Gor'kii Library of Moscow State University.

Pokrovskii, S. A. *Iuridicheskie proizvedeniia progressivnykh russkikh myslitelei.* Moscow, 1959.

Pokrovskii, S. P. *Demidovskii litsei v g. Iaroslavle v ego proshlom i nastoiashchem.* Iaroslavl, 1914.

— — —. "Stranitsa iz professorskoi deiatel'nosti K. D. Ushinskogo v Demidovskom litsee." *Vestnik Vospitaniia,* no. 9 (1911), pp. 57-77.

Polonskii, Ia. P. "Moi studencheskie vospominaniia." *Niva: Ezhemesiachnye literaturnye prilozheniia,* no. 12 (1898), pp. 641-87.

Polovstov, A. A. "Iz dnevnika A. A. Polovtsova." *Krasnyi Arkhiv* 33 (1929) : 170-203.

Pravikov, Fedor. *Grammatika iuridicheskaia.* St. Petersburg, 1803.

— — —. *Pamiatnik iz zakonov.* First volume published St. Petersburg, 1798.

Prints, N. G. "Sluchainosti vliavshiesia na sudebnoe preobrazovanie 1864 goda." *Zhurnal Ministerstva Iustitsii,* no. 2 (1894), pp. 1-26.

Przheslavskii, O. A. "Vospominaniia, 1818-1831." *Russkaia Starina,* no. 11 (1874), pp. 451-77.

Pushkin, A. S. *Dnevnik (1833-1835).* Moscow, 1923.

Radishchev, A. N. *Polnoe sobranie sochinenii,* vols. 1-3. Moscow and Leningrad, 1938-52.

— — —. *A Voyage from St. Petersburg to Moscow.* Cambridge, Mass., 1958.

Raeff, Marc. "The Domestic Policies of Peter III and his Overthrow." *American Historical Review*, 75 (June 1970): 1289-1310.

— — —. "La jeunesse russe a l'aube du XIX siecle: André Turgenev et ses amis." *Cahiers du monde russe et sovietique* 8 (October–December 1967): 560-86.

— — —. *Michael Speranskii: Statesman of Imperial Russia, 1722-1839.* The Hague, 1969.

— — —. *Origins of the Russian Intelligentsia.* New York, 1966.

— — —. *Plans for Political Reform in Imperial Russia, 1730-1905.* Englewood Cliffs, N.J., 1966.

— — —. "The Russian Autocracy and Its Officials." *Harvard Slavic Studies* 4:77-91.

Ransel, David. "Bureaucracy and Patronage: The View from an Eighteenth-Century Letter Writer." In *The Rich, the Well-Born and the Powerful: Studies of Elites and Upper Classes in History.* Edited by Fred Jaher. Urbana, Ill., 1973, pp. 154-78.

— — —. "Nikita Panin's Imperial Council Project and the Struggle of Hierarchy Groups at the Court of Catherine II." *Canadian Slavic Studies,* Fall 1970, pp. 443-63.

Reddaway, W. F. *Documents of Catherine the Great.* Cambridge, England, 1931.

Redkin, P. G. *Iz lektsii P. G. Redkina,* vol. 1. St. Petersburg, 1889.

— — —. *Kakoe obshchee obrazovanie trebuetsia sovremennostiu ot russkogo pravovedtsa.* Moscow, 1846.

Rennenkampf, N. *Sud'by privellegirovannykh i neprivellegirovannykh iuristov.*

Repinskii, G. K. (*soobshchil*). "Mery protiv neblagonadezhnykh chinovnikov." *Zhurnal Ministerstva Iustitsii,* no. 2 (1897), pp. 275-83.

Rieber, Alfred J. *The Politics of Autocracy: Letters of Alexander II to Prince A. I. Bariatinskii, 1857-1864.* Paris and The Hague, 1966.

Romanovich-Slavatinskii, A. *Dvorianstvo v Rossii.* St. Petersburg, 1870.

Rovinskii, D. A. "K sudebnym sledovateliam." *Vek,* no. 16 (1861), pp. 545-47.

Rozhdestvenskii, S. V. "Poslednaia stranitsa iz istorii politiki narodnogo prosveshcheniia Imperatora Nikolaia I-ogo." *Russkii Istoricheskii Zhurnal* 3-4 (1917): 37-59.

— — —. *Sankt-Peterburgskii Universitet, 1819-1919,* vol. 1. Petrograd, 1919.

Rubinshtein, N. L. *Russkaia istoriografiia.* Moscow, 1941.

Russkie erot. Ne dlia dam. n.p., 1879.

Ruud, Charles. "The Russian Empire's New Censorship Law of 1865." *Canadian Slavic Studies,* Summer 1969, pp. 235-45.

Salias, Graf E. A. "Poet Derzhavin: Pravitel' namestnichestva, 1785-1788." *Russkii Vestnik,* September 1876, pp. 66-120; October, pp. 567-627.

Segel, Harold B., ed. *The Literature of Eighteenth-Century Russia.* 2 vols. New York, 1967.

Seleznev, I. *Istoricheskii obzor Imperatorskogo byvshego tsarskosel'skogo nyne Aleksandrovskogo Litseia za pervoe ego piatidesiatiletie, 1811-1861.* St. Petersburg, 1861.

Semenov, N. P. "Victor Nikitych Panin." *Russkii Arkhiv* 3 (1887): 537-66.

Semevskii, V. I. *Krest'ianskii vopros v Rossii v XVIII i pervoi polovine XIX veka.* 2 vols. St. Petersburg, 1888.

Seredonin, S. M., ed. *Istoricheskii obzor deiatel'nosti Komiteta Ministrov.* 5 vols. St. Petersburg, 1902.

Shakovskoi, Kniaz' Ia.P. *Zapiski.* St. Petersburg, 1872.

Shemanskii, A., and Geichenko, S. *Krizis samoderzhaviia: Petergofskii Kottedzh Nikolaia I.* Moscow and Leningrad, 1932.

Shil'der, N. K. *Imperator Nikolai Pervyi, ego zhizn' i tsarstvovanie.* 2 vols. St. Petersburg, 1903.

Shimanovskii, M. V. *Petr Grigor'evich Redkin.* Odessa, 1891.

Shubin-Pozdeev, D. P. "Nekrolog Zarudnogo." *Russkaia Starina,* no. 2 (1888), pp. 477-84.

Shuvalova, V. A. "Podgotovka sudebnoi reformy." *Kandidat iuridicheskikh nauk* dissertation, Moscow State University, 1965.

Siuzor, Georgii. *Ko dniu LXXV iubileia imperatorskogo uchilishcha pravovedeniia, 1835-1910.* St. Petersburg, 1910.

Sluchevskii, V. K. "Iz pervykh let zhizhni sudebnykh ustavov." *Zhurnal Ministerstva Iustitsii,* no. 9 (1914), pp. 181-233.

Smirnov-Rosset, A. O. *Avtobiografiia.* Moscow, 1931.

Soloviev, S. M. *Istoriia Rossii s drevneishikh vremen.* 15 vols. Moscow, 1959-66.

Speranskii, M. M. "Imperatorskoe Uchilishche Pravovedeniia." *Russkaia Starina,* no. 12 (1885), pp. i-iv.

――――. *Obozrenie istoricheskikh svedenii o Svode Zakonov.* St. Petersburg, 1833.

――――. "O sushchestve svoda." *Russkaia Starina,* no. 3 (1876), pp. 586-92.

――――. *Proekty i zapiski.* Moscow and Leningrad, 1961.

――――. *Rukovodstvo k poznaniiu zakonov.* St. Petersburg, 1845.

Starr, S. Frederick. *Decentralization and Self-Government in Russia, 1830-1870.* Princeton, 1972.

Stasov, V. V. "Aleksandr Nikolaevich Serov." *Russkaia Starina,* no. 8 (1875), pp. 581-602.

――――. "Uchilishche Pravovedeniia sorok let tomu nazad, 1836-1842." *Russkaia Starina,* no. 12 (1880), pp. 1015-42; no. 3 (1881), pp. 393-422; no. 4, pp. 573-602; no. 5, pp. 247-82.

――――. *Vospominaniia tovarishcha o D. A. Rovinskom.* St. Petersburg, 1896.

Stoianovskii, N. I. *Kratkii ocherk ob osnovanii i razvitii Imperatorskogo Uchilishcha Pravovedeniia.* N.p., 1885.

――――. "Rech'―v Sankt-Peterburgskom Iuridicheskom Obshchestve." *Zhurnal Grazhdanskogo i Ugolovnogo Prava,* no. 9 (1882), pp. 8-12.

――――. *Vospominanie o 5-om i 7-om dekabria 1860 goda.* St. Petersburg, 1860.

Strakosch, Henry E. *State Absolutism and the Rule of Law.* Sydney, 1967.

Strube de Piermont, F. H. *Ébauche des lois naturelles et du droit primitif.* Amsterdam, 1744.

――――. *Programma v kotoroi ravnuiu pol'zu voennoi i sudebnoi nauki pokazyvaet: I kupno zhelaiushchikh upraizhniat'sia vo osnovatel'neishem uchenii na svoi lektsii prizyvaet Fridrikh Genrikh Shtrube Akademii Nauk professor.* St. Petersburg, 1748.

Struminskii, V. Ia. *Ocherki zhizni i pedagogicheskoi deiatel'nosti K. D. Ushinskogo.* Moscow, 1960.

Sudebnye ustavy 20 noiabria 1864 goda za piat'desiat' let. 2 vols and apps. St. Petersburg, 1914.

Sumarokov, A. P. *Polnoe sobranie sochinenii v stikhakh i proze.* 10 vols. Moscow, 1781-82.

Sushkov, N. *Moskovskii Universitetskii Blagorodnyi Pension.* Moscow, 1858.

Sverbeev, D. N. "Vospominaniia." In *Vospominaniia o studencheskoi zhizni.* Edited by V. O. Kliuchevskii; P. M. Obninskii; and D. N. Sverbeev. Moscow, 1899, pp. 66-111.

Svodnyi katalog russkoi knigi grazhdanskoi pechati XVIII veka. 5 vols. Moscow, 1962-67.

Szeftel, Marc. "Personal Inviolability in the Legislation of the Russian Absolute Monarchy." *American Slavic and East European Review* 17 (1958): 1-24.

――――. "The Form of Government of the Russian Empire Prior to the Constitutional Reforms of 1905-06." In *Essays in Russian and Soviet History.* Edited by John S. Curtiss. New York, 1965, pp. 105-19.

Tanabe, Kohji. "The Processes of Litigation: An Experiment with the Adversary System." In *Law in Japan: The Legal Order in a Changing Society.* Edited by Arthur Taylor von Mehren. Cambridge, Mass., 1963, pp. 73-110.

Tatishchev, S. S. *Imperator Aleksandr II, ego zhizn' i tsarstvovanie.* 2 vols. St. Petersburg, 1903.

Tel'berg, Georgii. *Pravitel'stvuiushchii Senat i samoderzhavnaia vlast' v nachale XIX veka.* Moscow, 1914.

――――. "Uchastie Imperatora Nikolaia I v kodifikatsionnoi rabote ego tsarstvovaniia." *Zhurnal Ministerstva Iustitsii* 22 (January-March 1916): 233-44.

BIBLIOGRAPHY

Tikhomirov, M. N., ed. *Istoriia Moskovskogo Universiteta*, vol. 1. Moscow, 1955.

Tiutchev, I. Z. "V Uchilishche Pravovedeniia v 1847-1852 gg." *Russkaia Starina*, no. 11 (1885), pp. 436-52.

Torke, Hans-Joachim. *Das russische Beamtentum in der ersten Hälfte des 19. Jahrhunderts*. Berlin, 1967.

Troitskii, N. A. *"Narodnaia Volia" pered tsarskim sudom*. Saratov, 1971.

Troitskii, S. M. *Russkii absoliutizm i dvorianstvo v XVIII v.: Formirovanie biurokratii*. Moscow, 1974.

Tynianov, Iurii. *Arkhaisty i novatory*. Leningrad, 1929.

Ushinskii, C. D. *Sobranie sochinenii*. 11 vols. Moscow and Leningrad, 1948-52.

Uvarov, S. *Desiatiletie Ministerstva Narodnogo Prosveshcheniia, 1833-1843*. St. Petersburg, 1844.

Valuev, P. A. "Dnevnik, 1847-1860." *Russkaia Starina*, no. 1 (1891), pp. 339-59; no. 2, pp. 167-82, 603-16; no. 3, pp. 71-82, 265-78; no. 4, pp. 547-62; no. 5, pp. 139-54.

— — —. *Dnevnik*. 2 vols. Moscow, 1961.

— — —. "Zapiska Aleksandru II — O polozhenii krest'ianskogo dela v nachale sentiabria 1861 g. 15, sent. 1861." *Istoricheskii Arkhiv*, no. 1 (1961), pp. 65-81.

Vasil'ev, I. I. *Dela pskovskoi provintsial'noi kantseliarii*. Pskov, 1884.

Vedomost' ob obrazovatel'nom tsenze lits sudebnogo vedomstva. St. Petersburg, 1889.

Veretennikov, V. I. *Ocherki istorii general-prokuratury v Rossii do ekaterinskogo vremeni*. Kharkov, 1915.

Veselovskii, A. N. *V. A. Zhukovskii: Poeziia chuvstva i "serdechnogo voobrazheniia."* Petrograd, 1918.

Veselovskii, K. S. "Vospominaniia." *Russkaia Starina*, no. 12 (1901), pp. 495-528.

Viazemskii, Kn. P. A. *Zapisnye knizhki, 1813-1848*. Moscow, 1963.

Vigel', F. F. *Vospominaniia*. 7 vols. Moscow, 1864.

Viktor Antonovich Artsimovich: Vospominaniia-Kharakteristika. St. Petersburg, 1904.

Vilenskii, B. V. *Sudebnaia reforma i kontrreforma v Rossii*. Saratov, 1969.

Vinogradova, L. V. "Osnovnye vidy dokumentov Senata i organizatsiia ego deloproizvodstva." In Glavnoe Arkhivnoe Pravlenie S. S. R, *Nekotorye voprosy izucheniia istoricheskikh dokumentov XIX-nachala XX veka*. Leningrad, 1967, pp. 111-32.

Vodarskii, Ia. E. *Naselenie Rossii za 400 let (XVI-nachalo XXvv)*. Moscow, 1973.

Voskresenskii, N. A., ed. *Zakonodatel'nye akty Petra Iogo*. Moscow and Leningrad, 1945.

Weber, Max. *On Law in Economy and Society*. New York, 1967.

Whelan, Heide Wolker. "Alexander III and the State Council: The Politics of Equilibrium." Ph.D. dissertation, University of Chicago, 1973.

Wortman, Richard. "Peter the Great and Court Procedure." *Canadian-American Slavic Studies*, Summer 1974, pp. 303-10.

Yaney, George L. *The Systematization of Russian Government*. Urbana, Ill., 1973.

Zabelin, I. A. *Vospominanie o D. A. Rovinskom*. St. Petersburg, 1896.

Zaionchkovskii, P. A. "Gubernskaia administratsiia nakanune krymskoi voiny." *Voprosy Istorii*, September 1975, pp. 33-51.

— — —. *Rossiiskoe samoderzhavie v kontse XIX stoletiia*. Moscow, 1970.

— — —. "Vysshaia biurokratiia nakanune krymskoi voiny." *Istoriia S.S.S.R.*, July and August 1974, pp. 154-64.

Zarudnyi, S. I. "Iz vospominanii." *Sbornik Pravovedeniia*, no. 3 (1894), pp. 1-6.

— — —. *Okhranitel'nye zakony chastnogo grazhdanskogo prava*. N.p., 1859.

Zhemchuzhnikov, A. M. *Ibrannye proizvedeniia*. Moscow and Leningrad, 1963.

Zhirmunskii, V. *Gete v russkoi literature*. Leningrad, 1937.

Zhukovskii, V. A. "Iz bumag V. A. Zhukovskogo." *Russkii Arkhiv* 3 (1875): 317-75.

— — —. "Neizdannoe pis'mo D. N. Bludovu." *Raduga*. Leningrad, 1922, pp. 19-20.

— — —. *Polnoe sobranie sochinenii*. 12 vols. St. Petersburg, 1902.

BIBLIOGRAPHY

Zolotnitskii, Vladimir. *Sokrashchenie estestvennogo prava, vybrannoe iz raznykh avtorov dlia pol'zy Rossiiskogo obshchestva.* St. Petersburg, 1764.

INDEX